AMERICA'S ASSEMBLY LINE

AMERICA'S ASSEMBLY LINE

DAVID E. NYE

THE MIT PRESS

CAMBRIDGE, MASSACHUSETTS

LONDON, ENGLAND

MIT Press books may be purchased at special quantity discounts for business or sales promotional use. For information, please email special_sales@mitpress.mit.edu or write to Special Sales Department, The MIT Press, 55 Hayward Street, Cambridge, MA 02142.

Set in Engravers Gothic by the MIT Press. Printed and bound in the United States of America.

Library of Congress Cataloging-in-Publication Data

Nye, David E., 1946–
America's assembly line / David E. Nye.
    p.   cm.
Includes bibliographical references and index.
ISBN 978-0-262-01871-5 (hardcover : alk. paper) 1. Assembly-line methods—United States. I. Title.
TS178.4.N944 2013
20120302276
670.42—dc23

10 9 8 7 6 5 4 3 2 1

dedicated to Helle Bugge Bertramsen Nye

CONTENTS

I have been thinking about the assembly line off and on since the summer of 1970. It began with an accidental visit to Greenfield Village in Dearborn, Michigan. I was on a road trip with a German exchange student. We were meandering from Minneapolis to Boston by way of Montreal. Perhaps because he was studying mechanical engineering, when we got to Detroit my friend wanted to see what Henry Ford had put into his outdoor museum. I wanted to see a baseball game. He prevailed, and we went to Ford's Greenfield Village. We spent a sunny afternoon there, and my interest was piqued enough to include Ford in an undergraduate course I taught the following fall, then to include him in the outline of my dissertation.

I expected that my dissertation would focus on the cultural meanings of "the machine" during the 1920s. Instead, it turned into a dissertation on Henry Ford, which marginalized my attention to the assembly line. In subsequent publications, however, the assembly line reappeared at times. I even outlined a book on the subject 25 years ago, but other research pulled me away from the project. That was almost certainly a good thing, because since then some excellent scholarship has emerged on the subject, and Japanese production methods and automation have revamped the assembly line, providing new complexities to its story.

The assembly line—invented without much fanfare in 1913—soon attracted enormous attention and admiration, followed by controversy and protests. This book will examine the context that fostered it (chapter 1), how it came into being (chapter 2), the excited but somewhat confused initial public response (chapter 3), its diffusion to all parts of the world in little more than a decade (chapter 4), and the growing chorus of criticism leveled at this form of production, which by the 1930s had become synonymous with dehumanizing work (chapter 5). The assembly line became a central icon of capitalist productivity during World War II and the early Cold War (chapter 6). During the 1960s, however, many intellectuals attacked it as inherently dehumanizing, and increasingly workers were disaffected and preferred other forms of work (chapter 7). At the same time, however, the assembly line was being reinvented in Japan, whose carmakers beat Detroit at their own game (chapter 8). The globalization of Japanese production systems was accompanied by further innovations, but they did not raise wages as much as they raised executives' salaries. Indeed, much new assembly-line work was done for low wages in non-Western economies (chapter 9). Today, rising global productivity has encountered environmental limits, and corporations are searching for ways to become greener (chapter 10).

Like the assembly line itself, this book draws on a wide range of sources and inspirations. Although this is a centennial history focused on the United States, it includes an international, comparative perspective, particularly in chapters 4, 6, and 9. Throughout, I focus not only on executives, workers, and intellectuals, but also on a full range of cultural expressions, including film, photography, music, and fiction, in order to understand the assembly line's evolving meaning in American society since 1913.

ACKNOWLEDGMENTS

My intellectual debts for this work stretch back to my dissertation and a 1973 research trip to Greenfield Village and what were then called the Henry Ford Archives. I returned in 1975 to turn that thesis into a book. I went back in 1977 to do research on Thomas Edison, and again in 1986 when writing a book on the history of electrification. Some materials, ideas, and impressions gathered during these earlier visits are used here for the first time. When reading secondary sources, it was a great benefit to have seen the Ford factories, indispensable to have studied original source materials, and invaluable to have spoken with the archivists at the Henry Ford Museum, including Cynthia Miller, whom I first met in 1977 and who was there when I returned in May of 2011.

Few subjects have been studied more intensively than the assembly line. A library's worth of books, articles, and archival materials deal with the themes of these ten chapters. For the present synthesis I needed to visit many libraries to get a grip on this vast literature. The library at the University of Southern Denmark provided standard works, access to online databases, and some rare works through interlibrary loans. However, it would have been impossible to research this book without the opportunity to work briefly but intensively in the libraries of the Massachusetts Institute of Technology, the University of Pittsburgh, Cornell University, the University of Michigan, the California State Polytechnic University in Pomona, and Harvard University's Baker Library, and in Cleveland's and Boston's excellent public libraries. I thank them all for generously allowing access to their collections.

Many people offered suggestions and advice, and I fear that I may not recall everyone. Daniel Arturo Heller shared his knowledge of Japanese business history, the automobile industry, and lean production. John-Eric Bigbie told me about the work of the Boston Consulting Group and others

involved in the transfer of Japanese methods to the United States. Peter
Feniak shared his extensive knowledge of popular culture. Several members
of the SDU History Department, notably Per Boye, Nils Arne Sørensen,
Terkel Stræde, and Jørn Brøndal drew my attention to useful examples and
encouraged me. An early exploration of the subject appeared as "Samle-
båndet og det accelererende Amerika" in *Den jyske historiker* (volume 108,
2005, pages 47–58). In 2011, John Carlos Rowe and the American Studies
faculty at the University of Southern California invited me to lecture on
the assembly line, and in the subsequent discussion they made many helpful
suggestions, particularly with regard to the assembly line in film and fiction.
In May of the same year, Irving Salmeen opened many doors for me inside
the Ford Motor Company; he also introduced me to Jim Tetreault, Ford's
Vice President for North American Manufacturing, who gave freely of his
expertise in an interview and took me on a guided tour of Ford's Michigan
Assembly Plant in Wayne, where the new Focus was being built. He and
Irving also arranged for me a special in-depth tour of the famous River
Rouge Plant, including views of areas no longer in use. At the River Rouge
Plant I benefitted from the knowledge of Anthony Hoskins, Plant Manager
of the Dearborn Truck Plant; Don Pijor, the New Model Launch Manager; and Dan Klebe, the Launch Coordination Manager. Edward Krause of
Ford's Research and Advanced Engineering Division also took part in these
tours and meetings, giving me the benefit of his extensive experience. All
the Ford people gave me far more time and information than I could have
hoped for. If any inaccuracies remain in this volume, none of these persons
or corporations bears any responsibility. I was also fortunate to receive help
in finding the illustrations for this book. Margaret L. Baughman, the photograph collection librarian at the Cleveland Public Library was extraordinarily
resourceful and energetic. Cynthia Miller, the photographic archivist at the
Henry Ford Museum, shared with me her knowledge of the vast Ford collections. Margy Avery, my editor, also pointed me toward some excellent
collections, and her assistant, Katie Persons, helped with the illustrations and
the process of getting permissions for their use. Finally, I thank the many
others at the MIT Press who have helped me to complete eight book projects since 1984. Writing is not assembly-line work, but the continuity of
working for decades with a fine publisher has made me a happier and more
efficient writer.

I CONTEXT

The Fast Man must certainly be an American, because nobody lives and propagates as fast as he.

—English critic[1]

The assembly line was invented in 1913 and has been in continuous operation ever since. It has spread to every industrial nation and has become the most familiar form of mass production. Some corporations that adopted it made enormous profits; others went bankrupt. It has been praised as a boon to all working men and women, yet it has also been condemned as a merciless form of exploitation. It has inspired novels, poems, popular songs, and even a short symphonic work, but it has also inspired satire and visions of apocalypse. It was embraced by both Nazi Germany and the Soviet Union, yet Americans believed that the production lines of Detroit ensured the victory of democracy in both World War II and the Cold War. More recently, it was reinvented in Japan and exported back to the United States.

As the assembly line spread, its effects varied. Between 1914 and 1940 a few nations and some industries embraced it rapidly, others slowly, and some not at all. European nations adopted it more slowly, even after World War II, preferring the flexibility of skilled workers over the standardization of semi-skilled work on assembly lines. In more recent decades, mass-production industries have gradually moved away from the expensive labor markets of Western Europe and the United States to less costly venues in Asia and Latin America. Once the engine of US prosperity, the assembly line now increasingly drives competing economies elsewhere. Its complex social and economic effects have become global. This book examines the assembly line's history, uses, and changing significance, primarily within the

United States, but with an awareness that this system of production has spread throughout the global market.

The assembly line emerged in a specific place (Detroit), at a specific time (between 1908 and 1913), in a specific industry (the automobile industry). But it also expressed trends in American society that can be discerned during the nineteenth century. It was the culmination of decades of labor-saving devices, new management ideas, improvements in metal alloys, increasing precision in machine tools, and experimentation with production. Yet that this technology of production should be invented in the United States was not inevitable. The elements that came together to form the assembly line could also be found in France, in Germany, and in Britain. Any of the other industrial nations might have hit upon it first. Nevertheless, the United States proved particularly suitable for its emergence. A cultural context either fosters or resists a new technology. Before Henry Ford was born, speed, acceleration, innovation, interchangeable parts, uniformity, and economies of scale already were valued in the United States,[2] where the values that the assembly line would embody were woven into everyday life.

The assembly line is a complicated artifact, an assemblage of many parts. What kind of story can be told about it? George Basalla noted that in discussions of technological innovations two approaches are common: some argue for revolutionary change, others for gradual evolution.[3] Non-historians often imagine inventions as a series of brilliant breakthroughs. The popular story usually is one of a great inventor changing the world by creating some device, such as the cotton gin, the electric light, the telephone, the airplane, the radio, or the laser. Such narratives are common in popular biographies and television documentaries. On this view, the Ford assembly line was a breakthrough that revolutionized both production and consumption, and it might be called the "innovation that changed the world." However, few historians of technology see the same developments as sudden revolutionary changes. Instead, most of them usually accept the "Darwinian-inspired idea that technical progress is the result of cumulative change."[4] Taking this approach, historians have found close relationships between Eli Whitney's cotton gin and other machines, including an earlier cotton gin that failed to work with the short-staple cotton that was commonly grown in the American South. Whitney didn't have a fundamentally new idea. Rather, he improved a previous artifact. Likewise, most inventions, when closely studied, turn out to be largely recombinations of existing practices and ideas. From this perspective, the history of the assembly line is a story of slowly accumulating technical knowledge that eventually led to a new synthesis. Both of these perspectives are compatible with a vision of history as the story of progress. However, the belief in human progress is more common in the popular stories of breakthrough inventions and technological revolutions. In contrast, Basalla rejects "the popular but illusory concept of technological progress."[5]

This book takes as its starting point the evolutionary view of how inventions emerge. Yet, as Basalla is the first to admit, this gradualist view is not able to explain why the public embraced and used some inventions more than others. Basalla's example of the early competition among three forms of automobiles (electric, steam-powered, and gasoline-powered) is particularly apt. In 1900 there were about 5,000 cars of all types in the United States. Less than 20 percent of them were gasoline-powered. Electric cars were the quietest and the least polluting. Steam-powered cars were the fastest and used the most familiar technology. Gasoline-powered cars were the noisiest, the most polluting, and the least familiar. Only in retrospect does the victor in this contest seem obvious. Consider a counterfactual question: What if the Ford Motor Company had developed the assembly line to manufacture steam cars or electric cars? Would Ford still have become the world's largest automobile manufacturer? Would the public still have preferred the gasoline car? Might the assembly line have been discredited and forgotten after the gasoline-powered car emerged as the standard type? The triumph of the steam car might seem an unlikely outcome, but in fact the fastest racing car in the world, for a few years, was the Stanley Steamer. The Stanley brothers built an excellent vehicle, but they didn't pioneer the assembly line.

History is replete with examples of innovations that were overlooked or underutilized. The Chinese invented gunpowder but used it only for fireworks. The Aztecs invented the wheel but used it only on children's toys. The ancient Greeks invented a small steam engine but thought it a mere curiosity. The Romans invented poured concrete, but the process was forgotten and was reinvented centuries later. As these examples suggest, technologies evolve from one artifact to the next. Their adoption and their use are not guaranteed; rather, they are shaped by their historical context. A technology may cease to be developed. Innovation on a particular device may cease for decades or even centuries before someone reconceptualizes its design or its use.

These generalizations apply to the assembly line. In the United States it developed rapidly between 1908 and 1913, more slowly from 1914 to 1930, and thereafter at a modest pace until the Japanese reinvented it after World War II and doubled its productivity. The popular notion of invention as the work of genius is clearly inadequate when it comes to understanding the invention, the stagnation, and the reinvention of the assembly line. The evolutionary approach, with its emphasis on the gradual accumulation of ideas from many different sources (or the discouragement of such accumulation), seems far more historically accurate. As this approach implies, the assembly line has a pre-history.

American society has long been fast-paced. Foreign visitors often notice that Americans seem to be in a hurry. They take less time for meals, and often they eat and hold meetings at the same time. The breakfast meeting, relatively rare in Europe, is common in the United States. Americans want things to happen quickly. They have little patience with delays, and what seemed fast a decade ago is too slow today. Over time, Americans have internalized acceleration as a value, and workers and consumers think it is "natural" that tempos increase. Once people have internalized acceleration, it becomes its own justification, and adapting to an increasing pace seems inherently right.

In 1851, English observers saw that the machines displayed by the United States at the Crystal Palace Exhibition were generally easier to use and more rapid in their operation than those from other nations.[6] One visitor to the exhibition felt that the love of speed applied to individual Americans as well: "Who is this celebrated individual, whom nobody can overtake? . . . the Fast Man shows nothing but his back, as he is outstripping all pursuers. He is undoubtedly an American, who can run through ten miles of fortune quicker that anybody else. Certainly he sails the fleetest ships, and drives the steamer most rapidly. Who eats so quick as he?" As early as the 1820s, a traveler staying at the finest hotel in Boston was astounded at how quickly the 150 guests dispatched their meals. Many were at the table only five or ten minutes. The traveler found himself "quite unable to keep pace at meals with the Americans," especially at midday.[7] They ate so quickly, it seemed, because they had so much business to attend to. The English journalist at the 1851 Exposition ventured the opinion that "the Fast Man must certainly be an American, because nobody lives and propagates as fast as he." Apparently "from a mere feeling of impatience he has been obliged to apply steam to navigation and invent the telegraph." And by 1851 Americans also had created a host of other labor-saving devices, including the mechanical reaper and the Colt revolver, which in a dispute would "settle the matter for a dozen at once."[8]

The development of the United States into a highly accelerated society began at the latest during the late eighteenth century and appears to have occurred in five steps. First came the standardization of space. For most of human history, space had been unique. Every piece of land had quite particular dimensions, and no two spaces were considered to be alike. In addition, there were characteristic cultural differences in land use. For example, the layout and the dimensions of agricultural fields differed from France to Germany to Britain. In the late 1780s, rejecting such differences, the U.S. government standardized into squares all the land put up for sale west of the thirteen original states, imposing a grid on the continent from the Appalachian Mountains to the Pacific. This grid had the effect of erasing the past. It declared that parcels of land should be regarded as raw material, waiting to be acquired and developed.[9] The imposition of the geometrical pattern on much of North America suggested an imagined order of interchangeable and standardized parts.

In the Colonial period, not the individual but the community had been central. The theocratic order of the first settlers was visible in the layout of the land. Americans reproduced the European village, with a church at the center and with roads radiating outward. The local governments of the first settlers didn't conceive of land as generic but rather evaluated it and divided it into woodlots, pasture, and farmland, distributing some of each to every household. A family's land wasn't all in one location, and the shape of a lot was by no means regular and was seldom a perfect square.[10] In contrast, the new grid system erased distinctiveness, hierarchy, and centrality from the landscape, substituting the values of individuality and equality.[11] Once all space was uniform, there was no need to linger in, or to identify too much with, any particular place. The grid was a precondition for acceleration, erasing differences.

Once Americans had homogenized space, the next step was to find ways to move rapidly through this new grid. They made this possible with successive waves of investment in roads, canals, and railroads. As transportation accelerated, individual Americans moved house more often. Dissolving local bonds was a precondition for increasing the speed of the individual's circulation through society. In contrast, European citizens of the same period retained stronger local ties. Even today, the regional and the local remain stronger in much of Europe than in the United States.

The third step was the rapid circulation of information. Americans invented and deployed the telegraph in the 1840s. In addition to speeding up the flow of information, telegraphy and the new wire services worked toward the standardization of news and facilitated the formation of chains of newspapers that could run identical stories.[12] The telegraph was also a precondition for centralizing trade in New York (the stock market) and Chicago (the commodity market). The Chicago Board of Trade not only concentrated and accelerated the flow of information; it also standardized the values of different sorts of grain for different moments in time, eliminating the individuality of a particular farmer's products.[13] By the 1860s, Americans had become accustomed to a national market and a rapid flow of information. The flow of information continued to accelerate with the advent of the telephone, cinema, and radio.

The fourth step was the standardization of time. The harmonizing of the nation's clocks didn't come from the government; it was instituted by the railroads[14] in order to increase the reliability and safety of transportation by making train schedules accurate. Americans standardized time not only out of a desire for order or uniformity but also as a logical outgrowth of the acceleration of transportation.

Fifth, the earlier forms of standardization culminated in the invention and dissemination of the assembly line as a fundamental principle of both production and consumption. The assembly line completed the institutionalization of the values and practices of acceleration. Nor is it incidental that this new system was first applied to manufacturing automobiles, which themselves embodied the values of speed, interchangeability, standardization, and the homogenization of space and time. Automotive manufacturers developed the most important industry in the United States, embodying these values and inculcating them into the population. By the 1930s, automobiles and paved roads had become "natural" in the United States.

Even before the assembly line, American factories had accelerated production relative to European practice. In 1897, a Frenchman who observed American steel mills, silk factories, and packing houses found that everywhere the pace was considerably faster than in France and that heavy work was mostly transferred to machines. He noted that the manufacturers believed that these changes benefited workmen both "as sellers of labor, because the level of salaries has been raised" and "as consumers of products because they purchase more with the same sum." But laborers didn't agree, reproaching the factories for exhausting them, for demanding enervating and continual attention, for "degrading man by transforming him into a machine," and for "diminishing the number of skilled workers."[15] A faster pace and deskilled work prepared laborers for something like an assembly line.

A useful version of the assembly line was created at Ford's factories between 1908 to 1913. It was not a final result, but a part of an ongoing cultural process. As Basalla noted, "technological evolution has nothing comparable to the mass extinctions that are of interest to evolutionary biologists."[16] Things that are discarded for a time may be taken up or rediscovered for use in a new context. Technological evolution does not necessarily have a regular pace. A society may create a variety of separate objects without ever combining them to make something that, when finally invented, seems obvious in retrospect. Rather than see the members of the Ford team that invented the assembly line as extraordinarily gifted, it is more accurate to see them as the heirs of centuries of development in machine design and manufacturing processes. Throughout the nineteenth century, other factories had intermittently worked on the problem of how to speed up production, contributing various technical elements that came together in the Ford solution. Just as important, the assembly line wasn't finished in 1913; it has been in constant development ever since then. Other automakers and other industries took it up and added refinements. It was more productive in 1923 than it had been in 1913. The American version of the assembly line was less innovative by the 1950s, but in part because managers focused on what seemed the imminent adoption of automation and robots. They believed that the next avatar of the assembly line would eliminate most workers. Elsewhere, however, particularly in Japan, corporations developed an entirely new approach, later to be called "lean manufacturing," which proved that human beings on assembly lines could be twice as productive. These ongoing developments are one strand of the story this book has to tell.

The assembly line spread to a wide range of industries; it also became a subject of intense debate and a basis for new cultural practices. Many intellectuals detested it, as did many workers. It was parodied and denounced both on both the right and on the left. Nevertheless, it was widely imitated in factories producing foods, consumer appliances, household and office equipment, tools, bicycles, toys, and games—in short, most of the things one finds in any large chain store today. The principles of the assembly line were also embodied in the cafeteria (an assembly line for meals), in the supermarket, and later in the limited-access highway (which resembles a vast conveyor belt carrying consumers past goods and services). The assembly line became a common way to organize experience.

The use of assembly lines has increased efficiency and lowered manufacturing costs. Largely because of mass production, standards of living have probably risen more in the last 100 years than in any comparable period in human history. Just before the assembly line emerged, an automobile cost at least three times as much to build as it did afterward, and much of the higher cost was for labor. A sudden increase in productivity meant two things that seemed to contradict one another: prices could fall, yet wages could rise. People therefore could afford to buy much more. That created new demand, which in turn made mass production feasible in more and more industries.

Clearly the productivity revolution began before the assembly line, but just as clearly the assembly line multiplied productivity to such an extent that the world of consumption was markedly different after 1913. Likewise, the high value attached to speed and acceleration predated the assembly line, but the radical increase in productivity reinforced those cultural preferences. In a 1916 book on the "romance of the automobile industry," James Doolittle declared that speed was "one of the most important factors in the development of humanity." Indeed, according to Doolittle, speed became "more important with each progressive step in the life of the world." With both the automobile and the assembly line in mind, he asserted: "Nothing more flagrantly false was ever said than that speed is inherently bad. Speed is the difference between doing and not doing. Speed is the measure of efficiency. Speed marks the line between misery and well-being—the difference between civilization of today and the benighted squalor of the Dark Ages."[17] Few stated the idea that speed was the measure of cultural progress quite so baldly, but none could doubt that the acceleration of production and consumption had a profound effect on human sensibilities.

Some philosophers have shown interest in how technical systems foster new sensibilities. Notably, Martin Heidegger argued that in the modern world technology provides a pre-theoretical "horizoning of experience." As technological rationality becomes dominant, human beings learn to perceive all of nature as a "standing reserve" of raw materials awaiting use. In the 1780s, Americans already had moved decisively in that direction by imposing the grid on the landscape. The transformation of the standing reserve of "raw nature" for human advantage became "natural." A child born after about 1840 accepted without thought the use of the railroad and telegraph to further homogenize American space, time, and information and to create a single continental market. In contrast, that child's grandparents regarded the telegraph, the railroad, and the stock market as innovations that had disrupted the "normal." But the child unquestioningly accepted these technical mediations of experience as the pre-theoretical "horizon" of perception.

One might argue that the child's life became richer and fuller, but many recent philosophers of technology have concluded that "disenchantment set in."[18] As the technological domain encroaches upon or mediates all experience, it overtakes and delegitimizes older perceptions of the world. A highly "technological character" is "concentrated in its liberating powers to be anything, that is, to be new, to never repeat itself."[19] This apparent liberation comes at a cost. The penetration of technology into all aspects of being means that "our new character is grounded in human-technology symbiosis," and "prior to reflection, technology transforms character."[20] The transformation imposes itself on each child, becoming part of its generation's understanding of what is normal.

These generalizations apply to all societies, but the particular machines that become "naturalized" vary from one culture to another, as does the pace of change. What are the psychological effects on Americans of living within a technological lifeworld that standardizes space, information, and time—a lifeworld that wraps them in a cocoon of machines that continually accelerate the pace and intensity of experience? The five steps identified earlier in this chapter correspond roughly to five generations. Americans of circa 1800 embraced the standardization of space, which simplified land sales, erased the perception of local differences, and accelerated national settlement. Their children internalized the grid and, in turn, developed and celebrated an extensive transportation system that accelerated the flow of goods and united the nation in a single market. In the mid 1840s, a third generation accepted these changes as "natural" but became excited at the prospect of the rapid circulation and standardization of information through the development of the telegraph, the creation of the wire services, and later the telephone. By the 1880s, a fourth generation had synthesized those changes with the standardization of time, erecting a universal standard for punctuality. Together these developments created the preconditions for the assembly line that consolidated acceleration as a social value. By 1920, American society had embraced a socio-technical system that reified the increasing tempo of experience and the homogenization of space, time, and information, thereby eliminating resistance to acceleration. Such socio-technical systems are not neutral; they establish directions and constraints.[21]

Since the early twentieth century, Americans have been constrained by habits of perception and systems of artifacts linked to the assembly line that naturalized acceleration. The great world's fairs in Chicago (1933) and New York (1939) assured visitors that every aspect of their lives would continue to accelerate in the future. One of the most popular exhibits at the 1939 fair was Chrysler's, which depicted the history of transportation from horse-drawn chariots to rockets (expected soon to be carrying tourists to London in just an hour).[22] Though the prophecy of rocket tourism proved fallacious, Americans often understood technical developments in terms of acceleration. In automobiles, they favored speed over either safety or fuel efficiency. They patronized thousands of fast-food restaurants that sacrificed taste to speed of preparation. Today, as in 1851, corporations find that Americans want things that are easy to use and that make it possible to do more in less time.[23]

Yet not everyone has accepted acceleration as a basic social value. Many Native Americans have rejected the homogenization of space, the erasure of the local, and the standardization of time.[24] Some people consciously choose a life with fewer possessions and a slower pace. Henry David Thoreau resisted the increasing tyranny of industrial time and the accumulating mania for acceleration. In an essay titled "Walking," he celebrated sauntering at a slow pace and opening all the senses to allow the unexpected to impinge on one's consciousness.[25] But Thoreau appealed to only a tiny minority in the 1850s. He wasn't a "fast man." He didn't want to eliminate the resistance of the world.

In contrast, the tinkerers, engineers, and mechanics of late-nineteenth-century America were enamored of speed, standardization, and mechanical improvements. One of them was Henry Ford. Although he read Ralph Waldo Emerson avidly and made a pilgrimage to Walden Pond,[26] Ford also presided over the development of the Model T and the assembly line.

I don't know who thought up the idea of putting the whole car on a moving line.

—Richard Kroll, Ford worker[1]

In 1910, the Ford Motor Company's new Highland Park plant provided a setting that was conducive to innovation in manufacturing. When the men arrived there from Ford's Piquette Avenue plant, Richard Kroll recalled, "there was no conveyor system built. It was all hand work."[2] There was no plan to invent something like the assembly line, and no single individual invented it. Rather, a collaboration of people drew on knowledge acquired in many different industries. One precursor emerged at the Olds factory in Lansing, where workers began to put chassis on wooden platforms that had furniture casters underneath so they could be rolled from one work area to another.[3] Others, including the manufacturers of the EMF and Brush automobiles, also saw that it was a good idea to move the partially assembled car along. Each of those firms had a rudimentary organization that might have become an assembly line by 1911.[4] There was considerable mobility in Detroit's rapidly expanding auto industry, and some workers left EMF and Brush for jobs at Ford. There are few useful contemporary records. The best sources are oral histories gathered 40 years afterward, but such histories are often fallible when it comes to the timing and order of events. Precisely when the assembly line became a conscious idea, and who was responsible, may forever elude us.

FIGURE 2.1
The Highland Park plant, where the assembly line was invented in 1913, with one day's production of identical Model Ts parked outside. Courtesy of Henry Ford Museum.

Yet in seeking an originator we may be asking the wrong question. John B. Rae, after looking into the matter, concluded that "the claim that Henry Ford invented mass production must be dismissed as absurd," and that "the introduction of the moving assembly line at Highland Park in 1913 was a momentous and epochal innovation, but it was essentially the capstone of an edifice that had been rising for over a century."[5] The technology scholar Anthony F. C. Wallace concluded, more generally, that inventions are collective efforts in their very nature: "We shall view technology as a social product and shall not be over much interested in the priority claims of individual inventors, for the actual course of work that leads to the conception and use of new technology *always* involves a group that has worked for a considerable period of time on the basic idea before success is achieved."[6] This generalization applies with particular force to both the assembly line and its later reconception as lean manufacturing. In each case, a group worked together for years to rethink the fundamentals of production.

Manufacturing processes that in hindsight look much like an assembly line can be found long before Henry Ford founded his company in 1903. The idea of moving work to the workers, who remained in fixed locations along a line and repeated a single function, had been developed before the Civil War in slaughterhouses, where the process of disassembly began with live animals being driven into the building and ended with cuts of meat, hides, tallow, and other products.[7] In a sense, Ford reversed this process. Another indispensable element in any form of mass production is interchangeable parts, which Charles Fitch examined in detail in his 1881 "Report on the Manufacture of Interchangeable Mechanism" (published as a part of the *Tenth Census of the United States*). The canning industry, by mastering continuous-flow production, offered another precursor to the assembly line. Historians have noted other precursors, some of which Henry Ford or his staff may have been aware of; two early examples are the Venetian Arsenal's production of ships and arms and Josiah Wedgwood's manufacture of pottery to a high and uniform standard. In the United States, Oliver Evans devised grist mills that produced a continuous flow of flour almost without the touch of a human hand before 1800. By 1804 the British Navy was manufacturing biscuits at a rate of seventy a minute. Dough was mixed in "an ingenious machine," and the subsequent work was divided into six tasks, the last being to place the biscuits in a long oven through which a conveyor belt passed. By the 1830s, most of the work involved in the first five tasks also had been mechanized.[8]

FIGURE 2.2
Swift Company slaughterhouse, Chicago, 1906. Courtesy of Prints and Photographs Division, Library of Congress.

The Chinese Han Dynasty's factories (ca. 80 BC–10 AD) also have been proposed as precursors to the assembly line. One historian concluded that "the artisans' labor was divided along very fine lines of specialization as part of a production process similar to the modern assembly-line," and that they made "thousands of nearly identical lacquer vessels on a short production schedule."[9] By 20 AD the division of labor had increased, raising productivity. When the process was fully developed, between twenty and thirty people were involved in making each cup or bowl—"counting the officials and clerks and the unrecorded men who gathered and processed the raw materials."[10] The eight to ten semi-skilled artisans at the heart of the process used lathes and specialized hand tools. However, nothing even remotely like a conveyor belt seems to have been in use.

Rather than look for manufacturing processes that prefigured the assembly line, other historians have traced the development of a new mentality among workers, engineers, and managers. Lindy Biggs studied the American pursuit of "the rational factory" from Oliver Evans and Thomas Jefferson in the late eighteenth century to the Ford manufacturing system. Biggs was concerned less with particular technologies than with the development of a mentality in search of rationalization and an incentive system that rewarded it. For example, in the textile industry, "mill mechanics quickly learned that production enhancing innovations earned rewards, and these bright, skilled men had little trouble introducing regular changes that increased speed or lowered skill requirements."[11] Industries rationalized in different ways. The paper industry didn't seek to lower wages but to increase productivity. The arms industry sought greater precision in order to make interchangeable parts. In contrast to these fabrication industries, processing industries such as steelmaking, canning, and oil refining didn't so much need machines that replaced skilled work as they wanted to speed up throughput and to reduce waste. Biggs also documents how, near the end of the nineteenth century, engineers invented elements of what would now be called systems management, including cost accounting, inventory control, incentive wages, and standardization of work routines. Labor-saving machinery, accelerated materials handing, and systems management all came together in the Ford assembly line, which culminated more than a century of effort.

Robert Friedel found that "a culture of improvement" characterized Western societies as a whole for at least 1,000 years. Rather than focus on brilliant inventors and their breakthroughs, Friedel argues that incremental improvements and the sharing of knowledge account for the West's mechanization and industrialization from the eleventh century on. In the case of the assembly line, he notes, it "was not, apparently, the result of some sort of overarching plan to reform manufacture. It instead grew out of the Ford engineers' effort to reduce perceived inefficiencies—their pursuit of step-by-step improvement of the production process."[12] The ability to perceive inefficiencies itself was the cultural outcome of centuries of practical knowledge gained through hard effort in many different industries. Those working at the Ford Motor Company when the assembly line was created had experience in arms manufacturing, bicycle production, meat packing, steelmaking, and brewing. The assembly line synthesized practices from all those industries, and became more than the sum of its parts. It thus exemplifies Wallace's observation that inventions emerge from a group, illustrates Friedel's argument that even the most important innovations are created incrementally, and offers the logical conclusion to Biggs' study of the how the rational factory evolved.

David Hounshell's *From the American System to Mass Production, 1800–1932* remains the most important study of the evolution of American manufacturing methods.[13] To explain the emergence of the assembly line, Hounshell makes use of case studies, based on archival sources, of a number of sewing machine manufacturers, several woodworking companies (including the Studebaker wagon works), the McCormick reaper factory, and several bicycle manufacturers. Hounshell focuses on fabrication industries that produced complex machines. These industries developed the division of labor, specialized machine design, metal stamping (rather than casting), rationalization of the flow of work, and improved shop layouts, all of which converged in the assembly line. Most industries moved only haltingly toward fully rationalized production. Neither the Singer Sewing Machine Company nor the McCormick reaper works, for example, adopted the New England armory practice of specialized single-function machines or the goal of fully interchangeable parts until they had been in operation for decades. What forced them to change? Not abstract logic, but the pressure of increased sales. The woodworking and furniture industries incorporated many elements of production that eventually were used in the assembly line. However, because consumers wanted variety, and because styles changed often, their "product lines could not be maintained long enough to justify the construction of special purpose machinery and other 'efficient' production techniques."[14] The Pope Bicycle Company continued hand forging of many parts until near the end of the nineteenth century, and it didn't solve the problem of efficient assembly before demand for its high-wheel cycles declined. In short, each of these industries contributed to the eventual emergence of the assembly line, but none managed to integrate all the separate improvements into a new system of production. One reason was the form of the factory itself.

What was the physical context for the invention of the assembly line? With few exceptions, the factories of circa 1900 were powered by steam and had a completely different architecture than the later assembly-line plants. A steam-powered facility was almost always built several stories high, with the power source centrally located on one of the lower floors. Power was transmitted to the machines by means of gears, shafts, and belts, and most of the machines were arranged in straight lines beneath the drive shafts. Because power was transmitted as physical movement, a great deal of power was required to run the transmission system itself. The larger a factory became, the greater the investment in shafts, belts, and gears had to be and the more power had to be used to turn them. In the largest factories it was necessary to build and maintain several power systems, with power radiating outward from each.

Electric motors made it practicable to lay out a factory to suit the nature of the work. Practical electrical generators first became available in the 1880s, and reliable motors in the 1890s. As late as 1900, only 3.6 percent of factory power came from electric motors; ten years later, the percentage was 18.7.[15] In many factories, electric motors were simply attached to the overhead drive shafts that already existed, or were rigged up to drive small clusters of machines. Setting up an assembly line required a further step. Every machine had to have its own motor before the machines could be moved into more efficient positions. Once transmitting power over a distance ceased to be problematic, a factory didn't have to be a multi-story structure with the power source in the middle. A sprawling single-story structure was often best suited to the handling of materials. Production was further accelerated by electric cranes, elevators, ventilation, and illumination. With electric lighting there was no need to halt production because of darkness, and a factory could operate day and night if demand warranted it. Each of these changes accelerated production. Collectively, they were preconditions for the assembly line.

Though the components of the assembly line all preceded it, there seems no doubt that their integration first occurred in Henry Ford's factory between 1908 and 1913. Electrical drive spread quickly in fast-growing new industries such as automobile factories. They were a likely place for production innovation because the demand for cars outpaced the supply. Furthermore, automobiles were suited to developing something like an assembly line because they were made from a large number of parts. An early Model T had about 10,000 parts, and the number increased somewhat between 1908 and 1916. In the early years, workmen moved each part to the embryonic car, which was stationary. Every team of workmen had to be familiar with a large number of operations and procedures. That system wasted time as workers moved about a large floor looking for parts, and it created chronic inventory and supply problems. It wasn't practicable to keep all the parts close to all the cars under construction. As orders for new cars poured in, the search for more efficient methods intensified. One possibility was to send teams of workers, each of whom had a certain specialty, from one car to the next. But specialized crews were only slightly more efficient. It was still difficult to keep all the parts that each crew needed nearby, and at times one crew had to wait for another to complete its tasks. It proved more efficient to move the parts to the men, and to subdivide the work. However, moving parts and materials continuously was difficult in a traditional factory building.

In order to produce a standardized car for a large market, Ford built a new factory in the Highland Park section of Detroit. It opened on January 1, 1910. If not designed with the assembly line specifically in mind, it was a new kind of facility, built on the assumption that electrical light and power should be available everywhere. The floor plan was more open and more flexible than those of older facilities, and it encouraged innovation. Good lighting facilitated precision work, which was essential in order to achieve the standardization needed to make interchangeable parts. Ventilation was just as important, as dust makes machines malfunction when working at close tolerances. At Highland Park, electric fans, operating continuously, swept out approximately 26 million cubic feet of air per hour. Dust was extracted from the air by passing it through a dense mist. The air was then dried and pumped into work areas. Pure air improved the workers' health and kept the machinery cleaner and more accurate.

Ford's Highland Park facility brought together managers and engineers who collectively knew most of the manufacturing practices used in the United States. So many individuals were involved that who originated what isn't certain. Henry Ford's precise role in the invention of the assembly line is also unclear. Ford had worked for Detroit Edison as an engineer in an electric power plant, as a mechanic in machine shops, and as a watch repairman, and thus had gained a grounding in electricity, mechanics, and precision work. He grasped the importance of both electric drive and interchangeable parts. At the least, Ford deserves credit for his support of the process of experimentation, and for holding many discussions with his staff. He also deserves credit for recognizing that there would be a large market for

automobiles if their prices could be greatly reduced. But Ford also hired talented managers who made major contributions to the assembly line. Some
of them were machinists who had started out as workers. Collectively they
had a great deal of expertise. William Flanders knew the sewing machine
business and championed interchangeable parts and single-function machine
tools.[16] Max Wollering had worked for International Harvester and for a
gas engine company. Oscar Bornholdt had direct experience with canning
and food processing. William Klann had worked as a machinist in flour
mills and in breweries. A whole crew of men who were expert at punching
and stamping steel moved to Detroit when Ford acquired their company
in 1911; among them was William Knudsen, who later would direct several assembly-line plants. He eventually left for General Motors, where he
became president. Another Ford manager, P. E. Martin, toured Chicago's
meat-packing plants in search of new ideas that could be used in automobile
assembly.[17] These men, and many others, created the assembly line so rapidly that who contributed what idea or implemented what process at what
date may forever elude historians. They were too busy to make notes at the
time, and many changes occurred simultaneously. In any case, it appears that
Henry Ford didn't first conceive of the assembly line and then delegate its
development to his managers. Rather, development came from the bottom
up as managers synthesized their knowledge and drew on the experiences
of workers.

Consider the testimony of Richard Kroll, who worked at Ford's Piquette
Avenue plant and then at Highland Park and who was involved in the development of the assembly line. "I don't know who thought up the idea
of putting the whole car on a moving line," he declared in an interview
years later. It appears that the intensive subdivision of work began with sub-
assemblies in the spring of 1913. Later, someone began to pull cars along by
a rope from one work station to the next. Later still, rails were put down to
guide the cars as they moved. Kroll thought that Clarence Avery, a former
teacher of Henry Ford's son Edsel who had come to work for the company,
had pushed the idea of a moving line and had been the first to bring the idea
to Henry Ford's attention. But "Mr. Ford didn't like it at first. He went on
a trip somewhere, and while he was on that trip, they put the line in."[18]
Pulling by rope proved a nuisance, and eventually a chain was hooked to
each car's front axle. Gradually the operations were strung out along the
track on which cars moved, and the full idea of the assembly line came into

view. Apparently at the same time, in another proto-assembly-line setup, a system of conveyors was first used in the assembly of motors. Several college-educated engineers, including Clarence Avery, teamed up with the machinist William Klann.[19] Klann recalled rigging up a chain conveyor that transported crankcases to another building, where a crankcase was painted and then passed into a drying room, "then up over the roof to the motor assembly building" to "right where it was needed."[20]

Such reminiscences are tantalizing, but it isn't possible to sort out the sequence of innovations and assign credit to individuals. We can say that 1913 was the year, that the experiments that led to the assembly line apparently began in April with sub-assembly of flywheel magnetos and then spread to other parts of the plant, and that by the autumn of 1913 an embryonic assembly line for entire cars was emerging at Highland Park. However, we cannot assign a precise date, or cite a "Eureka" moment that anyone recognized at the time or recalled later. We can be certain only that successful experiments with work subdivision and layout began in the spring of 1913, and that over a period of six months they spread from magnetos to the transmission system and elsewhere. In August came the first attempt to organize chassis assembly as a moving line. A rope attached to a windlass pulled the cars along. Parts were located in the proper sequence along the route, and a small team of rather skilled assemblers walked with the vehicle, installing the parts as they came to them. That cut assembly time in half. Experiments continued. By October 7 "140 assemblers had been placed along a 150 foot line," and by the end of the year 191 men were strung along a 300-foot line.[21] "By November 1913, Klann, Emde and others put the entire engine assembly—made up of several subassemblies—on an integrated assembly line."[22] In short, by the late autumn of 1913 Ford managers were quite consciously pursuing a new production system. The cars were still being pushed along manually until January 1914, when a chain was introduced. By April 1914, several assembly lines were in full operation, and cars were being put on raised tracks. (See figure 2.3.) Experiments continued, and further gains in productivity were achieved in subsequent months. But it seems evident that in April 1913 the assembly line wasn't an intended outcome. It emerged gradually. By late August or early autumn, a moving line had become a goal.

Five features define the assembly line. One is the subdivision of labor, described in the famous passage on the manufacture of pins in Adam Smith's *The Wealth of Nations* (1776). Smith notes that sometimes a person working

FIGURE 2.3
Model T assembly line, Highland Park plant, circa 1914. Courtesy of Photographic
Department, Cleveland Public Library

alone couldn't make twenty pins in a day. Strict division of labor made for
an enormous difference in productivity. "One man draws out the wire, another straightens it, a third cuts it, a fourth points it, a fifth grinds it at the top
for receiving the head; to make the head requires two or three distinct operations; to put it on, is a peculiar business, to whiten the pins is another; it is
even a trade by itself to put them into the paper; and the important business
of making a pin is, in this manner, divided into about eighteen distinct operations, which, in some manufactories, are all performed by distinct hands,
though in others the same man will sometimes perform two or three of
them."[23] A team of ten or more people with only minimal skills could produce and package 48,000 pins in a day. Smith notes that such enormous increases in productivity occurred in every industry in which division of labor
was introduced, and attributes them to "the increase of dexterity in every
particular workman; secondly, to the saving of the time which is commonly

lost in passing from one species of work to another; and lastly, to the invention of a great number of machines which facilitate and abridge labor, and enable one man to do the work of many."[24] Smith also notes that specialized machines often were created or proposed by workmen who focused all their attention on a single operation, and surmises that repetition of a single operation led them to imagine better tools and physical arrangements.

At the Ford Motor Company, managers subdivided work into small operations of nearly equal duration. By the early 1920s, Ford had a Time Study Department with more than sixty employees. Every time a part was changed, its production and its installation were newly timed. A former Ford employee named Anthony Harff recalled that "they followed engineering changes very closely . . . and immediately would study the job and adjust their time study."[25] The person timed had to be experienced, as new employees went through a period of adjustment—"a breaking in period." Harff continued: "You get toughened to the job in a matter of weeks and from then on its doesn't bother you . . . you are using muscles like a swimmer or athlete."[26] A job was reduced to repetition of a precise task that usually lasted less than a minute. A study conducted in 1952 found that the typical job on an assembly line consisted of performing one or two small tasks that together took two minutes. For the assembly line to work smoothly, it was important that the precise time needed for each task be calculated so that the correct number of workers could be allocated to each station on the line. There was variation. Some jobs took less than a minute, and a few might require as long as eight minutes, including some walking along the line, but the norm in 1952 was two minutes per job.[27] (The evidence suggests that on the 1914 line the typical job took less time. In 2011 the norm was a bit less than a minute in most factories.) To keep the line moving steadily, four times as many men were needed for eight-minute tasks as for those that took only two minutes. In 1913, bottlenecks, accidents, slowdowns, or parts shortages were reported immediately and dealt with as quickly as was possible. The company kept bicycles on hand so that troubleshooters could rush to areas where problems arose.[28]

One advantage of making the tasks brief was that every job could be learned quickly. Not only could virtually anyone work at Ford; workers could be moved around. Most jobs required almost no training. Managers found that blind or disabled individuals could do certain jobs just as well as anyone else. The company did a comprehensive analysis and found that there were 7,882 different jobs in the factory. Of these, only "949 were classified as heavy work requiring strong, able-bodied" men. Another 3,338 jobs could be done by anyone in ordinary physical condition. The "remaining 3,595 jobs were disclosed as requiring no physical exertion and could be performed by the slightest, weakest sort of men."[29] In fact, 670 could be done by legless men, 2,637 by one-legged men, 715 by one-armed men, and two by armless men. On the basis of this analysis, Henry Ford asserted in his autobiography that the greater the subdivision of industry, the more likely it was there would be work for everyone. He didn't say, but surely he knew, that blind or one-legged workers seldom quit. Healthy workers without disabilities were more likely to flee the repetition of the assembly line. Alternately, the talented might escape the monotony of the line itself into the skilled work of keeping the line in repair and constantly improving it.

A second idea essential to the assembly line was that of interchangeable parts that fit smoothly together without the need for any last-minute sanding, filing, or polishing. The origin of this idea can be traced back at least as far as the early eighteenth century. As Ken Alder has noted, "in the 1720s, Christopher Polhem, a Swedish inventor, manufactured clocks composed of interchangeable parts." In France a locksmith did something similar. By the end of the eighteenth century, one private French manufacturer was able to produce 10,000 gunlocks a year, using a process that divided labor into 128 separate steps.[30] In the United States, Eli Whitney promoted the idea of interchangeability, but Whitney didn't achieve results as impressive as those achieved by Samuel Colt or the federal arsenals later in the century.[31] Whitney convinced Thomas Jefferson of the advantages of interchangeable parts for the production of weapons, and received a contract to realize the idea in practice. However, he proved unable to make metal parts to the precision required. Pursued in armories and by clockmakers and other manufacturers, it was gradually realized during the nineteenth century. Interchangeable-parts manufacture required such high standards of precision, however, that for generations it cost more than older methods of production, which in some industries remained competitive until well after the 1860s. Yet continual small improvements in the accuracy of machine tools made parts more closely alike and cheaper to produce. Ford managers achieved exacting standards of precision partly by adopting the armory practice that each machine should perform only one function. A machine tool could be adjusted to make an almost infinite range of parts, but much time was needed to make each adjustment. For assembly lines to be efficient, each machine was designed to perform only one thing, and to do that as quickly as possible. As the scale of production increased, it became economically advantageous to invest larger sums in specialized machines, including some that no small manufacturer could afford. At Ford, the value of plant and equipment nearly doubled between 1909 and 1917, reaching $1,606 per employee.[32]

Single-function machines were necessary but not sufficient to make parts precisely identical. To improve precision, electric drive was needed. Mechanically driven shafts inevitably had a tiny wobble that imparted a slightly different speed to machines farther from the power source. Likewise, a drive shaft moved slightly more slowly when every belt was engaged than when some were disconnected. One specialist noted that "each shaft oscillates, each belt slips and creeps," and that the "variation of speed caused by one class of machinery is reflected to the other machines all over the mill."[33] These slight variations in the speeds of different machines translated into slight variations in the products they manufactured. It was difficult to make absolutely standardized parts with machines not driven by individual electric motors. Likewise, electrical heating spoiled fewer materials than other kinds of heating and increased the speed of some steps in the assembly process, such as drying paint on individual parts. Overall, electrification permitted a higher and more predictable standard of parts production.

A fourth idea that Ford managers developed was that machines should not be grouped by type (e.g., all punch presses together) but instead should be arranged according to the sequence of work needed to create each product. Ford could rearrange production because machines driven by electricity could be placed in any order on the shop floor. Furthermore, stronger construction techniques made it possible for Ford to place heavy machinery and even a foundry on the top floors of its 1914 Highland Park factory. Before then, the weight of machinery and the problem of vibrations had made it advisable to have such work done on the lowest floor. The new arrangement meant that the upper floors fashioned raw materials into parts, which then "flowed" to sub-assembly lines on lower floors before arriving at the main assembly line on the ground floor. Completed cars could then be driven out of the building into the parking lot.[34] These changes had immediate effects. In 1911, the new plant made it possible almost to double the number of cars being produced per man.[35] Thus, two years before the full assembly line was put into place, four of its five major features—subdivision of labor, interchangeable parts, single-function machines, and the sequential ordering of machines—had doubled productivity

Much of the productivity improvement realized at Highland Park was achieved through more efficient in-house production of parts. In the first years of Model T manufacturing, the cost of parts from outside suppliers was high. Fully two-thirds of the cost of parts was attributable to the inefficient production of (as well as the profits made by) outside suppliers. Gradually, Highland Park manufactured more of its own parts, and did so more cheaply than suppliers could, driving down the percentage of outside components in a Model T. One team of historians found that between 1909 and 1916 the cost of materials per vehicle (including raw materials and manufactured parts bought elsewhere) dropped from $590 to $262.[36] Moreover, the increased capability to produce parts in house pressured Ford's remaining suppliers to lower their prices or risk losing their contracts. By comparison, the cost of wages per Model T was a far less important factor, and it remained relatively constant, between $64 and $70 per vehicle, except for much higher costs during the year Ford moved into Highland Park.[37] To put this another way, in 1914, when Ford doubled wages to $5 a day, productivity per worker had already doubled, and labor costs were less than one-fifth of the total cost of production.

The fifth feature of the assembly line was that parts and sub-assemblies were moved automatically from one stage of production to the next. The most conspicuous elements of the assembly line—its gravity slides and continuous moving belts—are often mistakenly thought to be the most important elements. Meat packers had used somewhat similar "disassembly lines" for much of the nineteenth century. Before 1900, flour mills, bakeries, breweries, and cigarette plants also operated continuous-process machinery, particularly in conjunction with ovens. Henry Ford himself had seen a striking application of materials processing and handling at Thomas Edison's iron-mining facility in Ogdensburg, New Jersey. Since Ford idolized Edison, this example is particularly important as a precursor. In the early 1890s it briefly seemed that high-grade iron ores were running out. That led Edison to develop a way to extract iron from low-grade magnetite. His operation blasted five-ton boulders out of a mountainside, smashed them into progressively smaller pieces, ground those pieces into sand, then pulled the iron particles out of the sand by pouring it past a series of powerful magnets. Although the idea was simple in conception, realizing it in practice required an enormous

93-ton steam shovel, a small railway system, and a crane to move the boulders to the 130-ton rollers that ripped the boulders into football-size chunks of stone. The progressively smaller stones were transported on rubberized conveyor belts that had been developed at the site by Edison and a young rubber products salesman named Thomas Robbins. Edison's mining site and mill integrated machines with conveyors in a single overall plan that moved materials continuously.[38] Ford and his managers, emulating the practices of breweries, meat-packing plants, canneries, and flour mills, used gravity slides and moving belts to bring tasks to workers at a height that would eliminate heavy lifting, bending, eyestrain, and other discomforts.

In the new system, the amount of space devoted to production shrank as Ford's managers sought to reduce in-process inventories and to keep handling of materials to a minimum. The distance an engine block traveled shrank from 4,000 feet to 334 feet, reducing the number of partially completed engine blocks along the line by more than 85 percent.[39] At the same time, more than twenty jobs for hand-truckers were completely eliminated. Thus, the assembly line was not only a matter of bringing the work to the worker, but also a matter of shrinking the distances and the inventories involved.

Together, these five practices—subdivision of labor, interchangeable parts, single-function machines, sequential ordering of machines, and movement of work to workers via slides and belts—define the assembly line as a physical technology. A sixth factor, factory electrification, was a necessary precondition before these elements could be improved individually and combined into a new form of production. And the value of electric lighting should not be overlooked. As late as the 1930s, Ford managers found "a direct relationship between the maintenance of adequate illumination and the production efficiency of the various departments"—so much so that lighting was seen as "another production tool which is just as important as are modern types of machine tool equipment."[40] These practices came together at Highland Park, resulting in an immediate leap in productivity in 1911, smaller increases in 1912 and 1913, and another leap in throughput in 1914 (the first year the assembly line was in full operation).

Another essential idea was to make only one product and freeze its design. Adam Smith's pin makers, the British Navy's bakery, and Han Dynasty lacquer factories had all grasped this idea. Like them, the Ford Motor Company understood that offering a variety of models would require a separate

assembly line for each, and each of those lines would need its own continuous stream of parts. Likewise, changing the design of a car required closing
the entire assembly line for time-consuming retooling.

Ford offered the Model T in only a few colors. In 1909, the only colors
were red, gray, and dark green. From 1911 until the end of 1914, all Model
Ts were dark blue. Black then became the only color available until 1925.
There was a choice between a hard metal top and a retracting leather top
that folded down like an accordion behind the back seat. There were only a
few other options, more in some years than in others.

The standardization of the Ford car created an opportunity for smaller
manufacturers who catered to consumers' desires for variety. They produced thousands of accessories: horns, wheels, specially designed beds, tents,
storage devices, even complete bodies. Hundreds of patents were granted.
In addition, thousands of suggestions for improvements—great and small,
practical and foolish—were submitted to Ford, to General Motors, and to
the other automakers. People proposed new oil gauges, foot-operated turn
signals, anti-glare windshields, heated steering wheels, and battery-powered
hot plates.[41] Almost all such suggestions were rejected, but both the public's
impulse to be in dialogue with manufacturers and the widespread customization of cars suggest the creativity that manufacturers would tap generations later in the era of mass customization.

Ford's new assembly line reduced the waste of motion and the incidence
of bottlenecks, most obviously in final assembly. In 1909, when older methods were still in use, assembling a single Model T took more than 12 hours;
by 1914 it took only 93 minutes. The same number of workers could assemble 775 percent more automobiles in 1914 than in 1909. (Looking only
at final assembly overstates the productivity of the assembly line, however.
Savings achieved in manufacturing individual parts weren't always as dramatic.) The assembly line made monitoring individual worker performance
easier. The responsibility for correct installation of each part was clear, and
any slacking on the job quickly created a bottleneck in the flow of production. The assembly line also reduced the quantities of spare parts that once
had been lying around as floating inventories and thus saved the capital
previously tied up in them. Because assembly lines sped up production and
reduced inventories, companies that adopted them had a tremendous competitive advantage. When Ford was the only auto company with this new
production technology, it could simultaneously undersell its competition,

raise wages, and increase profits. The assembly line appeared to be a new engine of progress that benefited consumers, workers, and management.

Knowing what the assembly line was after it was invented does not explain why the Ford Motor Company developed it. No master plan seems to have existed from the start, and certainly no one imagined the final result. Rather, Ford managers and engineers were struggling to make cars quickly enough to meet the accelerating demand. They looked for efficiencies, and they discovered that simple changes in how workers moved or were positioned or received the materials saved time. Along with these adjustments came subdivision of each job into many smaller tasks. That was hardly a new idea, but Ford took it to an extreme. Making a magneto took a single workman twenty minutes. The same task, subdivided and laid out along a moving line at the perfect height, could be done in seven minutes. The idea of the assembly line emerged from such sub-assemblies. The whole system might be diagrammed to look much like the skeleton of a fish, with all the short lines for parts manufacture leading into the assembly line.[42]

The ultimate incentive for creating the assembly line was the insatiable demand for the Model T. Had the American public wanted only 100,000 new cars a year, the older form of manufacture would have been appropriate. That was the scale of European production at the time. Mass production made sense only if there was mass demand. Henry Ford thought he could enlarge the market by lowering the price. Against the advice of his executives and stockholders, he continually reduced the price of the Model T, which in turn raised demand and made greater economies of scale possible. After Ford bought out all the other stockholders, no one could obstruct this policy. By 1926, a new Model T could be had for less than $300.

Higher-volume production not only required more factories; it also required new kinds of factories. The series of plants Ford built in the two decades after the founding of his company in 1903 trace the transformation of architecture that accompanied changes in production. The 1904 Piquette Avenue building resembled a nineteenth-century textile mill. It was three stories high, a block long, and only 39 feet wide. Built specifically for manufacturing automobiles, it nevertheless was obsolete in only five years. It was suited to artisan laborers and the production of only a few thousand cars a year. As Klann noted, at the Piquette Avenue plant the "process was to build a car in one spot on [saw] horses and build it up the way you would a house."[43] By 1909, Ford was making 14,000 cars a year, and a larger facility with a different design was needed. The Highland Park plant was much larger than the Piquette Avenue plant. It was more open, it facilitated the handling of materials, and all the machinery was driven by electric motors. It was built of steel-reinforced concrete, which made it much more solid than a brick building and reduced vibration. However, the workers got sore legs standing on concrete all day. To make them more comfortable and to reduce absenteeism, wooden flooring was installed in work areas.[44] In that plant the assembly line was invented incrementally, and production skyrocketed. In 1910–11 it more than doubled, to 35,000 automobiles. The following year it rose to 78,000, and by 1913–14, when the assembly line was installed, it reached 248,000. Ford then built an additional factory complex at Highland Park; it was the first automobile plant designed with the assembly line in mind. Biggs has rightly emphasized the importance of the 1914 New Shop in Highland Park as the first rational factory.[45] Completed in August 1914, its two parallel buildings, each six stories tall, were built of steel-reinforced concrete. The New Shop was the full expression of the Ford assembly line. In the 1920s, the Highland Park complex produced more cars in a week than the Piquette Avenue plant had produced in its best year.[46]

Three additional aspects of Ford's assembly line must be emphasized. The first of these was the $5 day, introduced early in 1914, when the usual pay for a day's work was $2.50. The Ford Motor Company explained the higher wage as a form of profit sharing; it paid workers more because they helped make the assembly line more efficient. (An additional motive for the $5 day, reducing labor turnover, is discussed in chapter 5.) Workers' pay statements listed both a wage and a bonus. Higher pay clearly encouraged workers to be more productive. Despite the cost of paying a higher wage, Ford's profits rose to $30.3 million in 1914 and to $40.3 million in 1915.[47] These profits were achieved while prices were reduced. Ford lowered the price of the Model T by $50 in 1913 and by $60 in 1914. As table 2.1 shows, the real price of a Model T, in constant 1910 dollars, fell from $950 to just $214 in 1921.

The higher wage and the falling price of the Model T made it possible for Ford's workers to purchase their own automobiles. Henry Ford understood that mass production required mass consumption. In 1910, when a Ford worker typically was paid $2.50 a day, a $950 automobile cost 380 days'

FIGURE 2.4
The Piquette Avenue plant, where the Model T was designed and where it was manufactured before the assembly line. Photograph by David E. Nye.

wages. In 1921 a new Model T cost $397—only 80 days' wages at $5 a day. A used one, of course, cost even less.

Ford's $5 day linked production and consumption. When wages doubled, consumption could rise accordingly. More recently, American and European corporations have exported manufacturing of products intended for high-income markets to low-wage nations in Latin America, Asia, and Eastern Europe. Mass-production workers in developing countries aren't seen as potential consumers. Instead, corporations maximize profits by minimizing wages. In 1914 Henry Ford might have done the same thing. Instead, he raised wages, increased productivity, and relentlessly drove down the price of his car in order to maximize the size of his market. By the early 1920s, his company was making half of the world's automobiles.

A second important aspect of the assembly line, as the Ford Motor Company conceived it, was an insistence on recycling and eliminating waste. For example, in the 1920s many parts of a Model T were made from wood. In this area, as in many others, Ford pursued vertical integration, purchasing

TABLE 2.1
Data on Model T automobiles, 1910–1921

	Nominal price	Real price (1910 dollars)	Number of cars produced
1910	$950	$950	19,051
1911	$780	$787.90	34,070
1912	$690	$669.40	76,150
1913	$600	$585.90	181,951
1914	$550	$526.80	264,972
1915	$490	$448.60	283,161
1916	$440	$359.30	534,108
1917	$360	$236.70	785,433
1918	$450	$263.10	664,076
1919	$525	$269	498,342
1920	$507	$227.90	941,042
1921	$397	$214	971,610

Sources: Ford 1922, p. 145; Department of Commerce 1975, p. 224; Casey 2003, p. 51.

a forest in northern Michigan and building a factory there to manufacture wooden parts. Shipping finished parts to the River Rouge plant cost far less than shipping wooden boards, for much of the wood in unfinished boards later became waste. The sawdust was burned as fuel. Larger fragments left over after manufacturing were converted into charcoal. In every area of production, the goal was to reuse by-products and minimize waste. The River Rouge plant made its own coke from coal, in the process producing ammonium sulfate (which was sold as fertilizer), benzol (which could be mixed with gasoline and used in cars), and gas and tar (both of which the plant burned as fuel).[48] One story had it that during the years 1910–1914, when Ford bought engines from John and Horace Dodge, the packing cases they came in were used to make wooden panels for the sides of Ford's cars. Apocryphal or not, that story caught the essence of this aspect of the Ford system. Ideally, the factory was to convert all of the materials it received into useful products.

The Model T is often thought of as having changed little between its introduction in 1908 and 1927, when the 15 millionth unit was built. In fact, the Model T underwent many changes in the two decades of its production.

Notably, electric lights and an electric starter were added. The car's styling underwent some modest changes, too. In all, "the Model T underwent thousands of detail changes,"[49] and it was a far better car in 1927 than it had been in 1908. The transmission, the magneto, and the four-cylinder engine were changed less than other parts, but the product was hardly static. In 1913 alone, Ford made more than 100 design changes every month. As those who purchase and restore a Model T quickly discover, the general appearance may be much the same from 1912 until 1927, but the model year does matter. For example, the electrical system was completely redesigned twice. Alterations weren't ballyhooed in annual model changes but instead were introduced piecemeal. Most of the changes were scarcely visible to the average customer.

However, incremental changes couldn't postpone the need to develop a better vehicle indefinitely. Richard Kroll, an important figure in the development of the Model A, was quoted as saying "I think Mr. Ford stayed with the Model T so long with the idea that as long as you sell all you make, why should you change?"[50]

Ford's assembly line did not develop from or much resemble Frederick Winslow Taylor's concept of scientific management. Both systems sought to rationalize work and to improve efficiency, but they weren't at all the same. Taylor's system, which emerged first, focused on making workers' movements more efficient. Instead of allowing workers to decide how they wished to tackle a task, such as shoveling, Taylor determined the ideal weight for a man to lift, then designed specialized shovels for each task, so that a shovel for moving a light material, such as sawdust, held a greater volume than one for lifting something heavier, such as sand. Taylor also regulated work routines, telling men when and how long they should relax and specifying how much work they should do. By examining the movements of the most efficient workers and breaking them down into small sequences, Taylor determined "the best way" to perform a task and then retrained workers to complete a job with a minimum of effort and movement. To motivate workers to do more, Taylor relied upon incentives. There were normal wages for achieving a prescribed daily quota, and there were bonuses for exceeding the norm.

Essentially, what Taylor did was modify the piece-rate system. Managers who worked in a similar spirit often used a stopwatch to establish how long each movement on every job should take. The scientific manager demanded that workers give up personal routines for standardized movements made with standardized tools and paid them according to an incentive system. Those who cooperated produced more. In return, Taylor expected employers to raise workers' pay, though not all corporations did so.

Taylor's methods aroused strong opposition. In *Taylorism at Watertown Arsenal*, Hugh Aitkin notes that workers prevented Taylorism from being put into effect by demonstrating that they knew more about their tasks than those who attempted to reformulate them.[51] Despite such setbacks, Taylor's ideas circulated widely. His book *The Principles of Scientific Management* sold widely in French, German, and Russian translations, and was praised by Lenin. "Taylorism" had enormous resonance beyond the factory in many areas, including home economics, education, and popular culture. Experts appeared in every area of life, proclaiming that they had discovered the "one best way" to (for example) arrange a kitchen, regulate traffic, or plan a community.

Nothing could have been further from Taylorism than Ford's assembly line. Whereas Taylor designed ideal shovels, Ford abolished shoveling by using electric cranes, moving belts, and other devices as aids to continuous-flow manufacturing. Taylor retrained a worker to do the same job more efficiently; the assembly line redefined and simplified jobs. Taylor offered workers incentives to do piecework more quickly; Ford made piece rates pointless, because the assembly line paced the work, pushing everyone to move at the same speed. Instead, workers received a high fixed wage. Taylor maximized efficiency in existing production technologies; Ford transformed the means of production. Taylor saved time; Ford sped up time. In 1914, after Taylor put his system into operation at the Packard Motor Company, its 4,525 workers produced 2,984 cars a year—only about two-thirds of a car per employee. That was still fabrication by artisan methods. In the same year, 13,000 Ford employees, using conveyor belts, electric cranes, and 15,000 specialized machine tools, manufactured 260,000 cars—that is, 20 per man. Ford's workers outperformed Packard's Taylor-organized workers by 3,000 percent. In four days they assembled more automobiles than Packard constructed in an entire year. Taylor had maximized what was possible in the older artisan tradition. The assembly line was still in its infancy, and it would become far more productive. People often measured the productivity of the assembly line not by output per worker, but rather by how fast the cars were made. Before the assembly line, Ford workers took more than 750 minutes to assemble a car. Once the assembly line went into operation, in less than 100 minutes a car was already outside the factory, waiting for its top to be added.[52]

Because the manufacturing systems of Taylor and Ford differ so sharply, some historians have contended that they represent two distinct historical stages, "Taylorism" and "Fordism." Implicit in such arguments is the idea that manufacturing as a whole evolves through distinct historical stages, culminating in "Fordist" mass production. However, Phillip Scranton has shown that this approach to manufacturing history does not square with the complexity of historical fact. In *Endless Novelty*, rather than see large corporations such as Standard Oil, General Motors, Ford, and DuPont as the most advanced form of capitalism, Scranton examines the success that various firms achieved with customized and small-batch production. Far from being

FIGURE 2.5
The end of the assembly line outside the Highland Park plant, 1914. Photographer unknown. Records of Bureau of Public Roads. Courtesy of National Archives

unprofitable businesses destined to be converted to Taylorism before adopting assembly lines, such companies remained financially successful, and they proved just as important to an advanced economy as those that embraced mass production. Companies fabricating elevators, turbines, switchboards, and precision instruments didn't "fail" to become mass producers. Nor did they want to deskill labor. Rather, they prized skilled workmen who could respond flexibly to demands for varied goods. Such workers made possible the endless novelty that was the hallmark of the consumer society, and such companies were innovative and profitable. Taylor's prescriptions were more useful for the production of identical things than for batch production of fine carpets, furniture, jewelry, cutlery, hats, and ready-to-wear clothing. Large profits accrued to flexible firms with skilled workers who could supply variety. Assembly lines were suited to making identical things, but many products of advanced technology had to meet customers' requirements for installation at specific locations, and department stores' customers wanted variety and novelty.

Specialty production wasn't a sideshow. It grew just as fast as mass production, but it did so with different central actors. Instead of the "visible hand" of corporate managers advised by scientific experts, at the center were skilled workers and technologically adept owners. When it suited them, they drew on new work systems, of which Taylorism was only one. Instead of the rigidity of Taylor's "one best way," they valued flexibility. Instead of standardization of production at capital-intensive plants, they fostered diverse production at labor-intensive mid-size factories, and such factories proved to be technologically innovative. In short, industry as a whole didn't move through stages from artisan production to "Taylorism" to "Fordism." There was no single path for successful corporate development. Rather, the assembly line was ideal for long runs of identical goods, but specialty production was ideal for products that were distinctive, and it could change rapidly to meet the demands of fashion. Likewise, complex machines, such as steam locomotives, elevators, and switchboards, had to be crafted to meet the needs of particular buyers. They were never produced in numbers great enough to justify setting up an assembly line. Instead of a single path to development, there were many.

Nevertheless, the assembly line was extraordinarily productive in comparison with the craft-labor assembly of cars that preceded it. Daniel Raff examined the Ford Motor Company's records from the years 1909–1914 and concluded, after making adjustments for changes in raw material prices and the cost of living, that Ford was an extraordinarily efficient and profitable company compared to the rest of American industry in those years.[53] Its annual productivity growth was an astounding 22 percent, versus 1.5 percent for the economy as a whole. Many industries, including those producing electrical machinery, durable goods, and textiles, were almost stagnant during those years, with productivity growth at less than 1 percent. Some industries, including chemicals, furniture, and primary metals, even became slightly *less* productive between 1909 and 1919. Clearly the assembly line broke these patterns dramatically, and the productivity increases continued during the 1920s.

Defining the elements of the assembly line and demonstrating how it differed from Taylor's scientific management does not explain how the assembly line came into being. The process of breaking down conventions, throwing out inherited work routines, building new equipment, and arranging equipment in new ways demanded a special atmosphere of experimentation and an exceptional openness to change. That the elements of the assembly line were all available does not mean that it was inevitable that they would be combined. Had Henry Ford behaved like all the other automobile manufacturers in 1910, he would still have made a good deal of money. But Ford's managers weren't driven only by a desire for profits. They had a vision of accelerated production and efficiency, and that vision became an end in itself. They briefly created a dynamic of discussion, feedback, and continual improvement much like the one that would be created several generations later in Japan. That dynamic was carried over from Highland Park to the River Rouge plant, which was built around the company's evolving understanding of the most efficient form of an assembly line. Rather than credit Henry Ford for these developments, it is more accurate to say that he was the fortunate beneficiary of synergies among the exceptionally talented people he recruited. Ford gave authority to people who were willing to buck convention. In retrospect, something like the assembly line might seem to have been the inevitable result when strong consumer demand stimulated managers to look for more efficient manufacturing methods. But the assembly line could have emerged later, or somewhere else, making another product. It conceivably could have emerged sooner—perhaps in France, where the goal of interchangeable parts was briefly pursued in the late eighteenth century.[54]

But technological innovations aren't always remembered. As Alder has emphasized, "a technology (even a technology today accounted superior) can
be rejected, discontinued, and forgotten."[55] This happened to the achievement of interchangeability of parts in French arms production when Napo-
leon reverted to the artisan production of the *ancien regime*.

In contrast, once the assembly line was up and running, it most certainly
wasn't forgotten, but it has often been oversimplified and mis-remembered.
The majority of the cost savings achieved at Ford's Highland Park factory
were not due to the introduction of the moving line itself; rather, they
resulted from efficiencies realized through subdivision of labor, improved
accuracy in making interchangeable parts, rearrangement of machinery, and
better work-flow layouts. These changes were possible only in an electrified
factory. The assembly line is best understood not as a rigid system, and not
as an imagined historical stage called "Fordism" following an equally imagi-
nary "Taylorism," but rather as a moment of synthesis for a still-evolving
processing technology.

3 CELEBRATION

Mass production is not simply large-scale production. It is large-scale production based upon a clear understanding that increased production demands increased buying, and that the greatest total profits can be obtained only if the masses can and do enjoy a higher and ever higher standard of living. For selfish business reasons, therefore, genuine mass production industries must make prices lower and lower and wages higher and higher, while constantly shortening the workday and bringing to the masses not only more money but more time. . . .

—Edward Filene, *Successful Living in This Machine Age*[1]

When they first heard about the assembly line, many people burbled with excitement. In 1913 newspapers reported that Ford produced "one complete car every forty seconds."[2] The idea that mankind could produce more while working less was a staple of progressivism. Thousands of plant managers, engineers, and scientists constantly looked for labor-saving techniques and devices. They believed that rapid progress had occurred during the nineteenth century and that such progress could be measured objectively.

A leading engineer in the 1880s was Robert Thurston, a professor at Cornell University and a president of the American Society of Mechanical Engineers. In an article in the *North American Review* he extolled the rising standard of living that industry made available to all Americans, and the *Literary Digest* condensed his ideas for the popular audience.[3] Thurston illustrated progress with charts and with diagrams whose lines moved insistently upward.[4] He concluded that the value of a typical American family's

FIGURE 3. 1
A meat-packing line of 1910, with the individual machines driven by overhead belts rather than by electric motors. Courtesy of National Archives.

consumer goods, including clothing, appliances, and home furnishings, had risen rapidly. In just 20 years, production per factory hand had increased almost 30 percent, and real wages had risen 20 percent even though working hours had decreased.[5] Workers had more leisure time, higher real incomes, and more material goods. Such gains throughout the nineteenth century had improved people's lives radically. "Our mills, our factories, our workshops of every kind are mainly engaged in supplying our people with the comforts and the luxuries of modern life, and in converting crudeness and barbarism into cultured civilization," Thurston wrote in 1895. "We are fifty percent more comfortable than in 1880, sixteen times as comfortable as were our parents in 1850, and our children, in 1900 to 1910, will have twice as many luxuries and live twice as easy and comfortable lives."[6] Commissioner of Labor Carroll D. Wright advanced a similar argument at Chautauqua meetings and in a book titled *The Industrial Evolution of the United States*.[7] A generation before the assembly line, many believed that improved production technologies reduced working hours and increased real wages. When the assembly line appeared, it seemed a particularly good example of that general trend.

Some innovations are anticipated—even intensely sought after—years before they become reality; a notable example is the airplane. Others get extravagant press attention well before they become practical, as was the case with radio. But the assembly line wasn't anticipated or ballyhooed. It emerged with so little fanfare that it scarcely had a name before it existed. At first, the term "assembly line" was used only in the technical press, as in this example from a 1914 issue of *Engineering Magazine*: "Finishing and assembling of front-axle components shows how labor-costs may be . . . reduced . . . by the use of sliding assembly lines, chain-driven for the final assembling, but having the partial assemblies moved by hand."[8] The *New York Times* didn't use the term "assembly line" even once in the full-page story on the Ford factory that it ran in January 1914, nor did any of the six photographs that accompanied that story show an assembly line. Likewise, a 1918 story in the *Los Angeles Times* called Highland Park a "wonderful place" but didn't use the term "assembly line" at all; indeed, the absence of that term was obvious—the author labored to convey how it was possible for the motor department to create new motors at a rate of one every 30 seconds, citing the "amazingly well-developed organization with every man, and every piece of machinery and conveyor system assigned to some definite work or part in the process of assembly."[9] The *New York Times* seems not to have used the

term "assembly line" until 1923, when it appeared in an article about Studebaker.[10] Contrary to what one might expect, "assembly line" wasn't widely
used between 1914 and 1920. "Mass production" was more common.

That "assembly line" took some time to become a familiar term is evident from presidential speeches. Woodrow Wilson apparently never used
it, nor did any of his three successors during the 1920s use it in reference to
industry or productivity. Warren Harding, Calvin Coolidge, and Herbert
Hoover all had met Henry Ford, and they saw Model Ts on the roads.
However, the first president to use the term "assembly line" frequently was
Franklin D. Roosevelt. His predecessors had known that Ford had created a
new kind of production, but "assembly line" hadn't yet been universalized
as a term to describe a widespread system. It took at least ten years for it to
become a common expression. As late as 1941, a two-volume engineering
encyclopedia didn't have an entry for "assembly line," though it had one
for "progressive assembly." That entry focused on "conveyor systems" and
their speed without mentioning interchangeable parts, electric motors, the
division of labor, or standardization of the manufactured product.[11]

Although the assembly line was neither anticipated nor quickly named,
the public was well aware of the idea of mass production. In 1853 a paper-
folding machine was introduced that enabled just three workers to produce 2,500 envelopes per hour. In the 1860s petroleum refiners developed
continuous-process systems that tripled output while cutting costs in half.
By the end of that decade the Bessemer process enabled steel production to
speed up, and in the 1870s iron, copper, zinc, and glass companies adopted
continuous-process technologies.[12] By 1908 sheets of glass could be rolled
out in any size desired.[13] Similar developments occurred in food processing.
Consider the canning industry. In 1865 each can was produced by hand, and
a good worker could make between 200 and 400 in a day. By 1883 Heinz
and Borden had mechanized production, and a dozen unskilled workers
operating largely automatic machines could make 30,000 cans a day. For
a few more years the tops of cans were soldered on, but soon that too was
mechanized.[14] Likewise, in 1882 continuous-process production of oatmeal
meant that a single plant could supply the entire nation's needs. In each of
these industries, costs went down and quality improved.

When the assembly line emerged, the public already knew about continuous-process production, even if people seldom used the term "mass production" to talk about it. At Ford's factories they saw the culmination of

developments that had been occurring for two generations. For example, Ford had a machine from which a continuous glass sheet 51 inches wide rolled out at a rate of three and a half miles a day—more than a thousand miles of glass per year.[15] For a generation before the assembly line, advertisements had emphasized the reliability of standardized goods and the desirability of economies of scale in large factories that produced for the national market. From the last few decades of the nineteenth century until World War I, "companies put a strong emphasis on converting the population to the modern ways of mass production and factory-made goods."[16] Food processors, the companies that pioneered the conveyor belts and flow production Ford would later adopt, were keen to show consumers the scale of their production. At the 1893 Columbian Exposition, in Chicago, the maker of Quaker Oats distributed a lithograph of an entire train of railway cars packed with its breakfast cereals. The company's magazine advertising also emphasized that it was "shipped in trainloads." Mountains of California oranges, pyramids of Heinz pickles, and other gargantuan displays were typical of nineteenth-century expositions. Sheer volume was also a frequent advertising theme. In 1905, Wrigley's ran an advertisement claiming that it had made the largest rail shipment of chewing gum in history—60,000 boxes.

Companies proudly featured bird's-eye views of their factories in magazine advertisements. Many also threw open their doors to factory tours. Visitors to a Heinz plant saw spotless rooms and hygienic production areas presided over by young women in clean white aprons, and presumably came away convinced that Heinz pickles and condiments were of the highest quality.[17] Thousands of visitors each year saw pools of Hershey chocolate in cavernous stainless steel pots being stirred automatically, then followed the process as it was made into candy bars. At the Pan American Exposition held in Buffalo in 1901, General Electric displayed a working model of its largest factory. Several corporations brought full-scale factories to the Louisiana Purchase Exposition held in St. Louis in 1904.[18] The Pennsylvania coal companies displayed an "operating" anthracite mine, a cement factory, and an oil drill. This tendency culminated in 1915 at the San Francisco Exposition, where US Steel poured molten steel in an operating mill and Heinz showed how its jars were sterilized, filled with various foodstuffs, and hermetically sealed. Fairgoers evidently delighted in seeing the movement of actual production.

When the assembly line suddenly appeared, it was understood both as something new and as a culmination of earlier trends. Because it wasn't seen even in embryonic form outside the Ford Motor Company until 1914, it made a powerful initial impression. Newspaper stories and magazine articles on it began to appear in 1914 and 1915, stimulating public interest. Those not content with a few pages of description could buy *Ford Methods and Ford Shops*, a detailed and well-illustrated book that documented the new production methods.[19] But much of the public wanted to see an assembly line in action. The Ford Motor Company was besieged by an unending stream of visitors, and by 1916 it had 25 full-time tour guides. When it was noticed that the visitors often distracted the workers, Ford let more and more visitors in until they were no longer a novelty.[20] Former president William Howard Taft came and pronounced the assembly line "wonderful, wonderful." One journalist called the Ford factory "a national landmark and a new Niagara Falls." Twenty businessmen from Rochester, New York made a special trip to see the Highland Park factory, like pilgrims going to a shrine.[21] A journalist declared that Highland Park "is to Detroit what the Woolworth Building is to New York. It stands out like a beacon in the fog."[22] Even branch assembly plants conducted tours. In 1916, Ford's Omaha factory had 20,000 visitors, and just as many toured a plant in Minnesota.[23]

Building on this public interest, Ford set up a working assembly line to produce Model Ts at the 1915 San Francisco World's Fair. Every day, thousands of people, mostly men, watched cars being assembled from parts shipped in by rail from Detroit. Henry Ford himself was in San Francisco for several weeks, adding to the crowd's excitement. The Ford exhibit proved to be the most popular at the fair. When it opened, police had to restrain the crowds from pressing forward to get a closer look. Every day, people waited as long as two hours to get a good viewing position. Back in Detroit, tours of other automakers' assembly lines were also popular. Thousands trooped through the Dodge and General Motors plants.

Gold Shod, a 1921 novel about the automobile business, described how white-collar employees were given factory tours when first hired. A guide conducts one through the plant. "He had never visited a factory before. He had always thought of motor cars in terms of flight over fragrant country roads." But after his visit, he "saw them . . . in terms of enormous presses smashing steel plates into fenders, of a tangle of revolving belting in machine shops, of painting, woodworking, upholstering, and the final assembly." In contrast to his previous job writing advertising copy for an old-fashioned shoe business, "here was a business that gave him something to get his eyes on, something to get his hands on. It was stimulating to see the product being made, to see big men at work." Until this point in his life, the man had drifted, without much sense of purpose, in "dreamy apathy." But seeing the assembly-line factory "quickened his pace and his mind."[24] The idea that powerful machines and new technologies enlivened and inspired those who saw them was fundamental to the ideology of the technological sublime. As early as the 1830s it was not unusual for Americans to speak of railroads as "moral machines" that elevated the mind.[25] Visitors appreciated assembly-line factories in the same spirit.

In the 1924 novel *Temper*, an auto worker senses "a beating that always comes inside of you when you are in the factory. It made your heart beat change, and your breathing change until you got into step with it. Every man's body on every machine swung backward and forward with it—not with each other, with *it*, the beating." This insistent, overwhelming rhythm set a pace that "bosses had to change when they wanted more production, and they found it a very hard thing to do." Workers at each machine found what felt like the right pace. "It came into you through the floor on which you stood, through every lever that you put your hand upon, through every breath that you breathed, and even through all of the clamor that kept your ears filled with the good sound of men at work."[26] Such factory jobs could seem fiercely attractive to some workers. Even after the protagonist is injured and loses the use of one hand, the factory still casts a spell over him. When he returns to a lesser job, he still feels the beating of the factory. He draws a deep breath, "drinking the spirit of the place down into his lungs," and begins "to feel once more the 'iron in his blood.'"[27] However, with nearly ten years' experience, he is aware of the danger of immersing himself in the machine rhythm. "He was not going to let himself be carried away by it." Few visitors remained long enough to gain such wary insights.

Ford's River Rouge plant, completed in the 1920s, was even more popular with tourists than Highland Park. As late as 1940 it attracted 166,000 visitors per year.[28] The world's largest factory, it exemplified vertical integration. Here workers didn't merely assemble cars; they also smelted steel, produced light and power, and made virtually every part that went into each car. Guides enthusiastically cited statistics, informing tourists that the complex employed 100,000 workers, had 16 million square feet of floor space and 92 miles of railway track, and consumed 86 tons of soap every month. Its powerhouse made enough electricity to light all the homes in Chicago. It used more water than Detroit and Cincinnati combined. Working at top speed, the factory could transform iron ore, sand, and other raw materials into a functioning car in just 28 hours.

Albert Kahn, the architect for the Highland Park plant, also designed the River Rouge plant. He used steel-reinforced concrete to create large interior spaces without many columns or other supports, and worked closely with the company to lay out the floor plan. The factory's overall design was functionalist, but the use of space wasn't rigidly preconceived. The builder, William Verner, studied the process of making the Model T and laid out each section of the new factory in consultation with the managers of each process. The flow of the work determined the placement of each building. Since a Model T's main ingredient was steel, Verner began with the railroads and

FIGURE 3.2

An aerial view of Ford's River Rouge plant circa 1940. Courtesy of Photographic Department, Cleveland Public Library.

canals that transported the raw materials needed to produce it.[29] Once the location of railroads and canals had been worked out, he built a steel mill, then a foundry for engine blocks, rolling mills, and all the facilities needed to make sheet steel and stamp it into parts. The transportation of raw materials and parts between buildings was also designed into the architecture, and the details of every section of the new plant were developed in consultation with the Highland Park managers who were going to move to River Rouge. Logan Miller helped lay out the new motor department, making use of his experiences at Highland Park. "In the new motor building," he recalled, "we changed the flow of material considerably" as many conveyors were added. By contrast, at Highland Park "parts were kept in stock bins and there were few conveyors." In a 1915 book titled *Ford Methods and the Ford Shops* Horace Arnold and Fay Faurote had praised part bins and their replenishment as a form of efficiency, but at River Rouge managers tried to get rid of buffer inventories. Instead, "some conveyors acted as storage places from one operation to another." This might suggest that because River Rouge was large the work was spread out. But, Miller noted, "the machine shop setup was more compact. We studied the setup of machinery so there was no wasted space. We tried to move the machines as close together as possible to eliminate the movement of stock."

Yet the new factory had space for later innovation. Miller emphasized that there was no permanent layout for the machine shops, because the "production people . . . had the idea that there were going to be many changes in the makeup of the automobile."[30] Thus, the River Rouge plant was built to accommodate the flow of production without creating a rigid arrangement that might constrain further innovations in the work process. By the mid 1920s, a modern factory was no longer merely a container for work processes; it was a master machine that organized and expressed the whole system of production.

At both River Rouge and Highland Park, Ford ensured that visitors had elevated views so that the factories could be seen as a vast landscape of harmonious production.[31] One journalist described the overall effect on a visitor: "He sees these units not only in their impressive individual and astounding collective magnitude, but he also sees each unit as a part of a huge machine—he sees each unit as a carefully designed gear which meshes with other gears and operates in synchronism with them, the whole forming one huge, perfectly-timed, smoothly operating industrial machine of almost unbelievable manufacturing efficiency."[32]

Not content to reach only those who visited Detroit, the Ford Motor Company also used print and film media. In 1922 Henry Ford published the ghost-written *My Life and Work*, which became a best-seller in many countries; the British edition alone went through seven reprintings in its first year.[33] The company also distributed films of assembly-line factories to movie theaters across the United States. The ten-to-fifteen-minute Ford Animated Weekly films covered a wide range of topics, including American geography, current events, and sports. Some of them told the "Ford story" from the first quadricycle to the Model T. Moviegoers saw a recreated sequence. In the first scenes, cars were being assembled on sawhorses. Next came the changeover to pushing cars along the line, then the introduction of a track through the Highland Park plant, and finally the emergence of the full assembly line in 1913. In 1917 and 1918, Ford publicized the use of assembly lines to manufacture Liberty Ships and Fordson tractors. In the 1920s, Ford's films showed all aspects of production at the River Rouge.[34] Other short films showed the far-flung operations that made Ford a tightly integrated corporation. It owned half a million acres of forests and extensive iron mines in Northern Michigan. It owned coal mines in Kentucky and West Virginia. It owned a railroad and steamships to transport these raw materials to River Rouge. Eventually it would acquire a Brazilian rubber plantation.[35] In 1924, Ford exhibited a model of the River Rouge plant in New York City.[36]

Not only in the United States but also in other parts of the world, people praised the sheer size of such factories and the enormous number of cars produced. Newspaper stories continually raved about the rising output of automobile assembly lines and marveled at consumers' eagerness. In 1916, observers were amazed that sales of American automobiles might reach 100,000 a month. Five years later, Ford alone was selling more than 100,000 cars a month. Moreover, prices kept falling. In 1916 the price of a Model T coupe fell from $420 to $360. The *New York Times* calculated that anyone with an income of $1,200 a year could afford such a car, and that there were 5 million potential buyers in the United States.[37] In subsequent years, salaries would rise, while the cost of a new Ford would continue to fall. Moreover, many people began to buy used cars, and automobiles became common among every social class but the destitute. In 1920 used cars accounted for 38 percent of all cars bought; by 1927 they accounted for more than half. In such a market, as the price of a Model T continued to fall, Ford's competitors found it virtually impossible to produce a car of equal quality at such a low price. Yet if they couldn't produce a basic car more cheaply, they could offer a variety of automobiles at higher prices.

Ford's most important competitor was Alfred P. Sloan, a graduate of the Massachusetts Institute of Technology who had made a small fortune working for the Hyatt Roller Bearing Company in Newark, New Jersey, which manufactured ball bearings for the auto industry. General Motors bought out Hyatt in 1918 and made Sloan an executive in charge of parts manufacturing, then a vice-president in 1920, then president in 1923. At 48, he was totally dedicated to his job and an extremely talented organizer. He also realized that a corporation as large as GM needed to decentralize responsibility. Ford remained under the nearly autocratic control of its founder. In contrast, under Sloan's guidance, GM developed into the exemplar of the modern American corporation. Each of its divisions—Chevrolet, Pontiac, Buick, Oldsmobile, and Cadillac—was expected to focus on a particular segment of the market, and each was expected to make a profit. GM's central management demanded detailed reports on a regular basis but didn't try to control the day-to-day work on the shop floor. Instead, management focused on changes in the market, studied the competition, decided on strategy, coordinated advertising, and developed long-term plans and perspectives. It told the divisions how many cars each should produce but allowed them some autonomy. GM fully embraced the assembly line in its manufacturing, but far more than Ford it also focused on styling, on marketing, on positioning its products, and on developing a system of selling on credit that would permit customers to "move up" to more expensive vehicles.[38]

"In 1921," Sloan later recalled, "Ford had about 60 percent of the total car and truck market in units, and Chevrolet had about 4 percent. With Ford in almost complete possession of the low-price field, it would have been suicidal to compete with him head on." Sloan decided that General Motors couldn't beat Ford "at his own game" and should instead devise a "strategy . . . to take a bite from the top of his position, conceived as a price class."[39] Sloan thought some of Ford's consumers might be willing to pay a bit more to get a little more luxury, a variety of colors, and new accessories. He also thought automobiles might become a way to display wealth and to show friends and neighbors that one was getting ahead. GM's cars ranged in price from $450 to $3,500. Each division used assembly-line production, and economies of scale were realized through the sharing of some parts and some suppliers. However, divisions building higher-priced cars could afford to spend more time on assembly, could install more expensive components, and could devote more resources to design. Sloan thus offered a ladder of consumption that Americans could climb as high as their incomes permitted. The strategy worked so well that Henry Ford's company lost market share every year, and in 1927 it had to replace the Model T with a new model.

Many companies outside the automobile industry adopted the assembly line. GM's Frigidaire division used it to produce refrigerators. Almost all of the factories making radios, washing machines, toasters, and tires adopted it. In the 1920s, factories churned out millions of electric irons, vacuum cleaners, corn poppers, coffee percolators, and other household appliances. A survey found that as early as 1921 three-fourths of the households in Philadelphia had an electric iron and half had a vacuum cleaner.[40] By 1930, mass-produced electric fans, radios, and washing machines had become as widespread as the automobile.

In the nineteenth century, flour mills and canneries had made standardized production not merely acceptable but a sanitary ideal. In the twentieth century, the assembly line was applied to food processing. In the fruit canning industry of the 1920s, fruit was still peeled, pitted, and packed by hand. (See figure 3.3.) Those tasks and others were gradually mechanized, but not until the 1950s were all steps done by machines.[41] Similar changes took place in the candy industry. In 1910 two-thirds of the bread in the United States had been made in the home, yet by 1924 two-thirds of all bread was made in automated factories and the baking industry was being consolidated through mergers. What had previously been a craft became a science, with precise measurements, temperature controls, and automatic timing.[42] The assembly line also spread to farms. Cows had been milked by hand for thousands of years, but in 1930, with "automatic machinery that resembles an assembly line," they could be bathed and milked several times a day. A cow simply walked into one of a farm's 50 stalls and was kept in place by a stanchion that closed after it came in. A giant rotary combine milker or "rotolacter" could wash and milk 50 cows simultaneously in 12½ minutes—nearly 250 cows an hour. The milking apparatus was automatically cleaned after each use, and the milk was immediately carried off by hoses to refrigerated storage. However, that innovation didn't spread quickly in the depressed economy of the 1930s, and the Borden Company could still display it as a novelty at the New York World's Fair in 1939.[43]

FIGURE 3.3

"Food—Hawaii—Canning. Native girls packing pineapple into cans." Photograph by Edgeworth for Katakura & Company, November 20, 1928. Records of the Women's Bureau. Courtesy of National Archives.

The *Encyclopaedia Britannica* asked Henry Ford for an article explaining mass production for its thirteenth edition (1926). Ford didn't actually write the article (which explained mass production as management's application of "the principles of power, accuracy, economy, system, continuity, speed and repetition," in order to produce "continuous quantities" of "a useful commodity of standard material, workmanship and design at minimum cost"), but he approved it. The importance of mass production, particularly in the automobile industry, also was evident in the census of 1930. It reported that 49 companies were producing automobiles and 1,154 companies were supplying parts. They paid $732 million in wages to 447,000 workers, who created just over $2 billion in added value.[44] One-third of those workers were in two states: Michigan and Ohio.[45] Nine times as many people were making automobiles as were building railroad cars and locomotives, even though railway manufacturing had tripled in size since 1900.[46] In practical terms, this meant that in 1929 there was "1 motor vehicle to 4.6 persons or 1 family" in the United States.[47] The automobile industry's average annual wage in 1904 had been $594 a year. In 1914 it was $802. By 1924 it exceeded $1,600.[48]

That other industries also adopted the assembly line was evident from a startling statistic. Between 1919 and 1929 the number of factory workers declined 1.8 percent, despite enormous increases in manufacturing. In contrast, between 1899 and 1919 the number of industrial workers had doubled. Yet if during the 1920s the number of workers remained static, output soared. The census calculated that the total production of industrial goods had nearly tripled between 1899 and 1929.[49] Much of that increase had been achieved after the assembly line was introduced. Moreover, wages rose more in mass-production industries than in other areas. Workers in factories producing cars and automotive parts received 30 percent more in 1929 than they had in 1919; workers in other industries that used assembly-line methods, such as baking and radio manufacturing, had done even better.[50] Moreover, women were taking some of the new factory jobs.

Outside industry, mass production began to seem the answer to many problems, notably the shortage of working-class housing. *Popular Science Monthly* ran an enthusiastic article on building an "all-steel house" of standard parts. Photographs showed the framework and the staircases being bolted together in just 100 minutes. According to that article, "the easily standardized parts of a house represent probably 75 percent of the total cost." The demand for "individuality" could be met by giving customers "complete freedom of treatment of inclosing walls, roof covering, color, location and shape of entrances and porches, location and design of chimneys." Solid, affordable housing would soon be available to all through "the magic of mass production."[51]

During the 1920s, when New York City had a chronic shortage of decent housing for its working-class population, the International Ladies' Garment Workers' Union and several other organizations wanted to "mass produce" apartments. As the *New York Times* explained, housing construction remained artisanal, with many small builders. The builders didn't benefit from economies of scale in purchasing materials, and they paid higher interest rates than large companies. As a result, it had become unprofitable to build small houses or apartments for the less affluent factory workers, police, firemen, and young people, particularly in cities where land was expensive. The *Times* writer asked "If Henry Ford built only a half dozen automobiles a year in a small construction yard with only a few dozen workmen, instead of almost two million a year, in the largest and most highly organized factories in the world, how much would the Ford car cost?" For working-class and lower-middle-class people, mass production made less expensive housing and transportation possible. Had the assembly line not been invented, "only the wealthiest people could afford to buy cars" or to own homes, and "the great nine-tenths of the population would go without."[52] The *Times* writer emphasized economies in purchasing and construction time without discussing how the building trades might react to the reorganization of work that assembly-line principles would entail. In practice, these problems would not be solved until after World War II.

During the 1920s and the 1930s, architects exhibited drawings and prototypes that they wanted to see mass-produced. R. Buckminster Fuller, for example, advocated mass-produced housing that could easily be moved. In 1927 he had designed a "4-D House" and had circulated 200 mimeographed copies of the plans. The Chicago retail firm Marshall Field & Co. asked Fuller to build a scale model for display at its main store in Chicago. Fuller's model attracted interest but not investors. After the stock-market crash of 1929, demand for housing all but vanished, and innovative architects had even more difficulty attracting backers. However, model houses "of the future" were presented at world's fairs.[53] Actual mass production of houses and apartments may have been rare, but mass production was widely advocated as a solution to the shortage of inexpensive housing.

Industrial workers didn't reject mass production per se. They saw potential benefits in the powerful systems of production in which they were immersed. A man who worked in factories and mines briefly in order to study workers' attitudes found that workers repeatedly told him that they felt both indispensable to the larger operation and empowered by the use of powerful machinery: ". . . the man who works largely with his hands comes with amazing ease completely to dominate and to absorb into himself the great black beast of steel and steam or electricity before which we head workers stand awed and impotent." The blue-collar worker "finds no difficulty in breeding out of his tools in combination with himself a new blood-and-iron creature which he is perfectly willing to call familiarly, 'WE'!"[54] Even in the most repetitious jobs "on the evolving car or motor as it moves up to and then away and beyond him" the workers are aware of participating in a vast process in which every action is part of the larger result. At the same time, the worker's mind is "coasting" and largely "disengaged from the process and therefore free to daydream or perhaps to frame effective wisecracks." This participant observer found that workers didn't necessarily view assembly-line labor as deadening and repetitive; indeed, they often took pride in the larger accomplishment, sensed empowerment from operating large machines, and enjoyed the camaraderie of the line.[55]

Many workers enjoyed contemplating the future uses of what they produced. Such attitudes often emerged among those building a unique structure such as a cathedral, a dam, or a skyscraper, but they could also be found among mass-production workers. "Several hundred machinists enjoyed the thrill of shared exploit when, on their own bulletin boards, one historic morning, they saw the pictures of the engine which they had fabricated, while above it stood the proud legend, 'How we all helped Lindbergh get to Paris!'"[56] In short, workers weren't necessarily deadened, depressed, or alienated because they were no longer individual craftsmen. The vast factories of modern industry gave every worker a role in an interlinked process. As in an orchestra, every player was needed. Indeed, this had become one of the larger meanings of the assembly line. The new mode of production was understood as a form of the technological sublime, impressing some workers (particularly when first employed) and fascinating many onlookers with a sense of human mastery.

Mass production of automobiles also suggested new perspectives on historical and geographical development. During the 1920s, the frontier thesis of Frederick Jackson Turner was widely accepted as the blueprint for American history, seen as the story of westward expansion. John Long, a professor at the University of Wisconsin, proposed an extension and modification of Turner's thesis: "What happened, in short, was that along certain wagon trails, canals, and railways, the pioneer pushed westward and took the country, but in between these gridiron lines of communication vast territories remained undeveloped." The automobile would allow Americans to fill in these residual spaces "confined neither to rails nor to water."[57] The automobile opened a new "radial frontier" in sparsely settled areas, and it facilitated growth on the outskirts of cities. As early as the decade between 1910 and 1920, suburbs were growing more rapidly than urban centers. In all parts of the country, Long asserted, the automobile "makes this new territory available, [and] satisfies a pioneering desire."[58]

The public's interest in automobiles remained intense throughout the 1920s. In a typical American town, a working-class family that couldn't afford both a bathtub and a car was more likely to opt for a car. When Ford's new Model A went on display at the end of 1927, crowds descended on the showrooms. (See figure 3.4.) Perhaps it was understandable that 100,000 people might do this in Detroit, but excitement was just as intense in Cleveland, Chicago, and Kansas City.[59] A New York newspaper estimated that a million people tried to see the Model A on the first day it was shown.

The popularity of his automobiles made Henry Ford a celebrity. In 1924, when there was a grassroots movement to draft him as a candidate for the presidency, the magazine *Forum* joked that if elected Ford would put conveyor belts in the White House and make his cabinet a cost-accounting bureau.

During the prosperous mid 1920s, the assembly line, the Model T, and Ford were often treated humorously. The word "Fordism" didn't exist yet, and the assembly line was seldom seen as a threat to labor or as an embodiment of soulless mechanization.

"Between 1908 and 1940, more than 60 songs were composed and dedicated either to Henry Ford or his car."[60] On April 16, 1927, Serge Koussevitzky directed the Boston Symphony Orchestra in the world-premiere performance of Frederick Converse's "Flivver Ten Million," a symphonic evocation of the Model T that added to the usual symphonic instruments a factory whistle, a wind machine, an anvil, and an automobile horn. The work had eight sections. First came "Dawn in Detroit." In the opening bars an automobile horn resounded amid an awakening of nervous rhythms reminiscent of modern traffic. In "The Call to Labor" automobile workers reported to the factory. Third came "The Din of the Builders," evoking the sounds of the working assembly line. This led to "The Birth of the Hero—He Tries His Metal." The hero in this was is the automobile, which drove out into the world looking for adventures. The fifth section imagined a "May Night by the Roadside." The sixth movement, titled "The Joy Riders—America's Frolic," built up to a crashing climax: "The Collision—America's Tragedy." In the final movement, "Phoenix Americans," the hero rattled back to the highway and continued the journey. Two years later the piece was played at the London Proms. The British *Musical Times* declared "The idea of putting the motor-car, speed, joy-riding, and the atmosphere of the automobile works in Detroit into music is quite a good

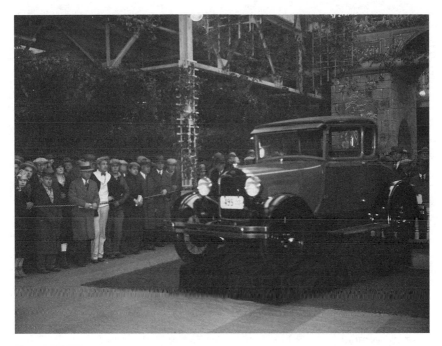

FIGURE 3.4

A crowd that turned out on December 5, 1927 to see the new Model A at Detroit's Convention Center. Courtesy of Photographic Department, Cleveland Public Library

one, nor need we be so severe as to take exception to a humorous use of percussion and klaxon horns." However, the reviewer, who failed to notice the piece's debt to George Gershwin, sniffed that "the thing had no style" and "was a pastiche of Strauss and Respighi."[61]

The enthusiasm for assembly lines and mass production carried over into education and the arts, and the language of the assembly line appeared in influential educational texts. Franklin Bobbitt's 1918 book *The Curriculum* argued that education could learn from manufacturing and called for the setting of "definite standards for the various educational products."[62] The division of knowledge into many small units for students to assimilate and the use of standardized tests that were thought to assure quality control built on analogies with factory practice.[63] More generally, "in the 1920s and 1930s a machine aesthetic dominated virtually all modern styles and movements"— it could be "detected in Russian constructivism, in the Dutch de Stijl, in Germany at the Bauhaus and in the Neue Sachlichkeit (or new objectivity) movement, in Italian futurism, in Dada, in French cubism and purism, and in America, in precisionism," in the poetry of William Carlos Williams, and in the photographs of Alfred Stieglitz.[64] International examples of the new aesthetic were displayed in 1927 in New York at a "Machine Age Exposition," sponsored by the *Little Review*, that interspersed among paintings, photographs, and sculptures "machines and machine parts—gears from the Boston Gear Works, valves from the Crane Company, a Curtiss airplane engine . . . and a Studebaker crankshaft."[65]

As the inclusion of the crankshaft suggests, mass production had become integral to the iconography of modernism in film, photography, and dance. Fernand Léger's *Ballet mécanique* asked performers to move repetitively like machines to the accompaniment of a frenetic pounding piano used as a percussion instrument, overlaid by sirens, traffic noises, and sounds of industrial production.[66] Georges Antheil, the composer, claimed that the music was based on mechanical (rather than human or natural) noises.[67] *Ballet mécanique* charged along at high volume, with many repetitions, including loops where the same pattern recurred many times, like a factory machine repeating the same movement over and over. Some of Antheil's music was used in a Dadaesque 1924 film version of the ballet that began with a woman endlessly swinging back and forth to the same rhythm as a clock's pendulum, intercut with and gradually replaced by images of gears and mechanical movements, including a dynamo. At times, images of rushing automobiles appear, and every object or person shown makes the same movements repeatedly.

In the same years, chorus girls began to dance in synchronized lines, kicking and gesticulating in unison, each "girl" appearing to be an interchangeable part of the line. Performers were recruited on the basis of uniform height and weight criteria, and were dressed identically. Such chorus lines mimicked the aesthetic of the assembly line, and crowds paid to see showgirls express the logic of mass production as applied to the human body.[68] Siegfried Kracauer noted this connection in 1927, and argued that the chorus line represented the mechanical aspects of the capitalist system. In Berlin he had seen a British troupe that had previously performed in New York. The troupe's very itinerary immediately suggests the rapid internationalization of such performances. Kracauer concluded that the identity of the individual woman disappeared, and that such spectacles were objectifications of interchangeable parts moving on the assembly line.[69] When the dancers undulated across the stage like a snake, they were asexually athletic, divested of individuality. He concluded that "when they raised their legs with mathematical precision over their heads, they joyfully affirmed the progress of rationalisation; and when they continually repeated the same maneuver, never breaking ranks, one had the vision of an unbroken chain of automobiles gliding out of the factory into the world and the feeling that there was no end to prosperity."[70] Their dance suggested the repetitive movements in a mechanized workplace.

During the same years it became popular to organize masses of people wearing identical uniforms to perform patterned gymnastics, often in sports stadiums or on parade grounds. Synchronized swimming was another voluntary activity that translated the industrial values of interchangeability and the flow of production into popular art. In 1916 the University of Wisconsin may have been the first to add synchronized swimming to its physical education program. The sport's popularity grew in the Chicago area during the 1920s and was featured at the 1933 Century of Progress Exposition. Sixty "Modern Mermaids" so pleased the crowds that similar aquatic entertainments were staged at both the New York and San Francisco Expositions at the end of the decade.[71] New York's famous Rockettes also donned swimsuits, as well as dancing. (See figure 3.5.) The repetition of industrial forms was also taken up as a trope in both advertising and artistic photography. During the 1930s this aesthetic was particularly prominent in the business magazine *Fortune*, which sent photographers to factories, warehouses, and display rooms.

The painter and photographer Charles Sheeler developed the new industrial aesthetic in a series of landscapes. Commissioned by the Ford Motor Company to depict the River Rouge factory, Sheeler first made a series of photographs as part of a larger public-relations campaign orchestrated by A. J. Ayer. Sheeler spent six weeks at River Rouge in late 1927, just as the Model A was going into production. "The subject matter," he wrote to a friend, "is incomparably the most thrilling I have ever had to work with."[72] He submitted 32 photographs to the Ford Motor Company, which it subsequently used in advertising and publicity. Curiously, at the time the images weren't exhibited together as a group.

Sheeler's photographs became the basis for a series of landscape paintings that he worked on until at least 1935. He concentrated on exterior views, showing mountains of coal, iron ore, and other raw materials, heaped symmetrically alongside the company's shipping canal and railroad tracks. In

FIGURE 3.5

"Precision plunge. Internationally famous for their precision, 36 members of the Rockettes . . . as one girl . . . thrust dainty toes into a New York pool" (April 13, 1938). Courtesy of Photographic Department, Cleveland Public Library.

American Landscape (figure 3.6) there is not a single bush or tree or even a blade of grass, nor are any workers visible. The only signs of activity are the smoke from the powerhouse chimney and the railroad cars along the canal. The immediate impression is one of stasis, calm, order, and absolute control over the environment. The image is not an example of realism, for it is cleansed of any messiness. The cultural historian Constance Rourke wrote approvingly: "He has accepted industrialism and renders what he sees as its essential forms."[73] Sheeler subtly simplified every object into an almost platonic form. His static Rouge factory was emptied of people and almost etherealized. Many critics praised his landscapes, notably in the magazine *The Survey*. His work was also reproduced in *Fortune*. Eugene Jolas, one of the editors of the literary journal *transition*, claimed to have "felt . . . a remarkable sense of dynamic magic" in Sheeler's photographs.[74]

Sheeler's aesthetic not only embraced the Ford factories but linked them to a developing American taste for the vernacular tradition that included Shaker furniture, old barns, folk art, and handcrafted objects. Sheeler's work

FIGURE 3.6

Charles Sheeler, *American Landscape* (oil, 1930). Courtesy of Museum of Modern Art.

linked such artisanal objects to industrial forms as parts of a continuous design tradition. (Henry Ford agreed with this view and collected thousands of early American tools.) Sheeler deemphasized the assembly line itself in his depictions of the River Rouge plant, for mass production was a radical break with craft tradition. By focusing on rhythmic patterns and formal aspects of the industrial landscape, Sheeler managed to unite the vernacular past and the present of the 1930s.

Sheeler and several contemporaries are often classed together as "precisionists." As Sharon Corwin notes, their paintings not only deal with machines and factories but also efface the artist's labor from the canvas. The brushwork becomes invisible, as if the canvas were produced without human intervention. This was the visual correlative of modern industrial efficiency. Sheeler declared that he wanted "to eliminate the evidence of painting as such and present the design with the least evidence of the means of accomplishment." Similarly, a critic said of Stefan Hirsh that "his pictures seem to have been done without any effort."[75] Likewise, mass-produced goods bear no marks of individuals; an assembly-line worker leaves no personalized trace of his labor on a car, a refrigerator, or a toaster.

The Boston department store owner and philanthropist Edward Filene became concerned about the larger meanings of the assembly line. In 1929 he argued in *The Atlantic* that "America's increasing general prosperity and high standards of living are due chiefly to the rapidly increasing use of scientific mass production and distribution."[76] Filene explored similar themes in a book titled *The Way Out: A Forecast of Coming Changes in American Business and Industry* (1924), which had chapters on mass production, mass distribution, and eliminating waste. He championed "Fordizing America" as the certain road to progress. As one biographer put it, he "wanted more standardization of production . . . less interrupted production, better stockpiling of materials and more prosperity for everyone" through a high-wage policy.[77] (However, Filene rejected Ford's anti-Semitism, as might be expected of anyone of Jewish descent.) In another book, titled *Successful Living in this Machine Age*, Filene declared:

Mass production is not simply large-scale production. It is large-scale production based upon a clear understanding that increased production demands increased buying, and that the greatest total profits can be obtained only if the masses can and do enjoy a higher and ever higher standard of living. For selfish business reasons, therefore, genuine mass production industries must make prices lower and lower and wages higher and higher, while constantly shortening the workday and bringing to the masses not only more money but more time. . . .[78]

Filene continued to champion these ideas after the stock-market crash of 1929. In 1936 he called for making high wages "compulsory."[79]

The crash of 1929 didn't immediately throw the assembly line into question. During the first years of the Great Depression, it still seemed the best way to organize work. In 1931 the Empire State Building was completed in less than two years with the use of assembly-line principles. Interchangeable parts sped up the installation of windows, for example, and stone was delivered pre-cut in standardized sizes. Indeed, "spandrels, steel mullions, and stone were all designed so that they could be duplicated in tremendous quantity and with almost perfect accuracy."[80] Temporary narrow railroad tracks were installed on the perimeter of each floor, and huge hand carts, each the size of eight wheelbarrows, expedited the delivery of parts. "There was almost such a thing at the Empire State as a factory assembly of standard units," including tons of bricks and stone that literally weren't touched by anyone before set into the wall by a bricklayer.[81] At the peak of their activity, masons erected fourteen stories of the building in only ten days.[82]

Despite hard times, public enthusiasm for the assembly line didn't immediately wane. To many it still seemed to promise a better future, if only society could increase consumption as rapidly as it had increased production. Just after World War I, Thorstein Veblen had argued that engineers were better able to run society than capitalists. Rather than exploit mass production for selfish, personal gain, the argument went, a technical elite would maximize efficiency, raise wages, and ensure full distribution. During the Depression, Harold Loeb expanded on these ideas. In a book titled *Life in a Technocracy: What It Might Be Like*, he argued that mass production made possible a comfortable life for all with a work week of just 16 hours. Machine production meant that in a Milwaukee factory just 208 men could make 10,000 auto frames every day. Loeb contrasted the hand production of glass bottles with "the Owens bottle machine": "Three thousand six hundred bottles are turned out in an hour," and only "a few such machines are needed to produce all the standardized bottles."[83] Under capitalism, these new capacities led to stockpiles of unsold goods and to severe unemployment. A technocracy would share the reduced workload equally and distribute consumer goods. Loeb predicted an "inevitable" triumph of technocracy as the logical outcome of social evolution.

In 1933—the year in which *Life in a Technocracy* was published—the "Century of Progress" Exposition opened in Chicago. Its planners rejected the neo-classical architecture of earlier fairs and embraced sleek, modern designs that harmonized with the exposition's slogan, "Science Finds, Industry Applies, Man Conforms." Various examples of industrial production were "the main focus of action-filled exhibits" that "demonstrated the creation of modern products on assembly lines, like the canning machine in the American Can Company display." Visitors could see Firestone produce new tires, Kraft make mayonnaise, Coca-Cola bottle soft drinks, or a bacon-slicing machine produce 400 pieces per minute and put them onto a conveyor belt to be packaged by "lovely girls in trim, natty uniforms."[84] The most popular pavilion was the million-dollar General Motors building, designed by Albert Kahn. (See figure 3.7.) It featured an assembly line larger than the one Ford had erected at the San Francisco Exposition in 1915. The guidebook declared that the building contained "a complete automobile assembly plant" that could be viewed by "1,000 people at a time." They saw several hundred workers on an assembly line a fifth of a mile long. "Raw materials enter through one door and by the time they reach the opposite exit, they have become finished cars." The exhibit was a participatory spectacle that could be viewed from many angles, and it often ended with a purchase. "A visitor may select the materials for his car as it enters the door, follow its progress along the assembly line, and get in and drive it off at the other side of the room."[85]

The men who managed the Ford Motor Company were so angry that another car company had "stolen" their idea that they erected an even larger exhibit for the Chicago Exposition's second year. It became twice as popular as GM's assembly line. Walter Dorwin Teague designed the building to resemble a gigantic gear system. Inside, a 600-foot photo mural circled the main rotunda. It aestheticized the factory tour with a "selective

FIGURE 3.7
General Motors' assembly line at the Century of Progress Exposition, Chicago, 1933. Courtesy of National Building Museum, Washington.

representation of the dynamism and modernistic beauty of the Ford plant."
The imagery drew upon Charles Sheeler's photographs and the aesthetics of
the painted murals that were popular during that era. The Ford photo mural
gave the impression of monumentality and also of "communal, public service," evoking the "plain-folks Americanism" that corporations had begun
to adopt "as a way of associating the narratives of their businesses with those
of the nation at large." In keeping with this message, Ford didn't present
itself as a self-sufficient company, but rather emphasized how its factories
bought cotton, wool, and soybeans from farmers and aluminum, copper,
and iron from miners. It exhibited not its own assembly lines but those of
suppliers. Teague chose to display processes that were visually interesting
and easy to grasp, using dioramas, photographs, and models.[86] The Ford
Motor Company thus showed how its business was woven into the lives
of farmers, miners, and workers all over the United States, and it showed
how suppliers everywhere had adopted the assembly line. Mass production
was no longer uniquely Ford's. It enhanced production for, and it belonged
to, all Americans. A similar realization prompted New York's Museum of
Modern Art to stage an exhibition called "Machine Art" in 1934. Its curator, Philip Johnson, wrote in the catalog that the aesthetic of the machine
included "precision, simplicity, smoothness, [and] reproducibility."[87] These
were essential qualities for both interchangeable parts and the operation of
the assembly line.

From 1914 until 1934 the public embraced the assembly line because
it seemed the crowning example of a century-long trend toward greater
efficiency and prosperity. The assembly line's division of labor potentially
provided a work niche for everyone, including jobs for the deaf, the blind,
and even the armless. It seemed conducive to every form of social progress,
including higher wages for labor, cheaper transportation, better housing, and
lower consumer prices. The assembly line was celebrated at expositions, in
music, and in modern art. It had critics, but during its first two decades an
enthusiastic chorus drowned them out.

No symphony, no Eroica, compared in depth, content, and power to the music that threatened and hammered away at us as we wandered through Ford's workplaces, wanderers overwhelmed by a daring expression of the human spirit.

—Otto Moug, a German engineer, on visiting the Ford factories in the late 1920s[1]

In Europe, Daniel Rodgers observed, "the 'new era' was the machine age, and Ford was its prophet."[2] Inexpensive automobiles promised to revolutionize mobility, Fordson tractors replaced horses and increased farm productivity, and the assembly line seemed to guarantee abundant consumer goods for all. The promise of abundance was also carried by the American-style advertising that became ubiquitous in Europe, as did Woolworth stores and their imitators. Moreover, by 1925 American films depicting a consumer's paradise were ubiquitous in European cinemas.

The American automobile industry and the assembly line attracted foreign attention even before World War I. The French automaker Louis Renault toured the Highland Park plant in 1911, and was particularly interested in the semi-automatic specialized machine tools. He concluded that the Ford factory "was the best organized in the country." Renault wanted financial details and sent an accountant to Dearborn to compile an analysis, unfortunately now lost. In 1912, Renault began to plan a shift from artisanal methods to American-style mass production.[3] A manager from Germany's Benz company declared the Ford plant "the most remarkable in the world" and "the very best in equipment and method."[4] These visits occurred even

FIGURE 4.1
Caviar being packaged on an assembly line near the Caspian Sea, 1936. Courtesy of Photographic Department, Cleveland Public Library.

before the assembly line was introduced. Interest revved up further after 1913. The British Institute of Automobile Engineers organized a tour to Cleveland and Detroit in 1913, and several British automakers visited Ford in 1914.[5] In the midst of World War I, the French auto firm Citroën sent a team to study Ford's Highland Park plant. That team's report, several hundred pages long, dealt not only with production but also with Ford's foundries and its research-and-development department. Citroën decided to produce in the "American style" after the war, and sent a second team back to Detroit.[6] After a third visit, in 1923, Citroën's production manager said: "Of all the industry leaders who welcomed me, it is Henry Ford who has impressed me most. He is an astounding figure." Citroën purchased many American machine tools and hired six American engineers to help put them to use in mass production. Peugeot also studied American methods, and after a 1926 visit its CEO suggested the French needed an organization that would send a constant stream of industrialists, merchants, and financiers on educational tours to the United States. Peugeot's team was most impressed with General Motors, not Ford, which by then was rapidly losing market share to GM's more varied line of cars. By that time, however, it was less necessary to travel to America, because Ford was the third-largest automobile producer in France, with a factory in Bordeaux. Nevertheless, between 1925 and 1928 Renault sent groups to study Ford's operations no less than nine times. Some visitors wrote a report every evening, and some of the reports included sketches of machines and factory layouts.[7] By this time, all the major French car manufacturers regarded regular trips to the United States as essential to keeping up to date, and such journeys continued during the 1930s despite the deterioration of world markets.

Not all attempts at adopting American methods were successful. Marius Berliet was one of the leading French car manufacturers before 1918. He ambitiously bought American machinery and copied the Dodge Company's production methods. However, he lacked qualified engineers, and his rush to become the leader of the French industry ended in a loss of market share. As Yves Cohen concluded, in France "seven to eight years were needed by each of the principal manufacturers to master the assembly line."[8] At Renault, for example, until the mid 1920s cars were assembled on a line; however, they were pushed manually from one work station to the next, and they remained at each station for 40 minutes. The three major companies only achieved moving assembly lines with an appropriate division of labor after 1928. By then elements of the assembly line were spreading widely to French factories outside the automobile industry.[9]

As the French examples suggest, European manufacturers didn't blindly stick to their traditions, but early sought to understand the assembly line and integrate it into their operations. Furthermore, World War I made mass production an urgent necessity. All the combatants recognized that interchangeable-parts manufacture of weapons and munitions was essential to military success, and governments gave lucrative contracts to arms makers capable of mass production.[10] The automobile companies were heavily involved. In the United States, automobile production fell by 700,000 units in 1917 as companies converted to war production of cars, trucks, boats, and artillery carriages. Ford supplied 15,000 ambulances and light delivery trucks. Dodge produced 4,000 heavy trucks, Packard 6,000. Studebaker, Packard, and Hudson converted entirely to war production.[11] In Manchester, England, Ford produced shell containers for 18-pound guns and ambulances.[12] The Allies found that the Model T, because of its lightness and its greater road clearance, often could negotiate bomb-damaged roads better than other vehicles. Many British reports praised its hardiness and versatility. An affectionate bit of doggerel based on Rudyard Kipling's "Gunga Din" went as follows:

You exasperating puzzle Hunka Tin,
I've abused you and I've flayed you,
But by Henry Ford who made you
You are better than a big car—Hunka Tin.[13]

Ford's new tractors also helped with food production when many horses and farmers had been sent to France. Citroen used mass production for the first time when it made artillery shells. For this purpose it rearranged machinery into lines, with individual electric motors in each machine, which was then unusual in French industry.[14] But the most important effect of the assembly line on the war was motorized transport for supplies and the troops. Together, Ford's many factories supplied an estimated 125,000 vehicles to the front.[15]

During the war, the Europeans not only had a crash course in how to work assembly lines; they also learned from the Americans that it was more efficient (and more profitable) to produce a smaller number of models, even though they weren't ready to cut back to just one model as Ford had. Nor were they prepared to adopt the high-wage, low-price policy that Ford had pioneered. French workers made modest advances in real income, but few of them owned cars. Patrick Fridenson concluded that in the 1920s "French car makers did not believe yet in the possibility of a mass market."[16] Yet the wider French public was receptive to the new methods. Indeed, after reading the newspaper serialization of Ford's book *My Life and World* many of the French "appeared to take the claims of Ford's ghost-written books at face value, seeing them as 'primitive socialism'; Ford's prognostication of a car for every family was a sign of the well-being to come."[17]

Some architects, including Le Corbusier, argued that mass-production methods could be applied to housing. Standardization and prefabrication could make more space available to ordinary families at a modest cost.[18] Ernest Mercier, a leading French industrialist, held similar views. In the midst of the 1925 French financial crisis, Mercier launched the "Redressement Francais," which called for the French economy to be led to recovery by technocratic experts through a combination of Taylorism and mass production.[19] Mercier's enthusiasm for such ideas increased after he visited the United States, which he saw as offering a model for the future. He envisioned a victory of "Ford over Marx."[20] According the Charles Maier, "the Redressement condemned not a parasitic financial network but the inefficiency of the traditional small producer," and "the small factory that resisted centralization and standardization was allegedly a threat to progress."[21] In the same spirit, Le Corbusier wrote pamphlets about modern housing for "Redressement Francais," which also distributed a magazine to about 25,000 readers. However, disillusionment with American mass production set in after the stock-market crash of 1929—"America's model of industrial productivity lost its catalytic inspiration."[22]

Though European industrialists eagerly visited the factories of Ford and other manufacturers after about 1910, that wasn't the only way the assembly line was transferred abroad. Ford installed assembly lines in its overseas factories, and engineering and scientific publications, world's fair exhibits, and government programs spread the word about the new manufacturing methods. There were also private initiatives—notably that of Edward Filene, who created the Twentieth Century Fund and who spread the ideas of scientific management and mass production through international meetings and publications.[23]

Ford's first automobile factory in Japan began operation in October 1921. It assembled cars from parts sent from Michigan, much as Ford's branch plants in Los Angeles and New York did. A "knocked down" car was far cheaper to ship than a finished one, and branch plants often consisted only of a final assembly line, making few parts if any. The Japanese factory was a small operation at first. It could produce only 200 cars a month—about ten per working day, or a little more than one per hour.[24] Since it didn't produce parts and didn't subdivide the labor as much as the larger US plants did, local workers and engineers couldn't learn the details of Ford's system from it.

As Stephen Tolliday emphasizes, Henry Ford decided to sell cars worldwide shortly after the founding of his company in 1903.[25] At first, Ford simply exported to foreign sales offices. Then, not long before the start of World War I, Ford began to build European plants. Attempts to consolidate those plants and give them central direction during the 1920s and the 1930s were often frustrated, however, by "European protectionism and the fragmentation of markets."[26] Characteristically, both French and German tariff legislation forced Ford to stop assembling cars from parts made in the United States and to open full-scale plants in both of those countries.

The most important of Ford's early European plants was the one in Manchester. Its factory in Cadiz doesn't seem to have produced many automobiles. One in Copenhagen proved profitable, and a larger facility was opened there in late 1924. The following year it produced almost 25,000 automobiles, and by 1926 the Danish branch had produced 100,000 Model T's. Located in the harbor area, it received some parts directly from Detroit, but it used Danish suppliers as much as it could. It exported to the entire Baltic region. That factory remained profitable even in the 1930s, despite the generally weak economy and the tariffs and restrictions imposed in other countries.[27] Ford added plants in France, Belgium, the Netherlands, Sweden, and Germany, but as late as 1931 the Danish plant had larger net earnings than any other Ford plant on the Continent, double those in Germany and 20 percent more than France. It paid a 10 percent dividend.[28] European factories often had American managers, and they received the same information as domestic branch plants, and were operated according to American standards and specifications.[29] Each gave local engineers, managers, and workers a taste of mass production. In larger markets, notably Britain, France, and Germany, local factories made some parts, reducing imports from the United States.[30]

FIGURE 4.2
Ford factory in Copenhagen, ca. 1930. Courtesy of Arbejdermuseet, Copenhagen.

In general, American corporations targeted Europe more than Asia. American investments in Europe went from $700 million in 1919 to $1.3 billion in 1929. Exports also grew rapidly. In 1925 the United States' export trade with all parts of the world had reached $4.8 billion. The largest single export item was raw cotton ($1 billion), but automobiles ($309 million) and machinery ($234 million) were impressive growth areas.[31] Many of the largest American corporations, including General Motors, General Electric, Ford, Monsanto, DuPont, IBM, and Kodak, set up or expanded European divisions. They approached the foreign market with American-style advertising and public relations, spearheaded by J. Walter Thompson and other American agencies who followed their clients abroad. Mass-produced products also became conspicuous in Europe as Woolworth's, Montgomery Ward, and other retail chains expanded there.

During the interwar years, Europeans generally saw the United States as "synonymous with efficiency, advanced technology and industrial dynamism, the worship of machines and assembly lines, 'streamlined' and standardized products, commercialism, mass consumption, and the emergence of a mass society."[32] An experienced American businessman who toured Europe in 1926 told the *New York Times* that European wage levels were too low to support mass consumption. "Europeans," he opined, "fail to realize how much our quantity-production enterprises depend for their success upon the quick and sure way in which the American public responds in volume buying to national advertising." He found Europeans avidly adopting "scientific management, labor-saving devices, and large-scale production."[33] Nevertheless, the desire for American methods seldom resulted in their full adoption. For the same reasons, the scale of American penetration into the European market was limited to particular product areas. Notably, the American share of the world automobile market rose dramatically. As late as 1907 France had 57 percent of the world's automotive exports, but that fell to just 6 percent in 1928. The British share declined from a high of 16 percent in 1913 to just 2 percent in 1923. By 1928 the United States' share of world automobile exports had risen to 72 percent.[34] With such dominance, the significance of American forms of production, business, and advertising was not lost on Europeans.

Yet the success of American automotive exports didn't always translate into dominance of individual national markets. Britain offers a fascinating example of initial success followed by many problems. Ford cars were first offered for sale in Britain in 1904. The market was so responsive that in 1911 an assembly plant was built in Manchester and a tractor factory in Cork, Ireland (then part of the United Kingdom). The Manchester plant began by building cars in the old way, but in September 1914 it was the first foreign Ford factory to install an assembly line. By the end of that year, 8,352 cars had been built there. Ford consistently paid higher wages than other British carmakers, but kept unions out until near the end of World War II.[35] Yet despite high wages, Ford struggled with a clash of work cultures. Detroit didn't understand the style of its first English managers and replaced them with Americans, who tried to run the Manchester factory as though it were in Detroit. For a time they even insisted on manufacturing cars with left-hand drive, which no British consumer wanted. British workmen regularly stopped the assembly line for tea breaks. Managers resisted getting their hands dirty and spent little time on the shop floor. One manager declared "I'm a carriage builder by trade and my father was a carriage builder by trade and my grandfather and my great-grandfather."[36] He wore a white shirt and white cuffs, and he refused to get his hands dirty making motorcars. A team of senior managers who came from Detroit to put matters right found that in "many of the cars . . . being produced . . . the top gear did not function" and that "90% of the pistons received in the plant were defective"; in addition, the welding was poor, and many defective rear axles had been installed in the hope that they would "wear in."[37] Everywhere the Detroit team found sloppiness and waste. After the managers were fired and the workers retrained, the factory functioned better. However, Ford long refused to allow the Manchester plant to design and manufacture a smaller vehicle suited to Britain's narrow streets, short distances, and high gasoline prices. The Model T, a modest car in the United States, was considered a large one in Europe. By 1928 the *New York Times* reported, in an article that was read and preserved in Ford's Detroit office, that "Ford cars of the old type [i.e., of the Model T era] have been driven off the English roads by English mass-produced cars such as the Morris and Cowley and very few of the new Fords have yet made their appearance here."[38] The Model A was even larger and more powerful than the Model T, and in the first year of its production the new Ford factory at Dagenham on the Thames, just outside London, made only five. That plant had been optimistically expected to produce vehicles for both Britain and the Continent. In 1929 Ford was also planning to upgrade its service network. "The [Model A] has a great reputation everywhere," Charles Sorensen (a skilled pattern maker of Danish immigrant background who had gone to work for Ford in 1904 and had risen to a high position in the company) wrote from Stockholm, having toured much of Europe. "[But] service is very bad on all cars."[39] He suggested setting up service centers in major European cities.

In 1930, as one response to the balkanizing European market, some design changes in Ford's European models were planned. A team of designers went to Europe, studied the competition, discussed the situation with local experts, made drawings for new designs, and sent them to Sorensen. A European Ford was to have less ground clearance. Its fenders and running gear were to look more massive, and the body was to be simpler, with "no adornments" and with more sweeping lines. Moreover, all the "panels must look heavy and well-formed. There is a particular stigma on panels which look like stampings . . . and the body should carry as few earmarks of 'mass production' as possible."[40] These were superficial changes. Not until 1931 did Edsel Ford convince his father that a different car was needed for the British market. Between 1913 and 1929, with poor management and an inappropriate product, Ford's British market share fell from 24 percent to just 4 percent. Britain had a growing domestic automobile market, and Ford might have remained a leading manufacturer there. Merely exporting the Model T and the assembly line wasn't enough to ensure success. A new car suited to the British and Continental markets finally emerged with the Model Y in 1932.[41]

Meanwhile, British car manufacturers had selectively adopted elements of the Ford production system. Both Morris and Austin saw the advantages of specialized machine tools that could produce parts to a higher degree of accuracy. But Morris didn't subdivide work as much as Ford; moreover, its assembly line moved by hand power from its introduction in 1919 until 1934, which meant that workers controlled the pace. Both Morris and Austin rejected a uniform high-wage policy, instead using piece rates to encourage higher productivity. Design also remained more flexible than on the Ford assembly line, as Morris body construction remained a matter of craftsmanship. That was more expensive, but it permitted frequent style changes. The British adopted some Ford methods that could improve quality and throughput but were less eager to achieve absolute standardization and quantity production.[42] By Detroit standards, volume remained low and manufacturing slow. The British firms didn't become capital intensive but continued to rely on skilled labor and thereby retained flexibility in responding to varied consumer demand.[43] Overall, during the 1920s, in Britain Ford's manufacturing system wasn't entirely a success in its own factories, and it was only partially adopted by local rivals. However, the assembly line became important in industries producing new consumer goods, notably vacuum cleaners, electric irons, and radios. Even in these new factories, however, British management had to cede some control over the shop floor to the powerful labor movement.[44] "In America," one manager at Morris observed, "you have to employ methods which a crowd can carry out, but the British individual will not have that." Indeed, he proudly declared, "the Britisher will not have 'herd' methods."[45]

Ford encountered different problems when it transferred its technology to the Soviet Union. In 1909 the Model T was for sale in six major Russian cities. Sales were modest before 1914. In all of Russia there were only 6,000 automobiles, fewer than in the state of Wisconsin, and the majority of them were German or French.[46] Immediately after the Russian revolution, Lenin pushed Taylor's ideas as the inspiration for industrial transformation. *The*

Principles of Scientific Management was translated into Russian, and American experts were brought to Russia to speed the transition. Lenin also supported the work of Aleksei Gastev, who developed exercises and routines designed to adapt the workers' bodies to the demands of machines. The revolutionary ideal was a proletarian with iron sinews and a physique like tempered steel.[47]

In this atmosphere, the Ford assembly line was officially embraced with enthusiasm. *My Life and Work* (1922) was reprinted four times by 1925 and reportedly was "read with a zeal usually reserved for the study of Lenin."[48] An assembly line was even used to package caviar. (See figure 4.1.) During the early years of the revolution, Ford sent a businessman named Julius Hammer to Moscow. Hammer wrote back in June 1923 that a Ford factory using local labor to make parts and assemble them would be extremely welcome. Indeed, owing to the loss of many horses in the Great War, the need for tractors seemed particularly desperate: "Mr. Belinky, the Chief of the Trade monopoly of the Southeast of Russia, assures me that to replace the draught-animals lost in that region alone would number between twenty and thirty thousand tractors and these are urgently needed at once. No efforts are being made to replace these lost animals. The land must wait untilled for the coming of tractors." There were additional "hundreds of thousands of acres" that could be cultivated. It seemed that "a large factory would have its entire output absorbed for many years to come."[49] Despite Hammer's enthusiasm, however, Ford wasn't ready for a Russian branch plant. Instead, the Russians imported Ford cars, trucks, and tractors. In 1925 they signed an agreement with Ford to buy tractors, to send fifty Russians to the United States for training each year, and to permit Ford managers to come to Russia to study the possibilities for setting up a factory there.[50] After making the trip in 1926, five Ford managers declared that building "any kind of manufacturing plant on Soviet soil would be nothing short of madness." They had concluded that getting raw materials would be expensive and difficult, that "political commissars" and labor representatives would constantly interfere, and that government would insist on fixing the price of the finished product. Moreover, they worried that the Soviets might take over the plant with little compensation. No factory was built.

The ideology of communism wasn't merely receptive to the assembly line; it made factories social and cultural centers. Peasants and workers were taught to read, and writers searched for ways to feature factories in their works. As Karen MacCauley notes, even before the factory became central to the Soviet novel, a "factory aesthetic had firmly established itself in the visual arts."[51] The factory's "transformation into the status of cultural icon in art and literature during the twenties stemmed from the productionist effort to salvage an aesthetic space that included the proletariat while excluding the bourgeoisie." By the mid 1920s, the goal of many dramatists and writers was to "make the reader perceive the world of production on an immediate visceral level."[52] The desire for assembly-line factories wasn't simply based on a demand for engineering efficiency; it expressed a larger determination to help workers build a new world. The factory was to embody new cultural values, and "labor acquired poetic qualities while the engineer's and worker's struggles became analogous (either implicitly or explicitly) to that of the writer who, not surprisingly, began to view himself as involved in the production process, that is, more specifically, as an engineer."[53]

In view of the centrality of the factory to the implementation of the revolution, the Soviet government wanted assembly-line training for both workers and managers, and it continued to seek help from Detroit.[54] It persuaded General Motors that the Soviet government was stable and that how it governed was not the corporation's concern.[55] However, GM's involvement was to be on a smaller scale than Ford's. In 1929, after considerable negotiation, Henry Ford agreed to sell complete plans for the construction of two factories, each able to manufacture Model A cars and Model AA trucks, to the Soviet government. Ford further agreed to supply the manufacturing equipment and to sell parts for 72,000 vehicles. (In fact, only half as many parts would later be purchased, as the Soviets began to make their own.) The contract also was accompanied by an exchange of hundreds of engineers and managers. The Russians saw American production firsthand, and the Ford engineers helped to build up manufacturing expertise in the Soviet Union. The original contract optimistically included a clause that gave the Soviets the right to modify and alter "the chassis of said Ford models in the cars to be produced" to adapt them "to the service and road conditions" of the USSR, and in return gave Ford the right to make use of such improvements in its American factories.[56] However, there seem not to have been any significant Soviet improvements. On the contrary. After the American-equipped factories were constructed, Ford specialists confronted "Russian bungling, a poor workforce, and awful living and working conditions."[57] Nevertheless, the main Soviet plant at Nizkny Novgorod began manufacturing Model A cars in January 1932, and by April 1935 100,000 had been built. Soviet Model As were still being assembled, in modified form, after World War II

By 1934 there were, by some estimates, 200,000 Fordson tractors in the Russian countryside. But not all of them were in use. In practice they often proved too light, and the heavier machines produced by John Deere, International Harvester, and other American companies were preferred. The Soviets developed their own assembly-line factories to produce similar machines, but the technology transfer did not go smoothly.[58] Inexperienced Russian peasants with little or no mechanical experience could quickly ruin new farm equipment, and there were few mechanics to make repairs. They also made poor industrial workers, and many of the tractors they built were shoddy. The Soviet Fordson tractor plant had great difficulty achieving interchangeability, and as a result it employed "an inordinately large number of fitters"[59] who ground, filed, and sanded parts to make them fit. Fitters were almost unknown in American mass-production factories. Soviet modernizers grasped only some of the technical aspects of the American system of mass production. As David Shearer found, they focused on production technologies without understanding the importance of such things as internal factory transport systems and modern accounting. Soviet factories had squadrons of workers shoveling and hauling materials and managers who often lacked the expertise necessary to evaluate their production system.[60] Progress was uneven despite the presence of American engineers to supervise factory construction and advise their Soviet counterparts.

It was difficult to transfer manufacturing methods from American private enterprise to state industries. In the Soviet context, "Fordism was seen as a method for controlling the workspace, boosting output to increase state power, and breaking the 'conservatism' of established engineers."[61] Often, when managers were appointed, good Party credentials counted for more than technical knowledge. Likewise, Ford's emphasis on high wages to enable increased consumption didn't fit well with an official ideology that attacked the middle class and the accumulation of private property. But perhaps the most fundamental problem was that of disciplining and training peasants with few or no skills. At the Fordson plant, the assembly line "was almost never implemented"[62] even though the Soviet tractor looked just like its American cousin.

If the Soviet Union enthusiastically attempted to import the assembly line, American manufacturing methods met a more mixed reception in

Germany. On the one hand, shortly after the end of World War I, Carl Friedrich von Siemens founded the Reichskuratorium für Wirtschaftlichkeit (RKW), whose purpose was to foster adoption of American manufacturing methods pioneered by Taylor and Ford.[63] It served as an umbrella organization linked to corporatist institutions from the different industrial sectors. It "hoped to enhance economic recovery through Fordist and Taylorist methods of improved management and industrial organization rather than by negotiating wages and work hours."[64] The public was also interested in these new methods. Ford's autobiography was translated and sold more than 200,000 copies, and interest in mass production extended to the universities as well. In 1924 three of the most influential German academics co-authored a volume that praised the Ford system of production as the epitome of rationality and efficiency. Max Weber, Werner Sombart, and Friedrich von Gott-Ottlilienfeld explained the Ford system, correctly emphasizing that it required the standardization of the product, interchangeable parts, and the use of assembly lines to produce high quality at a low unit cost.[65] In the same year, RKW leader Carl Köttgen made a tour of US industry that led to the publication of his book *Das wirtschaftliche Amerika* (*Economic America*).[66] Another German engineer, Otto Moug, toured the River Rouge plant in the late 1920s and found it an uplifting, almost religious experience. "No symphony, no Eroica, compared in depth, content, and power to the music that threatened and hammered away at us as we wandered through Ford's workplaces, wanderers overwhelmed by a daring expression of the human spirit."[67]

Yet if Weimar Germany discussed American methods a great deal, the industrial establishment was often wary of adopting them.[68] Opel introduced assembly lines to make its small cars in 1924, but didn't attain interchangeability until the end of the decade, when General Motors took an 80 percent share in the company.[69] During the 1920s few individual German companies proved ready to accept a full program of mass production. There was widespread agreement that industry could become more efficient through rationalization and the use of more interchangeable parts, but German managers didn't attribute the economic crisis of the 1920s to inefficiency. As Mary Nolan observes, industry "viewed mechanization, flow production, the assembly line and standardization much more negatively, and considered full-scale Fordism to be utterly unrealizable."[70] To industrialists, the crisis seemed rooted not in technology but in the welfare policies of left-leaning politicians who had raised taxes and introduced the eight-hour day. Some leading industrialists, particularly in the machine-tool industry, saw "mass production as a threat to the essence of German economic success, which they defined as specialized quality products made by skilled workers."[71] Remarkably, these arguments were common even within the automobile industry. Many "insisted that Germany could not sustain a Fordized automobile industry" because it lacked both the capital to build up production and the large consumer markets needed to absorb higher output. It seemed that "the most German auto makers could learn from Ford was how to reduce inventories and speed materials through the plant."[72] In Germany it was often not management but trade unions that advocated conversion to mass production. "Social Democrats could imagine rationalized capitalism as the basis of a reformist welfare state or as a building block of a socialist society."[73] Labor leaders saw that Ford had combined the $5 day with shorter hours and lower consumer prices, and argued for a transition to a society of mass production and mass consumption. But corporate managers rejected shorter hours and higher wages as ruinous. Overall, "assembly-line and flow production techniques were not widely introduced in Germany in the Weimar era."[74]

In 1925, the Ford Motor Company reentered the German market, having sold very few automobiles in Germany since 1914. The new subsidiary began by selling cars made in Copenhagen and Antwerp, but soon it opened an assembly plant in Berlin. Many small German car companies went bankrupt, however, and pressure to "buy German" was intense. Tariffs on parts imported from the United States were another problem. Ford invited German capitalists to invest in a larger plant, to be built in Cologne, that would not merely assemble vehicles but would also manufacture motors, transmissions, and many other parts. Machinery for the plant was shipped from Britain.[75] When the plant opened, in 1931, Carl Duisberg, chairman of the board of the German chemical conglomerate IG Farben, which had invested in the factory, declared its product "a purely German automobile." Nevertheless, in contrast to GM's Opel, Ford "did not succeed in being recognized as a German brand" even though its cars were manufactured locally and contributed to the German economy.[76] As one Ford executive later concluded, GM prospered in Germany because it first submerged its involvement by purchasing an existing German company, then introduced "American methods of production."[77]

FIGURE 4.3
Ford factory at Cologne, 1936. Courtesy of Rheinisches Bildarchiv.

Ford's Cologne plant was expected to threaten Opel's dominance, but sales were poor because the German economy was in crisis. In the summer of 1931, the Cologne plant operated at only 13 percent of its capacity.[78] Price was the problem, as one German expert wrote to Detroit. The American price of a new V8 Ford was $500, but in Germany the car was considered too large and the price, at $1,300, too high. Only a smaller car made entirely in Germany seemed to have a chance of success.[79] In June 1933 the Cologne plant abruptly decided "that no more parts for the production of cars should be imported into Germany" and canceled its orders from both Britain and the United States, including one order for parts that were en route.[80] A week later, Edsel Ford received a letter from Cologne explaining that "the Nazi organization issues Certificates of German origin, without which it is almost impossible to do business."[81] By December 1933, Charles Sorensen wanted to fire the German manager, but he was advised that if he did so the Nazi Party would almost certainly impose an even worse replacement. Already there were Nazis "in uniform parading the works."[82] By the following year, some Ford officials were wondering whether Ford should close down completely in Germany, because it was losing control.[83] GM's Opel had nearly a 50 percent share of the German market, versus a mere 5 percent for Ford. And as the Nazis seized more and more power, the Germanization of Ford accelerated. By the autumn of 1934, the German government was telling Ford to move its plant away from Cologne as part of a program to relocate all vital industries farther from France.[84] Ford suspected that letters to the German managers were being opened, and preferred face-to-face meetings. New Ford models received German names and a German logo, and more German managers were added.[85]

The Nazis sought to legitimize their rule through the mastery of mechanization. They used mass production to reduce the prices of certain "people's goods," including radios, cameras, and refrigerators. The Volkswagen was intended to be a part of this program, but it didn't go into mass production until after World War II. More immediately, the regime used economies of scale to offer workers 45 million inexpensive packaged vacations and excursions between 1934 and 1939.[86] This widespread implementation of American methods was also applied to the rearmament of Germany.[87] In addition to the fascination with aviation and the mass festivals in which thousands marched in rhythmic unison, after about 1936 the Nazis promoted a cult of productivity that made factories (often those with assembly lines) central sites of nationalism.[88] As a result, Ford and mass production became associated with the Nazi government and with "Nazi Modernism."

The Nazis didn't want factories to become alienating environments that produced proletarians ready to join the Communist Party. Rather, as Michael Allen has argued, the Nazis' goal was "a world where all conflict might disappear, where every German might know his or her station and understand it as just. Their industrial policy sought a uniquely German vision of Betriebsführung and Betriebsgemeinschaft (factory leadership and factory community), which could transform the production hall into a place for the 'spiritual mobilization of the people.' In often mixed metaphors, the factory became the smithy of the German soul."[89]

One might think that transferring the assembly line to other countries wouldn't have been problematic. But in practice every country—indeed every company—that adopted the assembly line also transformed it. To a casual visitor, an assembly-line factory in Russia might have looked much like one in Germany, Britain, France, or the United States, but there were significant variations. Each country had a different market for automobiles, shaped by local geographies and consumer desires. Relative to the United States, Western Europe had higher gasoline prices, narrower roads, and shorter distances between cities, all of which favored smaller cars with more economical engines. Western Europe also had a differentiated class system, and most of the demand for consumer goods came from the wealthier groups. This situation dictated producing a variety of models, rather than producing one model as cheaply as possible. In the Soviet Union, however, production of one car for everyone accorded well with revolutionary orthodoxy, and the Model T was readily embraced, even if universal car ownership proved unattainable. In Europe as a whole, mass production wasn't attractive to most manufacturers, because mass consumption didn't seem feasible. Wages weren't high enough. However, corporations did profit by adopting elements of the assembly line, such as moving work to the worker when possible or arranging machine tools to suit the assembly sequence rather than putting all the lathes in one location and all the drill presses in another.

Countries also had different cultures of work, shaped by their unions, their craft traditions, and their educational systems. At Ford's Manchester plant, workers insisted on stopping the line for tea breaks, and many managers, impeccably dressed in suits and white shirts, minimized their direct contact with the shop floor. The assembly line was only partially adopted in the UK. French automakers were more enthusiastic, but they didn't have real assembly-line production until about 1928, and even then they produced relatively small runs of large and expensive cars. In the Soviet Union, the whole Ford system was embraced, but a poorly educated workforce undermined both quality and productivity. In Weimar Germany, managers who valued craft traditions and flexible production talked about American methods more than they actually adopted them. In contrast, the Nazi regime embraced the assembly line as a way to legitimize its political power.

The reception of mass production was complex. Charles Maier summarizes:

The ideological breakdown between the enthusiasts and the indifferent or hostile did not follow any simple left-to-right alignment. Generally during the early postwar years technocratic or engineering models of social management appealed to the newer, more syncretic, and sometimes more extreme currents of European politics. Italian national syndicalists and fascists, German "revolutionary conservatives" and "conservative socialists" as well as the so-called left liberals who sought to mediate between bourgeois and social democracy, and finally the Soviet leaders, proved most receptive. Later in the decade, as the American vision of productivity was divested of its more utopian implications, it came to serve a useful function for business conservatives.[90]

Enthusiasm for mass production could be found at many points on the political spectrum, and to a considerable extent it hinged upon who was seen to be in control of the new productive technologies. Those on the left, notably in the Soviet Union, embraced mass production controlled by the working class but rejected mass production controlled by capitalists. Corporate managers were enthusiastic about American innovations if they could lower production costs, increase efficiency, and increase profits, but few of them believed that Europe was about to become a mass market with higher wages and shorter working hours.

Outside business and engineering circles, Europeans manifested a complex cultural response to mass production. To some, it promised escape from class conflict into utopian plenty for all. To others, it seemed to threaten European culture with mindless repetition, standardization, and uniformity. But whether critics thought mass production a benefit or a bane, they tended to assume that it was an unstoppable wave of history. In contrast to the majority of industrialists in Britain, France, and Germany, who remained dubious about adopting the assembly line, intellectuals tended to see mass production as both inevitable and regrettable.

In France, André Sigfried's 1927 book *The United States Today* sold 130,000 copies and was quickly translated to other languages. Sigfried recognized that the United States was able to provide housing, indoor plumbing, automobiles, and radios to most of its citizens, but asserted that Americans paid a "tragic price" for those worldly goods. The millions of workers were transformed into automatons, and "Fordism" made the worker little more than a standardized mechanism.[91] "By turning the worker into a cog in a vast machine, they have robbed him of the intense mental activity of the artisan or even the peasant who can think in terms of the finished product." As a result, American manufacturers lost out to their European counterparts in the markets for individualized goods. "The Americans," Sigfried wrote, "are so bound up with their machines that they are losing interest in making anything that cannot be turned out by mass production."[92]

Georges Duhamel, Sigfried's countryman, proclaimed his antipathy to American culture in the very title of his 1931 book *America the Menace:*

Scenes from the Life of the Future.[93] He described Americans as slaves in thrall to a society of consumption, marshaled into conformity by mass entertainment. Duhamel and Sigfried sounded an alarm that would be repeated for the rest of the twentieth century. As Richard Kuisel put it, they "contrasted French civilization with the wasteland of American mass culture and Gallic individualism with American conformism." They thought Americans were "dominated by businessmen like Henry Ford who trained their fellow Americans to be mass producers and consumers—creating a society of comfortable conformists and cultural philistines."[94] Similar arguments pervaded another anti-American French book published in 1931, Robert Aron and Arnaud Dandieu's *Le Cancer américain*.[95] Aron and Dandieu were members of a younger generation of intellectuals who feared the destruction of European humanism and saw the United States as a threat to their culture.[96] Rebuttals to this spate of anti-American books were rare, yet the tone of the French debate was on the whole defensive. In the eighteenth century Frenchmen had seen the New World as an exotic garden, and in the nineteenth century Americans could be treated with disdain as provincials. But after 1920 French anti-Americanism had an air of resignation. The intellectuals saw themselves as already conquered, already colonized.[97] The only hope seemed to lie in unity against a common cultural foe.

An incident in the world of fashion is highly revealing of French attitudes toward the United States and mass production. Jean Patou, a leader in the French fashion industry, went to the United States and held extensive auditions to select new models who could embody a leaner, more angular look than that common among models in the Paris salons. He imported American models to Paris with great fanfare. The response of the French press was "vociferous, chauvinist, and protectionist." Patou asked the Americans to keep their "flapper slouch," and at times he dressed them identically and "reduced them to abstract patterns." They became symbols of modernity, as though they were interchangeable parts. Only the dresses were expected to vary. The models were "cold, unavailable, detached, at work." The fashion show, a new institution, "strung the mannequins together like false pearls: too lustrous, too uniform, and too perfect for plausibility."[98]

One of the most influential French attacks on mass production appeared in Louis-Ferdinand Céline's novel *Journey to the End of the Night*. Applying for a job at a Ford plant in Detroit, the protagonist is told: "Your studies won't be any use to you here. . . . You haven't come here to think. . . .

We've no use for intellectuals. . . ." Once he enters the factory, he is over-whelmed by "the vast crashing sound of machines." "The whole building shook, and oneself from one's soles to one's ears was possessed by this shak-ing, which vibrated from the ground, the glass panes and all this metal." The noise of the factory overwhelms thought and takes over the body. "One was turned by force into a machine oneself, the whole of one's carcass quivering in this vast frenzy of noise, which filled you within and all around the inside of your skull and lower down rattled your bowels, and climbed to your eyes in infinite, little quick unending strokes."[99] Yet when compiling examples of French antipathy to the United States it is wise to keep in mind Rob Kroes' observation that "the French history of attitudes toward the United States is one of great ambivalence, of infatuation vying with revulsion, alternating over time."[100] Particularly in moments of self-doubt or internal crisis, such as the 1930s, the French tended to disparage America.

British worries about Americanization emerged even earlier. W. T. Stead's 1901 book *The Americanization of the World; or, The Trend of the Twentieth Century* was complimentary to the United States but neverthe-less articulated many British concerns about its rise to world power. Stead believed that America's economic might would propel it to the center of the world stage, and that Europe would be gradually Americanized.[101] He noted that most British people already used American mass-produced goods every day—safety razors, Waterbury watches, breakfast oatmeal, New Eng-land bedsheets, and so on. Concern about American technology became more focused after World War I. D. H. Lawrence famously sneered: "The Perfectability of Man! Ah heaven, what a dreary theme! The perfectibility of the Ford car! The perfectibility of which man? . . . I am not a mechanical contrivance."[102] Lawrence valued organic personal growth and passionate unpredictability, the antithesis of mechanization.

British and Continental writers were often inclined to criticize mass pro-duction, which seemed dehumanizing in its mechanical predictability and standardization. In *We*, a dystopian novel set in the future, the Russian novelist Yevgeny Zamyatin was one of the first to imagine what such values might lead to. In the regimented world of *We*, people have their basic needs satisfied, but unexpected events and even dreams have been eliminated. The citizens lack inner lives and inhabit glass buildings. Every movement can be seen by all. Aldous Huxley drew on Zamyatin in his 1932 novel *Brave New World*, writing of the assembly-line production of babies with carefully regulated abilities. In Huxley's dystopia, many popular sayings refer to "Our Ford" rather than "Out Lord," and the T has replaced the Christian cross.[103]

German attitudes toward the assembly line and Americanization were complex. Had not the Americans tipped the balance in World War I? Had the United States remained neutral, its armies and mass-produced armaments would not have given victory to the Allies. Well before the Great War, Germans had been fascinated by the industrial progress of the United States. Werner Sombart had written a famous short book that had asked why socialism was so weak there.[104] One reason, Sombart concluded, was that American workers had significantly better housing, clothing, and food than their European counterparts. Greater productivity had been translated into a better material life. The millions of German-Americans had, on the whole, a higher standard of living than their cousins in the fatherland.

Yet many remained highly critical of the culture of the United States. Oswald Spengler, like many European intellectuals, concluded that Americans were shallow; they lacked the "deepened and educated souls of the European." "Life in America," he declared, "revolves solely around its economy and lacks depth, the more so as absent from it is the element of true historical tragedy."[105] In a similar vein, Peter Mennicken contrasted the practical American "*homo faber*" with "the European *homo sapiens*, who created *Kultur* and embodied *Geist*."[106] America was successful on a material level, but it seemed a superficial land of pragmatism and conformity. Mennicken saw these differences personified in the contrast between Henry Ford, an organizer with little education or culture, and Walther Rathenau, head of Allgemeine Elektricitäts-Gesellschaft (the German counterpart of General Electric), a highly educated man who could discuss business, art, or philosophy with equal ease. Not all German critics were as harsh, but many contrasted a homogeneous and materialistic United States with a more nuanced Germany where centuries of high culture and historical traditions anchored social identity. From this perspective, Americanization represented the triumph of uniformity over *Kultur*, and the assembly line was an instrument of banalization that undermined quality and difference. Thinking in such dichotomies, intellectuals of the Weimar period couldn't embrace the Ford manufacturing system. Even Social Democrats who advocated adoption of mass production had difficulty imagining what consumer goods might be suited to German needs. They were constrained by material circumstances. Real wages didn't return to the levels they had reached before World War I until 1928. Half of all workers lived in apartments without toilets or electricity, and they had little disposable income. "Efforts to develop a more positive picture of German mass consumption," Nolan writes, "proved singularly unsuccessful."[107]

Just after the stock-market crash of 1929, a German journalist studied working conditions in the factories of Philadelphia, Pittsburgh, and Detroit, including the Ford factories. He admitted that many American workers owned houses and automobiles, and that their wages were higher than those of their German counterparts, but he also noted the weakness of the unions and how easily a worker could be fired. Most depressing, he found the workers completely drained by their jobs. After observing the fast pace of an assembly line and hearing its din, he left the factory during the change to the evening shift. He looked at the men going home. "None of them seemed undernourished, but all of them wore an indescribably tired, exhausted expression, and when they sat down on the streetcars and buses many of them fell asleep at once." He concluded that "mechanized labor" could transform "a man into an inanimate hammer or lever." In such factories, man became "an inanimate machine repeating the same gesture again and again."[108]

In the most ominous European visions, machines seemed inseparable from human oppression. Fritz Lang's 1927 film *Metropolis* depicts a future society divided sharply between the rich, who live with ease and abundance in a skyscraper city, and the poor, who live and labor underground. The workers have no names, only numbers, and in the opening scene they march in lockstep through a tunnel to an elevator that takes them down to their jobs. Because the men are dressed in identical gray clothing and close-fitting caps, they appear interchangeable. A patrician who wanders into this subterranean world for the first time sees the men frantically tending a vast machine—the city's electrical works. When it overheats and explodes, he is thrown against a wall. Delirious, he has a vision in which the machinery is transformed into Moloch, whose enormous mouth devours the workers. When he revives, he sees the killed and the maimed being carted away and replaced by identical workers. After this scene there are no more images of production in the film, but antipathy to "the machine" is pervasive.

René Clair's 1931 film *À nous la liberté* (*Give Us Liberty*) is a critique of mass production intertwined with comedy. An escaped convict becomes a successful entrepreneur. His factory's production line is reminiscent of a prison. One overhead shot shows men in identical uniforms evenly spaced along a line, almost faceless, endlessly repeating the same movements. (See figure 4.4.) They are producing phonographs. The film contrasts the grim discipline of the factory with vagabondage, fishing, dancing, and other forms of play.[109] In one scene, a man falls behind in his work and follows the unfinished piece to the next work station, interfering with the worker there. Soon both men are interfering with a third man. The problem cascades into chaos, and the line has to be stopped. (This scene seems to have inspired later scenes of assembly-line humor in other films, including Charlie Chaplin's *Modern Times*.) The monotony and stress of the factory are abolished when the hero creates an automated production system. He gives it to the workers, who then become leisurely supervisors. Then, with his friend, another escaped convict, he leaves the factory and settled life to wander the open road. Though *À nous la liberté* is sometimes seen as a European rejection of the assembly line, its ending is curiously American: technological development ensures leisure for all, and the two heroes run away from society, preferring to be vagabonds.

Clair depicted a frictionless transfer of factory ownership to the workers, but Marxists saw mass production as a final stage of capitalism that would

FIGURE 4.4
Still image from the 1931 film *A nous la liberté*, directed by René Clair.

provoke workers to revolution. The assembly line both increased workers' alienation and created a contradiction between surplus production and weakening consumption. Corporations, unable to sell their goods to unemployed consumers, would go bankrupt, and each corporate failure would further undermine the entire capitalist system until it collapsed from its internal contradictions. Classical Marxist theory had anticipated the crisis of the 1930s, and the only solution, apparently, was for workers to seize control of industry and create a new economic order. The assembly line therefore was not in itself an evil, but rather the harbinger of an inevitable transformation.

Antonio Gramsci advanced a somewhat different view. He was one of the first to use the term "Fordism," which was coined in Europe and which later spread to the United States. The *New York Times* first used it in a 1927 article on European critics of mass production.[110] Gramsci considered "Fordism" to be a new stage in capitalist development in which production was being further rationalized. He recognized that workers received higher wages in America than in Europe, and attributed this in good part to the persistence in Europe of a parasitic class of landowners, who were the last vestiges of pre-capitalist social systems that had never existed in the United States. Just as important, however, the Americans had a temporary monopoly on the new production methods, and Gramsci argued that high wages were "a transitory form of remuneration" that would keep workers from deserting the assembly line. He concluded that wages would fall again once mass production was "generalized and diffused." A new, more subservient worker was being molded as "the apparatus of material production" was perfected. Before long, high unemployment would force workers to accept mass production, and "high wages [would] disappear."[111] The $5 day therefore was only a temporary phase. In the long view, Gramsci argued, the assembly line would not bring prosperity to workers but would force them to adapt, both physically and psychologically, to new conditions. He considered it possible that Fordism was "a malignant phenomenon which must be fought" because it could "lead to the physical degeneration and to deterioration of the species, with the consequent destruction of all labor power."[112] Yet he considered it more likely that the assembly line could be modified and adapted to benefit workers once they gained control.

Gramsci didn't believe capitalism was about to collapse, however, because the corporations had developed a hegemonic system that dominated workers less through force than through displays of cultural power. This observation seems particularly apt for the Italy of his time. Gramsci started university in Turin in 1911 and remained there as a labor leader. He observed Fiat's factories and the Agnelli family that owned them. Fiat was the assembly-line corporation that Gramsci knew firsthand. With the interesting exception of Fiat, the Ford-style assembly line was not widely or fully adopted in Italy during Gramsci's lifetime. Beginning in 1916, in Lingotto, just outside Turin, Fiat erected a plant modeled on Ford's Highland Park. Its moving assembly line didn't become fully operational until 1925. Unlike Ford, Fiat produced not one model but several. Peak production was only 300 cars a day, and that was rarely achieved. Later, Fiat sought greater vertical integration in the larger Mirafiori factory, which was based on Ford's River Rouge plant but was considerably smaller. It produced more components in sub-assembly lines that fed into the final assembly. Yet Mirafiori was built to be flexible, and Fiat didn't use as many single-function machines there as Ford did. And Mirafiori didn't have overhead conveyors.[113] In neither of Fiat's factories was mass production fully developed by Detroit standards. However, Fiat did seek to control as many of its manufacturing processes as it could, and until about 1920 it focused on just two models. Because of high tariffs against foreign cars, more than 80 percent of all cars in Italy were Fiats. With such protection, Fiat didn't have to compete on price and efficiency to the same degree as manufacturers inside the American market. Gramsci's ideas of hegemony and "Fordism" were based on Fiat's tariff-protected, partially developed form of mass production.[114] This lack of direct experience with either full mass production or truly competitive markets doesn't necessarily invalidate Gramsci's analysis of Fordism, but it does suggest that he really was writing about Fiatism.

The Ford Motor Company itself was scarcely present in the Italian market, with a small assembly plant in the free port of Trieste. In 1929, just before the stock market crashed, Ford was negotiating with the Italian government for permission to build a factory in Livorno. "We shall never beat up a very big business in Italy so long as the present excessive duties have to be paid," someone in Ford's London office wrote to Charles Sorensen.[115] Ford was ready to build the factory, but the Italians suddenly pulled out of the agreement and began to insist that any contract would have to include Fiat as a partner. Benito Mussolini was directly involved in these long and fruitless discussions. Tariffs were raised several times as the discussions proceeded. By 1934, the tariff on the British-produced Model Y automobile was 300 percent and that on a Ford truck was higher still.[116] By 1934, Ford's managers realized that after the "introduction of the new duties on 22nd January, 1934, it is obvious no further business can be done in the sale of cars and trucks,"[117] and that only a few tractors could be sold in Italy. France likewise imposed stiff duties, and as early as 1931 Ford in France was paying an average of 90 percent in duties on all imports (which were considerable, as only about half the parts were made inside the country).[118] In Germany, even with an improving economy, Ford sold only 13,085 cars and trucks in 1935.[119] Everywhere in Europe, government interference and tariff barriers hindered full development of mass production, which requires large and open markets. The balkanized market protected inefficient producers and allowed elements of older production systems to survive until World War II.

Europeans' disdain for mass production was based, in large part, either on their having read about it or on their experience with transplants of partial assembly lines. However, a few Europeans had worked on both American and European assembly lines. In a book titled *Robots or Men?* a French worker named Hyacinthe Dubreuil reported on his experiences during fifteen months in the United States during 1927 and 1928. Dubreuil, an admirer of John Ruskin and William Morris, wanted to see for himself whether American factories were as insufferable as many French intellectuals claimed. After employment in a number of factories, including a Ford plant, he concluded "I cannot condemn what are called 'American methods.'" Rather, he admired the rationality and the flow of work in American plants. Dubreuil worked under the Taylor system in one Cleveland factory, and found it quite a contrast to the Ford assembly line, which he praised as the epitome of mass production. "When it comes to feverish activity," he concluded, "it should be sought rather in our French factories, where often frantic workers rush about in unorganized production."[120] In short, at least one astute French observer with firsthand experience of the American assembly line found it preferable to European production.

Another neo-Marxist critique of the assembly line emerged in Germany, among the scholars who later would become known as the Frankfurt School. They focused less on the factory than on mass consumption's invasion of other aspects of modern life. As Martin Jay summarized, Theodor Adorno and Max Horkheimer argued that "leisure was the continuation of labor by other means" and that "the culture industry enslaves men in far more subtle and effective ways that the crude methods of domination used in earlier eras."[121] Writing to Leo Lowenthal, Horkheimer asserted that "the mechanisms which govern man in his leisure time are absolutely the same [as] those which govern him when he works." Just as work was subdivided into small repetitive tasks, social life was being packaged into experiences that could be repeated just as a phonograph record could be played over and over. Life was divided into tiny pieces with no continuity. Horkheimer complained of "those terrible scenes in the movies when some years of a hero's life are pictured in a series of shots which take about one or two minutes, just to show how he grew up or old, how a war started and passed by." Such collages of images turned "existence into some futile moments which can be characterized schematically."[122] The audience imbibed a segmented vision of existence that mimicked the division of labor on the assembly line, robbing life of coherence.

Perhaps the most famous essay along these lines was "The Work of Art in the Age of Mechanical Reproduction," in which Walter Benjamin argued that sculptures and paintings had a unique aura of originality and authenticity, and that mass-produced copies of such works destroyed that aura because the copy lacked the uniqueness, the permanence, the physical location, and the tactile properties of the original. Making copies removed the object from its context and tradition, creating the illusion that all objects exist in the same social and historical space. Benjamin also recognized that the invention of mechanical reproduction made possible new kinds of consumer goods for which there was, in a very real sense, no original.[123] Just as every issue of a magazine, every print of a photograph, and every recording was identical, so too every car that rolled off an assembly line was identical to all the others. What was the meaning of a copy for which there was no original? An original oil painting by Leonardo da Vinci had a unique historical and cultural location, but mass-produced goods floated free of any context. They had no authenticity. In mass-produced goods, in contrast with the artisanal goods of an earlier era, there was no trace of human labor. The new goods had no "depth" and quickly lost their monetary value. The automobile, unlike the durable goods a person inherited in pre-industrial times, was a transient possession that seldom lasted more than ten years. Objects were becoming ephemeral, and all that was solid was melting into the air.

Benjamin's rejection of mass production articulated in theoretical terms the distaste that many European intellectuals had for American material culture. Exporting the assembly line had proved more difficult than Henry

Ford had imagined. Not only did each of his branch factories have to adapt to local circumstances—designing a new car for the British market, accepting unneeded German investors, struggling with peasant laborers, party interference and technical imprecision in the Soviet Union—but the idea of mass production itself met considerable European resistance. Perhaps most crucially, no European economy fulfilled the preconditions necessary for the assembly line to become the cornerstone of its productive system. These preconditions included sufficient capital for conversion of factories, a large market free from tariff barriers, and high wages for workers so that they could become consumers of assembly-line goods. No European nation could develop an American-style production system unless it also embraced mass consumption. Had most European economies been stronger, such a mass market might have developed. Instead, Ford and General Motors made large investments in European factories that, despite great efforts, were always less productive and less efficient than their American plants. Ford's Dagenhem

FIGURE 4.5
Ford's Dagenhem factory on the Thames near London, January 29, 1967. Courtesy of Photographic Department, Boston Public Library

plant, outside London, had the capacity to make 300,000 vehicles per year. But Ford's sales of trucks and cars in all of Europe fell from 80,176 in 1931 to just 26,243 in 1932.[124] Dagenham would recover somewhat by 1933, but even then it hardly was engaged in mass production by American standards. A comparative study found that American auto workers were three times as productive as their British counterparts in 1935. As late as 1955, it took five British workers to do as much as two Americans.[125]

Paradoxically, European intellectuals such as André Sigfried and Peter Mennicken attacked an Americanization that in fact was scarcely taking place. Europeans had smaller factories, less efficient workers, less mass production, and far less mass consumption. Critics bemoaned a standardization and an interchangeability that were still uncommon in Europe. Even when mass production was embraced, as in the Soviet tractor plants, parts often had to be filed by hand before they would fit together, and mass production remained less an actuality than a conflicted aspiration. The assembly line was a metaphor for an unwanted modernity. Europeans discussed and often disdained the idea of an assembly line they were only beginning to know firsthand.

In contrast, during the same years Americans questioned an assembly line that already was deeply embedded in their society.

15075-1

5 CRITIQUE

We was a mighty cocky nation. We originated mass production, and mass-produced everybody out of a job with our boasted labor-saving machinery. It saved labor, the very thing we are now appropriating money to get a job for. They forgot that machinery don't eat, rent houses, or buy clothes. We had begun to believe that the height of civilization was a good road, bathtub, radio, and automobile.

Will Rogers, New Year's Eve, 1930[1]

Europeans understood the assembly line both as a form of Americanization and as a worrisome new stage in the history of industry. It was embraced most wholeheartedly by totalitarian regimes quite unlike the United States, in Nazi Germany and Soviet Russia. In contrast, most Americans celebrated the assembly line until the early 1930s.

In the United States, critics were, at first, a minority. After a burst of initial enthusiasm for the $5 day, workers focused their criticism on the repetitiveness and deskilling of assembly-line work and on "the speed up." They also found that sudden layoffs occurred whenever there was a lack of parts or a mechanical problem with the line.[2] Worker criticism of mass production persisted after 1918, although at first non-workers paid little attention.

The term "Fordism" was neither invented in nor frequently used in the United States. "Mass production" was the common term, and it referred not to a potential system but to a realized fact. The debate was not about whether to adopt the assembly line or not but rather about its meanings and social consequences. In 1914 some businessmen worried that Ford's new manufacturing system would foster labor unrest. In the 1920s some

FIGURE 5.1
The Battle of the Overpass, May 26, 1937. Courtesy of Franklin D. Roosevelt Library.

intellectuals feared that it would undermine American individualism. From the late 1920s on, sociologists and planners were alarmed that it might lead to widespread technological unemployment, a fear that seemed justified during the Great Depression. These concerns coincided with growing worker dissatisfaction that culminated in sit-down strikes and successful unionization of the automobile industry. Overall, however, Americans tended to question not the assembly line itself but rather the way it was being used. The general assumption was that increased productivity and efficiency were desirable if they didn't lead to exploitation of workers and mass unemployment.

In 1914, some businessmen didn't understand the linkage between the assembly line and the $5 day. The *Wall Street Journal* declared that Henry Ford "has in his social endeavors committed economic blunders, if not crimes." *The Nation* suggested that the inequality between highly paid workers at Ford and workers at other companies could lead to social unrest. The *New York Times* worried: "The Ford Company cannot hire all the men, yet there will be unrest and dissatisfaction in the shops of other companies. Strikes are likely enough, and conditions of peace cannot be looked for until the equilibrium is somehow restored."[3] In Detroit, the First Unitarian Church held a lively debate in which some condemned the $5 day as destructive of local prosperity on the ground that it would scare away other businesses since they would not be able to match this wage. But others at that meeting defended the $5 day as a form of profit-sharing.[4] In Cleveland, 350 workers and their friends turned out to hear a debate on the merits of Ford's system. At the end, by far the loudest applause was for this new form of profit sharing, which the crowd decided was based on improved efficiency.[5] In Columbus, Ohio, a similar throng debated the issue hotly with a group of socialists, and the discussion was resumed a week later.[6] Ford won plaudits from many social reformers, including Felix Adler, president of the Ethical Culture Society in New York.[7] The debate raged in all parts of the nation, from Boston to Atlanta and from New York to California.[8] One editorial cartoon depicted a farm hand demanding $5 a day. Another showed workers and managers sharing a car on Easy Street.

At first, the radical press tended to praise both the assembly line and the $5 day. A reporter named Kate Richards O'Hare informed the 160,000 readers of the socialist monthly *The National Rip-Saw* that Ford's system was far preferable to Taylor's scientific management. After spending two days

FIGURE 5.2
Cartoon celebrating the $5 day, *Los Angeles Times*, 1914. Courtesy of Ford Archives.
Photograph by David Nye.

FIGURE 5.3

Cartoon of farmhand demanding $5 a day, *South Bend Tribune*, 1914. Courtesy of
Ford Archives. Photograph by David Nye.

touring the Highland Park plant and interviewing many workers, she concluded that the work was less demanding and the workers were much better paid than in most industries. Moreover, she was convinced that if other manufacturers "were to suddenly become converted to Ford's ideas and put the 'Ford plan' into operation" the effects would be beneficial. She admitted that the assembly line and the $5 day "would not solve the social problems, eliminate the class struggle or inaugurate the co-operative commonwealth," but suggested that it "would advance the cause of social justice, demonstrate the soundness of the socialist theories and bring the mighty pressure of education to hasten the final and complete emancipation of the working class."[9] She illustrated these generalizations with anecdotes about particular workers who had better living conditions or who, because Ford had instituted the eight-hour day, had time and energy to patronize the library. Similarly, in 1916 John Reed praised Henry Ford as "industry's miracle maker," noting that he had both raised wages and lowered prices.[10]

Socialists praised the new factory methods largely because workers' early responses to the assembly line were positive and focused on the $5 day. In 1913 that was twice the average day's pay. Workers who had felt fortunate to make $500 in the year 1912 suddenly had the chance to make $1,000 in 1913. At the time, many workers walked away from a manufacturing job after just a few months. Yearly worker turnover in some industries was over 100 percent. The Department of Labor found that in meat-packing plants, textile mills, machine shops, and automobile factories the average was 115 percent.[11] Corporations in these industries had to hire and train about 10 percent of their workforce every month. The situation at Ford in 1913 was worse. Shortly before the assembly line was introduced, annual labor turnover had reached 370 percent. An internal Ford Motor Company report found that 71 percent of those who left didn't bother to give notice; they simply failed to show up. In March 1913, when Ford had a workforce of 13,623, every month 5,000 quit and another 1,300 were fired. Of those quitting, only one in nine gave notice. Absenteeism had reached a level of 10 percent, and 1,300 substitute workers were needed every day.[12] The disruption and the demoralization were tremendous. Keeping enough men in position on the assembly line was a managerial nightmare. And even with a man at every post, many were still learning how to do their job. In assembly-line operation, a few slow workers can impede the entire line. Sluggish production was expensive. The $5 day was introduced to reduce turnover and generate more worker enthusiasm. To be eligible for the higher wage, a worker had to stay with the company for six months. By November 1914, annual turnover had fallen to 54 percent, still high but far below the 370 percent of the previous year.[13]

Ford's employees were initially enthusiastic about the high wages, but most disliked the monotony of the work and the fact that management could use the assembly line to control them. Workers benefited from shorter hours, higher wages, and falling consumer prices, but they worried about loss of freedom on the shop floor, about endless repetition of the same movements for eight hours, and about jobs that deadened the soul. Their complaints, scarcely audible before 1920, grew louder until they became predominant in the late 1930s. A Yale student who worked on an assembly line one summer complained: "You've got to work like hell in Ford's. From the time you become a number in the morning until the bell rings for quitting time you have to keep at it. You can't let up. You've got to get out the production and if you can't get it out, you get out."[14] Another worker declared: "Henry [Ford] has reduced the complexity of life to a definite number of jerks, twists, and turns. Once a Ford employee has learned the special spasm expected from him, he can go through life without a single thought or emotion. When the whistle blows he starts to jerk and when the whistle blows again he stops jerking. . . ."[15] A General Motors worker also complained of the repetition: "If I keep putting on Nut No. 86 for about 86 more days, I will be Nut No. 86 in the Pontiac bughouse."[16] Charles Madison, a skilled man who had worked at Studebaker and at Dodge, disliked his experience at Ford and soon quit because he "felt too fatigued after leaving the Ford factory to do any serious reading." "The painful Ford interlude," he later recalled, "was a rancorous memory—a form of hell on earth that turned human beings into driven robots." Madison especially "resented the thought that Ford publicists had made the company seem beneficent and imaginative when in fact the firm exploited its employees more ruthlessly than any of the other automobile firms."[17]

Madison had worked at Highland Park, which he regarded as "a mammoth plant,"[18] but it was far smaller than the River Rouge plant, where the assembly line reached both its most complete expression and its logical dead end. Electrical power made such a factory possible, but did not make it wise. Its enormous size, coupled with Ford's determination to produce every component of his cars at one site, tied up an enormous capital investment and made workers into anonymous cogs in a vast machine. Meant to demonstrate the scope of the assembly line as a production form, instead it pointed to its defects and limitations not least its devastating effect on labor. In 1925, Carter Goodrich wrote of the "fascinating and horrible spectacle" of work in the auto industry, singling out "the jobs along the famous assembly line at Highland Park out of which the last residue of workmanlike interest has been relentlessly squeezed." He noted further that the availability of cheap energy was essential to the transformation of skilled work into machine tending. Low energy costs seemed to bring a more "complete subordination of the individual to the machine's routine." In 1925 organized labor was weakest in the new assembly-line industries and strongest in fields where the work was less mechanized, such as coal mining.[19] Observers, of whom there were many by the late 1920s, saw that assembly-line production took decision making away from workers and eliminated variety from their day. It made work so dull, repetitious, and monotonous that many workers stayed less than the six-month probation period, and therefore never received $5 a day. The assembly line forced compliance with an entirely new working environment that had little use for skills. Workers lost control over even small elements of the day. Except for a fifteen-minute lunch break, they could scarcely move from their spot on the line during an eight-hour shift. Nor were they supposed to talk to one another unless the talk was work related. Worst of all, there was no let-up. No one could go to the bathroom until the foreman found a replacement. The assembly line was a mechanism that management used to control the organization of space, determine the work pace, and make most of the choices in the factory.

A common corporate response to worker discontent in the 1920s was welfare capitalism. The Ford Motor Company had savings plans, pensions, free gardening space, a medical staff at the factory, and educational programs, as well as the $5 day. The company also shortened the working day to eight hours. Even with welfare capitalism, higher wages and shorter hours, however, Ford and other assembly-line manufacturers found it difficult to hold on to employees.

Attacks on the assembly line appeared in labor unions' publications, in poems, in songs, in novels, and in theatrical works. Amy Koritz found that in the staged dramas of the 1920s "the artificial and alien rhythms of machines" were "treated with a combination of fascination and horror."[20] In Eugene O'Neill's *The Hairy Ape*, Elmer Rice's *The Adding Machine*, and

Sophie Treadwell's *Machinal*, human rhythms clashed with the demanding, repetitive rhythms of the machine. Likewise, in Robert Lynd and Helen Merrell Lynd's famous "Middletown" study of Muncie, Indiana, the machine-governed work processes of local factories stand in contrast to earlier artisan labor, in which "the speed and rhythm of the work were set by the human organism."[21]

Nor are the effects of mechanization and the assembly line limited to the workers. O'Neill's stage directions for *The Hairy Ape* describe wealthy New Yorkers at a party as "gaudy marionettes" whose movements suggest "something of the relentless horror of Frankensteins in their detached, mechanical unawareness."[22] Rice viewed the effects of the machine on American society as being just as dire, in his autobiography characterizing *The Adding Machine* as "a case study of one of the slave souls who are both the raw material and the product of a mechanized society."[23] During the 1920s Sigmund Freud was in vogue, and many intellectuals, including Rice, saw the machine as part of civilization's apparatus of repression of the individual's organic development and sexual instincts. The same qualities "associated with machines—standardized conformity, mindless repetition of tasks, inflexibility—Rice also associated with repression, particularly sexual repression,"[24] notably in the character of an accountant named Zero. Similarly, in Treadwell's *Machinal* the main character, "The Young Woman," finds it difficult to conform to office routines. One reviewer concluded that the play was "a tragedy of submission" that pitted "an individual character against the hard surface of a mechanical age."[25] Sherwood Anderson admitted in an article he wrote for *Vanity Fair* that he "could get a thrill any time looking at the machines" but they also frightened him: "Solve all the problems of my life for me by industrialism, by standardization, and you leave me a dead man." Anderson had "the individualist's fear of mass production." He feared that "the age of the individual [had] passed." His "inheritance" was being taken away "by mass production, by the great factory, by inventions, by the machine."[26] Anderson's novel *Poor White* described how the industrialization of a small town led to conflict between the workers and the factory owners, who expected to outsmart labor with new machines: "Pretty soon we'll do all the work by machines. Then what'll we do? We'll kick all the workers out. . . ."[27]

Rising productivity seemed to mean lost jobs. Unemployment caused by technology first worried government statisticians in 1926, when they found that productivity had increased in various industries between 40 and 59 percent since 1919 while employment had declined. By the autumn of 1927, in the midst of a small recession, the nation had begun to discuss the concept of technological unemployment, an idea that "was firmly entrenched in the public mind" by the middle of 1928.[28]

If articles in the popular press often saw a direct cause-and-effect relationship between mass production and higher unemployment, many professional economists did not. More than a century of theory, including the work of Jean Baptiste Say and David Ricardo, argued that displacement of workers by new machinery didn't lead to a permanent shrinkage in the workforce, but rather to new kinds of jobs. Say's *Treatise on Political Economy*, which went through six American editions by 1855, argued that "the mere circumstance of creation of one product immediately opens a vent for other products."[29] Greater productivity expanded the market. Indeed, during the nineteenth century increases in productivity made possible by new machinery increased the general wealth, and when it threw people out of work in one industry the temporary unemployment was offset by new jobs. Such arguments were more difficult to maintain, however, after the stock-market crash of 1929. By 1933, unemployment exceeded 25 percent. As late as 1929, more than 125,000 people had toured Ford's River Rouge in a single year. But in the early years of the Great Depression the annual total fell to less than half that.[30]

Stuart Chase, a Harvard-educated accountant, examined the new relationships between business, labor, and the machine in a series of widely read books. In *The Tragedy of Waste* (1925) he argued that, although capitalist industry was becoming much more productive, it was often inefficient and wasteful of both men and natural resources. The best factories were at least 50 percent more efficient than the average, and most of the difference was due to poor management. There were too many contractors, small stores, and little businesses of all sorts, many idle much of the time. Worst of all, 90 percent of the $1.2 billion spent on advertising each year served only to shift consumption from one product to an almost identical alternative. Chase was one of the founders of Consumer Research, which investigated the quality of goods and helped consumers choose products that were safe, well designed, and durable. In 1929, he warned in *Men and Machines* that regulations were needed to slow down the pace of technological unemployment. Chase disparaged the idea that people were becoming a race of robots, calculating that only 5 percent of the populace had endlessly repetitive jobs and that the number of new, high-skilled positions was increasing. Rather, Chase worried that mass production could transform war into mass slaughter. He also warned that any system that yielded high profits while paying low wages would produce starvation in the midst of plenty. In his 1931 book *The Nemesis of American Business* Chase concluded that the Depression had been caused by overproduction, and that it should be curbed by planning and by an "Economic Disarmament" agreed upon at an international conference. Bread lines could be seen all over the United States, and Chase seemed a prophet. Soon he was an advisor to President Franklin D. Roosevelt. In his 1934 book *The Economy of Abundance*, Chase argued that electrification had transformed industry and had made it far more productive; a declining number of workers produced an increasing number of goods. As technological unemployment increased, Chase concluded, competitive capitalism became unsustainable; only some form of state capitalism or socialism could balance production and consumption. If business were turned over to a staff of technicians, he argued, Americans could raise their standard of living and yet shorten the work week to perhaps 25 hours.[31]

As the Depression wore on, many discussions of the assembly line followed a similar pattern. Capitalism seemed an inhumane system that condemned many to bread lines and tormented those who did work. Prominent authors protested technological unemployment. Upton Sinclair asserted that the coming of mass production to steel mills had "put tens of thousands of the most highly paid roller men out on the streets."[32] John Steinbeck described how small farmers lost their land to agribusiness, and fled to California seeking agricultural work, only to discover that much of it was being mechanized. Likewise, in the South a cotton-picking machine eliminated hand picking. Theodore Dreiser traveled the country and found that on the docks conveyor lines had replaced stevedores, and that at the phone exchanges automatic switchboards had replaced most operators. In cotton mills highly automated looms displaced many workers, and in tobacco factories cigars were rolled by machines. Everywhere, Dreiser complained, "the developing machine age speeds, reduces, and discards men."[33] A 1934 science fiction story imagined a future in which human beings had lost all initiative and robots ran a meaningless world. As Amy Bix summarized, such Depression-era science fiction "operated according to an extreme Social Darwinism; without either the need or the opportunity to maintain their physical and mental health through work, humans would deteriorate biologically and move toward extinction." At the same time, improved machines "would be more fit than human beings and have a better chance of surviving in a new Machine Age."[34]

The fear of technological displacement pervaded 1930s popular culture. With the advent of sound films, theater musicians, who had had regular work at movie houses during the 1920s, suddenly were unemployed. They circulated a poem about people being replaced by machines. In it, one workman complains about a new machine: "You simply cannot tire it out, 'twill work both day and night / Pretty soon we'll lose our jobs, the end of work's in sight."[35] Similarly, a carpenter complained that robots were erecting houses and a factory hand reported that a new machine did the work of ten men. Industrial-scale bakeries had machines to slice the bread. One of the few jobs left for a human being to do was package it, and soon that would soon be automated too. The humorist Will Rogers declared in his newspaper column: "We was a mighty cocky nation. We originated mass production, and mass-produced everybody out of a job with our boasted labor-saving machinery. It saved labor, the very thing we are now appropriating money to get a job for. They forgot that machinery don't eat, rent houses, or buy clothes. We had begun to believe that the height of civilization was a good road, bathtub, radio, and automobile." Rogers didn't blame "Hoover, the Republicans or even Russia." "I think the Lord just looked us over and decided to set us back where we belonged," he concluded.[36] Rogers' argument that technological "pride goeth before a fall" may have persuaded many in 1930; however, as the Depression wore on, ordinary Americans were less ready to think the Almighty was admonishing them whenever they lost a job.

During the Great Depression, the centralization and vertical integration that in prosperous times had seemed the great advantage of Ford's River Rouge plant became a serious problem. Alfred Chandler put it this way: "Ford was the world's most integrated automobile company. To be sure of constant, tightly scheduled flows of materials through his huge plants . . . and thus to enhance the economies of scale, Ford made massive investment in the production of steel and glass, parts and accessories." When output declined, however, Ford couldn't escape the high fixed costs, and the "unit costs rose much more rapidly than did those of his competitors."[37] General Motors and Chrysler had more suppliers. They therefore didn't

FIGURE 5.4
Russel Lee, "Wrapping Sliced Bread, Bakery, San Angelo, Texas, November, 1939."
Courtesy of Prints & Photographs Division, Library of Congress.

own as much equipment, much less hardwood forests and Brazilian rubber plantations. Since Ford's investments in extraction of raw materials and in machinery couldn't be reduced, to stay competitive Ford had to wring more work out of every man and woman on the line. To management a speed-up seemed a logical necessity in order to save money on labor and thereby keep the cost of cars from increasing. Yet, as workers immediately realized, the speed-up was physically hard, and it meant fewer people had work.

Mass-production jobs had become harder and less regular. The annual model change alone ensured that workers were always laid off for at least a month in the summers, and usually longer. Slackening of demand or a shortage of parts would trigger unemployment (usually for a shorter period). The Department of Labor found as early as the mid 1920s that work in the automobile industry was "seasonal." The "year" was only ten months in the best of times, and it shrank further during the Great Depression.[38] Auto workers had no job security, and increasingly faced the pressure of the speed-up.[39] Sherwood Anderson described a Ford assembly plant in New

Orleans as a "place where no one stops to play" and "no one fools around or throws things, as they used to do in the old factories." That was why the assembly line "put the old-fashioned factories, one by one, out of business." Anderson sensed "calculation" in the atmosphere of the plant: "You feel it when you go in. You feel rigid lines. You feel movement. You feel a strange tension in the air. There is a quiet terrible intensity." And always "The belt moves. It keeps moving." The men and even the boss feel that "the belt is God."[40]

Edmund Wilson recorded the musings of an Englishman who worked for Ford: "Ye get the wages, but ye sell your soul at Ford's—ye're worked like a slave all day, and when ye get out ye're too tired to do anything."[41] In *The Big Money*, John Dos Passos focused on the sudden profitability of mass production during the 1920s, when "the big money was in economical quantity production, quick turnover, cheap interchangeable easily-replaced standardized parts."[42] Dos Passos devoted a section to the rise of the Ford Motor Company, but focused more on exploitation of workers than on the assembly line. His language mimicked the repetition of the job: "At Ford's production was improving all the time; less waste, more spotters, strawbosses, stool-pigeons (fifteen minutes for lunch, three minutes to go to the toilet) the Taylorized speedup everywhere, reachunder, adjustwasher, screwdown bolt, reachunderadjustscrewdownreachunderadjust, until every ounce of life was sucked off into production and at night the workmen went home gray, shaking husks."[43]

The assembly line was numbing. A character in Jack Conroy's novel *The Disinherited* comes to a realization after years of work: "I never really escaped by quitting and changing jobs. All the factories had the same conveyors, the same scientific methods for extracting the last ounce of energy. The same neon tubes pulsing with blue fire and the same automatons toiling frantically beneath the ghastly rays that etched dark shadows under their eyes and blackened their lips to resemble those of a cadaver."[44] Behind the blank looks of these automatons the minds were still active, if disengaged. "When I come in the gate in the morning," one worker who knew something about human psychology declared, "I throw off my personality and assume a personality which expresses the institution of which I am a part." He kept "just enough consciousness to operate my body as a machine." In this state he seldom made mistakes but hardly paid attention either. "My subconscious," he concluded, "is more capable of this monotony than my personality." Wives reported that many workers came home with "the shakes" and were "too tired to do anything but eat and go to bed."[45] Such men were desensitizing themselves in order to get through a meaningless job. They coped with the situation in a variety of ways, including using a great deal of profanity and occasionally howling: "The work will not absorb the mind of a normal man, so they must think. . . . Suddenly, a man breaks forth with a mighty howl. Others follow. We set up a howling all over the shop. It is a relief, this howling."[46]

In an article in the *Atlantic Monthly*, Gene Richards complained of factory noise: "The noise is deafening: a roar of machines and the groaning and moaning of hoists; the constant pssfft-pssfft of the air hoses. One must shout to be heard." Even so, after some time in the factory, the din became "part of what is natural and goes unnoticed."[47] As early as 1920 the Department of Labor was convinced that noise was counter-productive: "Few employers of labor appear to realize that there is no greater enemy of efficiency in industry than mere noise. The noise of machinery is accepted as being almost commonplace. The din and bustle of a warehouse is regarded as part of the daily routine. That this clatter, this din, are eating away profits is not recognized. . . ."[48] Because the assembly line packed workers and machines more closely together than the traditional shop, the noise also was more concentrated. The continuous hum of electric motors, the high-pitched grinders, and the whirring of drills and lathes were punctuated by the periodic crash of metal presses, the pneumatic hiss of compressed air, the clank of metal against metal, and a hundred other sounds, ranging in pitch from the bass of heavy objects such as engines and dashboards falling into place through the whine of drills and the higher tones of metal rasping on metal to the shrill screeching of distant whistles. Also in the din were occasional shouts of supervisors trying to be heard. New workers often couldn't hear their bosses' instructions.[49]

One novel described this noise and rhythm from the point of view of an auto worker regaining a job: "It was good to get back in the noise and the racket; it was like getting back to city streets after being in the country a long time." The distinctive soundscape "made you feel like you were a part of the factory. On the line there was the rat-a-tat-tat of pneumatic hammers, the sharp pft-pft-pft and snarl of air hoses, the whine of electric drills and the hum of power wrenches and screw drivers. But above it all rose the beat and peculiar vibrating hum of the high-speed automatics. The vibrations from these filled the whole place and got into your blood and nerves. It made you breath faster, work faster; if you wanted to go slow you couldn't, and if your work didn't keep you busy you jiggled around on one foot, or made some extra motions with your hands or your arms just to keep in time to the noise."[50] If the men often complained about being driven on the assembly line, being part of this intense activity was also satisfying. A novel attacking work conditions in Detroit contained this admission: "Just to be there—to be making your share of the noise—it made you feel good. It made you feel as though you were a part of something pretty darn big and important."[51]

Joel Dinnerstein has argued that African-American music adopted and transformed these factory sounds and rhythms. He asks "How can a human being reclaim his or her human motor from workplace demands, and how can a person integrate the newly revved up, machine-driven human motor into the entire human organism?"[52] The answer lay in mastering mechanical repetition through the imposition of human rhythm, both incorporating and countering the logic of mass production. Tap dancing and swing music, he argues, were aesthetic responses to the increasingly mechanized tempo and soundscape of industry. As the bandleader Paul Whiteman put it, "the rhythm of machinery became the rhythm of American civilization, a clanging, banging, terrific rhythm, full of energy."[53] The rhythms of assembly lines were translated not only into precision swimming and chorus lines, but also into swing music that moved at 200 beats per minute, making it faster than any previous American popular dance music. A tap dancer was "a vision of the industrial body retooled for a rootless, mobile future." The tap dancer "took the speeded-up machine-driven tempo of life and the metallic crunch of cities and factories and spun it all into a dazzling pyrotechnical display of speed, precision, rhythmic noise, continuity, grace, and power."[54] Two veteran dancers declared that they wanted to "fight back against the roar of jets, the boom of factories, the whirr of air conditioners, the slamming of doors, the battering of jackhammers."[55] Tap dancing returned control to the individual, but at a demanding tempo. The stylish rhythms of swing and tap were ingenious vernacular responses to the pounding repetitions of the machine age.

Yet these responses did not change the actual work on the assembly line. They offered therapy through improvisation and submergence in shared social experience, but the underlying demands of work didn't abate. Nor could musical innovations alone overcome racial barriers between white and black workers. In Detroit, African-Americans were initially not interested in joining unions. Henry Ford had made it his policy not to discriminate in hiring, and in the 1910s and the 1920s, a time of considerable "negro-phobia," he hired many African-Americans, supported the work of George Washington Carver, gave generously to the Tuskegee Institute in Atlanta, and was a philanthropist to the local black community. At the Highland Park plant alone, which was "whiter" than many other Ford plants, there were 1,171 African-Americans in 1930, half of them women.[56] Henry Ford remained personally popular with his African-American employees well into the 1930s. They took little interest in unionized labor, especially as it was still organized along craft lines and African-Americans were concentrated in less skilled positions.[57] This began to change in the late 1930s as the United Auto Workers grew stronger and as employment increased after the outbreak of war in Europe in 1939. Before then, however, unions often ignored blacks in mass-production industries. Both the UAW and the CIO focused on organizing white labor, arguing that racial problems would have to be tackled later.

Novels of the period suggest how difficult things were. In the ironically titled *Nobody Starves* (1932), Catharine Brody described the anonymity of automobile workers in the highly mechanized world of Detroit.[58] Her book was less about work than about how unemployment first impoverished and then destroyed families. In *Conveyor* (1935), James Steele wrote angrily of the effects of the speed-up on assembly-line workers and of the plight of men and women thrown out of work during the Depression. Even before 1929, some families lost their homes because of the irregularity of automo-bile work. In many jobs women were preferred because they were paid less than men for the same job. They too were pushed at the fastest pace possible. "Their bare arms flashed in and out of the presses like piston rods. Their faces were tense and nervous; their eyes fixed on the dies. The women on the slower presses were strained and panicky. All of them, behind on production, were driving their bodies in an effort to catch up."[59]

The 1938 novel *F.O.B. Detroit* begins with men outside an automobile plant looking for work, then focuses on the harsh demands of the assembly-line factory and on the irregular employment and poverty of 1930s Detroit. In the opening scene, two unemployed men manage to get inside a factory by slipping through the gate when most of the other unemployed men waiting there fall into an ugly interracial fight. On a winter night, lying on a bed in a rented room, its narrator realizes that "the only thing that stands between you and the cold and an empty belly is your little, thin hold on a job that you've got no control over and that's liable to be somebody else's any morning when you come to the factory; look for your card in the rack and find it's not there."[60]

Charlie Chaplin's 1936 feature film *Modern Times*—made after Chaplin visited the Ford's River Rouge plant—was a forceful satiric critique of the assembly line. Though it is difficult to tell what is being manufactured,[61] the Little Tramp's job is repetitive in the extreme. He must use two large wrenches to tighten two bolts on the items that pass by on an endless conveyor. The foreman regulates the speed of the line, periodically running it faster, until at top speed the workers become frantic in their efforts to keep up. At one point, the Little Tramp becomes so fixated on turning bolts that he leaps onto the conveyor belt and rides the assembly line down into a system of gears. The entire line must be halted so that he can be extracted. At the lunch break, the factory management selects him as the guinea pig to test a new machine designed to feed workers so that they need not stop working to eat lunch. During its trial run, the new machine, like the assembly line itself, begins to speed up. It stuffs the Tramp with food faster than he can swallow it, and rather than daintily wiping his face after each serving, it repeatedly smacks him. It also forces metal parts into his mouth, so that he is literally eating the machine. That afternoon, when the line halts during a break, the Little Tramp can't stop the convulsive nervous movements of his arms and hands. He starts to jerk uncontrollably and begins a wild dance, racing around the factory, wrenches in hand, until just outside its doors he confronts a large-breasted woman. When arrested, he is brandishing a wrench over each of her breasts.

Like the cinema, museums sought to acquire art that depicted modern factories and workers. The Detroit Institute of Art commissioned Diego Rivera to adorn its most prominent interior walls with murals that powerfully depicted mass production. Curiously, although Rivera was a communist who admired Trotsky, his patron was Edsel Ford, Henry's only son. In 1932 Rivera spent several months studying Detroit's history and visiting factories, gradually working up sketches and then a detailed plan for the murals. Divided into 27 panels, they presented modern industry as the culmination of a long evolutionary process that began in pre-history. In Rivera's own words, his art was "making plastic the beautiful, continually ascending rhythm moving from the extraction of raw material, product of nature, to the final elaboration of the finished article. The product and expression of human intelligence, will and action." Rivera intended to interpret this rhythm and depict "its social implications for the life of the producers."[62] The murals covered all the walls in a courtyard. They weren't in the style of Socialist Realism; rather, they synthesized pre-Columbian art with industrial imagery. They depicted not the immediate present of mass unemployment, but rather the "golden age, before the 1929 stock crash, when industrial productivity, employment and wages were at their height and Detroit was a boomtown."[63] As the single panel reproduced here as figure 5.5 suggests, Rivera traced automobile manufacture from the raw materials to the blast furnaces (in the background) to the movement of engines and the assembly line. He made the workers prominent, whereas Charles Sheeler's depictions of automobile factories were nearly devoid of human presence. But Rivera erased much of the workers' individuality, so they appear as a unified class moving in common work rhythms. In another panel, tourists appear as somewhat cartoonish figures who look out at the museum visitors. They are smaller than the workers and more diverse in dress and in facial expressions. The workers are too engaged in their tasks to notice them.

Initially, many patrons of the Detroit Institute of Art disliked Rivera's work. The *Detroit Free Press* complained that a foreign artist couldn't capture "the spirit of an American city" and argued that "true art" had to "be indigenous to the soil from which it springs."[64] The *Detroit News* angrily suggested that the museum "whitewash the entire work completely and return the Court to its original beauty." Conservatives thought the murals "communistic." However, many factory workers appreciated them. Rivera's Detroit murals are now popular with the public and praised by art historians. The curator Linda Downs argues that Rivera "presented a vision of industrial order based on the sacrifice of the working class, just as the ancient Aztec order was maintained by human sacrifice."[65]

The *Daily Worker*, a communist newspaper, criticized the Ford Motor Company for lunch breaks so short that men weren't able to digest their food, claimed there were many industrial accidents in Ford's factories, and asserted that the mood in those factories was bleak because of continuous espionage against the workers and daily searches of their lunchboxes and their pockets. It concluded: "To the tens of thousands of production slaves out of whose

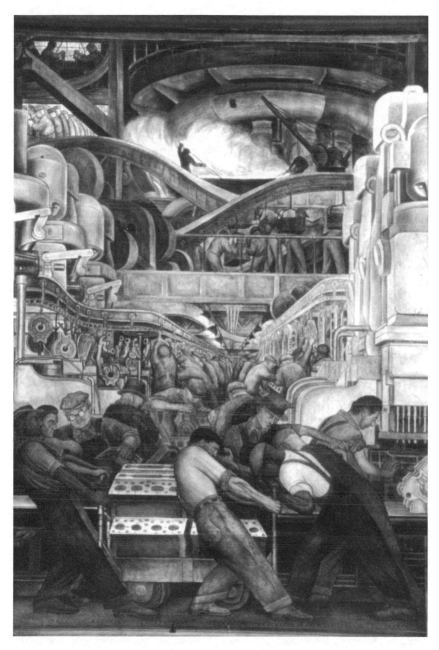

FIGURE 5.5
Diego Rivera, panel from mural at the Detroit Institute of the Arts, 1932–1933.
Courtesy of Walter Reuther Library, Wayne State University.

very hides are tanned the hundreds of millions of Ford profits, [Henry Ford] is looked upon as a mean, heartless miser and a hypocrite par excellence."[66] A 1932 biography of Ford summarized the common view of "the Ford factory, the workmen with their dull eyes, their rapid dull hands, obeying their mechanical drill masters as slavishly as if they were valve-stems yielding to the superior force of the cam-shaft."[67] The assembly line had become the agent of oppression and over-production, guaranteeing not prosperity but unstable employment. By 1932 one-fourth of all Americans were out of work, but unemployment was even worse in the automotive industry. Ford had laid off 91,000 workers, keeping just 37,000. Parts suppliers and tire manufacturers had followed suit. In Detroit, one journalist wrote, men were "sitting in the park all day long and all night long," and hundreds of thousands had no jobs.[68] "From the early 1930s through the early 1940s," the historian Steve Meyer writes, "American automobile workers felt angry, degraded, and emasculated . . . [until] the swift rise and the gradual consolidation of the United Automobile Workers Union reversed the social and economic decline of automobile workers' lives, permitted a venting of deep-seated anger and hostility, and sanctioned a reassertion of dignified masculine aggressiveness."[69]

In 1932, Detroit's auto workers were desperate. Thousands had used up their savings, cashed in their life insurance, and lost their homes. More than 3,000 joined a march to the gates of the River Rouge plant, where their protests met armed resistance. The marchers moved freely through Detroit, but once they reached the city limits of Dearborn police demanded that they turn back. When they refused, the police fired tear gas; the workers responded by pelting them with rocks. As the police retreated, the workers marched forward until they reached the Ford factory. There the police and private security forces opened fire, killing four and wounding many more. This "Dearborn Massacre" angered workers in all parts of the United States. In Detroit more than 20,000 people turned out for a defiant funeral. In these years the work discipline imposed by the movement of the line itself was supplemented at Ford by a strong security presence. One labor organizer believed that "at least 15 out of every 100 employees" were either foremen, security personnel, or spies. The undercover men were instructed to use violent methods to quell disturbances. One Ford worker testified to the National Labor Relations Board that he had been told to swing a lead pipe freely and to hit anyone he had to hit in order to quell disturbances that might erupt on the shop floor.[70] Ford also made an alliance with the American Legion for support in case of labor troubles.[71]

In the nation as a whole, work remained irregular. New Deal programs siphoned off some of the unemployed to the Works Progress Administration and the Civilian Conservation Corps, but government programs weren't long-term solutions. New industries were needed to absorb the displaced millions whose work had been mechanized out of existence. In 1937 *Life* called the automotive manufacturers "good employers" who "have never had a serious labor strike" but who might become "victims" of one. They hadn't quite "realized what a perfect target they would make." Each auto company was "a giant assembly line, fed by bodies, tires, windows, upholstery and all sorts of parts." It would not be necessary for all the workers to strike, *Life* explained, because a "small minority of workers, by shutting off the supply of a few parts, could shut down the entire assembly line."[72] *Life* said nothing about the Dearborn Massacre or about other protests; it also overlooked the fact that jobs had become almost as interchangeable as the parts themselves and the fact that supervisors could quickly train replacements for strikers.

The CIO therefore developed a new strategy: the sit-down strike. Instead of walking out, workers barricaded themselves inside the factory, preventing production from continuing. So many of the skills needed to make automobiles had been transferred from men to machines that a walkout was no longer an effective tactic. The factory itself had to be taken hostage before workers' demands would be heard. Management didn't dare to use force to evict sit-down strikers, because the machinery might be damaged in any confrontation. It cost a great deal, and, unlike the men, required a long time to repair or replace.

Before developing the weapon of the sit-down strike, the union movement struggled with the Detroit automobile companies for a generation. Between 1913 and 1929 the generally high wages paid in the industry weakened the union's appeal, as did the "Red Scare" of 1919–1920. The underlying problem was that auto workers weren't as highly skilled as the plumbers, electricians, metal workers, or carpenters that the American Federation of Labor (AFL) customarily organized. The AFL successfully controlled such skilled crafts, and if its members went on strike employers couldn't easily find replacements. In contrast, strikers against the automobile industry repeatedly saw others being hired and quickly trained to replace them. A different union strategy was needed. When the AFL refused to change its craft approach to organizing, the Congress of Industrial Organization (CIO) broke away and organized by factory, not by skills. Rather than walk out, they stayed in, paralyzing all possibility of production. The first sitdown took place in South Bend, Indiana, where in November 1936 workers occupied the Bendix Corporation and forced it to recognize the union as their bargaining representative. After that success, the tactic spread rapidly. A popular union song contained these lines:

When the speed-up comes, just twiddle your thumbs.
Sit down! Sit down!
When the boss sees that, he'll want a little chat,
Sit down! Sit down![73]

The most famous of the sit-down strikes targeted General Motors' plants in Flint, Michigan. (See figure 5.6.) It lasted 44 days, starting on December 24, 1936 and lasting until early February. The corporation first responded by getting a court injunction from a judge whose GM stock was worth $219,000. It also tried to intimidate the strikers and especially the organizers.[74] These actions only fanned the flames of resistance, and the sit-down spread to other GM factories. By January 11, 1937 there were 113,000 GM workers on strike, and the corporation found that neither the governor of Michigan nor President Roosevelt was willing to intervene on its behalf. GM tried a frontal attack using police and strikebreakers, but workers turned firehoses on them and drove them back. GM turned off the heat in the factories and tried to prevent delivery of food and other supplies, but the strike only spread further. By the end of January 1938 there were 140,000 workers on strike, and GM was at a standstill.[75] As this solidarity over an extended period suggests, the sit-down strikers were disciplined and highly organized. They didn't merely occupy the factories; they organized a temporary local government, including a court to deal with infractions of rules. The executive committee in each factory gave every striker particular responsibilities. Some were to patrol the factory's perimeter, some to guard against sabotage by individual workers, some to prepare food, and some to tend to sanitation, recreation, and even postal services. Men who had scarcely known any of their fellow workers other than those next to them on the line discovered a sense of community like that among soldiers holding a fort under siege.

Songs were an important part of this new camaraderie. Some of the singing was purely recreational, but much of it referred directly to the strike. Two workers at the Chevrolet No. 4 plant in Flint, Michigan composed this protest song early in the sit-down strike:

Oh, Mister Sloan! Oh, Mister Sloan!
We have known for a long time you would atone
For the wrongs that you have done,
We all know, yes, everyone.
Absolutely, Mister Travis!
Positively, Mister Sloan![76]

These lyrics targeted Alfred P. Sloan, president of General Motors, and helped to sustain the wave of strikes in which the union won the right to represent the workers. "Mister Travis" was Bob Travis, the CIO organizer for Flint. By calling him "Mr." the workers asserted his equality with Sloan.

The striking workers had a great deal of support. Local merchants and some farmers sent over food, and some of the National Guard troops stationed nearby wore union buttons. The National Guard was not called on to force the men out of the factories for fear of the property damage that might result. Furthermore, many wondered if they would be willing to attack the strike, which had widespread national support.[77] Indeed, by the time the confrontation was nearing its end, the National Guard was actively protecting the strikers against a planned attack on the Flint plant by 330 private police.[78] President Roosevelt pointedly refused to condemn the sit-down strike, and "behind the scenes he made it clear that, in principle, he sided with labor."[79] The workers also had a great deal of support in academia. (Shortly after the strike, the Yale University Press published a book that criticized the automobile industry sharply: "[M]otorcar manufacturers still lack, toward their workers, even that rudimentary sense of responsibility which prompts any dirt farmer to pasture a faithful horse." The Detroit car companies "remain indifferent to how fast the men wear out as long as there are others to replace them."[80])

The striking workers had a cheer:

Knuts to Knudsen,
Slush to Sloan,
Boos for Boysen,
The Union's our Own!

Knudsen was the fireman,
Sloan rang the bell,
Parker started the speed-up,
And GM went to hell![81]

William Knudsen had thrived at anti-union companies—first at Ford and then at General Motors, where he worked his way up to become Alfred P. Sloan's right-hand man. Nevertheless, the strike forced him to sign a contract that recognized the right of the United Automobile Workers to organize the workers and to serve as their bargaining agent. GM's lost production during the sit-down amounted to 280,000 automobiles, and its market share for that quarter fell from 43 percent to 34 percent. However, Chrysler and Ford too were soon subjected to successful UAW strikes. Chrysler was struck shortly after the GM contract was signed, and it too capitulated.

Ford, the last bastion of anti-unionism, resisted violently. On May 26, 1937, four UAW men, including Walter Reuther, went to an overpass near Gate 4 at River Rouge to hand out leaflets urging workers to support the union. Men from Ford's so-called Service Department (a security force) beat them severely in an incident that became a national news story and subsequently came to be called "The Battle of the Overpass." The United Auto Workers continued to organize and to press for recognition for more than two years. For example, in January 1938 the UAW erected large billboards close to the River Rouge factory that read "STOP speed up, service spies, discrimination. GAIN real seniority, labor rights, collective bargaining."[82] The UAW waited until a new European war had begun, when business was picking up, before forcing Ford to the bargaining table. They won exclusive right to represent the workers, after which they held union elections inside the Ford factories.

After a decade of the speed-up, strikes, and mass unemployment American manufacturers had a bad public image. As unions organized workers and reduced the corporations' power on the shop floor, the auto companies turned to public-relations campaigns and world's fair exhibits to counter the barrage of bad publicity. They proclaimed that the Depression was temporary and that mass production would bring a better tomorrow.

General Motors outfitted 28 specially designed vehicles to take its Chicago "Century of Progress" exhibits, which emphasized corporate science as the key to future growth, on the road. This "Parade of Progress," also touted as a "Circus of Science," toured the United States for several years,

FIGURE 5.6
A sit-down strike. Photograph taken by Sheldon Dick at Flint, Michigan, January 1937. Courtesy of Franklin D. Roosevelt Library.

starting in 1936. It primarily visited cities of less than 70,000 people, such as Greensboro, North Carolina, or Eureka, California. In such communities it became the center of attention during the two or three days it was there, hammering home the message of greater abundance through corporate science and the promise of continual improvements in the standard of living.[83]

In 1938, having decided that it should find common ground with its restive workers, General Motors began to publish a magazine titled *GM Folks*. As Ronald Marchand writes, it "unabashedly mimicked *Life*," notably with a front cover that featured a full-page black-and-white photo in which three workers walk toward the camera, smiling and waving.[84] Similar in-house magazines had appeared near the end of World War I, and others had been published during the 1920s, but many of them ceased publication in the early 1930s. General Electric's *Works News* had pioneered this kind of in-house publication, which insistently presented ordinary workers as the embodiment of the corporation. In the late 1930s, corporations copied the visual styles of *Life* and *Look* to sell workers the idea that the corporation

FIGURE 5.7
Ford workers taking part in a union election at the River Rouge plant, April 1942.
Photograph by Arthur S. Siegel, Farm Security Administration/Office of War In-
formation. Courtesy of Prints & Photographs Division, Library of Congress.

was a family, with many shared life experiences. Such publications seldom
depicted assembly-line work. When they showed labor at all, they showed
skilled men working at their own pace.[85]

World's fairs provided an opportunity to show consumers putative homes
and cities of the future. The New York fair of 1939 presented an idealized
world of 1960, with streamlined cars cruising through skyscraper cities on
limited-access highways. In this corporate utopia, the machine had largely
eliminated hard physical labor, and citizens enjoyed the benefits of mass
production. Corporations had brought models of their factories to expositions between 1901 and 1934, but assembly lines were scarcely in evidence
at the 1939 fair. Instead, Westinghouse, General Electric, DuPont, and the
other large corporate exhibitors showed off their research laboratories and
the products of the future.[86]

At New York's "World of Tomorrow," GM's "Futurama" was the most
successful exhibit. People patiently waited for hours to see its vision of 1960,

shown in a simulated airplane flight over an immense miniaturized land-scape. In this future world, everyone had a job and an automobile. Immense freeways were filled with futuristic cars.[87] While Futurama displayed how consumers benefited from mass production, Ford literally put the consumer in the driver's seat on an aerial "road of tomorrow" that pierced the exhibit building and circled its walls, giving visitors a half-mile ride in a new car. The elevated road provided a fine view of the fairgrounds and suggested that "skyways" could relieve the congestion on the surface roads below, making traffic safer for pedestrians and drivers alike.[88]

Ford also idealized production. Its "cyclorama" exhibit was a 30-foot-high, 152-ton rotating carousel, with figurines inspired by children's car-toons depicting the "cycle of production" from 27 raw materials to finished automobiles.[89] Walter Dorwin Teague's office arranged for it to be fea-tured in *Newsweek*, in *Popular Mechanics*, and in *Esquire* just before the fair opened.[90] On the bottom layer of this giant wedding cake, raw materials (oil, rubber, wood, wool, ores) were extracted; then as the eye moved ever higher, they were smelted into metal parts, transformed into tires, woven into fabrics, molded into plastic, then assembled into cars. Crowning the exhibit were three full-size automobiles. The 142 cyclorama figurines were also featured in a cartoon film, "Symphony in F," that explained how Ford automobiles were made from many raw materials, creating employment for farmers, miners, and suppliers. The film was shown both at the exposition and in a new theater added to Ford's visitor center in Detroit.[91] The Ford Rotunda, as it was called, drew 951,558 visitors in 1940 and more than 600,000 the following year.[92]

In the foyer of Ford's fair pavilion, an animated mural greeted visitors. (See figure 5.8.) Designed by Henry Billings, it showed how solar energy constantly pours down on the earth and how industry controls "the channels through which this energy flows" and "harnesses its power to do the work of man."[93] In the foreground, the towering three-dimensional structure had six gear wheels, each taller than a man, that rotated. Above them, an enor-mous cross-section of a V-8 engine was surrounded by a collage of manufac-turing images, including ingots of molten steel, assembly lines, and smoke-stacks. As Marchand noted, "shafts, gears, and connecting rods protruded into the third dimension" and provided "a highly abstract, kinetic vision" that was meant to represent the accuracy and precision of mass production.[94] Workers were absent from this industrial artwork, just as they were absent

FIGURE 5.8
Mobile mural, Ford exhibit, New York World's Fair, May 12, 1939. Photograph by Gottscho–Schleisner Inc. Courtesy of Prints & Photographs Division, Library of Congress.

from Charles Sheeler's images of River Rouge. A member of the exposition's theme committee saw the mural as "an altar piece for science."[95] It rose above the grime and sweat of the shop floor, turning production into a magnificent abstraction.

Could such corporate displays blunt attacks on mass production or assuage fears of technological unemployment? Historical events intervened before these questions could be answered. On September 1, 1939, as the New York fair was about to close for the year, Germany invaded Poland. Ideal visions of the world of tomorrow gave way to an embattled present. In World War II, mass production would become a matter of life and death.

The real battle today is between the American assembly line and the Communist
party line.

—Paul Hoffman, Administrator, Economic Cooperation Administration, 1948[1]

On November 4, 1938, President Franklin D. Roosevelt gave one of his
famous radio addresses to the nation. It was the eve of elections to the House
and the Senate, and Roosevelt made a plea for the return of New Deal
legislators. He spoke of the threats to democracy from communism and fascism, and warned that the country needed to complete his program so that
it could "provide efficiently for distributing national resources and serving
the welfare and happiness of all." Roosevelt drew an analogy between society and industrial production: "The modern interdependent industrial and
agricultural society which we live in is like a large factory. Each member of
the organization has his own job to perform on the assembly line, but if the
conveyor belt breaks or gets tangled up, no one in the factory, no matter
how hard he tries, can do his own particular job. Each of us—farmer, business man or worker—suffers when anything goes wrong with the conveyor
belt." The job of government was to "keep the machinery humming, so
each person could benefit." Elsewhere, "dictators . . . keep the conveyor
belt moving—but at a terrible price to the individual and to his civil liberty."
In contrast, "the New Deal has been trying to keep those belts moving
without paying such a price. It does not wish to run or manage any part of
our economic machine which private enterprise can run and keep running.

FIGURE 6. I
Emerson radio assembly line, 1945, shortly after V-E Day. From records of Office
of War Information. Courtesy of National Archives.

That should be left to individuals, to corporations, to any other form of private management, with profit for those who manage well." However, the role of government was hardly passive, for "when an abuse interferes with the ability of private enterprise to keep the national conveyor belt moving, government has a responsibility to eliminate that abuse."[2] With this analogy, Roosevelt articulated a central trope of World War II and the Cold War.

The Democrats lost seats in the 1938 election, but the image of the nation as an assembly line didn't disappear from Roosevelt's rhetoric. Even before the United States entered the war he repeatedly linked the productivity of the assembly line with the power of democracy and victory over the Axis powers. "Our defense production is a gigantic assembly line," he declared, and it was the duty of the Home Front to speed it up. A few months later, he said: "Our Nation will and must speak from every assembly line, from every coal mine—the all-inclusive whole of our vast industrial machine. Our factories and our shipyards are constantly expanding. Our output must be multiplied." In a Fireside Chat immediately after the attack on Pearl Harbor, he spoke of the need to "build our American assembly lines of production." In the midst of the war, he declaimed "More cooperation, more teamwork, and more production, all the way from the farms and mines through the assembly lines, will enable us to win the war more quickly."[3]

The assembly line shed its problematic Depression-era image as it became a necessity for supplying the troops and ensuring victory. New York's Radio City Rockettes expressed the patriotic synergy between manufacturing and national defense. On a stage dominated by facsimiles of battleships, dressed identically in Navy uniforms, they celebrated mass production on the home front. (See figure 6.2.) The horrors of the speed-up were transformed into patriotic overtime. Women were drawn into the workforce to replace the men drafted into the army. "Rosie the Riveter" was celebrated in a 1942 hit song: "All the day long, whether rain or shine / she's a part of the assembly line." Rosie wasn't merely making money; she was "making history / working for victory."[4] The following year, Rosie was the subject of a factory poster first seen only by Westinghouse workers (figure 6.3) but then extensively reworked by Norman Rockwell for a cover of the *Saturday Evening Post*. The fame of this image was far greater in historical memory than during the war itself. Subsequently, Americans have honored women's contributions to the war effort and in the process accorded higher status to assembly-line work.[5]

FIGURE 6.2
The Rockettes during World War II, dressed as sailors. Courtesy of Photographic
Department, Cleveland Public Library.

During World War II, the Ford Motor Company and mass-production
industries in general were reconceived as the guarantor that the United
States would never run short of trucks, ships, planes, weapons, or supplies.
In 1940 *Life* magazine devoted eleven pages to a photographic essay on
Ford's River Rouge factory. In addition to a detailed diagram of the whole
plant and pages of photographs of the foundry and various machines, the
story also including some human-interest material, such as a photo of men
lined up at a lunch wagon and one of a man operating a large floor cleaner.
There was not a critical word.[6] The same issue of *Life* carried a long story on
Hitler's rise to power, with more than 60 photographs documenting his life.

Shortly after the United States entered the war, *Time* declared: "Something is happening that Adolf Hitler does not yet understand—a new re-en-
actment of the old American miracle of wheels and machinery, but on a new
scale. This time it is a miracle of war production, and its miracle-worker
is the automobile industry." On *Time's* cover, rows of tanks and bombers

FIGURE 6.3
J. Howard Miller, poster for War Production Co-ordinating Committee (NARA Still Picture Branch). Courtesy of National Archives.

flanked a portrait of Henry Ford. "Out of enormous rooms," the caption declared, "armies will roll and fleets will fly."[7] American mass production was expected to overwhelm the Germans and the Japanese. *Time* declared: "Endlessly the lines will send tanks, jeeps, machine guns, cannon, air torpedoes, armored cars. Ford's River Rouge plant, where Ford steamships dump coal and iron ore and limestone to be magicked into steel and glass and machinery, has turned its two square miles of self-contained industrial empire to the tools of war."[8] General Motors, Chrysler, Packard, Studebaker, and Hudson were also lauded. The government spent $315.8 billion on contracts with private firms, and just thirty companies received almost half

of this money, particularly automobile and aircraft manufacturers.[9] General
Motors, for example, produced trucks, airplanes, cannons, tanks, projectiles,
ball bearings and a myriad other items. Such facts strongly suggested that
mass production was considered essential to victory.

Yet the reality of wartime production was not so simple. Though the
War Department proclaimed that Willow Run was already churning out
B 24 bombers in the summer of 1942, in reality the factory was still tooling
up, and it only produced parts for aircraft manufacturers.[10] Once the assembly lines were running, however, the United States produced huge numbers
of planes. In the first half of 1944 alone it made 35,000, more than it had
produced from the first Wright Brothers plane in 1903 through the end of
1943.[11] Jonathan Zeitlin compared aircraft manufacturing in Germany, Britain, and the United States during World War II and found that it "required
not only the capacity to manufacture complex products in vast numbers, but
also considerable flexibility." "As fighters, bombers, and other types of aircraft were tested against one another under real battlefield conditions," Zeitlin continued, "military authorities demanded continual modifications to
overcome design flaws and incorporate new tactical and technical ideas."[12]
Flexible production, rather than the rigid uniformity of the classic assembly
line, delivered the best weapons. The war imposed demands for constant
innovation. In addition, material shortages at times forced manufacturers to
improvise. The British adopted the practice of making piecemeal changes
during manufacturing, and their planes improved incrementally during the
war. According to Zeitlin, "only at moments of extreme military urgency,
as at the onset of rearmament in 1934, after the Munich crisis in 1938, and
during the Battle of Britain in 1940, was the RAF's so-called doctrine of
quality relaxed in order to secure larger quantities of existing types, while
current designs were temporarily frozen."[13] Otherwise, improvements continued apace, with dramatic improvements in performance. For example,
the maximum speed of the Supermarine Spitfire fighter increased from 356
to 460 miles per hour, and its altitude ceiling from 34,000 to 42,000 feet.
Pilots caught in a dogfight also enjoyed the ability to climb twice as fast in
the newest models, fully 5,000 feet per minute. Flexible production, rather
than churning out identical planes on an assembly line, brought measurable
benefits.

German aviation factories were less successful than those in Britain in
both volume of production and in use of assembly-line techniques, largely

FIGURE 6.4

B-24E "Liberator" bomber production line, Ford Willow Run plant, February, 1943. Courtesy of Franklin D. Roosevelt Library.

because for much of the war there was little check on military demands for constant modifications. On the other hand, German tank quality and production were superior to either British or American efforts.[14]

Some German concentration camps had factories in which prisoners made uniforms and other clothing. The textile factory at the Ravensbrück camp proved capable of a kind of dictatorial flexible production. The supervisors were experienced manufacturers who trained the female prisoners and were willing to beat them and drive them like slaves. The prisoners operated new, state-of-the-art sewing machines, each with a built-in electric motor that made possible highly efficient production without special skills or years of training. In short, prototypes of flexible production emerged on both sides in the war, and they weren't necessarily synonymous with industrial democracy.[15]

The US military's desire for continual design changes was met through several strategies. In some cases, a design was periodically frozen to allow a run of about 1,500 identical airplanes. Alternately, Boeing developed the practice of pre-assembling sections of airplanes. These were ready for rapid final assembly, but could still be modified if that proved necessary. Yet another technique was to mass-produce planes at Ford's Willow Run plant, which at its peak made a bomber every hour, and then modify them at another factory in Birmingham, Alabama. Overall, the United States produced three times as many planes as Britain, using assembly lines that a Harvard Business School report found to be more flexible than traditional mass production.[16]

American manufacturing methods improved during the war, but not always as expected. The Office of Production and Research Development (established in 1942) made only modest contributions to war production, with the exception of scaling up the manufacture of penicillin and alcohol.[17] Many other improvements emerged from the shop floor, as Richard Muther detailed in his book *Production-Line Technique*. Muther, a professor at MIT, spent several years working on and observing assembly lines in Detroit and elsewhere. His book suggested ways to rearrange work and emphasized the need to continually "balance" the time allotted to every task on the line. This "balancing" of the assembly line was necessary because each worker became more proficient and because new techniques and processes constantly altered the time needed for each task. Muther advocated installing new equipment to help balance the line, and he saw the advantage of having men work in teams to do related tasks.[18] He showed how a radio manufacturer increased productivity by the simple expedient of installing fixtures on its assembly line that held each radio chassis in place, so that a worker had both hands free at all times.[19] Sunbeam Electric sped up the crating of refrigerators by having men do the job while standing on moving conveyors.[20] Work could also be sped up if some tools were suspended on flexible lines, so that workers could guide them to the right position, do the job, and then "drop" them in midair, where they would hang until needed again. Likewise, "floor platforms, tiers, scaffolding, and the like may be introduced where it is inconvenient to raise or lower the work on the conveyor. Pits are fitted into the floor on automobile assembly lines so that underneath work may be done more easily."[21] Muther's book summarized hundreds of practical discoveries and contained many illustrations that showed how time and materials could be saved. For example, a large metal clip could be redesigned to be stamped rather than machined. When producing 100,000 of them, this change saved 17,000 pounds of steel, eliminated 8,000 hours using machine tools, and produced the clips 150 times faster.[22] At Lockheed Aircraft, re-design of one component reduced the number of parts from fifteen to four, eliminated six sub-assemblies, and replaced time-consuming riveting with spot welding.[23] The innovations Muther described weren't necessarily new, but he disseminated them widely, and they came into more extensive use under the pressure of wartime production.

Another result of the war effort was the full emergence of "statistical quality control," which had been developing slowly before the war. The old method, taken from armory practice, was to examine parts produced by inserting them into jigs, gauges, and fixtures identical to those used to make them. This was tedious and time consuming. W. Edwards Deming and others developed both Statistical Quality Control and methods to involve workers more directly in ensuring quality. After the war, these discoveries won more rapid acceptance in Japan than in the United States or Britain.

Although not all war production was as well adapted to the assembly line as many believed, both government and corporate advertisements empha-sized the connection. In 1944 a characteristic Ford advertisement focused on the birth of the assembly line at Ford's factories in 1913 and the intro-duction of the $5 day shortly afterward. Beneath a single large illustration that showed men assembling Model Ts, it declared that "the assembly line eased working conditions" and "helped to increase the life span of workers," while it "also brought price reductions on Ford cars." It concluded: "Today, in the creation of equipment vital to victory, Ford men continue their search for better ways of doing things."[24] The assembly line, excoriated in the late 1930s, had become the harbinger of health, prosperity, and victory. When the war in Europe ended, the major manufacturers scrambled to retool and produce consumer goods for Christmas.

Not only did mainstream magazines and corporate advertising applaud the assembly line; so did thoughtful social commentators such as Roger Burlingame and Christy Borth. In the first chapter of *Masters of Mass Produc-tion*, Borth declared that "America welcomed the idea of mass production" in the eighteenth century.[25] In his account, European artisans long had mo-nopolized technical knowledge and reaped profits by charging high prices for items produced in low volume. Americans had pioneered mass produc-tion in order to spread the benefits of new technologies more widely. Borth argued that not only had mass production been essential to winning World War II, but also that it would be the basis of postwar reconstruction. He ended his book with a quotation from the former Ford executive Charles Sorensen: "The world as a whole will benefit through further knowledge of American mass-production methods."[26] Similarly, Burlingame's popular books presented American history as a story of inventors and advances in manufacturing. He admitted that "the assembly lines may be stultifying." He conceded that if run too fast they could become an "instrument of cruelty."[27] Yet he also recognized that, assembly-line workers labored 20 hours less each week than workers had in the late nineteenth century. The new factories were clean, with fresh air, potable water, and good light. "Ford boasts that a man can visit his tire plant in a white suit and remain immaculate, and the claim is true."[28] On balance, Burlingame concluded, factory work was better than before and could be expected to keep improving. Industry was at an "intermediate stage," but progress for both workers and consumers was unmistakable.[29] Such views prevailed in the United States in the postwar years. Commentators acknowledged some defects in mass production but assumed relatively frictionless social progress.

Americans seldom used use the word "Fordism" during the first years of the Cold War. Most, like the industrial designer Walter Dorwin Teague, envisioned higher levels of prosperity for all. In a 1947 book titled *Land of Plenty*, Teague rejected the 1930s' consensus that the United States had become a "mature economy" and couldn't grow much more.[30] He pointed out that horsepower per worker had doubled in a single decade after 1936. The Second World War had stimulated productivity and invention, and had opened Teague's eyes to enormous future potential. He foresaw inexpensive, high-quality, prefabricated housing, faster transportation, cleaner factories, and a rapidly rising standard of living.

Would such prosperity be possible in Europe? In 1945 much of Europe lay in ruins, and the factories that had survived five years of bombings were worn out. The Soviet Union rebuilt its factories with an emphasis on producer goods, not consumer goods. It resisted mass consumption and sought to establish a "dictatorship over needs."[31] According to Stephen Kotkin, "Soviet socialism not only greatly expanded the mass production of machines by machines, but also propagated a vision of an automated, heavy industrial world that equated technology with progress, while insisting that the elimination of private property made its version that much more progressive. Unencumbered by private property interests, Soviet socialism institutionalized comprehensive social welfare."[32]

The British, in contrast, continued their conversion to the production of consumer goods, which the war had interrupted. They studied German manufacturing and, although they admired the quality of Germany's skilled labor, decided there was more to learn from the Americans. They had gained experience with American methods during the war, for example by manufacturing Jeeps from US-supplied parts. (See figure 6.5.) After the war, the British took "mass production and the 'three charmed 'S's' of simplification, standardization, and specialization as their model for the reconstruction of the domestic metalworking industries, a message reinforced by the postwar Anglo-American productivity missions organized in the context of the Marshall Plan."[33]

In most Western European countries, American-style productivity seemed the key to revival, and to winning the Cold War. A good example

FIGURE 6.5
Jeep assembly line, Tidworth, England, September 8, 1943. A jeep was produced every three minutes. Photograph from Signal Corps. Courtesy of National Archives.

was the conversion of Volkswagen from war production back to its original purpose: mass producing a durable and inexpensive people's car. Because no other automobile manufacturer wanted to buy it, the British forces of occupation presided over this transformation between 1945 and 1949, laying the groundwork for production of the "Beetle," 20 million of which would eventually be built over four decades.[34] Volkswagen eventually became much stronger than Britain's own car manufacturers, most of which disappeared in mergers or bankruptcy.

American automobile manufacturers also transformed themselves after the war, none more than Ford. After the death of the founder in 1947, his grandson Henry Ford II spent a year converting the company to a modern managerial style. Then, in February and March 1948, he traveled to Europe, with Graeme Howard (a former vice-president of General Motors now serving as an advisor to Ford), to take a look at Ford's international division. Ford and Howard found that "England, in many ways, has the most difficult problem. In our opinion her industrial fabric must be subjected to what can only be described as revolutionary changes." They believed the problems were more with leadership than with labor. "A job-shop nation must be . . . converted to mass production. A philosophy of competitive individual enterprise must be substituted for a cartel, socialistic philosophy."[35] The Dagenham plant was Ford's most important foreign operation, but the cars needed more modern styling, and the heavier vehicles were outdated. In France, Ford was a smaller player but sales were improving. Ford and Howard judged Peugeot to be Ford's most serious French competitor, and they contemplated an association with it, with savings for both companies to be achieved through sharing of some design costs, engineering, and common standards. They didn't contemplate a merger, however. Ford in France had a fine physical plant and seemed prepared for growth, especially after the US Congress passed the European Recovery Program. "France appears to us to have a better economic outlook than it has had in any of the years between the wars." In contrast, Ford and Howard found "unbelievable destruction" in Germany, yet recognized that its people had an "extraordinary capacity" for hard work as well as "technical genius and managerial ability." Volkswagen had modern machine tools and had such a good reputation that Ford considered "acquiring a controlling interest in the Volkswagen Werke." The Volkswagen car (now back in production) had "operating economy, low purchase cost" and "ample room for improvement."[36] Ford and Howard even foresaw the possibility that Volkswagens might be exported "all over the world" through Ford's network of dealers. (A Ford-Volkswagen merger never occurred, of course.)

Yet if Henry Ford II was prepared for expansion and possible mergers in France and Germany, he and Howard rejected a potential monopoly of truck production in Spain. They didn't visit Madrid, and dealt only with intermediaries. Among smaller nations, Ford operations in Belgium, in the Netherlands, and in Sweden were found to be in good hands, but Denmark made an unfavorable impression. Ford and Howard judged it a "rich little country, critically dependent on international trade" and suffering from too much economic planning. "There is an eeriness and an unreality about the country," they thought, with its "restricted imports, directed exports, hothouse industries, agricultural subsidies" and its lack of competition.[37] Yet Ford's Danish branch had accumulated a large surplus of cash during the years of occupation, and Denmark was judged to be a good market. Ford and Howard concluded that letting the British manage Ford's European operations wasn't effective, and that Ford Canada should no longer oversee operations in the tottering British Empire. Instead, a single international office was needed to direct world operations. Ford and Howard also feared that the USSR might overrun Western Europe. They concluded that "the Ford Motor Company can make a great contribution—not only actual but by example—in supporting the Marshall Plan and United States' economic policy."[38]

The Marshall Plan institutionalized the drive toward European mass production, and by the time it ended, in 1952, fully half of its $5.5 billion had been used to purchase industrial goods needed to rebuild Europe's capacity for production. In just five years Germany again became the world's second industrial power, and France and Britain bettered their pre-war production levels.[39] For example, the automaker Austin rebuilt its Birmingham factory and was producing new models for export by 1949. (See figure 6.6.) In Italy, American loans helped Fiat to rebuild its war-torn factories and to reach full production ahead of most of its European competitors.[40] Improvement of European production was also a goal of the Economic Cooperation Administration, founded in 1948. The ECA established links between government and business. Its chief administrator, Paul Hoffman, declared "The real battle today is between the American assembly line and the Communist party line."[41] The ECA was hardly alone in taking this view. At Fiat a strong communist movement among workers periodically disrupted production, and in response the US military offered lucrative procurement contracts that included an "anti-Communist clause" that led to "the firing, relocation, and political reeducation of many Fiat employees."[42]

The young Arthur Schlesinger Jr., who had been in the Office of War Information, served as a consultant to the Economic Cooperation Administration. Its strategy was woven into his 1949 book *The Vital Center: The Politics of Freedom*, which called for "exporting technology rather than commodities."[43] By 1951 the ECA had brought more than 3,000 technicians from Britain and Western Europe to the United States to visit factories, farms, and businesses there. Aside from the specific production techniques they might learn, the ECA believed it was "crucial that foreign managers be exposed to the bulging shelves of supermarkets and shops crammed with inexpensive, mass-produced goods"[44] so that they would understand the

FIGURE 6.6
Austin cars made for export in a Birmingham factory rebuilt with Marshall Plan aid, ca. 1949. Photograph from Economic Cooperation Administration. Courtesy of National Archives.

consumption side of the American model. In the ideology of the Marshall Plan, "productivity would eventually emerge as the key concept" in the raising of living standards. "This would transform the ancient battle between reactionary capitalists and revolutionary workers into a constructive, dynamic relationship" that united "enlightened producers and contented consumers."[45] As "domestic opinion shapers increasingly linked U.S. greatness and 'identity' with quantitatively defined prosperity,"[46] such themes became central to American ideology during the early phases of the Cold War. President Dwight D. Eisenhower put it this way in 1953: "We know that there is but one struggle for freedom—in the market place and in the university, on the battlefield and beside the assembly line."[47]

By 1955, Western Europe's productivity had increased between 15 and 20 percent from the immediate postwar level, and the growth accelerated in the 1960s.[48] By no means were the gains due simply to transfers of technology. As in the 1920s, many employers and workers preferred craft production in smaller batches to assembly lines. In Italy and Britain, some companies were more prepared to adopt aspects of Taylor's scientific management than they were to embrace the more sweeping changes that the Ford assembly line required.[49] Hybrid systems emerged that anticipated later flexible production. They amalgamated craft traditions, local customs, and efficiency initiatives. Production technologies were embedded in local contexts. European technicians who toured American factories didn't go home and imitate them slavishly. Few adopted all aspects of Ford-style mass production.[50] Peugeot, for example, debated whether to adopt Detroit practices for several years, but instead decided, in 1954, to make durable cars for "that part of the public which viewed the car as a basic utility rather than a status symbol."[51] In contrast, Renault "concentrated on a large production of relatively small and inexpensive cars." Yet it didn't copy all things American, either. Renault worked with the French government to create welfare programs and foster good labor relations.[52]

In *Image of America*, a book that was widely read on both sides of the Atlantic, Raymond-Léopold Bruckberger, a French Dominican priest, devoted an entire chapter to Ford's production system and its social implications. He underlined the linkage between the assembly line, low prices, and high wages, turning every worker into a customer. Ford was "far more of a revolutionary than Marx or Lenin." Why? Because "Ford exploded the whole idea of the supposedly immutable 'iron law' of wages on which

Ricardo believed capitalist economy was founded and which was to provide every proletarian revolution with a spring board."[53] Peter Drucker applauded these Cold War sentiments in his introduction to the American edition.

Bruckberger was hardly alone in his admiration for the assembly line. Thousands of Europeans crossed the Atlantic in the 1950s, many with tickets paid for by the Fulbright Program, the US Department of State, or other agencies, such as the Anglo-American Council on Productivity. Many visited assembly lines and studied American methods of mass production. They came both in small national delegations and in multi-national groups of specialists. Often they studied a single industry, such as shoe making, textiles, concrete, or paint. When touring factories they saw large-scale processing and assembly lines. "Danes came to investigate meat packing. Belgians, French, and Dutch came to study American hotel methods."[54] Norwegians examined American mining methods. Two British groups studied the clothing industry and foundries. Delegations from Japan were amazed at their easy access to US factories. They used the information gained to develop a new electronics industry and to improve organization and management.[55] Each team wrote a report on its findings when it returned home. A British report on the American steel industry sold more than 25,000 copies and went through four editions.[56]

Although the Department of State paid for many of these journeys, there were other sponsors. For example, the non-profit Danish-American Foundation offered scholarships and advice to young people who wanted to study in the United States. In 1951 it published a pamphlet for Danish students that proclaimed: "Today, technique, commerce, and science look to America as the educational institution from which the greatest knowledge flows."[57] The United States as a whole was seen as a training ground for bright, ambitious Europeans. The same sentiments underlay the awarding of thousands of Fulbright Scholarships, given out by national committees. Some US corporations, notably Westinghouse, set up their own training programs for foreign engineers. These were genuine exchanges, in which Americans also learned. The Europeans who came were among the most talented and experienced, and during tours through American factories they sometimes had useful suggestions for their hosts. Merck & Company learned from British visitors an ingenious method for corking bottles containing fluids for syringe injection, and the American Drop Forge Association compiled a list of thirty useful suggestions made by visitors.[58]

Some critics have argued that the Marshall Plan and the Fulbright exchange were elements of a larger Americanization of Europe. In its most assertive form, as in George Ritzer's book *The McDonaldization of Society*, this argument contends that after 1945 US culture rolled like a mighty wave over the rest of the world.[59] Victoria de Grazia developed a more nuanced version of this position in *Irresistible Empire: America's Advance Through Twentieth-Century Europe*.[60] The hegemonic argument emphasizes intention, pointing to the cultural programs sponsored by the US Department of State and the marketing campaigns of US corporations.

Exporting mass production and the culture of consumption was hardly new, but had begun well before World War I with sewing machines, Kodak cameras, phonographs, silent movies, and Buffalo Bill's Wild West Show (which toured Europe several times).[61] The large internal US market stimulated the development of mass culture, in contrast to the fragmented markets of Europe. To supply foreign buyers, American manufacturers could, without new development costs, churn out more phonograph records, cigarettes, shoes, or nylon stockings. After the scarcity of World War II, most of the world was eager for such consumer goods. Moreover, the British Empire had spread the English language around the globe, and millions of people were able to understand American advertisements. The collapse of the British imperial network during the 1950s left a commercial and political vacuum. Who could fill it better than the United States? The war had savaged other countries' industrial plants, but the American manufacturing infrastructure was intact. How much help from the Department of State did Ford or General Electric really need to sell mass-produced goods to hungry markets? In 1947, one-third of the world's exports came from the United States.[62]

Europe had fewer assembly-line factories than the United States, and not many of these focused on consumer goods. When Europeans took on American manufacturing innovations, they often received technical assistance. By "licensing American technology, capitalizing on American producers' knowledge of mass-production methods, and adopting American personnel-management practices," Europe began to close the gap with the United States.[63] By about 1970 the Europeans had caught up, in part because they already had human capital and scientific knowledge and in part because they dismantled barriers to trade that each nation had erected to protect its own industries. With the creation of the European Union, a single large market made mass production (and economies of scale) more attractive.

However, "as the early opportunities for catch-up and convergence were exhausted, the Continent had to find other ways of sustaining its growth. It had to switch from growth based on brute-force capital accumulation and the acquisition of known technologies to growth based on increases in efficiency and internally generated innovation."[64] This demanded a shift from copying to creating, from extensive growth to intensive self-generated growth. During the first catch-up phase, the US government was eager to help Europeans acquire mass-production technologies. Afterward, European growth sustained itself.

In the United States, renewed enthusiasm for the assembly line brought tourists back to factories, not only in the automobile industry but in a wide range of industries. In 1953 a new board game called "The Game of Assembly Line" went on sale. Two to four players could learn to "assemble cars like motor czars." The players operated competing factories (Ford, Plymouth, Chevrolet, Studebaker). An advertisement for the game declared that it "offers a challenge to each player to manage his own automobile plant where he collects auto parts, assembles them, part by part, and then rolls completed cars off his assembly line."[65] The game fostered a managerial view of production and scarcely presented workers as part of the process.

During the first two decades of the Cold War, the field of American Studies also emphasized mass production as it sought to discover what made the United States different from other nations. Attempts to define the "American character" often described a nation of tinkerers and inventors. This technological prowess found expression in the immensity of its railroad system, the scale of its bridges, and the productivity of its factories, which became symbols for the new nation.[66] American mechanical ingenuity was woven into a narrative of rapid national development. The United States seemed a practical nation that had improved European devices, among them the axe, the plow, the railroad, and the textile loom. Many perceived an "American system" of manufacturing using interchangeable parts, particularly in the production of weapons, sewing machines, and other metal goods where precision was paramount. American inventors created entire industries based on new devices such as Eli Whitney's cotton gin, Cyrus McCormick's reaper, Alexander Graham Bell's telephone, Thomas Edison's electrical lighting system, and Henry Ford's assembly line. By 1920 the United States had the largest industrial capacity in the world. It had more automobiles, bathrooms, telephones, and electric lights per capita than any other nation. In 1925, there was only one automobile for every 100 Germans but one for every six Americans. Drawing on such examples, Louis Hunter argued that "the western steamboat, like the American ax, the revolver, and barbed wire, was a typical mechanical expression of a fluid and expanding frontier society which was ingenious in attaining ends but careless in the choice and use of means."[67]

Similar arguments could be found in John Kouwenhoven's *Made in America*, a widely read book of the early American Studies movement. Kouwenhoven argued that interchangeable parts and the assembly line were quintessentially American.[68] He contrasted American tools, locomotives, buildings, and machine design with their English counterparts. In each case, he found, American flexibility, disdain for tradition, improvisation, and a focus on ease of use contrasted with British rigidity, adherence to the past, formality, and impracticality. Kouwenhoven saw interchangeable parts as typically American and noted how this idea had spread from factories to fast-food restaurants and to higher education, with its easily transferable credits. Although Kouwenhoven wrote from a white, male, middle-class perspective and scarcely mentioned African-Americans or women, these weaknesses were removed and his approach further developed in John Blair's *Modular America* (1988).[69] Such definitions of American character suggested that what other nations needed from the United States were the very factory tours and short courses on mass production that the United States Information Agency had arranged for foreign businessmen and engineers.

The USIA wanted to reach not just engineers and politicians, but also the wider overseas public. It did so through films, conferences, and traveling exhibitions, notably one (developed with assistance from the Advertising Council) called "People's Capitalism—Man's Newest Way of Life." The head of the Advertising Council explained that the United States needed this campaign because it had "a serious propaganda handicap until we can hold up for the world a counteracting inspirational concept. We cannot be merely against communism; we suffer from the lack of a positive crusade."[70] The exhibition, test-marketed at Washington's Union Station, suggested that American society had already achieved what communism only promised. The first version of the exhibit traced the evolution from a "worker's home" in 1776 to a prefabricated steel house stuffed with appliances. It claimed that technological progress benefited rich and poor alike. A blacksmith making nails by hand was contrasted with a nail-making machine that produced

16,000 nails an hour, and visitors were given a small bag of nails as a souvenir. They were told that American workers produced five times as much per day as their ancestors had 100 years earlier and that their wages and quality of life had improved accordingly. The people as a whole had become capitalists. The 150 million Americans had 70 million savings accounts, and their pensions were invested in the stock market. The United States, the exhibit proclaimed, had "a new social system" in which differences between "very rich and the very poor have steadily diminished." "People's Capitalism" was not merely a slogan but a "trend . . . continuing to the point where America is becoming classless. Already worker and boss have much the same comforts and recreations."[71] Or as one exhibit placard put it, "people's capitalism—capitalism 'of the people, by the people, for the people.'"[72] Thousands of Americans visited the exhibit, including President Eisenhower, who asked that religious pluralism and toleration be incorporated into its message.[73] Others criticized the 1776 worker's home, which the USIA replaced with a pioneer's log cabin from the time of Abraham Lincoln. Some felt that the modern house looked "too slick," and in response the USIA "put in some used furniture and kitchen equipment to present a more 'lived-in' look."[74]

In the spring of 1956 the USIA sent the "People's Capitalism" exhibit to Latin America and to Ceylon, and the federal government decided to "conduct a domestic version of the People's Capitalism campaign." The Advertising Council was again asked for assistance, and academic respectability was sought through a collaboration with Yale University. It held an academic "round table" on the themes of the campaign. David Potter, a professor of history at Yale, digested these discussions into a pamphlet that was then sent free of charge to newspaper editors, to university teachers, and to businessmen. In 1954 Potter had published an influential book in American Studies, *People of Plenty: Economic Abundance and the American Character*. In it Potter didn't conclude that social classes had disappeared in the US, but he did argue that the class structure was more fluid there than in Europe and that "the factor of abundance . . . has constantly operated to equalize the overt differences between the various classes and to eliminate the physical differences between them."[75] Similar ideas circulated widely. General Electric declared, in a nationally distributed advertisement, "The 376,000 owners with savings invested in General Electric are typical of America, where nearly every citizen is a capitalist."[76] In fact only 5 percent of Americans owned stocks in 1956, and the percentage had fallen slightly since the 1930s.[77] Nevertheless, the Marshall Plan, the new Fulbright Program, the USIA's public-relations campaigns, and leading American Studies scholars such as Kouwenhoven and Potter all agreed that Americans were a technological people with a fluid class structure and a distinctive national character. All saw American economic abundance as a cause and a guarantor of this character. It seemed logical that exporting American mass production would weaken foreign class systems and build democracy.

Perhaps in response to these themes, the Swiss-born photographer Robert Frank chose to make Detroit the first stop in his exploration of the United States. Funded by a Guggenheim fellowship, Frank took 20,000 images all over the United States, then winnowed them down to 83 for his landmark book *The Americans*.[78] Spending two days at Ford's River Rouge factory, he was as mesmerized as Charles Sheeler had been three decades earlier. Indeed, Frank knew and admired Sheeler's images. "Ford is an absolutely fantastic place," Frank wrote in a letter to his wife. "This one is God's factory and if there is such a thing—I am sure that the devil gave him a helping hand to build what is called Ford's River Rouge Plant."[79] Whereas human beings were nearly entirely absent from Sheeler's almost static landscapes, Frank's factory images usually depict human beings in action. In some of the photos, blurring suggests the hectic pace of the work and draws attention to Frank as a moving presence behind the camera. With a documentary impulse much like that of his friend Walker Evans, Frank also photographed auto workers in Detroit's streets, parks, and other public spaces. Frank seemed almost to intend a visual investigation of what People's Capitalism looked like.

Frank was photographing Detroit at the high tide of its prosperity. From World War II until about 1980, American auto workers were the best-paid semi-skilled workers in the world. The United Auto Workers negotiated successfully for wage and benefit increases. Between 1948 and 1980, hourly wages rose from $1.50 to $10.77 and benefits grew to include not only pensions but also full health insurance for everyone in the family.[80] Wage increases always kept up with inflation, because the UAW had negotiated an automatic cost-of-living adjustment. After 1955 these benefits also included supplemental unemployment payments. For up to twelve months a laid-off worker was paid almost as much as one with a job.[81] Perpetual increases in wages and benefits seemed possible because productivity inched higher every year. Mass production seemed to ensure endless gains in both efficiency and compensation. Autoworkers appeared to have enviable security. Factory tours were popular again. In 1964, 227,561 people trooped through the River Rouge, which remained an American icon of productivity.[82]

And yet the lives of auto workers were constrained. The earlier goal of a shorter work week was gradually abandoned, and increases in productivity were translated not into more leisure time but into additional wages. Indeed, the many fringe benefits (pensions and medical care among them) created an incentive for employers not to hire new employees but to maximize the output of those they already had, even if that entailed overtime. This was a long-term trend. The pressure to work more hours rose as fringe benefits increased as a percentage of wages from 17 to 36 percent between 1955 and 1987.[83] Thus, the American labor market demanded more and more hours from those who had work, until jobs became all-consuming. "Where I work at the auto plant," one man said, "the workers are just dropping like flies. When there's a lot of work because of a new model coming out, they make people work 10 and 12 hours every day, 6 days a week. Lots of people, even the younger ones, are developing high blood pressure, having accidents on the job, or car accidents on the way to and from work," or other health problems.[84]

The hours grew longer, but the job didn't become more interesting. A British commentator, Geoffrey Gorer, concluded that an American worker had "no choice but to admit that his body can be used as an adjunct to a machine, that his muscular strength and coordination are raw materials to be exploited in the most efficient and economical way, that his work should consist in learning a few routines and repeating them endlessly." He argued "this is not consciously felt to be humiliating or degrading by the majority of workers." Yet there was still high turnover at mass-production factories, because workers felt no involvement with their jobs.[85]

A sociologist who worked on the assembly line before conducting long interviews with his fellow workers concluded that "routine jobs and a standardized wage structure take away men's uniqueness and reduce them to anonymous entities who can be easily managed and manipulated in accordance with the needs of a constantly changing mechanical technology."[86] Although "rags to riches" mythology was strong in popular culture, in the factory opportunities for advancement were few. Many workers dreamed of buying a farm or opening a small business. A handful hoped to become foremen; fewer still seriously imagined they could rise very far in the world. Among all those interviewed, "without dissent, assembly-line work was looked upon as the most exacting and most strenuous. Its coerced rhythms, the inability to pause at will for a moment's rest, and the need for undeviating attention to simple routines made it work to be avoided if possible. . . ."[87] The fervent wish of every man on the line was that it would occasionally break down. "You don't want it to break down so you get sent home, but you want it to stop for a little while and give you a chance to stop for a minute."[88] Those on production lines or working as inspectors all took home the same wages. The best jobs were in the maintenance, tool and die, and experimental departments, where one escaped the assembly line and got higher wages too. But beyond those positions, there was little prospect of further advancement. Almost no one made the transition from worker to management.[89] Despite the claims of the "People's Capitalism" public-relations campaign, most factory workers were resigned to their jobs, embracing security rather than striving for an elusive advancement. Most hoped that their children would not work in the factory. A 40-year-old line repairman said of his son "If he goes into the factory, I'll beat the hell out of him [unless he either goes] to engineering school or learns a trade first."[90]

The workers weren't as content as the "People's Capitalism" campaign claimed. Harvey Swados, a writer who had worked on aircraft production lines during World War II, spent several months in the spring of 1956 working at a new Ford plant in New Jersey. The following year, he published a widely discussed essay, "The Myth of the Happy Worker," in which he argued that workers hadn't suddenly joined the middle class. Relative to white-collar work, factory work was dirty and demeaning, and although wages had risen they weren't as good. "The working-class family today is not typically held together by the male wage earner, but by multiple wage earners often of several generations who club together to get the things they want and need."[91] Shortly after "The Myth of the Happy Worker," Swados published On the Line, a series of interconnected stories based on his factory experiences. Each of the eight chapters is devoted to a different assembly-line worker.[92] The pressure of the work keeps these eight men apart, and they make only sporadic efforts to know one another. An experienced man, Joe, remarks: "No one who comes here wants to admit that the place has any real connection to his real life. He has to say that he is just putting in his time here, and so no matter how friendly he is by nature he has to think of the people around him as essentially strangers. . . ."[93] To a young Irish immigrant the factory appears to be a fairyland of promise, but to his partner in the body shop it is a dirty and dangerous workplace. To an old Polish man, it is a refuge from an empty home. For a reformed alcoholic, it provides a routine that helps him resist his compulsion. For all the men, the factory is ultimately a place where "a man's life goes down the drain like scummy water."[94] Many, especially the young, remain only briefly before moving on in search of something better.

Many also criticized what came off the assembly line. If in theory Americans were supremely practical tinkerers, in practice the 1950s and the 1960s were a period of florid and at times downright wacky automobile design. The annual model change had become an ingrained part of American automotive culture, and in 1955 many car owners traded in perfectly good vehicles after only two years. In 1934 the average driver waited five years before trading in. The head of styling at General Motors openly admitted "Our big job is to hasten obsolescence."[95] He didn't mean that GM cars should last only two years, but rather that new features, colors, and styling in the annual model should be so enticing that potential buyers would feel, after 24 months, that their cars were no longer satisfactory. The dream at General Motors was to reduce new-car ownership to a single year. The need to create new models for every brand every year encouraged designers to invent elaborate exteriors that masked minimal changes under the hood. One automobile analyst in 1958 was particularly critical of the Oldsmobile and the Buick: "When the reckoning time comes at the end of the era of the automobile, anthropologists will look upon these two cars as prime examples of the age of excess. Huge, vulgar, dripping with pot metal, and barely able to stagger down the highway," they exemplified the triumph of style over safety and function.[96]

During the 1940s and the 1950s the assembly line was extended to new areas, notably housing. During World War II "mass-production carpentry and prefabrication" met emergency housing needs for defense industries. In 1941 more than a million homes and apartments were under construction in a frantic effort that began in factories where all the "sawing, planning, and nailing was done." At the site where a prefab building was installed, workers often needed only rubber mallets, screwdrivers, and wrenches.[97] The federal government alone built 273,476 units of new housing.[98]

A few architects advocated radical new designs. For example, R. Buckminster Fuller briefly mass-produced circular buildings for the military.

These structures prefigured his more thoroughly worked out "Dymaxion House" of the mid 1940s. A pre-fabricated structure of standardized parts, its sleek, aluminum design reprised the streamlining of the 1930s and was portable, affordable, and environmentally efficient. The idea was to sell it "for the price of a Cadillac" and ship it "worldwide in its own metal tube" ready for rapid deployment and assembly.[99] However, conflicts about how to translate Fuller's design into a manufactured product derailed the project.[100] Later, Fuller's geodesic domes could be found on every continent, including several erected in the Arctic to house the radar of the Defense Early Warning system. The domes could be assembled quickly from identical parts, even in harsh conditions, and they kept out the cold, the snow, and the wind. Geodesic domes were also erected at world's fairs and expositions, but ordinary people wanted more conventional homes.[101]

William Levitt, a contractor with more conservative taste, found a successful formula for mass-produced housing. On Long Island he constructed identical homes using standardized components, economies of scale, and specialization of labor.[102] Most of the parts were delivered to the site ready to be assembled, with little or no sawing or sanding needed. Windows, doors, flooring, rafters, and the other parts were absolutely standardized. One team of workers did only foundations, another walls, another roofs, and so forth. Levitt eventually built more than 140,000 houses in several locations. Long Island's Levittown, with 17,400 units, was the largest development ever put up by a single company.

Buyers literally lined up to purchase Levitt's houses, in part because they got more floor space for their money than elsewhere. Yet many criticized the Levittowns. Wouldn't such uniformity produce standardized, soulless people? The sociologist David Riesman likened the conformity of suburbia to that of a small college fraternity.[103] The architectural critic Paul Goldberger declared Levittown "an urban planning disaster." Moreover, the styles of the houses were retrograde. But Levittown wasn't an isolated example. Similar planned communities were built in much of the Western world. (A few of the builders were architecturally innovative—notably Joseph Eichler, who built more than 11,000 houses in the San Francisco Bay area.[104]) William Levitt responded to the criticism of his houses by commissioning Richard Neutra, a leading Californian modernist, to devise more innovative designs,[105] but none of them were ever built. Yet variation emerged gradually in each Levittown as the homes' owners expanded and remodeled them

FIGURE 6.7
Levittown, Long Island, ca. 1957. Courtesy of Photographic Department, Cleveland Public Library.

until no two houses looked alike. A few companies specialized in making additions to Levittown houses, commissioning architects to design expansions. They built new wings and dormers and even raised the roof ridges of smaller homes to add another floor.[106]

Some of the most memorable 1950s critiques of the assembly line were humorous. An episode of the television series *I Love Lucy* showed what happened when Lucy and her friend Ethel went to work on a line that produced chocolate candies. At first they barely have time to wrap each piece as it comes along the conveyor belt, but then the line speeds up and they cannot keep pace. Frantic to succeed in their new jobs, they begin to eat the candies they can't wrap. When they hear the supervisor coming, they stuff their cloth hats with more unwrapped chocolates. Next they stuff their mouths like hamsters. Falling ever further behind, Lucy shoves unwrapped candy down her cleavage. This *I Love Lucy* episode was so popular that in

2009 the US Postal Service issued a stamp commemorating it. The core idea of this episode wasn't new. The humorous depiction of fast-paced assembly-line work was a staple in vaudeville; as was noted in the preceding chapter, it provided one of the most memorable scenes in Chaplin's film *Modern Times*. In Jackie Gleason's version, he plays Penwick Babbitt, a man working on a small assembly line in a bakery. His job is to decorate cakes and put them in boxes.[107] As the line speeds up, he can no longer put on the whipped cream, nuts, and maraschino cherries accurately, and some of these toppings get on his face and clothes. Because he isn't quick enough, unfinished cakes begin to fall off the end of the conveyor belt. When his supervisor discovers the mess, Penwick is fired on the spot.

The popularity of such skits demonstrates that the public knew that assembly lines caused anxiety. A line can always be run faster, until human beings cannot keep up. The machine always "wins," and the humor lies in the individual's attempts to conceal defeat as long as possible. The Little Tramp, Penwick Babbitt, and Lucy all fail to keep up and are fired. The situation may not seem inherently humorous, but the comedy lies in the how it is told, allowing the viewer both to identify with the worker's predicament and to laugh at increasingly strenuous and ultimately futile efforts to conceal failure. The longer the comedian manages to stave off discovery, the greater the tension grows, until the crowning moment of defeat.

Henri Bergson argued that some humor originates in the "mechanical encrusted upon the living." It arises from the incongruity between human intelligence and mechanical repetition or rote physical activity. Humor resides in "the illusion of a machine working in the inside of the person" and "the attitudes, gestures, and movements of the human body are laughable in exact proportion as that body reminds us of a mere machine."[108] When Chaplin becomes rigid and precise in his movements on the assembly line, he becomes comic. When Lucy mechanically begins to stuff chocolates into her cleavage, the humorous contrast between the machine and the human widens. The assembly line is latently comic because it demands from human beings an ultimately impossible mechanical repetition.

Academic critics of the 1950s argued that mass production erased cultural differences, homogenizing people, places, and products. Just as all the assembly-line goods were the same, workers were becoming interchangeable and consumers identical. There seemed to be no escape. As technical systems became more complex and interlinked, the argument ran, human beings became dependent upon the machine and had to adjust to its demands. Critics worried that educational technology was shaping the personality and dominating the mental habits of future generations.[109] Many schools had adopted multiple-choice tests that could be graded by machine. In 1949, one writer protested in the *Journal of Higher Education* that universities were mass-producing students who were "completely adjusted to being grist for a bureaucratic mill" once their "education" had "deprived" them "of their spontaneity and individuality." A new college graduate would never "protest against regimentation" and was "ready to have his life routinized and procedurized. No large corporation need hesitate about hiring him; he will never cause it any trouble. . . ." Liberal arts education had become a sham, as "all sorts of devices are used to make the whole process mechanical, such as standardized true-and-false tests, fill in questions, multiple-choice questions, matching questions, and a host of other techniques which aid the teacher to mark the student without knowing whether he can think." Universities were mimicking assembly lines, and "the forces that are at work here as elsewhere are: mass production, standardization of product, interchangeability of parts," and, more insidious, "concealment of the structure behind an ide-ological façade which proclaims that all of this is democracy."[110] Adopting the values of the assembly line made the liberal-arts college "the medium for intensifying the anti-democratic influences."[111] Such arguments resembled those of the Frankfurt School, which achieved considerable American influence after some of its prominent members relocated to the United States during World War II.

Many academics began to share their view that mass production and communication technologies had become a primary means of imposing uniformity and social control.[112] Mass-market publishing, radio, and film seemed to package, standardize, and ultimately trivialize human complexities. Personal experience was being fragmented, simplified, and then reassembled for mass consumption. The modern man described in David Riesman's book *The Lonely Crowd* no longer actively directed his life but was shaped by outside forces and movements.[113] Riesman argued that large corporations rewarded not independence or self-reliance but compliance and cooperation. The assembly line, with its extremely limited range of choices, exemplified a culture in which people were expected to adjust to outside demands rather than assert their own needs. The more a society embraced mass production, apparently, the more uniform its cultural life became.[114]

FIGURE 6.8

A 1959 Ford on display at the Brussels World's Fair (Expo 58). *Boston Traveler,* October 21, 1958. Courtesy of Photographic Department, Boston Public Library.

In 1951, Riesman published "The Nylon War," a parody of the Marshall Plan in which he imagined American planes dropping consumer products on the USSR. The premise of "Operation Abundance" was "that if allowed to sample the riches of America, the Russian people would not tolerate masters who gave them tanks and spies instead of vacuum cleaners." Russian housewives, suddenly supplied with refrigerators, would demand more consumer goods, and the Soviet system would be forced to change.[115] There was a grain of truth in this parody. America's burgeoning shop windows, supermarkets, and high levels of consumption impressed the teams of Europeans who came to investigate American industrial methods. One female team member exclaimed: "Don't talk to me about economics! Tell me how I can buy a washing machine."[116] The visitors calculated that to afford a pair of nylon stockings a British woman had to work six hours, an American woman only one hour.

American consumer goods were highlighted at exhibitions abroad, notably the displays of automobiles at the 1958 world's fair in Brussels. At the 1959 American National Fair Exhibition in Moscow, Vice-President Richard Nixon showed Soviet Premier Nikita Khrushchev around a model home, expatiating on how mass production made such homes available to ordinary workers and extolling the many choices American consumers had. Nixon praised planned obsolescence, and said Americans wanted constant replacements and novelties. According to Nixon in that "kitchen debate," mass production was the engine of democracy, symbolically pitted against authoritarianism. Choices of kitchen appliances became conflated with political choices. As Nixon put it, the Moscow exhibit was meant to "show our diversity and our right to choose. We do not wish to have decisions made at the top by government officials who say that all homes should be built in the same way."[117]

During World War II, the assembly line had become the arsenal of democracy; after the war, it became the guarantor of prosperity and democracy. In the 1950s, at the height of the Cold War, American mass production seemed to ensure the victory of "people's capitalism." But criticism of the assembly line would become more vocal in the 1960s.

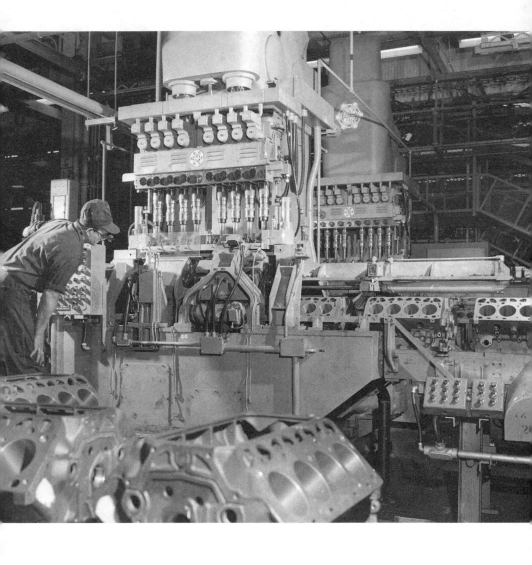

7 DISCONTENT

I protest the assembly-line production of our food, our songs, our language, and eventually our souls. . . .

—John Steinbeck, *Travels with Charley*, 1962[1]

Triumphant rhetoric about mass production vanquishing fascism and communism could assuage neither fears of technological unemployment nor fears of cultural homogenization. Businessmen promised a cornucopia for the common man, but working people worried that automation would push them into poverty. A wide spectrum of intellectuals, including both conservatives and radicals, believed that American life was becoming bland, repetitive, and uniform. Many who grew up in new suburban houses were later drawn to the Counterculture, which offered an escape from the standardized. In short, to workers, intellectuals, and many young people, mass-production society appeared to lack individuality, spontaneity, and creativity. Discontent with the assembly line grew.

In science fiction, automation and robots became more common themes after World War II than they had been in the 1930s. In *The Humanoids* (1949), Jack Williamson describes a world in which robots do everything for people, become overprotective, and thwart invention and risk taking.[2] Kurt Vonnegut's *Player Piano* (1952) depicts an automated world in which a few technicians maintain factories and robots and most of the population is utterly bored. In stark contrast, nineteenth-century workers had been "almost fierce with dignity and pride." In old photographs, "each face had a defiant

FIGURE 7.1
Automated engine production at Ford's Cleveland Engine Plant No. 2 in 1955. Courtesy of Photographic Department, Cleveland Public Library.

promise of physical strength" and these workers felt that they shared in the "mystery" of the new electrical technologies.[3] A century later, however, computers have largely eliminated all forms of work, and the remaining managers have little to do but watch meters and fix occasional malfunctions. One manager seeks renewal by purchasing a traditional farm, without electricity or running water, but quickly loses interest in living without modern technologies. A few discontented managers want to destroy the automated production system and recover the dignity of human labor. They ally themselves with under-employed Luddites who smash automated factories in some cities, but the rebellion is quickly crushed. Immediately afterward, people begin to reassemble the system. There seems to be no escape from people's impulse to improve themselves out of jobs.

In "Autofac" (1955) Philip K. Dick suggests that automation may lead to extreme overproduction. He describes a post-nuclear-war society in which automated underground factories supply all human needs. The factories work perfectly, but the citizens find it impossible to shut them down and they overproduce to such an extent that they threaten to exhaust the world's resources.[4] "Autofac" was a variation on the idea of a machine that operated ceaselessly and controlled itself, which was hardly a new story. Lewis Mumford traced it back to Aristotle and to Heron of Alexandria.[5] Centuries later the medieval clock tower became the model of a self-regulating machine, which in its most elaborate form not only kept track of time but also played music and paraded automatons at designated times during the day. Later, the precise regulation of time was deeply embedded in industrialization, and it was embodied in the act of punching in and out of work each day. Regulating human movement according to the clock was an essential part of an assembly line, which divided labor into discreet, repetitive tasks. The next step would be to transfer that repetitive work from human beings to machines.

Robots remained largely science fiction until World War II, but they had some popular appeal. At the 1939 New York World's Fair, Westinghouse presented an aluminum-sheathed robot named Elektro, a seven-foot-tall household servant that supposedly would be for sale in the 1960s. (See figure 7.2.) Elektro had a vocabulary of 700 words, and responded to some verbal commands. He could make 26 specific movements, could smoke cigarettes, and could sing. Elektro and his robot dog Sparky drew crowds to their hourly performances. If such robots could be built in 1939, by implication far more sophisticated and useful ones would soon be possible.

In practice, robots first replaced not domestic labor but some of the dirtiest jobs on the assembly line, such as spray painting and welding. These industrial robots didn't look at all like human beings. Each was designed for a specific job. Many had only one "arm" and had wheels rather than legs. Adoption was slow. By the mid 1970s there were still only about 6,000 robots in American factories. Humans had to keep an eye on them, and skilled workers were needed to set them up and to repair them.

Inventors and engineers long had dreamed of automated factories. One notable early success was Oliver Evans' fully automated flour mill of the 1780s.[6] In 1940 Roger Burlingame wrote: "We are moving toward the wholly automatic machine. Men are being replaced at every point by machines. This seems right and not a curse as some social philosophers suggest."[7] Shortly after World War II, a Ford vice-president named Dell Harder seems to have coined the word "automation" to describe the company's new Brooks Park plant.[8] The term became widespread after its use in a *Fortune* story, titled "The Automatic Factory,"[9] that extolled a plant with almost no workers. Brooks Park employed 4,500 people, but management expected to reduce its workforce continuously. By 1948 "automation" was being used in *American Machinist* to mean "the art of applying mechanical devices to manipulate work pieces into and out of equipment, turn parts between operations, remove scrap, and perform these tasks in timed sequence with the production equipment so that the line can be put wholly or partially under pushbutton control at strategic stations."[10] Gradually, "automation" also included the idea of feedback. Management began to imagine a factory with almost no workers, and therefore with no labor problems.

The federal government fueled such dreams by investing in automation. It sponsored General Electric's prototypes for machine tools that could endlessly mimic a skilled workman. The basic idea resembled the system used to produce piano rolls (which inspired Vonnegut, then a General Electric employee, to write *Player Piano*). As a machinist cut a part to precise specifications, a punched tape recorded his every movement. Afterward, just as a player piano can endlessly reproduce a sequence of notes, the machinist's movements could be "played back" as often as desired. By 1950 the dream wasn't merely that of speeding up production of individual parts. Norbert Wiener described "the automobile factory of the future" in an influential book titled *The Human Use of Human Beings*.[11] That factory would be controlled by a "high-speed computing machine" capable not only of carrying

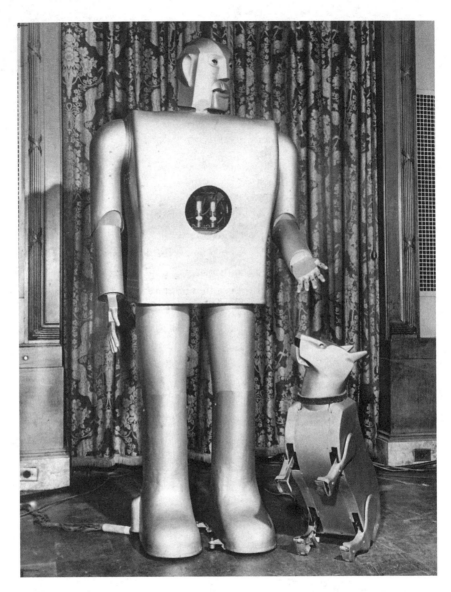

FIGURE 7.2
Elektro and Sparky, Westinghouse Robots, New York World's Fair, 1939. Courtesy
of Photographic Department, Cleveland Public Library.

out instructions but also of using "sense organs, such as photoelectric cells" to gather information and then determine how to take action. Such a computer would not be an isolated brain; it would be more like a "complete animal." Wiener noted that analogous industrial systems were already operating in "continuous-process industries like canneries, steel-rolling mills, and especially wire and tin-plate factories," in "paper factories, which likewise produce a continuous output,"[12] in oil-cracking refineries, and in chemical works. As early as 1932 a machine had been invented that could test the vacuum in 300 cans per minute and automatically reject those that weren't properly sealed. (See figure 7.3.) Because a computer-driven factory with such machines could automatically do quality control and keep statistics on output, Wiener noted, it would replace both white-collar and blue-collar work.[13] Wiener expected that within 20 years "deadly uninteresting" jobs would disappear. This development seemed inevitable, he thought, because the automatic factory "is the precise economic equivalent of slave labor" and anyone who tried to compete with it would have to accept slave wages. Wiener knew that severe unemployment might result, and asked that automated factories be "used for the benefit of man, for increasing his leisure and enriching his spiritual life, rather than merely for profits."[14] In 1949 he wrote a letter to Walter Reuther of the CIO in which he warned that automation could be an acute threat to employment in little more than a decade.[15] Reuther took the warning seriously and repeatedly called on the government to oversee an orderly transition to automation so that workers wouldn't be suddenly pushed into permanent unemployment.[16]

In 1950 Wiener assumed that automation would use the "record and playback" method. The recordings of the essential tapes had to be done on the shop floor with worker and union involvement. By 1958 there were 16,000 "automatic assembly machines" in the United States, half of them in the automobile industry and most of the others in factories that produced identical items in high volume. General Electric had three automated lines making electric motors at its Schenectady plant. Television and radio manufacturing was also being automated, as machines inserted components into pre-drilled holes on printed circuit boards. But the automobile industry, owing to its scale and its complexity, often took the lead in automation, notably among parts suppliers. The Timken Roller Bearing Company's automated plant in Detroit produced 30 million bearings a year and could sell

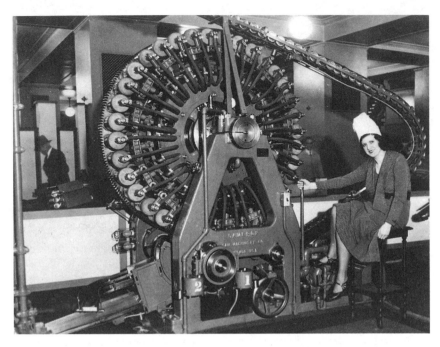

FIGURE 7.3

This machine, photographed in 1932 at a convention of the Canning Machinery and Supplies Association Convention in Chicago, used a vacuum process to test cans for leaks. It handled 300 cans per minute, automatically ejecting those that failed. Courtesy of Photographic Department, Cleveland Public Library.

them at prices 15 percent below the prices of bearings made in conventional plants. However, Timken's automated machinery was two and a half times as costly as the machinery used in non-automated factories. Moreover, there were still 700 workers. "People are required for this line. People to pull bearings out for spot inspections and to reset machines, people to sharpen tools and fit them precisely into position in tool blocks, people to snap these blocks in position replacing others that hold worn tools, people to oil, adjust, and repair the machines. And, on the six lines producing the inside bearing rings and their assembled rollers, people perform two operations that Timken engineers felt could be done better by hand."[17] The Timken factory made 400 percent more per worker than a traditional assembly-line plant; however, profits didn't rise correspondingly, because a more skilled workforce was needed to service the expensive machines.

Moreover, retooling cost much more in automated factories. Ford's first "automated" plant, in Cleveland, had been expected to produce engines for ten years, but consumers' demands for more powerful cars forced the company to scrap the line and rebuild it entirely after only five years. After that expensive lesson, Ford began to acquire more flexible machine tools that could be put to new uses. A few years later, Ford built a largely automated line at its Lima, Ohio plant to produce V-8 engines for the Edsel. After the Edsel failed in the marketplace, the whole line had to be redesigned to produce six-cylinder engines for the Falcon. Because Ford had learned from its experience in Cleveland, many of its machine tools could be adapted and reused. Even so, automated machines proved so complex that after installation it typically took weeks, and sometimes months, to get all the "kinks" out so that the line ran smoothly; during that period, production moved by fits and starts.[18] Moreover, in an automated factory the semi-skilled work of assemblers and machine operators had to be combined with maintenance and repair work to create the better-paid position of an "automation worker."[19] In view of the high cost of equipment, the complexity of setting up such a factory, and the higher wages paid to the workers who remained, automation didn't always save money. Whether it did so depended on the product. The more varied the goods produced and the more frequently models were changed, the less worthwhile automation became.

Playback systems clearly worked, but many engineers dreamed of sending specifications for a product directly from a computer to a machine, with no human mediation. This "numerical control" shifted power decisively from workers to management.[20] Numerical control was one element in the larger project of computer-aided design (CAD) and computer-aided manufacturing (CAM). The goal of CAD-CAM was to move directly from a designer's representation on a screen to instructions that told machines how to make a product. This ambitious vision required that the full repertoire of workers' skills and routines be translated into computer code. With numerical control, at least in theory, retooling to make something different would only take the few moments needed to change the computerized instructions. "Since the rate of production of such a machine [tool] is several times that of a conventional machine, work is effectively taken away from at least two or three skilled machinists."[21] Eliminating skilled workers was a specific goal.[22] Automated machines could work every shift. They would never get sick, ask for a raise, or go on strike.

During the 1950s one newspaper story explained how one Ford worker supervised automatic machines that produced 100 engines per hour, replacing 75 auto workers.[23] Another story proclaimed that "automation enabled one man" to direct a complex gas pipeline that stretched from New Mexico to Wisconsin. Using microwave communications, radar, and new tracking systems, that man could monitor and deliver gas thousands of miles away. The director of the House of Representatives' Subcommittee on Unemployment and the Impact of Automation declared in 1962 that the "fear of technological unemployment" was "a very real one in the minds of millions of American workers."[24] However, he believed that such worries were unfounded. Between 1870 and 1960 productivity had quadrupled, but total employment also had grown.

Yet jobs for the unskilled and some for the semi-skilled were disappearing. During the 1950s total industrial production rose 43 percent but the number of blue-collar workers fell by 10 percent. There were 94,000 fewer electrical workers, 80,000 fewer steel workers, and 250,000 fewer coal miners.[25] Yet coal production was up 96 percent.[26] About 40,000 elevator operators lost their positions as automatic elevators were installed.[27] In the telegraph industry, automatic equipment had eliminated 57,000 jobs.[28] A Pittsburgh steelworker complained: "New machinery, new methods in the mill did it to me—after nineteen years in the mill. They abolished my department completely."[29] Such workers often could find nothing else to do, because new jobs demanded skills they didn't have and were in entirely other fields.

A resolution put forth at the United Auto Workers' 1953 convention warned that automation could "create a social and economic nightmare in which men walk idle and hungry—made obsolete as producers because the mechanical monsters around them cannot replace them as consumers."[30] In support of that resolution, a delegate from Ford's Cleveland plant declared: "We have got 78 people in Cleveland doing the work of 770 people from the Rouge and we are out-producing them. . . . I am representing more machines than I am men."[31] When Ford Motor Company officials guided Walter Reuther through the company's Cleveland plant, they pointed out that not one of the new automated machines paid union dues. Reuther immediately replied "And not one of them buys new Ford cars, either."[32]

Fears of widespread technological unemployment cropped up in questions put to President Eisenhower at press conferences. In 1955 Eisenhower replied to one such question this way: "Exactly the same thing has been going on for a hundred and fifty years; exactly the same fears have been expressed right along; and one of the great things that seems to happen is that as we find ways of doing work with fewer man-hours devoted to it, then there is more work to do."[33] Two years later, Eisenhower declared: "Whatever saves the time and the effort of humans does give them greater opportunity for self development in their moral, their intellectual, and cultural sides. Therefore, I believe that automation . . . is not a wicked thing at all. I think, on the contrary, it is a great advance."[34] Many commentators shared the president's optimism, and newspapers ran headlines such as "Automation Aims at New Freedom" and "G.E. Head Depicts Automation Gain."[35] Edward R. Murrow was not as optimistic. He devoted an hour-long installment of his television documentary series *See It Now* to automation, tracing its history from Oliver Evans to IBM's latest computer-driven machines. He gave air time to enthusiasts but also to doubters, including Walter Reuther and unionized bakers who were losing their jobs.[36]

The Democratic Party's national platform of 1960 declared that the economy had to grow faster in order to absorb both the Baby Boomers emerging from colleges and the workers "displaced by the rapid pace of technological advances, including automation."[37] President John F. Kennedy's Secretary of Labor, Arthur J. Goldberg, in a feature article for the *New York Times*, recognized that James Watt's automatic controls for his steam engines and Charles Babbage's calculator "were the seeds for today's mammoth automatic processes that refine oil, make artillery shells, bake cakes, process chemicals, generate electric power, cast engine blocks, dig coal, produce atomic materials, and perform thousands of other jobs."[38] Goldberg saw the human costs of such advances. He cited Samuel Gompers' recollection of how the silk weavers of London had lost their jobs to new machines in the 1850s: "No thought was given to these men whose trade was gone." Goldberg declared that a century later the United States would do better. Retraining programs would prepare workers for new jobs. Like Eisenhower, he argued that the long-term effects of automation were good, lessening heavy physical labor, pushing the workforce toward a higher level of education, and giving society more leisure time. But he also recognized that "the shadow of technological unemployment has fallen across mill towns, mining towns, textile towns and manufacturing towns across the nation."[39] One newspaper article asked: "Is automation the answer to man's dream of more leisure time, inexpensive goods, and a continually growing economy? Or a Frankenstein's monster destroying jobs and men?"[40]

Representative Elmer J. Holland, a Democrat from Pennsylvania, wrote to President Kennedy: "When new mechanical or electronic devices are installed, assurances are given workers in many industries that they will not be hurt or fired. However, when they leave—due to retirement or resignation—no one is hired to replace them."[41] Arthur Goldberg told a similar story about manpower reduction, dealing with an insurance company that cut the workforce in one division from 198 to 85 by installing a mainframe computer. That company had successfully re-deployed the workers displaced, but automation had eliminated more than half of the jobs. Aware that jobs were being eliminated in many companies, Walter Reuther spoke of thousands of workers "relegated by automation to the ranks of the technologically unemployed."[42] His solution was to reduce working hours and spread the work available to more people.

The chairman of the board of General Electric declared that when "some people are temporarily unemployed because of technological change, both industry and government have a recognized responsibility to help families through any such periods of transition."[43] Transition to what? President Kennedy thought that technological unemployment was "the major domestic challenge, really, of the Sixties—to maintain full employment at a time when automation, of course, is replacing men." He believed that "we have to find over a ten-year period 25,000 new jobs every week to take care of those who are displaced by machines."[44] Some predicted that technological unemployment might reach 10 percent before 1970.[45] In 1962 Congress passed the Federal Manpower Development and Training Act to help displaced workers. But some commentators, including Peter Drucker, argued that automation would not lead to a permanent job crisis but rather would release energies for better jobs and more leisure.[46] Optimists extrapolated from the annual 3 percent rise in productivity since World War II (a 50 percent rise in total)[47] and predicted that soon most people would work fewer than 30 hours a week and retire before the age of 50. Such extravagant hopes were expressed at the 1964 New York World's Fair, in magazine articles, and in books that imagined automation emancipating mankind from toil.[48]

The same expectations permeated Europe and Japan, where automation coincided with the reconstruction of industries shattered by World War II. The German government gave companies tax incentives to adopt automation. Renault sought to use automation to increase productivity drastically. Japanese firms embraced automation, and Nikita Khrushchev praised it as the tool communism would use to outperform the West.[49] But European workers often had strong unions as well as considerable political power, and such changes couldn't be pushed through without consulting them. Socialist parties usually represented labor interests at the ballot box. Minimum wages gradually rose above US levels, and in Europe health care was not an employee benefit but a right attached to citizenship itself. American auto-industry unions achieved high wages and good fringe benefits but had less political influence than their counterparts in Western Europe. When harder times came in the 1970s, the US minimum wage stagnated and national health care remained an unrealized proposal. American union leadership as a whole had moved to the right. Allying themselves with anti-communists, in some cases as early as the 1940s, American union leaders seldom sided with foreign trade unions during the Cold War.[50] They disapproved of both the New Left and the loose confederation of radicals and antiwar protesters who made up the Counterculture. Indeed they became so conservative that they refused to support the Democratic candidate, George McGovern, against Richard Nixon in the 1972 presidential election. They had accepted both technical control of the assembly-line factory that workers despised and the Cold War policies that the youth culture rejected.

In 1970, one-fourth of Ford's workers quit and unexplained absences were common. At General Motors' plants, on any given day, 5 percent of the workers didn't show up. At the worst plants that figure rose to 7.5 percent, with absenteeism highest on Mondays and Fridays.[51] Nationwide, only one manager in fifty thought the workers of 1970 were more conscientious than those of a generation earlier; 63 percent found them to be worse. When interviewed, workers complained not of wages but of conditions. An intensive series of meetings and interviews with a group of GM workers in 1971 found that 70 percent hadn't expected to make a career of assembly-line work, and that every person interviewed would "choose a different trade or occupation" if he or she could "start life over again." None of these workers considered themselves to be radicals, and only 16 percent called themselves liberals, yet they were deeply disaffected.[52] The most disgruntled were younger workers, whose long hair, loose-fitting clothing, bell-bottom pants, and occasional peace button signaled their alienation from top-down control, whether from management or the union.

At the same time, on college campuses a vibrant youth culture imbibed a distrust of standardization and mass production from many intellectuals and authors active in the early days of the Cold War, notably Allen Ginsburg and the Beats, Lewis Mumford, David Riesman, John Steinbeck, and neo-Marxists such as Herbert Marcuse. In different ways, all criticized automation, homogenization, and the reduction of human needs to functions. One mid-century survey of American literature declared: "Mass production led in time to the production of mass thinking, mass feeling, mass recreation. . . . The Machine was Lord of Prosperity and King of Pleasure—enthroned, worshipped, hated, and despised."[53] Dwight Macdonald, in his widely read 1953 essay "A Theory of Mass Culture," railed against cheapness, standardization and "the 'editorial formula' which every big-circulation magazine tailors its fiction and articles to fit, much as automobile parts are machined in Detroit." In the era of mass production, he argued, "art workers are as alienated from their brain-work as the industrial worker is from his hand-work."[54]

Criticism of cultural homogenization became common. Ernest van den Haag declared in a 1957 essay in *Diogenes* that "the production of standardized things by persons demands also the production of standardized persons." The quality of American bread illustrated what was wrong. First, during "milling and baking, bread is deprived of any taste whatever and of all vitamins," after which some vitamins were added again. "It is quite similar with all mass produced articles. . . . Producers and consumers go through the mass production mill to come out homogenized and decharacterized—only it does not seem possible to reinject the individualities which have been ground out the way the vitamins are added to enriched bread." In the United States "this assembly line shaping, packaging, and distributing of persons, of life, occurs already. Most people perch unsteadily in mass-produced, impermanent dwellings throughout their lives. They are born in hospitals, fed in cafeterias, married in hotels. After terminal care, they die in hospitals, are shelved briefly in funeral homes, and are finally incinerated." In every aspect of American life, it seemed, "efficiency and economy are obtained and individuality and continuity stripped off."[55] According to van den Haag, the promise of freedom and choice that consumer goods offered was an illusion: "The rhythm of individual life loses autonomy, spontaneity, and distinction when it is tied into a stream of traffic and carried along according to the speed of the road, as we are in going to work, or play, or in doing anything. Traffic lights signal when to stop and go, and much as we seem to be driving, we are driven."[56]

Other critics complained that public schools were being modeled on assembly lines. Standardized testing using multiple-choice questions had spread to all parts of the country. Students applying to colleges had to take the College Board's Scholastic Aptitude Test, which was graded by machines. "You may mass produce intellectual goose-steppers, or rote learners," the editors of the *Journal of Teacher Education* complained, but not independent minds. Likewise, they complained, "hospitals and doctors gave the impression of not caring deeply about the human patient, leaving the feeling among patients that they were only bits of living meat on an assembly line."[57] In such statements the assembly line seems an inherently totalitarian technology rather than the bulwark of democracy. Just before the United States entered World War II this association had often been explicit. In 1941, Clyde Miller, an associate professor at Columbia University, wrote: "Collectivism, totalitarianism, authoritarianism—call it what you will—has come upon our generation with a terrifying rush. . . . Propaganda has popularized and made acceptable assembly-line production with its necessary regimentation of workers. The Ford Motor Company in Michigan, for example, might well have been taken as a model for the industrial plant of Hitler's Germany."[58] Such associations went out of favor during the early days of World War II, but became more common again after about 1960.

Many were uneasy with the accumulation of standardized goods and with measuring civilization in quantitative terms. In a best-selling book titled *Travels with Charley*, published in 1962, John Steinbeck mused about the quality of life as he had observed it while driving around the United States in a pickup truck equipped for camping. Steinbeck may have been in a mass-produced vehicle, but he wasn't happy with standardization: "I protest the assembly-line production of our food, our songs, our language, and eventually our souls. . . ."[59] In his 1939 novel *The Grapes of Wrath*, Steinbeck had described how landowners used mass-produced tractors to evict millions of sharecroppers, who then wandered across the country in search of new homes. Yet Steinbeck also saw that these displaced farmers, like most Americans, nevertheless could "admire the tractor—its machined surfaces, its surge of power, the roar of its detonating cylinders."[60]

The apparent standardization of the middle class suggested an irreversible movement toward bland homogeneity. Some saw the 1956 film *Invasion of the Body Snatchers* not as paranoid anti-communism but as a commentary on the mindless conformity of suburbia. Aliens grown in pods infiltrate and take over a typical American town, replacing one lively resident after another with a zombie-like replica. Many worried that Americans were becoming mere cogs in an impersonal machine, or, as the title of one best-seller put it, *A Nation of Sheep*.[61] Critics also attacked the emergence of the "throw-away culture" that seemed a necessary concomitant of assembly-line production. The low prices of mass-produced goods made it possible for consumers to replace articles that were still serviceable simply because they were tired of them or wanted something else in the latest style or color. Assembly lines filled houses with more and more goods that eventually landed in expanding dumps and landfills. By the 1960s there was a "garbage crisis." With the greater environmental awareness of subsequent years, burying tons of waste in the ground began to be understood as pollution. In 1948 New York City began to dump its garbage on Staten Island, creating by 1994 a land fill 25 times the size of the great pyramid at Giza.[62]

One widely read critic of excess was Vance Packard. Packard had lived through the privations of the 1930s and the rationing of World War II. The sudden proliferation of consumer goods dismayed him. He attacked the spending of millions of dollars on packaging that was immediately thrown away. He condemned giving credit cards to teenagers and the general increase in buying on credit. He revered frugal living within one's means, abhorred planned obsolescence and consumer over-spending, and called for restraint. His 1960 best-seller *The Waste Makers* was a jeremiad condemning American culture for losing sight of traditional values such as durability, prudence, and self-reliance. An increasing percentage of these mass-produced goods were made, at least in part, from plastic. By 1976, according to Ted Steinberg's environmental history *Down to Earth*, "more plastic was manufactured, in terms of cubic volume, than all the steel, copper, and aluminum combined."[63] When thrown out, plastic didn't rot or rust; it took centuries to degrade. It seemed to symbolize an artificial and wasteful society.

The Left mounted a critique of what it regarded as the bourgeois conformity of suburban life. Marxists denounced consumerism as "commodity fetishism." Marx had written of the change in values that occurred when products were disconnected from their production. In an artisanal society, when a carpenter made a table by hand, Marx argued, its use value and its connection to work were clear. But in a capitalist society the product lost its connection to the worker, and its value was expressed in the abstract form of money. As labor was subdivided and automated, moreover, an object's origin was effaced. In modern society, currency had become "the direct incarnation of all human labor." As a result, "men are henceforth related to each other in their social process of production in a purely atomistic way; they become alienated because their own relations of production assume a material shape which is independent of their control and their conscious individual action."[64] To this add the alienation that Harvey Swados found to have separated the men on the assembly line, who not only had no meaningful relationship to production but also lacked personal ties to one another.

Commodity fetishism meant that there was a widespread desire for what the assembly line produced but an equally widespread disdain for the work involved. This contradiction came sharply into focus in a musical extravaganza staged in 1965 to promote Ford's new Mustang. The Ford executive Lee Iacocca, seeking to yoke the new car to the appeal of rock music, got Ford to co-sponsor a ninety-minute program on the CBS television network with the federal Office of Economic Opportunity, which wanted to encourage young people to get summer jobs. Many of the performers, including Marvin Gaye, Martha and the Vandellas, the Supremes, and the Four Tops, were associated with Detroit's Motown Records. They were joined by Ray Charles, the Righteous Brothers, Johnny Mathis, Herman's Hermits, and Tom Jones. The show was called *What's Happening Baby?* and was hosted by the New York disc jockey Murray Kaufman, a.k.a. Murray the "K." In a precursor of the music video, Martha and the Vandellas pranced around a working assembly line singing their hit "Nowhere To Run."[65] (See figure 7.4.) As a journalist later summarized, the trio "skip like unruly schoolgirls along a Ford car production line in Detroit. Followed by her two backing singers, [Martha] Reeves hops in the back of a half-assembled Mustang—the vehicular symbol of rebellious youth at the time—and all three continue singing 'Nowhere To Run' as the car glides forwards and a gleaming engine is lowered onto the chassis." The workers in the background remain caught in the toils of the assembly line, and seem a bit bewildered.[66] The free dance moves of the three female singers contrasted sharply with the repetitive movements of the male workers, and the text of the song suggested to some viewers that during their shift these men had—as in the words of the song—nowhere to run to and nowhere to hide. The Office of Economic Opportunity wanted young people to take summer jobs, but Martha and the Vandellas' performance contrasted boring work with appealing images of femininity, leisure, and escape. Who wouldn't prefer to ride off with Martha and the Vandellas in a spanking new Mustang convertible rather than be tied to a churning assembly line for 8 hours?

The Mustang had been designed with Baby Boomers in mind and became immensely popular. Indeed, it was introduced in April 1964, shortly before the first of the Boomers graduated from high school. Celebrities such as Frank Sinatra and Debbie Reynolds owned one, and in *Bullitt* (1968) Steve McQueen wheeled a Mustang on a ten-minute car chase through the hilly streets of San Francisco in what was long considered one of the greatest stunt-driving performances.[67] The car was glamorous; the work of building it wasn't.

Despite popular culture's disdain for mass production, it readily spread into corporate agriculture and food processing. The early hippies began to embrace organic foods even as many plants and animals were redesigned to accommodate machines. Scientists bred new strains of tomatoes with thicker skins that could be picked green by metal fingers and then "ripened" with the help of chemicals in storage sheds. Consumers complained that these thick-skinned tomatoes were tasteless. Similarly, between 1935 and 1995, chickens were "redesigned" through breeding. Their average weight increased by 80 percent to 4.7 pounds, and they matured in less than half the usual time. These factory-hatched birds were permanently confined to small cages. They became identical parts in continuous-flow production that converted grains to animal flesh that was then processed through highly automated slaughterhouses equipped with feather pluckers and digital cameras linked to computers that analyzed birds for defects.[68] Such food production eventually spawned, in reaction, consumers' demands for organic meat and free-range poultry.

Fears of technological unemployment and worries about the standardization of social life, the proliferation of waste, and the mass production of tasteless food were discussed in leading newspapers, by special commissions, and at conferences, and many people were prepared to read Jacques Ellul's 1954 book *The Technological Society* when it was published in an English translation in 1964.[69] Ellul, a law professor and a historian at the University

FIGURE 7.4

Martha and the Vandellas at Ford's River Rouge plant. This photograph appeared in the *Detroit News* on June 15, 1965. Courtesy of *Detroit News*.

of Bordeaux, argued that the political system had become less important than the technological systems that posed a more serious threat to freedom than any ideology because they were engulfing all of society. Human beings were rapidly losing touch with the natural world and becoming technicized. Their lives were being redefined and reorganized in terms of only apparently neutral values, such as efficiency and order, which shaped new regulations, rules, and procedures that forced people to adapt to technical developments. "Enclosed within his artificial creation, man finds that there is 'no exit'; that he cannot pierce the shell of technology to find again the ancient milieu to which he was adapted for hundreds of thousands of years." Human beings apparently had no choice but to adapt to this artificial environment that Ellul felt was shaped and dominated by *Technique*. "In our cities there is no more day or night or heat or cold. But there is overpopulation, thralldom to press and television, total absence of purpose. All men are constrained by means external to them to ends equally external. The further the technical mechanism develops which allows us to escape natural necessity, the more we are subjected to artificial technical necessities."[70] The operation of *Technique* as a whole was analogous to the assembly line. Natural environments, work processes, and cultural values were fragmented and then recombined into new systems, and each individual was reduced to a small, pre-determined role.

Ellul's argument reinforced other radical critiques of an assembly-line culture. The Beats of the 1950s and the Counterculture of the 1960s denigrated mechanization. Allen Ginsberg attacked mass standardization in his poem "Howl," declaiming against the rationalized society, personified as "Moloch whose mind is pure machinery! Moloch whose blood is running money!"[71] In "America," Ginsberg declared "Your machinery is too much for me" and jokingly compared his poetic productivity with mass production:

I will continue like Henry Ford my strophes are as individual as his automobiles more so they're all different sexes
America I will sell you strophes $2500 apiece $500 down on your old strophe[72]

The Beats looked for authenticity away from factories, seeking the unexpected and the unique on the "open road."

Universities were the meeting point for Beats, critics of standardization and waste, neo-Marxists, and the antiwar movement. Each, in its own fashion, attacked mass production, and each was inspired by the successes and the moral passion of the Civil Rights movement. Lewis Mumford concluded that "the increasing number of mass protests, sit-downs and riots—physical acts rather than words—could be interpreted as an attempt to break through the automatic insulation of the megamachine, with its tendency to cover up its own errors, to refuse unwelcome messages, or to block transmission of information damaging to the system itself."[73] Protesters were attempting to resume two-way communication. But like the hierarchical factory, which seldom attended to worker comments, a society that was moving toward automation didn't promote dialogue. Mumford argued that "once automatic control is installed one cannot refuse to accept its instructions, or insert new ones, for theoretically the machine cannot allow anyone to deviate from its own perfect standards."[74]

Attacks on mass production were common in the student revolt. Mario Savio berated the University of California for conceiving of itself as a factory, with the president as manager, the faculty as workers, and the students as raw materials to be transformed into docile white-collar workers. He declared to cheering Berkeley students: "There is a time when the operation of the machine becomes so odious, makes you so sick at heart, that you can't take part; you can't even passively take part, and you've got to put your bodies upon the gears and upon the wheels, upon the levers, upon all the apparatus, and you've got to make it stop. And you've got to indicate to the people who run it, to the people who own it, that unless you're free, the machine will be prevented from working at all!"[75] Savio was hardly alone. Ken Kesey offered a similar critique of middle class life in his 1962 novel *One Flew Over the Cuckoo's Nest*.[76] A popular song from the same period by Malvina Reynolds complained of towns of "little boxes" and described how the identical people living in these boxes had identical children who all went to university where they were also put into boxes—"little boxes, all the same."[77] "The result of automation," Mumford argued, "is not a better product." Rather, automation enabled "the same product to be sold at a larger profit in a mass market." Often the mass-produced good was worse. "The growth of automated bread making has driven thousands of local bakers out of existence, but the result is neither a cheaper nor a superior loaf."[78] The standardization of goods tended to level down, not up. Mass-produced breakfast cereals, many believed, provided little more nutrition than the cardboard boxes they came in.

Counterculturists looked for alternative forms of production and consumption. They set up communes, food cooperatives, and small-scale enterprises under local ownership. They emphasized homemade goods rather than relying on mass manufacturing. They promoted recycling and saw themselves as "well-equipped refugees from technocracy"[79] who were creating an alternative way of life. *The Last Whole Earth Catalogue* (1971) suggested ways to help oneself rather than rely on pre-packaged solutions; indeed, its subtitle was *Access to Tools*. The *Catalogue*, which received a National Book Award, "celebrated small-scale technologies."[80] The millions who embraced alternative lifestyles, however briefly, were attracted to the idea that they could make their own furniture, grow and preserve their own food, supply their own energy, and build their own shelter. The loose, "unisex" clothing of the era didn't demand the skill of a tailor, and almost anyone could assemble a geodesic dome. To many, Thoreau provided the inspiration for new experiments in simple living and self-reliance. Rather than depend on corporate utilities for power, why not return to using wood, windmills, solar hot-water heaters, and kerosene lamps?

In *The Making of a Counter Culture* (1969), Theodore Roszak declared that the "prime strategy of technocracy" was "to level down to a standard of so-called living that technical expertise can cope with—and then, on that false and exclusive basis, to claim an intimidating omnicompetence."[81] The student revolt of the 1960s was more than a reaction against institutionalized racism, sexism, and the Vietnam War. The prestige of Gandhi for that generation lay not only in his anti-imperialism and non-violence but also his rejection of Western industrialization in favor of local production, even if it was less efficient. Roszak's point, which student radicals quickly grasped, was that local control of machinery and production made a group independent of outside authority. The Counterculture was a reaction against standardization, efficiency, and mass production that the young felt had come to dominate the university and most of the jobs society had to offer after graduation. Charles Reich put it this way in another best-seller, *The Greening of America* (1970): "When man allows machines and the machine-state to master his consciousness, he imperils not only his inner being but also the world he inhabits and upon which he depends." Americans were "forced to exist in a universe that is, in the most profound sense, at war with human life."[82] To escape this existence, the *Whole Earth Catalog* presented do-it-yourself ideas to help readers imagine and construct an alternative life. The hippies spawned their share of entrepreneurs, but they were promoting not identical ranch-style homes in the suburbs but the hand-made and idiosyncratic.

Communes didn't reject technology per se, but rather sought to make the human-technology relationship into a series of overt choices that gave control back to the individual.

The disaffection wasn't limited to communes and universities; it was also common among young assembly-line workers who had little or no sense of engagement with their jobs. At a General Motors plant in Warren, Ohio, workers listened to acid rock and regularly smoked marijuana in order to get through the day. Between 1960 and 1968, their absentee rate doubled and the employee turnover rate increased 250 percent. One worker commented: "Every day I come out of there I feel ripped off. I'm gettin' the shit kicked out of me, and I'm helpless to stop it." Worst of all, "I don't even feel useful now. They could replace me; I don't even feel necessary."[83] The lack of motivation or self-worth were the polar opposite to how essential American workers had felt during World War II.

During the Vietnam War and the rise of the Counterculture, the problems of industrial workers were seldom front-page news. Standard histories of the time scarcely mention that 400,000 workers struck General Motors, Ford, Chrysler, and American Motors in 1970 in the largest strike ever orchestrated by the United Auto Workers. It lasted 67 days, and in retrospect it marked the end of an era. The strike seemed an unambiguous victory for labor, which won a wage increase of more than 20 percent spread over three years and generous cost-of-living adjustments. Afterward, however, the number of auto workers employed in unionized plants would fall as foreign competitors ate into the market. A million fewer American cars were produced in 1970 than in 1969. Foreign manufacturers, notably Volkswagen and Toyota, made up some of the difference, selling 100,000 more cars. At the time this seemed to be merely a side effect of the strike, but Germany and Japan would continue to gain market share.

The 1970 strikes also marked a change in the unions, which then were dominated by older white ethnic workers, who held most of the skilled jobs. Younger workers (many of them unskilled African-Americans or immigrants) were under-represented in the unions' leadership. In practice, this under-representation weakened communication with the rank and file, and led to many wildcat strikes and some sabotage, such as intentionally ruining a new car's upholstery or its paint job.[84] In 1968, the Dodge Revolutionary Union Movement (DRUM) emerged, with an ideology of revolutionary nationalism. It was founded in response to the firing of seven black workers who were protesting a speed-up at the main plant of the Chrysler Corporation's Dodge division. "The Union," DRUM declared, "has consistently and systematically failed us time and time again. We have attempted to address our grievances to the UAW's procedure, but all to no avail. The UAW bureaucracy is just as guilty, and its hands are just as bloody, as the white racist management of the Chrysler Corporation. We black workers feel that if skilled trades can negotiate directly with the Company and hold a separate contract, then black workers have even more justification for moving independently of the UAW."[85] DRUM complained that 99 percent of the foremen and all of the superintendents were white, and argued that the seniority system was, in operation if not by intent, a racist arrangement than ensured white domination of the best positions.[86] It called on African-American workers to create their own separate union, an idea that wasn't supported by older activists but embraced by many of the young.[87]

Young white workers were also becoming restive. They didn't respect union leaders, and they were contemptuous of management. The political scientist and historian Ira Katznelson observed: "Predictable patterns of action have given way to significant minority political acts that range from the support of quasi-populist candidates of the right and left to plant sabotage. Assembly-line turnover in the automobile industry approaches 100 per cent in some factories, and almost all shop floors have developed significant drug and crime subcultures."[88] By 1969, Malcolm Denise, Ford's Vice President for Labor Relations, recognized that there had been "a big influx of a new breed of union member—younger, more impatient, less homogeneous, more racially assertive, and less manipulable" whose "attitudes and desires were not easily read by a sixty-two year-old labor leader"—or, presumably, by a corporate manager of the same age.[89]

The tensions and problems of the auto industry culminated in the early 1970s at General Motors' plant at Lordstown, Ohio. At first, Lordstown resembled other factories, with 7,000 workers producing slightly more than 60 cars an hour. Then in 1971, after changeover to production of the Chevrolet Vega (a small car that had been designed to meet the foreign competition), the speed of the assembly line was increased to one car every 36 seconds, or more than 100 cars per hour. The managers tried to achieve this rate with more subdivision of labor as well as with a speed-up. The sociologist Stanley Aronowitz (a former steelworker) found that "no line job takes more than a half-hour to learn," and that "most workers achieve sufficient speed in their operation to keep up with the line in about half a shift."[90] "[for] a lot of the jobs," a woman who had worked on the line recalled, "you had to get into the car, and do your job sitting on raw metal. And I can remember coming home with black and blue marks on the back of my legs. And I would go out to my car and it would hurt so bad that I couldn't even sit—that's how bad it hurt." Another worker designed a padded apron to protect herself, but "the guys were too proud to wear the aprons." Many assembly line workers experienced repetitive-motion injuries. One woman commented: "No one comes out of GM without an injury. It's the repetition. . . . It just wears you down in your bones, so I always have a sore shoulder."[91] The grueling pace exhausted even the most experienced workers. Moreover, managers made overtime mandatory. A ten-hour day became standard, and "young people are the only ones who can keep up to the killing pace of the line." The average age on the Lordstown line was only 28.[92] In February 1972, 97 percent of the workers voted to strike. In the previous months they had filed more than 1,000 work grievances and had tried to slow down the pace. They had been unable to keep up, and thousands of defective cars ended up in the repair lot.

Assembly-line workers developed many ways to cope with notoriously draining jobs in which "people break on the line."[93] Most dealt with the monotony and pressure by becoming buddies with those nearby, making jokes, playing pranks, and talking. Richard Sandler's sociolinguistic study of this behavior found "a recurrent theme of being victimized throughout the abundance of pranks and sexual tales in the factory." "This preoccupation with being a victim," he commented, "is not as prevalent in other occupations."[94] In the 1970s and the early 1980s, these workers shared a sense of victimhood. As one worker put it, "No one is better, or he wouldn't be here."[95] The humor, storytelling, and practical jokes affirmed a shared fate and, at the same time, countered the sense of failure. Often the pranks used grease, dirt, or automobile parts to emphasize the worst features of the factory environment.[96] The humor not only boosted morale but also commented on and rejected the working conditions. Alienation from the physical space of the plant was further expressed through continual and often wildly inventive profanity that vented anger and frustration.[97]

Assembly-line workers weren't passive; they constructed communities. As one industrial folklorist found, a man's "life on the assembly line was punctuated by an ongoing visual dialogue with his fellow workers, literally 'on the line.'" This dialogue took the form of drawings, verses, jokes, and commentary written in chalk on the black rubber conveyor belt that transported the products of their labor. It was humorous, irreverent, poignant, and lively, whereas the work was serious, repetitive, and numbing.[98] Workers also made jewelry, belt buckles, and other small things from waste and scraps. A few workers painted the factory walls; indeed, workers at an Oldsmobile plant and at a Dodge truck factory painted murals. Seeing the enthusiasm of workers for these images, management encouraged the artists, because "these painted murals provide visual relief from the austerity and mechanical repetitiveness of the assembly line."[99]

Wayne Kemp's song "One Piece At A Time," a hit for Johnny Cash in 1976, imagines another form of worker creativity. It tells of an assembly-line worker in a Cadillac plant who admires the cars as they roll by. Since he cannot afford to buy one, he decides to steal one part at a time. After decades, he has acquired all the parts needed to build a car. But when he tries to assemble them, they don't fit together. He has a transmission from 1953 and a motor from 1973, two headlights on one side but only one on the other, and a back end with only one big tail fin. Finally he manages to cobble everything together, and the whole town laughs when he drives down Main Street.[100] This song is less about the high cost of luxury cars than about one worker's inventiveness and persistence.

Although pranks, scribbling, profanity, fabrications, and wall murals testified to the vitality of worker culture in the face of repetitive monotony, these responses couldn't help the American auto industry meet the Japanese challenge. The intransigent opposition between management and labor created a barrier to change.

Discontent with assembly-line work was by no means limited to the United States. In Britain, women workers struck Ford's Dagenham plant outside London, demanding equal pay for equal work. Their strike spread to the women in other UK automobile factories and resulted in a sizable pay rise. In 1970 Parliament made wage discrimination against women illegal.[101] In France, in the aftermath of the student revolt of 1968, Robert Linhart, a young professor of economics, left his position at a university and took a job in a Citroën factory just outside Paris. His autobiographical account of that experience, *L'établi* (*The Assembly Line*), described how easy it was to be hired and how difficult it was to do what looked like an easy job: to use a blow torch to melt and smooth out a small amount of tin in the gap where two sheets of metal met over the windshield. Despite patient instruction, he couldn't master the task. Next, Linhart was given the job of putting a rubber strip on windows. When he failed at that too, the managers found that he was able to put the fabric on front seats. In each job he needed help from fellow workers, who covered for one another in small ways that made the grinding repetition of the work bearable.

Linhart went home each night with swollen hands and bloody thumbs.[102] He discovered "the constant exposure to the aggression of objects, all these unpleasant, irritating dangerous contacts with materials of all kinds: sheet iron with cutting edges, dusty pieces of scrap metal, pieces of rubber, fuel oil, greasy surfaces, splinters under the skin, chemicals which damage your skin and burn your bronchial tubes."[103] Many jobs in the factory involved specific hazards: benzene poisoning in the paint shop, tin poisoning in the soldering area, chemicals in the air. Raising efficiency was not an abstraction on the line. At first, five workers finished 300 seats a day, 60 each, but after a few months the company suddenly demanded that just four workers achieve the same output. After a few more months the company reduced the hours but wanted almost as much production. Management focused entirely on the cars, which were "smooth, shining, multicolored" whereas "we, the workers, [were] gray, dirty, crumpled." A car, Linhart writes, is "enriched with accessories and chrome, its interior is embellished with soft fabrics, all attention is on the car. It laughs at us. It scorns us. For it, and it alone, shine the lights of the main assembly line. As for us, we're enveloped in invisible darkness."[104] There was no negotiation. Management suppressed any worker input and made all decisions without even a show of consultation.[105] Louis Malle filmed the work that Linhart described for *Humain, Trop Humain* (1974), a 75-minute documentary.[106] Without voice-over, the film contrasts the narrative of a car's creation as it moves down the line with the repetition experienced by each worker.

By 1983, there was, as John Staudenmaier put it, widespread social pressure for "a cooperative model linking workers and management" in assembly-line manufacturing.[107] This was due at least in part to the Soviet Union's claims that its workers were treated more humanely than workers in Western capitalist factories. (See figure 7.5.)

The desire to improve the workers' lives led Swedish corporations and labor unions to create a more humane work process that eliminated the social

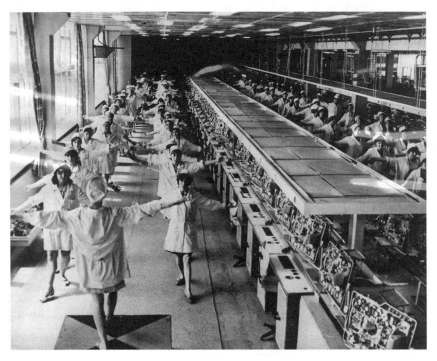

FIGURE 7.5
Workers exercising in a Soviet television plant, 1970. At precisely 2 o'clock every afternoon, production halted and seven different exercises were performed under the eye of volunteer gymnastics instructors. Courtesy of Photographic Department, Cleveland Public Library.

isolation that most assembly-line workers experienced. As early as 1952, Charles Walker and Robert Guest had noted in a book titled *The Man on the Assembly Line* that more than half of all workers "had infrequent social interaction" and that even those who were able to speak or gesture to those nearby had a small personal network based almost entirely on proximity. The workers who labored in "almost complete isolation" tended to be the most unhappy. In contrast, in a few areas, "usually not on a moving line," men "worked in teams. Geographically they were apart from other operations. Each man was functionally dependent upon his partner or his teammates, and social interaction was virtually constant. Jobs were usually rotated within the group." These teams of workers were markedly more satisfied. Indeed, they were "positive and cheerful."[108] Detroit automakers knew about such findings, but a large, coordinated effort to reconceptualize the assembly line wasn't undertaken in the United States. In contrast, Volvo and other Swedish manufacturers rethought the assembly line completely, creating what one critic later suggested was a form of "flexible Taylorism."[109] Around 1990, Volvo boasted in advertisements that if Henry Ford had started the assembly line Volvo had stopped it. Instead of a moving line, cars stood still much of the time, while teams of workers built them. Two indispensable elements of the original assembly line remained, however: interchangeable parts and reliance on electrical tools, each with its own motor. Two other aspects of the classic assembly line seemed to have been eliminated, however: the moving line and the extreme specialization of labor. (There was still considerable specialization of labor in the production of parts, however.) Parts were delivered in complete sets for each segment of the car assembly. Because small teams put together entire cars, it required 4 months to train an assembler, versus 4 hours on a conventional line.

How could the Volvo system possibly compete with a classic assembly line? It eliminated high worker turnover, because workers derived far more satisfaction from putting an entire car together than they did repeating a few identical movements for 8 hours a day.[110] Moreover, once given a view of how the entire vehicle was designed they were more likely to spot irregularities or problems than workers whose specialized labor denied them a larger view of production. The absence of a work hierarchy in the plant improved the flow of information from the shop floor to management. Indeed, at the Uddevalla plant the structure eventually consisted of "teams with their spokespersons and a workshop leader working with the plant director."[111] In contrast, an American automobile factory typically had more than 100 job classifications and an elaborate hierarchy.

The classic assembly line works best if the product is undifferentiated, allowing managers to focus on balancing the load and evening out the work to minimize idle time at any work station. The balancing problem disappeared entirely at the Volvo plant, where a team had a fixed amount of time to assemble the entire car. Some of their work might go slowly, but glitches or delays had no effect on the other teams. Likewise, when work went smoothly a team didn't have to wait for others to catch up. This advantage was particularly useful whenever a new model was introduced, for just one poorly defined work process or intricate task can slow down or even stop a classic assembly line, idling many people until it is dealt with. Even when no major problems emerge, a traditional line doesn't achieve an optimal division of labor until it has been operating for some time and the "balancing losses" have been rectified.

The Volvo method also made it easier to respond to increased or decreased demand. In slack times, instead of running the entire assembly line for fewer hours, Volvo had fewer teams working. During such times, assemblers might be reassigned to the less skilled work of materials handling or maintenance. When demand rose, these workers moved back into production, and there could be more shifts or overtime as well. Yet another potential advantage of the Volvo system was that many different models could be constructed without continually rebalancing the line. Indeed, a new form of specialization could occur, with some teams assembling only one model and others assembling only a different model. Workers seldom mixed up the parts and installed the wrong ones, because they were given, in a single container, all the components required for each vehicle. Absenteeism, a chronic problem ever since Ford had introduced the assembly line, declined markedly, and when it occurred it had less of an impact. Volvo used working teams of four or even two persons, which meant that most teams were complete most of the time. Such a workforce was quite flexible, and a few teams could quickly be asked to meet the deadline for a high-priority special order without disrupting production elsewhere.

The Volvo system would have been more competitive for a manufacturer relying on less expensive labor. (The minimum wage was higher in Scandinavia than almost anywhere else.) The Uddevalla factory didn't close because Volvo's alternate system failed; it closed because Swedish wages made it hard for Volvo to compete no matter manufacturing methods it adopted. (A Japanese variant of assembly-line manufacturing did outcompete the classic assembly line; it will be discussed in the next chapter.[112])

In 1980 the weekly magazine *Time* ran a cover story on robots. The advantages that had been touted for decades still seemed obvious: "Not only can the robot work three shifts a day, but it takes no coffee breaks, does not call in sick on Mondays, does not become bored, does not take vacations or qualify for pensions," and is "immune to government and union regulations."[113] Yet the United States was still producing only 1,500 robots a year. Some of these were doing extremely dangerous jobs, such as handling plutonium in nuclear reactors, but in ordinary workplaces human beings still did more than 99 percent of the work. In an uncertain economy, $110,000 was a lot to spend on just one Pragma A-3000 robot. It could be unplugged, but it couldn't be laid off. Automation remained more an expectation than a reality.

In 1970, Americans bought most of their cars from Detroit and believed they were the best mass-market vehicles in the world. By 1990, millions of Americans were buying Japanese cars. They were doing so because Honda, Toyota, Nissan, and Mazda vehicles had fewer defects and required fewer repairs. They gave more value for the money, and they were built on a new kind of assembly line that required fewer workers and less space. Not many Americans understood the new manufacturing system, however, which didn't even have a widely accepted English name until 1990, when a team of researchers at MIT dubbed it "lean production."

The Japanese had no idea—in any systemic, big-picture sense—what they were doing.

—Takahiro Fujimoto[1]

It is a myth that the Toyota system is a unique antithesis of [the] Ford system.

—Takahiro Fujimoto[2]

What do we want our kids to do? Sweep up around Japanese computers?

—Walter Mondale, 1982, cited in *The New Yorker*, 2003[3]

Just after World War II, workers in the United States were five times as productive as those in Japan and twice as productive as those in Europe. Indeed, at Toyota a then-unknown manager named Taiichi Ohno estimated that the productivity of the American automobile industry might be as much as ten times that of the Japanese.[4] Between 1950 and 1990, however, Europe and Japan closed the gap. In those years Italian and French workers increased their productivity per hour worked from just 40 percent of the US figure to 98 percent. Some nations, notably Belgium, Norway, and the Netherlands, exceeded the US in productivity. The speed of the change was especially

FIGURE 8.1
Two photographs featured in the *Boston Traveler* on August 14, 1970 (the anniversary of Japan's surrender in World War II). Original caption: "The assembly lines of the Toyota automobile company and Sony Trinitron, producer of electronic equipment, are contributors to the $164 million gross national product run up by Japan in 1969—less than 25 years after the atom and conventional bombs leveled Tokyo and Hiroshima to ashes." Courtesy of Photographic Department, Boston Public Library.

remarkable because the US was by no means standing still. Between 1960 and 1990 its overall industrial production rose 250 percent, even though the number of workers remained about the same.[5] The American population grew, but the fraction of blue-collar workers declined from one-fourth to one-sixth of all employees.

Between 1950 and 1990 Japan's productivity increased at twice the rate of US productivity, and Japan had pulled ahead in the automotive sector, although it lagged slightly behind in other areas[6] Moreover, Japanese workers put in four more hours each week than their American counterparts.[7]

As early as 1970 Japan was a major exporter of televisions and was producing about one-ninth of the world's automobiles. Just ten years later it was producing nearly one-third of the world's automobiles. Dominant in Asia, it had captured one-fourth of the US car market. Japan's share of automotive patents also grew, surpassing that of the United States and Europe combined.[8] By the 1980s, Japanese corporations, using "more re-source- and cost-saving methods," could produce "a greater variety of cars in smaller volumes with less defects."[9] The productivity of US trans-portation equipment industries as a whole had almost doubled from 1948 to 1965, but then entered a period of oscillation and little overall growth that persisted through the 1970s.[10] Many of the cars that came off Detroit's assembly lines were poorly made "lemons." In 1982, Secretary of Labor Raymond Donovan admitted that the US was "experiencing an extended period of absolute decline in our production efficiency." Symptomatical-ly, in 1980 the Chrysler Corporation needed a $1.5 billion federal bailout to avoid bankruptcy. In 1982, Secretary of Commerce Robert Dederick predicted that 200,000 jobs in the auto industry would disappear perma-nently within a decade.[11]

Few Americans had imagined that Japan would emerge as a world au-tomotive power. The Japanese had to import iron ore and coal to make steel, and to sell cars in the US they had to ship them across the Pacific. In the boom years of the 1960s, Detroit's automakers didn't see a threat from Japan. Conceivably, they thought, Japan could develop a niche market for compact cars, but Americans liked large cars with powerful engines. Sales of American-made cars rose from 7.1 million in 1970 to 9.7 million in 1973. Then came an oil embargo and an economic downturn. In 1974 Detroit only sold 7.4 million cars. In subsequent years sales varied, but for the rest of the century Detroit's "Big Three" never again sold 9.7 million automobiles in a year. Sales of Asian and European vehicles, almost all of them relatively small and efficient, reached 2 million in 1977 and 3.2 million in 1986.[12] Detroit's declining market share could no longer be attributed to the price of oil.

Leading companies seldom react quickly when endangered by a new technology.[13] Consider the leading typewriter manufacturers of 1960, Underwood, Royal, and Olivetti. They all produced high-quality manual typewriters. In the 1960s they introduced electric typewriters, and in the 1970s some of their machines had small screens that displayed the most recent line of text, held in a memory chip. But none of those once-dominant firms survived the transition to personal computers.[14] This is not an isolated example. In the 1880s, Columbia was the leading manufacturer of high-wheel bicycles. It long relied on craft production, selling durable cycles that were custom built to fit the lengths of clients' arms and legs. In the 1880s a Columbia bicycle cost as much as an ordinary worker earned in an entire year. When the "safety" bicycle emerged as the standard design in the 1890s, other companies mass-produced them from identical parts that could be bolted together quickly. Almost anyone could afford one, and suddenly the high-wheelers were dinosaurs. Like most corporations facing a paradigm shift in technology, Columbia was slow to change the form of its product and slow in adopting mass production. Newer competitors soon dominated the market.

Why do corporations resist change when better alternatives emerge? Why did Ford, Chrysler, and General Motors fail to adopt superior Japanese systems of production in the 1970s or the early 1980s? Economic historians explain such failures through the theory of path dependence.[15] By the 1970s, millions of American auto workers and managers could recall no other system than the classic assembly line. American industries led the world in manufacturing volume, and foreign delegations had been coming to the US to study their successes since 1910. European and Asian automobile industries seemed to produce only luxury cars or small cars. Dominant corporations seldom make radical innovations; they prefer to make incremental improvements in the systems they know. Moreover, in the words of the economist Douglass North, "Path dependence is more than the incremental process of institutional evolution in which yesterday's institutional framework provides the opportunity set for today's organizations and individual entrepreneurs (political or economic). The institutional matrix consists of an interdependent web of institutions and consequent political and economic organizations that are characterized by massive increasing returns."[16] By the 1970s, the assembly line was institutionally inseparable from a web of contracts with labor unions, training programs, relationships with suppliers, obligations to dealers, financial relations with banks, investor expectations, consumer habits, and links to state and federal agencies. The traditional assembly line was at the heart of a socio-technical system so familiar that it was difficult to imagine alternatives.

The business scholar William Abernathy offered a related explanation for the US automobile industry's stagnation, arguing that the pursuit of incremental productivity gains worked against fundamental change.[17] Process-management techniques spread into centers of innovation and became embedded in routines that focused "on easily available efficiency and customer-satisfaction measures. Although increased efficiency results from these dynamics in the short run, they also trigger internal biases for certainty and predictable results."[18] Historians of science likewise have observed that "normal research" is shaped by a dominant paradigm. Research refines an existing theory, while challenges to it are marginalized until internal inconsistencies become glaringly evident.[19]

During the 1970s, analysts attributed the decline of the American automobile industry to rising oil prices, high labor costs, excessive government regulation, managerial errors, and failures to anticipate demand for fuel-efficient cars. Yet the central problem was that Detroit's corporations were slow to understand, much less to adopt, the new Japanese manufacturing strategies. By the mid 1980s, when Detroit's automakers fully understood that they weren't so much being outcompeted by lower wages as by superior systems, Nissan, Honda, and Toyota were manufacturing millions of automobiles every year in the United States.

The production systems of the Japanese manufacturers differed in some ways. Nissan's strategy—volume production of a range of cars—was based on the strategy that Alfred P. Sloan had invented for General Motors in the 1920s.[20] Toyota originated what eventually came to be called "lean production"—a strategy of "permanent reduction in costs" that included "just-in-time" delivery of parts. Honda emphasized product innovation as a means of catering to consumers' shifting tastes and reaching new market segments. It used flexible production to develop new models quickly, and to abandon unsuccessful ones even more quickly.[21] To maximize flexibility, Honda didn't build as close a relation to suppliers as Toyota did. Despite these differences, however, it is possible to identify some general contrasts between Japanese and American assembly plants circa 1975.

Whereas an American auto company typically made only one model on each line, several models were produced simultaneously on a Japanese line, which had fewer work stations, with more tasks performed at each of them. There were smaller buffer inventories between machines, so less capital was tied up in parts. Indeed, parts were usually delivered "just in time" from suppliers, who paid wages one-third less than those of the Japanese automobile manufacturers; in the US, the differential between wages paid by manufacturers and by their suppliers was only 11 percent.[22] Yet such wage differences cannot explain the Japanese workers' higher productivity. Nor did the speed of the assembly line explain it. In fact, Japanese workers were expected to halt the line (and that was easy for them to do) if they needed to correct mistakes or if they needed to stop incomplete vehicles from proceeding to the next work station. Especially at Toyota, the speed of the line was subordinated to quality in order to reduce waste and rework. Japanese workers were treated less as individuals reporting to a foreman than as members of a team, responsible for both assembly and quality control. Most important, Japanese work systems were constantly upgraded, often on the basis of workers' suggestions.

As analysts began to comprehend these differences, some saw Japanese industry as a monolith, with one dominant system. Moreover, they argued that Japanese methods were largely non-transferable, because Japanese culture was fundamentally different from Western culture. On this view, Japan had industrialized so rapidly that it retained a neo-feudal system of fealty in which workers and employers forged a bond reminiscent of that between lord and peasant. Middle-class values hadn't taken root. Ethnic and cultural homogeneity, reinforced by religious values, created a strong group orientation, in striking contrast to American individualism. Japanese workers identified strongly with their employers, preferred working in teams, embraced quality control, and had low absenteeism.[23] To the extent that this view was correct, Japanese productivity systems wouldn't be transferable to culturally heterogeneous, individualistic nations with strong labor unions, such as the United States. Such conceptions of Japan, which were hardly original, found new adherents in the early 1980s. Some of these ideas could be found in Ruth Benedict's 1946 book *The Chrysanthemum and the Sword*, which depicted Japan as a homogeneous society averse to individualism.[24]

In contrast, other Western analysts thought that Japanese productivity gains were based on techniques that could be transferred. During the 1980s, the Japanese settled that question by establishing factories in the United States that successfully used their production methods. Many American companies outside the automobile industry also adopted Japanese methods. To some extent they were rediscovering earlier American practices, such as eliciting suggestions from employees. Another old practice that was recovered was tighter inventory control. In the period 1913–1930, Ford managers focused intently on reducing the amount of money that was tied up in parts inventories. Their successors paid less attention, and eventually there was considerable needless duplication. For example, General Motors once discovered that the cost of stocking both blue and black shock absorbers (whose color customers could only see if they crawled under a car) was $1 million per year. On a larger scale, GM's separate divisions were often more rivals who duplicated one another than collaborators who shared costs and learned from each other.[25]

Japan's creation of more flexible and more productive forms of the assembly line is a complicated story whose beginnings can be traced to before World War II, though most of the new practices stem from the 1950s and after. At Toyota, what later became known as "lean production" emerged from situational pressures and borrowings from other nations, including the United States. Takahiro Fujimoto later concluded that the Japanese manufacturers "did not set out to create new kinds of production systems. Rather, their systems emerged from piecemeal, ad hoc measures for addressing needs and issues that arose in their business and operations. The Japanese had no idea—in any systemic, big-picture sense—what they were doing."[26] In particular, "the Toyota-style system was not developed all at once by one-time strategic decision making, but evolved" over several decades.[27] Likewise, at Ford between 1908 and 1913, the focus had been on solving particular bottlenecks and problems, without any grand vision of a new production system.

In the 1930s, Japanese companies were well aware of American mass production. American auto companies, particularly Ford, then dominated the small Japanese auto market, and Fords sold in Japan were assembled from parts shipped in from the United States. Ford planned to build a factory that would produce parts in Japan, but in 1936 the Japanese government imposed a protectionist policy that shut down American production in Japan.[28] Domestic companies grew to meet the demand. Notably, Nissan sought to replicate American mass production.[29] Some innovations emerged within Japanese corporations. The tight orchestration of supply chains that later would be called just-in-time production was already being tried out in the 1930s. The Japanese also adopted some German manufacturing practices. For example, during World War II some Japanese aircraft companies adopted the German *takt* system—the practice of organizing work stations in sequence, then allocating a precise time for each station to complete its assembly tasks. When that time had expired, "the noisy plant suddenly turned quiet" and "workers pushed their section of fuselage forward to the next position. Next, the rising-sun flag was hoisted, and all the workers came together in the center of plant and lined up" before returning to work.[30] Moving together according to *takt* time (without the flag raising) would later be embedded in the lean system.

Japan had long been receptive to foreign ideas and techniques. For example, NEC was founded in 1899 as a joint venture with the American firm Western Electric. After an earthquake destroyed NEC's factories, in the early 1930s, NEC built a near-replica of Western Electric's Hawthorne plant. NEC also learned of experiments conducted by sociologists at Hawthorne (near Chicago) that suggested the importance of involving workers in production.[31] The sociologists had told workers that they were taking part in a study, then had done little more to change the work conditions than adjust the levels of lighting. The goal of the study had been to discover the optimal level of factory lighting, but productivity unexpectedly seemed to rise in response to the tests themselves. Even in semi-darkness productivity was higher than normal. The crews seemed to become more involved with their work because management was taking an interest in them.[32]

After NEC and other Japanese corporations recovered from World War II, they continued to learn from American sources. A small group of engineers and scientists read the literature on statistical quality control, which had been used in US defense industries. During 1948 and 1949, visitors from the Bell Telephone Laboratories held seminars for the Japanese Union of Science and Engineering (JUSE), providing practical examples of the utility of statistical control methods. In 1950, 1951, and 1952, JUSE invited the consultant W. Edwards Deming to explain how statistical control had improved American war production by enabling managers to identify problems as either systemic (i.e., requiring changes in the system) or personal (i.e., poor work habits or lack of expertise among particular workers). Once a company could make the distinction between system problems and personal ones, it could reduce the incidence of defective products from 15–20 percent to less than 5 percent. Statistical control led to large savings and to worker satisfaction. Deming also showed that reliable suppliers were valuable, even if their prices were higher than those of less reliable suppliers. If the materials supplied were uneven in quality, some of the parts made from them would be flawed, incurring replacement costs larger than any "savings" achieved by purchasing cheaper materials.[33] Deming mapped the whole system of production and consumption, and emphasized that the consumer was the most important part of that map. While the Japanese made good use of statistical control methods, most American corporations lost interest in them.[34]

Deming, an inspiring teacher, was willing to lecture almost every day, and he missed no opportunity to praise his Japanese hosts.[35] He worked essentially for free, donating his modest fees to JUSE. A few Japanese specialists already knew much of what Deming had to say, but he was a good teacher who spread the message to a large audience.

Between 1950 and 1970, JUSE organized intensive courses for more than 14,000 engineers, and the use of statistical methods became common in major Japanese companies.[36] Practical results soon demonstrated the value of the JUSE-organized courses. In 1951 a cable and wire company reduced the costs of rework to remove defects by 90 percent. A steel producer reduced the amount of fuel needed to produce a ton of steel by 29 percent. A pharmaceutical company was astounded to find that it could increase production by 300 percent while using the same machines, manpower, and materials.[37]

Such achievements made Japanese companies eager to learn more. Often they had the chance to do so through personal observation. Between 1955 and 1965, the Japan Productivity Council sent 6,600 people to the United States on "productivity missions." After returning to Japan, they gave lectures on their findings and wrote reports that eventually filled 40,000 pages in more than 165 volumes.[38]

Some practices later considered indigenous to Japan actually were based on American observations. For example, in 1950 two Toyota executives got the germ of the idea of getting continual input from workers from an employee suggestion system they saw in use at Ford's River Rouge plant.[39] Toyota reworked the practice, made it integral to their system of work teams, and three decades later re-exported it to the United States. Other Japanese businessmen observed that Hotpoint made several different models of refrigerators on a single line, and decided to try making several different models on one automotive assembly line.[40] A generation later this practice too was re-exported to the US. The pupil had become the teacher. NEC, which once learned from the US, was so far ahead of its US counterparts by 1986 that the telecommunications firm AT&T sent a team of managers to Japan to learn from NEC.[41]

The Japanese business community continued to learn from other outside experts after W. Edwards Deming's early visits. A General Electric consultant, Armand Feigenbaum, coined the phrase "total quality control" as early as 1957.[42] Though his approach was more bureaucratic than the approach the Japanese would eventually embrace, the phrase itself became part of the definition of lean production. More influential than Feigenbaum was Joseph Juran, who first traveled to Japan in 1954 to teach courses to engineers and to serve as a consultant to several companies. Juran's approach was less statistical and more pragmatic than Deming's.[43] He argued that quality control should become part of every employee's way of working and thinking. His approach harmonized with Japanese developments that shifted the focus of reform away from managers to workers on the factory floor. Process innovations often came about through an extended dialogue with workers; they became deeply involved in the synthesis that eventually came to be called "Total Quality Control." This "was not a simple knock-off of American managerial advances," but an adaptation of "American quality control methodologies to the specific context of postwar Japanese industry."[44]

Improving quality control became so important that it had its own Japanese society, with a journal and annual meetings. In 1951 JUSE created an annual Deming Prize. At first given only to Japanese firms, it evolved into a prestigious international award. However piously they honored Deming, however, the Japanese automotive and electronic firms didn't merely copy his ideas; they went beyond them. The Japanese engineers and managers learned from one another at regular meetings,[45] and they surpassed their American competition during the 1960s, although few realized it at the time.

The Japanese automobile industry combined American practices with home-gown innovations. In 1950 it was quite small, producing only 67,000 cars, half of them small three-wheelers.[46] But by 1961 it was producing more than a million cars a year. This rapid growth was reminiscent of the American auto industry between 1905 and 1920, when an enormous increase in demand stimulated production innovations. But Japan lacked capital, and thus couldn't invest heavily in machinery, and its market was smaller and more differentiated. Those conditions put a premium on labor-intensive innovation that was flexible and could produce a variety of models. The then-tiny Toyota Motor Corporation responded well to this challenge, creating a new system of production that was well suited to the prevailing conditions.

At Toyota, important changes began during World War II at a truck factory where Taiichi Ohno was a manager. Ohno had learned from his previous job in the spinning industry that a factory's layout should focus on the product (not mirror administrative divisions), should emphasize small-lot production, and should try to do each job right the first time so as to minimize rework. After 1945, Ohno focused on how to improve the use of Toyota's existing equipment and factory space. With no grand design, through trial and error, he found that incremental changes in layout, inventory, and materials handling improved efficiency quite significantly. At first his factory followed the American practice of pushing production and demanding that the sales force find a way to sell whatever was produced. In 1948–49, however, overproduction created a large inventory of unsold trucks that almost bankrupted the company. After that mistake, Toyota further developed just-in-time production, minimized inventories, and began to build vehicles in response to the "pull" exerted by actual orders. These changes brought with them a profound rethinking of how to organize an assembly-line factory. Rather than emphasize speed of throughput, as American companies did, Toyota began to emphasize minimizing error. Ohno introduced the *kanban* system, in which cards of various colors were used to indicate assembly sequences and to keep track of inventory. Kanban, he told his workers, "is like money: if you take out parts without *kanban*, you are stealing the parts."[47] If the workers didn't not use the cards, then management lost track of the parts.

At the same time, Toyota adopted some practices from Ford. Toyota's chairman, Eoiji Toyoda, and an executive named Shoichi Saito visited the River Rouge plant in 1950 in the course of a three-month industrial tour of the United States. The handling of parts and materials at River Rouge particularly impressed them. After their return to Japan, they introduced many more conveyor belts to the Toyota factory and brought in electric fork-lift trucks to move pallets around.[48] During the 1950s, Toyota kept innovating by selectively adopting ideas from Detroit and integrating them with its own innovations. "In short," Takahiro Fujimoto writes, "Toyota's production organization—during the prewar and early postwar era in particular—adopted various elements of the Ford system selectively and in unbundled forms, and hybridized them with their indigenous system and original ideas. There is an obvious continuity between the two systems."[49]

Surprisingly, a formal emphasis on quality control came later to the automobile producers than to much of Japanese industry. Nissan was the first to embrace it, winning the Deming Prize in 1960.[50] Toyota didn't relish falling behind Nissan or being criticized for inadequate quality. In an unusual top-down decision, it quickly adopted and enforced quality control,[51] which also helped it to achieve goals it already had set forth: to cut down rework, to reduce waste, to increase customer satisfaction, and to minimize the high expense of recalls. Toyota won the Deming Prize in 1965 and began transferring its system to suppliers in the late 1960s. By the early 1970s the Toyota system was fully developed, though refinements continued.[52] "Production of a limited range of products in large volumes gave way. . . to producing a large range of products in generally small volumes. That meant a shift in emphasis from maximizing equipment capacity and utilization rates to maximizing flexibility in responding nimbly to trends in demand."[53]

In contrast, a Detroit factory often produced a single vehicle, using machines that couldn't easily be redeployed to make anything else. In the late 1980s, General Motors made a colossal error of this type. Its executives decided to build three single-model plants—one in Georgia for the Oldsmobile Cutlass Supreme, one in Kansas for the Pontiac Grand Prix, and one in Oshawa, Ontario for the Chevrolet Lumina. However, the cars didn't sell well, and "one plant would have sufficed for the Cutlass Supreme and the Grand Prix."[54] But neither the Georgia plant nor the one in Kansas could be retooled quickly or cheaply. It was "virtually impossible to change course." GM had needlessly spent hundreds of millions of dollars to build and operate an unnecessary factory. No such error could have occurred at Toyota, where every line could transfer production from one vehicle to another. "Factories shifted to processing in increasingly smaller lots. People found ways to shorten changeover times and streamline layouts."[55]

When Taiichi Ohno of Toyota visited Detroit for the first time, in the 1950s, he could see that American production was efficient because of economies of scale and the extensive use of machinery. But Ohno also sensed that American companies had forgotten that a technological system includes both the machines and the knowledge and skills of the workers. He believed that productivity increases could be achieved by maximizing workers' contributions rather reducing the workers to automatons who did only what they were told. As Ohno later put it, Toyota went from "single-skilled to multi-skilled workers." He asked: "Which is better, the American system, where a lathe operator is only a lathe operator and a welder must only be a welder, or the Japanese system, where a worker can operate a lathe, a milling machine, a drill-press, and welding equipment, in short command a wide variety of skills?"[56] Multi-skilled workers were more satisfied, and flexible teams of workers could integrate quality inspection into assembly-line work, rather than treating it as a separate and time-consuming step. Process inventories also shrank. When one person used three different machines to fashion a part, no buffer inventories were needed between machines. Smaller inventories also meant that defective parts were discovered sooner. Under the older "push" system of manufacture, "parts may have been entered into the production chain days or weeks before their actual use. This means that if a problem is discovered at the point of use, several days' worth of parts must be discarded."[57] In a lean system, few defective parts can accumulate in the pipeline, because, in effect, that pipeline is very short. That is why Japanese auto companies wanted their suppliers to adopt lean production. Ford grasped this before General Motors, and sent some of its American suppliers to Japan to observe Mazda's suppliers and learn from them.[58] The lean system is not just a change at one factory but a new way of doing business between companies.

Another valuable aspect of "lean production" was the trust created between management and labor. In the 1950s, Toyota experienced ongoing labor unrest and occasional strikes. The company therefore created affinity groups based on hobbies, sports, workers' regional origins, and the like. More important, it organized workers into teams, gave them more responsibility, improved their job security, and built stronger bonds between workers and management. Many a man worked for and identified with Toyota for his entire career. Workers nearing retirement seldom were fired, but some were asked to work part-time. Their hours fluctuated more than those of younger workers who were starting families and buying their first homes. Because Toyota's workers had security within a strong corporate culture, they were relatively loyal and productive. American auto workers, by contrast, relied on their union for job security. Confrontations with management were frequent, and mutual loyalty between employers and workers was rare.

Not all Japanese workers enjoyed such a protective corporate culture as Toyota's. Smaller companies, which employed more than 70 percent of all Japanese auto-industry workers even as late as 1990, paid lower wages and offered fewer benefits. The fragmented Japanese unions were in a weak position to negotiate with the thousands of parts makers, who paid less than the large automobile companies. Furthermore, in the 1960s women's salaries were, on average, only half those of men,[59] and girls between 15 and 20 made even less than mature women.[60] American union officials and managers believed that low wages gave Japanese auto companies an unfair competitive advantage and were largely unaware of the Japanese automakers' development of more efficient production systems.

Toyota put worker teams into friendly competition, and they strove for "*kaizen* assembly," meaning continuous improvement through employee participation in a process-oriented corporate culture.[61] Japanese workers suggested how machines might be better arranged, waste movements eliminated, inventories reduced, bottlenecks avoided, and defects discovered. At a *kaizen*-based factory, it is assumed that everyone occasionally has ideas for improvements, and suggestions are solicited from workers in regularly scheduled meetings. No suggestion is considered too small, as lean production emerges from a myriad small improvements that collectively become quite significant.

Kaizen manufacturing uses, for the most part, existing employees and equipment rather than requiring huge investments in new machines. For example, a machinery builder in South Carolina brought in a consultant who worked with the employees to redesign its production line. They spent just $10,000 to reorganize and the changes raised productivity 31 percent. Throughput declined from 8 hours to only 2 hours, with fewer partially completed products in process on the line. Over decades the older line had accumulated many benches, racks, and tools that, though no longer needed, still cluttered the work area. When these were removed and the work process was redesigned, instead of fifteen work stations there were only six.[62] The redesigned assembly line took up only half as much space. This transformation was achieved in little more than a month, with the help of one outside consultant. It relied primarily on employees both for ideas and for implementation. After this successful conversion, the corporation continued to develop a lean work culture, as it redesigned three additional assembly lines.

By the 1970s, Japanese corporations had achieved dramatic gains in productivity, inventory control, and product quality. They had abandoned hierarchical communication down a chain of command in favor of dialogue.[63] They assiduously encouraged workers to make suggestions, and workers' suggestions then became the basis for innovation. Institutionalizing dialogue between workers, managers, engineers, designers, and marketers improved quality, efficiency, and safety. The new system also encouraged continuous learning on the job. What came to be called lean production emerged from, and ideally should remain, an ongoing process rather than a fixed system.

A lean company also increased the communication between managers, salesmen, designers, engineers, and suppliers. Japanese manufacturers discovered the economic advantages of putting production engineers on teams designing new models with the goals of reducing the number of parts and of making them easier to assemble. McKinsey and Company estimated that "design for manufacturing and other upstream arrangements that were facilitated by better internal communications determine 70 to 80 percent of manufacturing efficiency, cost, and productivity." For example, in 1989 Ford reduced the number of parts in the front bumper of its Taurus model from more than 65 to 10. In contrast, the bumper of GM's Pontiac Grand Prix had 100 parts. An internal GM study attributed 41 percent of the higher cost of making the Grand Prix to poor design.[64]

Japanese companies institutionalized the exchange of ideas that once had led Ford's employees to invent the assembly line in a burst of creativity that began around 1908 and lasted about 15 years. When Ford was small, it had a culture of innovation. Workers, foremen, and managers continually discussed how to improve production. Anticipating recent trends, Ford also focused on preventing waste of motion, waste of materials, and accumulation of unnecessarily large inventories. The company had lost this innovatory thrust by the 1930s. The assembly line gradually became more rigid, corporations were run from the top down, and the growing distance between management and the workers inhibited the sharing of ideas.

In contrast, Japanese companies saw that their most valuable resource was the collective talent of their employees. A few American firms had made similar discoveries. Notably, in 1929 the Marmon Motor Car Company demonstrated that it was possible to manufacture three models on the same assembly line.[65] But Marmon was a small company that disappeared. Toyota independently discovered that alternating models on the same line could "smooth" the flow of production. When just one model was being made, as on a classic Ford assembly line, some tasks always took a bit longer than others, and the idle or unused time at particular work stations couldn't be recovered. In the Toyota system, production engineers alternated the models coming along the line, providing not only more varied work but also a pattern of tasks that evened out demands on each worker. This reduced the wasting of time to a surprising extent.[66]

Some American companies also discovered the economic value of greater employee participation. In the 1960s, a small Michigan corporation producing mirrors removed its time clocks and put all employees on salary, with bonuses for everyone at the end of the year if business went well. After giving workers increased autonomy, more respect, and an economic stake in the bottom line, the company was able to lower prices, increase profits, and give a yearly bonus. When its workers asked for a raise in 1970, they found ways to pay for that raise by reducing purchasing costs, improving the system of production, and eliminating waste.[67] However, the large American automobile corporations learned little from such successes.

The Japanese auto companies made their innovations available to competitors, just as the Ford Motor Company had done in 1913. They opened factories to visitors and published articles about their methods. Japanese practices were copied in many parts of the world, but matching their quality and productivity often proved difficult. Technical systems are not only machines but also social constructions. Imitators often copied only the most visible aspects without making a change in corporate culture. Japanese firms also engaged in joint ventures. Mazda partnered with Ford in 1979, which allowed them to share some tasks. This relationship gave Ford a better understanding of Japanese manufacturing methods, while Mazda gained more expertise in styling and design. Toyota and General Motors made a similar arrangement, partnering under the name New United Motor Manufacturing, Inc. (NUMMI), with a factory that made small cars in California. NUMMI broke with American practices in many ways, emphasizing teamwork, guaranteeing workers that there would be no layoffs in exchange for other concessions, and applying principles of lean production to all aspects of the manufacturing system. As a result, the time needed to produce a car was reduced dramatically. Comparisons between the NUMMI plant and two GM plants showed that assembly time fell by 10 hours per vehicle, to just 19.6 hours. That made NUMMI nearly as fast as a Japanese plant in Takaoka, which did the same work in 18 hours. Moreover, the defects per 100 vehicles fell by 20 percent.[68]

At NUMMI, Toyota made a point of rotating in new Japanese managers every few months so they would learn how to work in a US factory environment and would be well prepared for the day when Toyota would open American factories. In contrast, relatively few GM managers were rotated through NUMMI, which limited the number who learned lean production firsthand,[69] and those who did spend time at NUMMI weren't kept together afterward, nor were they given a chance to apply principles of lean production in a GM factory. Dispersed as consultants throughout the company, they had only a diffuse effect.[70]

Japanese companies had learned from partnerships with foreign firms from the 1960s on, and they used this knowledge as they expanded overseas. As Ford had done between 1910 and 1920, the Japanese first established foreign factories that assembled parts sent from home. By the 1980s, Mitsubishi was manufacturing in Taiwan, Korea, Malaysia, Indonesia, Thailand, and New Zealand. It had the advantage of being part of a large conglomerate with long-established ties in many markets. Nissan also expanded vigorously, notably in Taiwan, in Thailand, and in Mexico (where by the mid 1980s it had become the largest producer of cars, with 29 percent of the market). Toyota was more reluctant to build complete manufacturing plants abroad, but had many plants that assembled knocked-down vehicles, including seventeen plants assembling trucks in Africa and in Latin America. By 1990, Toyota had only two complete automobile factories in Asia other than Japan, one in Indonesia and the other in Thailand. Most of its overseas plants were in English-speaking countries: Canada, New Zealand, Australia, Britain, and the United States.[71]

Japanese automakers had extensive experience with transferring their technology abroad before 1981, when the US government pressured them to negotiate "voluntary" import quotas. The US government was seeking to protect Detroit's manufacturers from foreign competition, but the quotas didn't apply to Japanese cars made in the United States. From a "lean" perspective, locating assembly plants abroad near consumers made economic sense whether there were quotas or not. Shortening the supply chain was a fundamental concept of lean production.

In 1982 Honda opened its first US plant, in the small town of Marysville in central Ohio, to make the Accord. In 2009 that factory employed 4,400, built Accords and Acuras, and had the capacity to produce 440,000 cars a year. In 1985 Honda began to produce engines in nearby Anna, Ohio; four years later it added another Ohio plant in East Liberty. Toyota was close behind. By 1992 Japanese plants inside the US were capable of building 2,380,000 vehicles a year and employed 30,800 people.[72] The factories were south of Michigan's traditional auto-manufacturing sites but still near enough to suppliers to make just-in-time delivery possible.[73] Whereas a GM plant or a Ford plant typically had more than ninety different job classifications, a Honda plant in the US had only three or four. Workers rotated frequently, not only to avoid boredom and muscular injury from repetition of one task, but also to ensure that each could do several jobs.

In the 1986 Hollywood comedy *Gung Ho*, a Japanese auto company purchases and reopens a factory in a Midwestern town.[74] The Japanese pay a lower wage than US workers are used to, they don't offer a union contract, and they demand more regimentation and a higher output. The workers accept this situation only because there are no other jobs. Yet because the American factory isn't as productive as its counterparts in Japan, the management threatens to shut it down. In response, the workers increase production, determined to match the Japanese level. Though they still fall slightly short of the target of 15,000 cars a month, the Japanese management is impressed by the improvement and the team spirit. The factory stays open, and wages are increased. In this fantasy, in less than a year Americans learn a new work discipline and Japanese learn to loosen up. Future harmony seems assured.

Despite what *Gung Ho* suggested, Japanese practices weren't rapidly adopted in the United States. A 1989 study of 34 "Japanese transplants" looked at 24 different work and management practices. A rating of 5 indicated complete adoption of Japanese norms; a score of 1 indicated complete retention of American practices. In certain areas, notably adoption of Japanese process technology and job rotation, 75 percent of the plants achieved high scores. But in other areas, the scores were far lower: maintenance (2.6), quality control (3.2), small-group activity (2.8), and the wage system (3.0). The average was 3.6, and it seemed that "any advancement in the real transfer of the Japanese system" would be "difficult."[75] These results were reminiscent of problems Ford had in the 1920s and the 1930s when it brought the assembly line to various European nations. In each case, the problems of transfer were less technical than cultural. Just as in the 1920s Ford found it necessary to staff foreign operations with some American engineers and supervisors, in the 1980s Japanese managers played a crucial role in transferring their production systems to the United States. Tetsuo Abo found that Japanese supervisors were "the key human element," emphasizing that lower and middle-level Japanese managers "take charge of almost all practices, particularly at the shop-floor level," and were perhaps more important in making transfer successful than top managers.[76] Nevertheless, they found it impossible to make quality control as central as it was in Japan, where all workers were actively engaged in it. Quality control remained voluntary in most Japanese firms' US factories, and only 20–30 percent of their American workers participated. Other Japanese practices were modified or simplified for the American context. The overall result was more productive factories, but they were still 10–20 percent less efficient than those in Japan.[77] The transfer was by no means complete, even with close supervision.

The American automobile manufacturers' slow response to the challenge of more efficient Japanese production methods is typical of established industries confronting a major innovation.[78] Analysis has shown that firms fight back in two ways.[79] First, a company further improves its existing production technology. The old methods reach their highest levels of efficiency as they are becoming obsolete. Second, when it becomes clear that a new system (such as lean production) outperforms the old, companies begin to adopt it, often piecemeal. Sometimes a company tries to pursue both strategies, as General Motors did in the 1980s. GM continued traditional assembly-line production with greater determination. It realized that after the parsimonious 1970s American consumers wanted larger cars and also wanted trucks (which were exempt from fuel-efficiency standards Congress had mandated). They used traditional assembly lines to produce such vehicles. In effect, they ceded part of the "family car" segment of the market to the Japanese. Hence a second strategy was also needed.

General Motors entered into the already-mentioned partnership with Toyota. The NUMMI plant in California proved 40 percent more efficient than GM's other plants, including a few where enormous sums had been invested in automation. As a result, "GM cancelled many automation projects—saving billions of dollars" and focused more on lean management.[80] GM's president, Roger Smith, decided that, in addition to gas-guzzling large cars, GM would use the Japanese approach to make a new small car, the Saturn. Instead of complex work rules and myriad job classifications, he negotiated a contract with the United Auto Workers that applied only to the new Saturn plant in Tennessee. There would be only a few job classifications, and workers would be trained to perform multiple tasks. Pay would not be based simply on hours worked, but would be linked to productivity and sales, so workers would have a stake in Saturn's future. Decisions would no longer be dictated from above; they would now emerge from discussions with workers. In short, GM tried to learn the new manufacturing system by establishing a single Japanese-style factory. At first, this strategy seemed to work, not least because in 1985 the public seemed to love the new Saturn cars.

Yet the Saturn Division ultimately proved a failure. It was a victim of corporate infighting, of management betrayal (no new models were developed for most of the 1990s), of union backsliding to old rules and work classifications, and of consumers' demand for larger cars. GM's attempt to support two radically different production systems was a recipe for internal conflict. The fate of the Saturn Division illustrates how difficult it is to change. GM had entered "a final state from which only a radical departure in product or process can liberate it."[81] Process innovation had largely been replaced by "overwhelming standardization and uniformity among producers."[82]

Ford did better. It bought a stake in Mazda in order to learn that company's production system, and it brought in W. Edwards Deming as a consultant. Deming's ideas had hardly remained static since the 1950s. He surprised the Ford executives by focusing less on statistical methods than they had expected. He presented a fourteen-point system that "tied together disparate process-oriented management ideas into a single, holistic vision of how companies can anticipate and meet the desires of the customer." He began with the consumer, then moved on to design and production, comprehending the whole as a single process that had to enlist "every employee, division, and supplier in the improvement effort."[83] Unlike General Motors, Ford didn't ask only a single part of the company to embody the change. It took a gradualist approach that pushed the entire corporation toward lean production. The consulting firm McKinsey & Company later praised Ford for its "holistic learning approach from the beginning, attempting to develop expertise in a wide range of production processes, including just-in-time inventory control, design for manufacturing, total quality management, and supplier management."[84]

Between 1979 and 1989 Ford reduced its vehicle-assembly time to 28 hours, and 75 percent of the improvement was attributable to process innovations. By comparison, to assemble a car in 1989 Chrysler and General Motors needed 42 and 43 hours, respectively—as many hours as Ford had needed in 1979. But in the late 1980s a GM factory in New Jersey adopted elements of lean production and eliminated one-third of the production workers and 42 percent of the foremen and supervisors.[85] Robots and computer-driven machines took over some of the routine work. The demand for skilled workers more than doubled, and they now made up 12 percent of the workforce. Line workers were organized into teams. Their jobs became less monotonous, although the increased tempo was stressful. The transition wasn't easy. Workers who tried to ensure quality control often ran afoul of management's demand for maximum output.[86] Managers resisted when workers stopped the assembly line (as they were supposed to do) in order to fix a problem. "It took Chrysler until 1992 and GM until 1997 to bring down assembly hours per vehicle to" the level Ford had achieved eight years before.[87] Moreover, as late as 2002 none of the American manufacturers matched the productivity of the "Japanese transplants."

Detroit's automakers had taken a generation to respond to lean production. Yet they had been warned that they would have to respond to it. A US Department of Transportation study conducted in the early 1980s showed that Detroit's factories spent between $1,000 and $2,000 more to build each car than Japanese factories did. Other industries learned more quickly. In the late 1980s a *New York Times* survey of 1,000 companies found that two-thirds were in the process of adopting just-in-time production. Dell Computers developed a system by which a customer selected the exact specifications of a computer and Dell then built and shipped the computer within five days.[88] However, many American employers wanted to keep or even to increase top-down control while somehow tapping into workers' creativity. This often meant "massive investments in advanced manufacturing technologies sugar-coated with some superficial application of Japanese production principles such as 'group work' and 'just-in-time' supply features."[89] It proved difficult to pick and choose certain practices used in Japanese factories without understanding the synergies of their systems. Even with a clear understanding of Japanese methods, copying Toyota or Honda also required a new corporate culture that redefined relationships between workers and management.

When an American corporation wanted to change its corporate culture, it often had to confront anti-Japanese feelings. Many Americans felt they were losing an economic war with Japan, which in the mid 1980s had a $50 billion annual trade surplus with the United States. Japanese investors bought Rockefeller Center, Columbia Records, and other prominent American companies and landmarks. A *Wall Street Journal* headline warned "Yellow Peril Reinfects America: U.S. Hostility Turns to Japan." Both Republican and Democratic politicians declaimed against Japan. "We've been running up the white flag, when we should be running up the American flag," Walter Mondale said in 1982. "What do we want our kids to do? Sweep up around Japanese computers?"[90] California's governor, Jerry Brown, complained: "'We are forming a type of colonial relationship with Japan. We ship her raw materials, she ships us finished goods."[91] The hostility wasn't merely rhetorical. The US Department of Justice reported that "incidents of violence against Asians jumped 62 percent between 1985 and 1986, accounting for 50 percent of all racial incidents in Los Angeles and 29 percent in Boston."[92] As "bashing" of Japan spread through popular culture, an American auto worker thought twice before buying a Toyota or a Honda, much less parking it outside a Ford or a GM plant. Indeed, signs went up outside some factories declaring that no Japanese cars were allowed there. In Michael Crichton's best-selling novel *Rising Sun* the hero declares "We are definitely at war with Japan."[93] With such sentiments widespread, to some people adopting Japanese manufacturing practices seemed like surrender.

Poor labor relations also obstructed rapid adoption of new production methods. Ben Hamper's *Rivethead*, a memoir of working for General Motors in Flint, Michigan, explains why.[94] The book seethes with loathing for assembly-line work and contempt for management. Could such workers easily be converted to a cooperative pursuit of total quality? Hamper was writing during the 1980s, when Japanese companies markedly increased their share of American sales. Yet from the workers' perspective, the lean system scarcely existed, though awareness of Japanese competition certainly did. In *Rivethead* the Japanese are primarily glimpsed in the peripheral vision

FIGURE 8.2

In 1981, the UAW local at a Ford stamping plant bought a 1974 Toyota and smashed it to pieces with sledge hammers. Courtesy of Associated Press.

of beer-drinking buddies grousing in a bar. Yet *Rivethead* displays American workers' ingenuity. In a succession of assembly-line jobs, Hamper learned to perform his tasks so efficiently that huge amounts of time opened up. In most cases he was able to "double up" with a fellow worker, so that only one of them was actually on the job at any moment. Hamper wasn't unusual. American workers found ways to save time, just as Japanese workers did. But their discoveries didn't lead to more efficient overall production. American workers became more efficient in order to create personal time off. The car manufacturers weren't harnessing their creativity. The informal teamwork that employees used to multi-task and "double up" could have been the basis for a different and far more efficient system. US companies could have used workers' ingenuity to create a homegrown version of lean production.

When in 1989 MIT's International Motor Vehicle Program examined more than fifty automobile plants in all parts of the world, the surprise wasn't that the Japanese plants in general were more efficient, but that efficient plants could be found in so many places. A few US factories (most of them Ford plants) needed only 19 man-hours to produce each vehicle, which was the Japanese average. "Japanese transplants" also proved efficient, averaging 19.5 hours per vehicle. In contrast, the best European automobile manufacturers (22.6 man-hours) were little better than the least efficient Japanese plants (24.2 man-hours). The slowest European factories needed 53 man-hours per vehicle.[95]

Lean production still worked best in Japan. Absenteeism there was half that in American plants. For every 123 worker suggestions the Japanese received, American and European factories got just one.[96] Japanese automakers had reduced defects to 60 per 100 vehicles, versus 82.3 per 100 for American factories. The "Japanese transplants" in North America came close to the Japanese level, with 65 defects per 100 vehicles; European manufacturers lagged, with 97. Nor was lean production averse to automation. Americans had invested heavily in robots and automation for four decades, but in 1989 Japanese companies used automation in welding and painting more than Americans or Europeans. Automation of the final assembly line was quite low, however, at 1.2 percent in North America and 1.7 percent in Japan. Europeans led in this category, at 3.1 percent, but overall they were the least efficient.

In 1990, a book titled *The Machine That Changed the World* summarized the Japanese productivity achievement and its transfer to other nations. The book also helped solidify "lean production" as the name for the system, primarily as developed at Toyota. Where fully introduced, the "lean" system outperformed older assembly lines. It used just half the space and half the investment in tools to produce a superior product, with less waste. The conclusion seemed unmistakable: lean production is "a superior way for humans to make things." Relative to the classic assembly line, "it provides more challenging and fulfilling work for employees at every level." Therefore, "it follows that the whole world should adopt lean production, and as quickly as possible."[97] However, Toyota wasn't the only story. Japanese industry had developed a range of production innovations. Other countries didn't simply "adopt lean production"; they created new hybrid forms. In *Beyond Mass Production* (1993) Martin Kenney and Richard Florida were likewise certain that the productivity gains of lean production gave early adopters a decisive competitive advantage.[98] But they were less sanguine about its benefits, concluding that in practice lean production often was accompanied by stress and by higher rates of injury. Moreover, the "Japanese transplants" weren't unionized, and they paid lower wages than UAW plants.

During the 1990s, the lean system became the new standard. In Austin, Texas, Dell assembled computers from screens made in Tijuana and components brought in from Taiwan, Korea, Malaysia, and China.[99] With only a four-day supply of parts, Dell relied on just-in-time deliveries. Rather than churn out computers and hope to find buyers, it responded to the pull of customers' orders. Dell was hardly alone. From 1993 to 1995 *Industry Week* examined hundreds of American manufacturers and annually awarded prizes to the 45 companies that were the best operated. These 45 produced a wide range of goods, including vacuum valves, ice cream, forceps, engines, sanitary napkins, computer work stations, single-use cameras, radial tires, air-conditioning compressors, anti-lock braking systems, ethylene, yogurt, and vinyl ceiling panels.[100] All but one of them had adopted a *kaizen* approach to continuous improvement. All of the best plants had adopted cross training of production workers. All had accelerated product development cycles, by an average of 46 percent. All of their design teams focused on creating products that were easier to manufacture, and 96 percent had adopted just-in-time production.[101] All the plants had employee problem-solving teams, all had operators inspect their own work, and 88 percent had self-directed work teams who made the day-to-day decisions. Most involved their suppliers early when making changes, and all involved workers in manufacturing-process development. Their productivity had increased an average of 59 percent. Moreover, employee satisfaction was evident, as these 45 award-winning factories had a median annual job turnover of just 2.5 percent a year.[102]

Yet if other American firms became more profitable through lean production, the automobile industry had difficulty making the full transition. Just as 1920s Europeans had many different responses to Ford's original system, automobile manufacturers who tried lean production had uneven results. In 1995 the International Motor Vehicle Program at MIT compared 88 auto assembly plants in Japan, the United States, Germany, the United Kingdom, Canada, Italy, France, Spain, Australia, South Africa, Korea, and Brazil.[103] The lean system was spreading at different speeds. In all parts of the world the plants that had most completely achieved the lean system were Japanese-owned. These companies scored high on their involvement of workers. They created few status differentials, organized production teams, rotated jobs often, established groups to solve problems, emphasized suggestion programs, got feedback, and sent workers to training programs. A second group, in Europe and in regions new to automobile manufacturing, had adopted lean production rapidly. In Germany, for example, unions had accepted elements of lean production in exchange for greater job security. Constructive dialogue existed between workers and management. The "leanest" company was Opel, a GM subsidiary. A third group consisted of firms that had adopted only some aspects of lean production. Fiat, Renault, and Seat had eliminated much of the management hierarchy and organized work teams, but they retained considerable top-down control by engineers and supervisors. The fourth group, in North America, remained closest to traditional mass production. Those firms had the fewest workers organized into teams—only 23 percent in the United States and just 4 percent in Canada, versus 70–80 percent in Japan and Europe. A few factories had tried lean production briefly and had then reverted to old practices, in a classic example of path dependency. In short, the American auto industry resisted change more than the rest of the world and more than other American manufactures.

The Machine That Changed the World trumpeted a single "best way" to produce cars, but General Motors was particularly slow to act on the message, partly because its multiple-division structure obstructed change.[104] Each division had considerable autonomy, and some plants adopted lean principles more than others. The new Opel plant in Eisenach adopted lean thinking successfully from its opening in 1992. It spearheaded the GM's second push toward lean production, which included creation of a "global manufacturing system" in which all GM factories adopted "the same operating system with common principles and elements."[105] Representatives from GM plants in all parts of the world convened in Eisenach and laid the groundwork for this universal system, which neared parity with the Japanese in 1997.

Auto companies also found new ways to design their products. Design, like manufacturing, became networked and global. As late as the 1980s, a new car had gone through a slow-motion design process that took 5 years to move from idea to production. Designs and prototypes moved back and forth between departments of marketing, design, engineering, accounting, and manufacturing. Changes requested in one department had to be analyzed and approved by the others. The marketing department might insist that consumers wanted a more powerful motor, but would it fit under the hood and work with the cooling system as currently designed? The engineers might want a new braking system, but would it cost too much? A more sculpted design might look fabulous, but would it be difficult or expensive to manufacture? Lean design eliminated the jockeying between departments. Instead, a team of people was formed drawn from all departments that could settle such questions internally. This new design paradigm meant that too much outsourcing could create problems. A company needed in-house manufacturing expertise on design teams, whose efficiency typically saved an entire year in developing a new car.

During the 1990s the design process accelerated further as computers became more powerful and software improved. The design team for a new vehicle might not be in a single place, but rather in many locations linked through high-definition screens. Teams no longer made as many sketches or clay models; instead they often worked with three-dimensional holograms. Computer-aided design had evolved since the 1950s, making it possible to build a virtual prototype, with engineers evaluating the strength and testing the manufacturing feasibility of each element.[106] This work could be globally dispersed. At least in theory, designers in Europe could work for 8 hours before handing off their ideas to mechanical engineers in Detroit. At the end of their shift, they could then pass the virtual prototype along to production engineers in Asia. Work could continue around the clock. When each team came back to work the next morning, 16 hours of work would have been accomplished in the interim. Furthermore, as each part or component received final approval, production engineers could use the specifications to design the tools, jigs, and dies that would be needed. (Implementing parts production had previously been a time-consuming bottleneck at the beginning of the process of manufacturing a new model.) Production engineers also could discover and solve problems on a simulation of the next assembly line. The combined savings due to teamwork and computerization were prodigious; the time needed to move from initial design to manufactured product was cut from four or five years to two years or less. For less complex products, such as clothing, automated design cut down the product cycle even more, from a year to a few months. Furthermore, using bar codes to track sales provided rapid feedback, allowing manufacturers to respond to the pull of consumer demand rather than push new styles to retailers and hope they could be sold.

A wide range of industries adopted new forms of production in the 1990s, but there wasn't a universal "lean" system. Just as the classic Ford assembly line was transferred selectively during the 1920s and the 1930s and soon found itself in competition with both Sloan's General Motors system and with forms of what is now called flexible production, in the 1980s and the 1990s Japanese approaches to manufacturing were transformed when adapted to different contexts. The assembly line had become global, but it wasn't one hegemonic system. New manufacturing techniques were inflected by culture and adjusted to different market situations. The Toyota approach was preferred for standard, mass-market products that appealed to a large market. The Honda approach was more suited to adventuresome products aimed a niche markets or new constellations of consumers. Even the traditional assembly line, making a single product at the lowest possible price and automated where possible, could still be a logical choice for some products. By the 1990s, the assembly line had many forms, each revamped to fit local circumstances and to manufacture particular things.

The redesigned production lines often weren't located where the old factories had been. Not only were Japanese factories located well south of Detroit; the US automakers also shifted production to new places. These relocations left their mark on Detroit. Just after World War II, Detroit had 280,000 manufacturing jobs. By 2002, only 38,018 remained. The poet Philip Levine grew up there, attended Wayne State University, and worked several years in the automobile industry. In the early 1990s, the night before writing the poem "What Work Is," he had "seen a horrible program on Public Broadcasting . . . about two guys, a father and son, who killed a young Chinese man in Detroit. They thought he was Japanese, and they had this animosity toward him because they were blaming the Japanese for the decline in the auto industry or the decline in their jobs or whatever marginal relationship they had with the auto industry. And they beat the guy to death. And there was this immense anger in me."[107] Levine's outrage at this murder is not an explicit part of the poem, but the incident stirred up memories from his time in automobile factories. He knew what it was like to "stand in the rain in a long line / waiting at Ford Highland Park. For Work."[108] Eighty years after it had opened, Levine still could be confident that readers knew that Ford factory. For decades men and women had gone there searching for work. The poem is less about jobs inside the factory than about waiting outside. "What Work Is" is about demanding, often eviscerating work, and about the deferral of ambition into jobs that are detours from more meaningful activity. In a sense, it is a poem about his brother who

FIGURE 8.3
Unemployed people seeking work, River Rouge plant, Miller Road, Gate 4, 1978.
Courtesy of Walter Reuther Library, Wayne State University.

disliked his assembly line work and preferred to sing Wagnerian opera. It is about swallowing one's pride and persisting in unloved jobs, about standing patiently in the rain, hoping to get work that, while repetitive and numbing, still offered good wages and benefits. But such jobs were disappearing. Detroit was in decline.

Detroit's decline was not only the result of Japan's success. The US automotive industry had relocated many factories, and was producing more cars with fewer workers. Downtown Detroit slowly collapsed as the city's population fell from 1.5 million in 1970 to just over 700,000 in 2010. Halfway through this collapse, Hudson's, once Detroit's largest department store, closed. By 1993, "Detroit had 66,000 vacant lots, about forty square miles of the 137-square-mile city."[109] Despite the uptick in the national economy that occurred in the 1990s, the city continued to shrink. By 2010 there were 80,000 empty houses and apartments.[110] Revisiting his old neighborhood, Philip Levine found "miles of mostly vacant lots" where once there had been lively neighborhoods.[111] His old haunts and the very fabric of the city had disappeared. There were vegetable gardens on abandoned land. Detroit wasn't just lean, it was anorexic.

Paradoxically, Japan too had economic problems. Its success in exporting automobiles and electronics had pumped up the value of the yen and fostered a gigantic real-estate bubble. When property values collapsed in the 1990s, stagnation followed. Domestic automobile sales, which had increased almost continually since 1950, fell for two straight years after 1990. The manufacturers were poorly prepared for that. Between 1984 and 1991 they had doubled the number of base models to 400, imposing more fixed costs.[112] The decade in which the rest of the world feverishly rushed to embrace Japanese techniques proved to be a decade of recession and stagnation inside Japan itself. As Koichi Shimokawa found, the Japanese had "forgotten the origins of Japan's success in the automotive industry—the lean production system." They had "gone from high efficiency and lean to a considerably high-cost structure."[113] Even as the Japanese domestic market shrank, foreign competition sharpened. Americans, Europeans, and other Asian nations became more efficient. After 40 years of rapid expansion, the Japanese economy, the second largest in the world, had stopped growing. If one looked beyond Detroit, the US economy was booming.

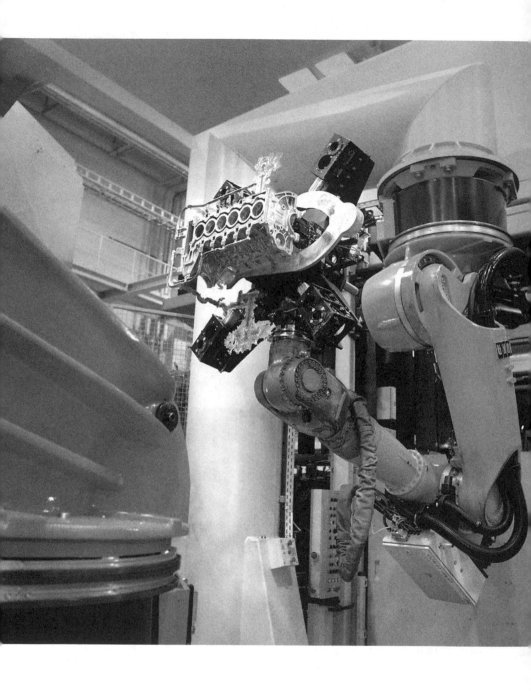

Those jobs aren't coming back.

—Steve Jobs to Barack Obama, 2011[1]

From labor's point of view, lean production meant lost jobs, as fewer people did the same work. Worse, the auto industry's "Japanese transplants" paid lower wages. Worse still, lean production emerged at the a time when management was moving millions of jobs "offshore" to foreign-based but often American-owned factories. Worst of all, automation and robots were gradually replacing human beings on assembly lines. Between 1970 and 2000 the population of the United States increased by 100 million, but the number of blue collar jobs of all kinds fell by 600,000 to 20.7 million. In the automobile industry, 700,000 jobs disappeared between 1979 and 2000.[2] During the 1980s the move to cheaper labor markets was widely called "deindustrialization." Older manufacturing such as the steel and auto industries were increasingly regarded as "sunset" industries whose jobs could be exported, in favor of high-tech replacements, or "sunrise" industries such as electronics, lasers, aerospace, and computers.

The lost jobs were lamented. In the song "Factory" on the 1978 album *Darkness on the Edge of Town*, Bruce Springsteen mourned the losses of a working-class life in decline—particularly in what came to be called the "Rust Belt."[3] The following year, in "The Day They Closed the Factory Down," Harry Chapin sang of jobs that moved to "another town / where they'll make shirts for less."[4] In "Allentown" (1982), Billy Joel sang

FIGURE 9.1
A KUKA robot lifting a motor. Source: www.kuka.com.

of Pennsylvania steel plants shutting down and workers "out in Bethlehem
. . . killing time / filling out forms / standing in line." Joel's song was in the
top twenty for the year and received a standing ovation when he performed
it in Bethlehem.[5]

A 1982 book titled *The Deindustrialization of America* argued that it had
become too easy for corporations to move manufacturing offshore, while
taking no responsibility for workers and communities that they deserted.[6]
When a factory moved away, some small businesses collapsed, the population declined, and unionized workers could seldom find wages and benefits
as good as those they had lost. Local government had a smaller tax base
but had to provide more social services. In contrast, European nations gave
workers more rights and made plant closings more difficult. They also provided better severance pay, retraining programs, and other benefits.[7]

For generations the American labor movement had sought shorter hours
and better wages. Those goals came closest to being achieved in the years
1945–1965. Nineteenth-century workers got only Sundays off, and twelve-
hour days weren't unusual. A work week ranged between 50 and 72 hours,
and some workers put in more than 3,000 hours a year.[8] Unions successfully
bargained for better conditions. In the US automobile industry, the number
of hours worked per week fell from about 60 in 1905 to about 40 in the late
1920s. After this dramatic initial decrease, working hours fell more slowly,
reaching their lowest point in 1968. Wages peaked in 1973.[9] By 1990, a
person had to work an additional 245 hours per year to make the same real
wages.[10] In the US automotive industry of 2010, the work week averaged
43.3 hours. With a two-week vacation and a month of layoffs, that was
1,992 hours a year.[11] By comparison, US workers as a whole averaged 1,778
hours per year—one week longer than the Japanese, nine weeks more than
the Germans, and ten weeks longer than the Dutch.[12]

According to the Bureau of Labor Statistics, between 1987 and 2009
productivity in the automotive industry increased an average of 3 percent
per year, but the total compensation for auto workers declined an average of 0.8 percent per year.[13] Compensation fell at the same rate in the
US electrical appliance industry, even though its productivity increased by
122 percent. The disparity was even more striking in the computer and
electronic industries, in which productivity increased an astonishing 11.2
percent each year while compensation rose a meager 0.8 percent. But at

least those industries survived. During the same 22 years, as most of the knitting mills and clothing factories in the United States were shut down, the apparel industry's output fell 9.3 percent per year. Between 1999 and 2009 alone, about 6 million manufacturing jobs disappeared,[14] even though productivity grew every year except for the recession year of 2008.[15] After this great reversal of fortune for blue-collar workers, the jobs that remained were more demanding and often paid no more (when adjusted for inflation) than they had in 1973.

This erosion of the size and the wages of the working class was already underway before lean manufacturing became an issue. In 1981 the magazine *Ms.* ran a story about "life on the global assembly line" depicting the exploitation of young women in the Third World.[16] Five years later, a television documentary titled *The Global Assembly Line*[17] examined plant closings in California and Tennessee that resulted from moving production to the Philippines and to Mexico. Most of the overseas apparel and electronics-assembly workers featured in the documentary were young women. Typically, they were hired at age 18 and let go well before age 30. American workers who assembled televisions at that time received between $4.50 and $5.50 an hour, versus $0.70 an hour in the Philippines. After American companies were well-established in the Philippines, they increased production by lengthening the hours and increasing the speed of the line.[18]

Criticism didn't slow the shift toward "offshore" manufacturing. For example, in the 1970s Nike (now an enormous company with more than one-third of the global market for sports shoes) had plants in New Hampshire and in Maine, but by the early 1980s it was manufacturing most of its shoes in Asia. Parts were made in five different countries and then assembled by women in South Korea, Vietnam, Indonesia, and China. Nike had revenues of $3.2 billion in 1992. It gradually closed its US factories and subcontracted much of its production to the Tsai family in Hong Kong, which ran 97 production lines and also produced shoes for Reebok and Adidas.[19]

Across Asia, poor women were recruited into assembly-line work, much as nineteenth-century New England textile mills had recruited farm girls. An official Malaysian brochure invited Western corporations to relocate, extolling "the manual dexterity of the Oriental female": "Her hands are small and she works with extreme care. Who, therefore, could be better qualified by nature and inheritance to contribute to the efficiency of a production line?"[20] In China, one of these "oriental females," Shu Ting, wrote a poem about how it felt to have such a job. It begins this way:

In time's assembly line
Night presses against night.
We come off the factory night-shift
In line as we march towards home.
Over our heads in a row
The assembly line of stars
Stretches across the sky.
Beside us, little trees
Stand numb in assembly lines.

The workers and the trees are dying from "smog and monotony," and the poet finds herself unable to feel any concern for her "manufactured fate."[21]

Asian women commonly were paid half as much as men and often were required to work overtime. The "women who take up these jobs typically have only primary schooling. Their earnings are generally sent to their families," who live "in rural areas" and "desperately need cash."[22] They made more money than they could in their villages, but they adopted Western clothing and makeup and often began to buy on credit. The factory work usually proved unstable, as layoffs came with little warning whenever demand slackened. Like American assembly-line workers in the 1920s and the 1930s, many fell into debt. Some had extremely low wages. In 1988, *Business Week* reported that some Chinese children as young as 10 years worked 14 hours a day and slept two or three to a bed in crude dormitories, often earning less than a dollar a day.[23] Their incomes were a tiny fraction of the prices charged for the toys, electronic devices, and clothing they made.[24]

US carmakers also closed factories at home and sent work abroad. During the 1990s General Motors shut down two dozen American plants, firing 75,000 workers. Chrysler also shut down factories, notably one in Kenosha, Wisconsin that had built cars continuously from 1902 until its closing in 1988. In *The End of the Line* Catherine Dudley analyzes how the community responded to this closure.[25] Kenosha's identity was intertwined with 5,500 highly paid factory jobs that pumped money into the local economy. The workers felt bitter and betrayed. Yet many in the local white-collar class felt that auto workers had been overpaid, that they had not valued education, and that the collapse of the automobile industry was partly the fault of organized labor. In the United States as a whole, blue-collar workers didn't always find sympathy or solidarity from those who had not shared their excellent benefits. Yet such views were short-sighted. Union wages had been negotiated on the basis of genuine increases in productivity, and UAW contracts had pressured other employers to increase pay and benefits.

In a book titled *Mollie's Job: A Story of Life and Work on the Global Assembly Line*, the journalist William Adler traced what moving jobs abroad meant to the workers involved.[26] Mollie James, an African-American, migrated from the segregated South in 1950 and took an assembly-line job in Paterson, New Jersey. It was a union shop, and she made decent wages and raised a family. But in 1963, induced by tax incentives and non-union labor, the company began to move jobs to Mississippi. Soon Dorothy Carter in Mississippi was doing the same work Mollie did for a lower wage. The company's profits increased. Then, in the 1980s, the company was absorbed into a conglomerate named MagneTek, and an additional plant was opened in Mexico. In 1989 MagneTek closed the New Jersey factory, and Mollie lost her job. A few years later, Dorothy Carter was fired when MagneTek shut down the Mississippi plant and concentrated all production in Matamoros, Mexico. The job was now done by Balbina Duque, who had migrated from a poor rural village to live in a crowded barrio without pollution controls, good public schools, a clean water supply, or the amenities that Mollie James had enjoyed in New Jersey.

As corporations moved their manufacturing offshore between 1973 and 1991, the number of American workers making appliances fell from 196,000 to 117,000. General Electric tripled its profits during these years, but its global workforce fell from 400,000 to 230,000. Such statistics alarmed the economist and activist Jeremy Rifkin, who published a book titled *The End of Work* in 1995.[27] Rifkin argued that lean manufacturing, continual advances in automation, and the exporting of jobs were creating severe technological unemployment. To a degree, Rifkin was rephrasing arguments that had been popular during the Great Depression and had resurfaced in the 1950s. The critics of those earlier eras had been wrong, for higher productivity had not led to mass unemployment but rather to a rising standard of living and new kinds of work. From that perspective, the problem was structural unemployment and the solution was retraining so that displaced workers could be hired elsewhere.

Rifkin's argument would be tested in the years immediately after his book was published. On January 1, 1994, the North American Free Trade

Agreement (NAFTA) went into effect, abolishing tariffs and facilitating the importing of finished goods from Canada and Mexico. In the next six years, corporations relocated 1.2 million semi-skilled and unskilled jobs to Mexico. Women remained the preferred employees because of their manual dexterity and their willingness to accept low wages.[28] After 2000, American companies continued to build new plants abroad. For example, "Mexican auto exports shot up by almost 70 percent between 2004 and 2007 to 1.6 million vehicles, the majority of which were destined for the U.S. market."[29] Moreover, the technological sophistication of Mexican factories and the quality of their products, including televisions and automobiles, kept improving, in some cases equaling or surpassing their US counterparts. In Mexico, hourly wages and benefits averaged $4.50, versus $40 in Detroit.[30]

Rifkin was vindicated. By 2001, there were 2,700 foreign assembly plants in Mexico, the majority owned by American firms but some owned by firms headquartered in Japan, in South Korea, in Taiwan, in Hong Kong, and in Europe.[31] This competition held down wages in New Jersey, Pennsylvania, Ohio, Michigan, and other industrial states, and it forced some factories to close. Likewise, tens of thousands of US garment workers lost jobs to "guest workers" on Saipan in the Northern Mariana Islands (a commonwealth, like Puerto Rico, that technically is US territory). By 1998, Saipan's clothing factories employed 40,000 people and shipped $1 billion in goods to the mainland United States per year. Among the largest customers were Levi Strauss, Tommy Hilfiger, Gap, and Walmart.[32] Workers on Saipan received half the US minimum wage, but there were even cheaper factory sites. None grew more rapidly than Shenzen. A mere fishing village on the Chinese mainland near Hong Kong in 1980, one generation later it was a city of 8 million. This astonishing growth was based on assembly-line production for companies such as Abercrombie & Fitch, Miss Sixty, American Eagle, Ann Taylor, Lands' End, Eddie Bauer, Next, and Benetton.[33]

At times, workers in developing countries tried to pressure manufacturers to pay better wages, end compulsory overtime, abolish child labor, and provide healthy work environments by informing consumers in Europe and North America about abuses. In 1996 the American public was scandalized to learn that Walmart sold a line of clothing made in Honduras using child labor. Walmart, with its high visibility, had to respond to the public pressure. Naomi Klein's 1999 best-seller *No Logo* described how, at times, local change became possible because of international consumer concern.[34] But that tactic didn't always work. In 2000, the Taiwanese-owned Chentex jeans plant in Nicaragua came to a standstill as a result of a confrontation with the garment makers' union. Yet despite a great deal of publicity, monitoring by non-governmental organizations, and attention from academia, the Nicaraguan workers lost the strike.[35] In other instances, consumers and stockholders scarcely noticed the abuses of foreign suppliers.[36]

For several decades, "offshore" factories used semi-skilled workers on traditional assembly lines. In the late 1980s there was little lean production in Mexico, even among the 180 Japanese transplants operated by companies such as Sony, Toshiba, and Nissan.[37] Lean production required fine transportation networks for just-in-time delivery and an educated workforce, but at the time both were in short supply in Mexico. Most of the *maquiladoras* (assembly plants close to the US border) did simple assembly work. The high-tech factories remained inside the US, requiring smaller numbers of skilled workers whose wages were a small percentage of total costs.[38]

However, the division between traditional assembly lines in poor countries and lean production using skilled labor in the older industrial centers began to break down. Developing nations improved their infrastructure and their educational levels, and at the same time the relationships between suppliers and manufacturers became much closer. Auto companies that once had bought individual parts increasingly bought entire sub-assemblies. In 1975, parts manufacturers might move to Mexico. By the 1990s, as large corporations contracted out sub-assemblies of entire components, these subcontractors were merging into larger companies that produced complex units. Instead of providing the many knobs, dials, and other parts of a dashboard, suppliers began to build and install the entire dashboard. Manufacturers, instead of buying the parts that went into a door from different suppliers and putting them together, paid a subcontractor to build and install complete doors. (Something resembling this post-lean system had briefly existed in US airplane manufacturing during World War II.) At GM's plant in Gravatai, Brazil, fifteen component suppliers built adjacent factories and put their workers on GM's shop floor. Likewise, eight suppliers installed pre-assembled components at Volkswagen's Brazilian factory.[39] The most efficient post-lean automobile plants required as little as ten hours for final assembly, half the time needed in 1990.

In order to handle these more complex sub-assembly jobs, parts manufacturers expanded or were absorbed into larger companies. Post-lean suppliers forged a tighter bond with manufacturers, who began to sign long-term contracts, in some cases for the lifespan of the model. When GM opened a Chevrolet Suburban assembly plant in Silao, Mexico, in 1994, many of its sub-assemblers moved there too.[40] They made the steel blanks for stamping, the doors, interior upholstery for roofs and doors, hoods, axles, wire harnesses, and sensors for anti-lock braking systems. In seven years the small agricultural city of Silao was transformed by 9,000 factory jobs, the majority not with GM but with its suppliers. Because companies didn't relocate individually, but as clusters, one corporation's move had a multiplier effect. For every person on an assembly line there were four or five more working in the local supply chain. Furthermore, the companies in Silao had a free hand to rearrange work and to introduce new equipment. The new jobs abroad no longer were clones of those lost in the US. *Maquiladoras* increasingly had robots, faster machines, and new layouts.

As technologically advanced factories proliferated abroad, complex parts began to be outsourced—even components of such high-end products as the Boeing 777 airliner. Designed in Seattle, its modules were made in thirteen different countries.[41] Henry Ford built the River Rouge complex as a self-sufficient plant that could make everything needed to build a car, including the steel, the electricity, the body, the engine, and all the automotive parts. Today parts come from all over the world, shipped in containers. This internationalization of production undermined well-paid workers in the United States and Europe, not only because Asian and Latin American labor markets were inexpensive but also because the new factories had no unions, demanded long hours, and spent little on pollution control or safety. Firms outsourced whatever they couldn't do more cheaply themselves. Some companies making smaller electronic goods, such as mobile phones or tablet computers, restricted themselves to engineering and design and outsourced all their manufacturing.

The world's largest electronics manufacturer was not in the United States or Japan, but in Taiwan. Foxconn's 1.2 million employees, many in mainland China, assembled products for Nokia, Sony, Hewlett-Packard, Apple, and other well-known companies. General Motors had employed half a million Americans in the 1970s. In contrast, Apple, the world's most valuable corporation in the winter of 2012, had only 40,000 US employees, while its foreign subcontractors had 700,000.[42] Apple had once prided itself on making products domestically. But eventually, like Nike, Apple chose cheap Asian labor. In 2011, President Barack Obama asked Steve Jobs, Apple's CEO, why that work couldn't be in the United States. Steve Jobs replied "Those jobs aren't coming back." "Apple's executives," the *New York Times* reported, "believe the vast scale of overseas factories as well as the flexibility, diligence and industrial skills of foreign workers have so outpaced their American counterparts that 'Made in the U.S.A.' is no longer a viable option for most Apple products."[43]

The situation looked considerably different from labor's perspective. As the *New York Times* observed, Chinese workers "assembling iPhones, iPads and other devices often labor in harsh conditions . . . [amid] serious—sometimes deadly—safety problems,"[44] that included excessive overtime, seven-day work weeks, child labor, exposure to toxic chemicals, and occasional explosions. (In 2011 an explosion at an iPad factory killed four and injured 77.) Apple wasn't uniquely reprehensible. Dell, Hewlett-Packard, IBM, Lenovo, Motorola, Nokia, Sony, Toshiba, and most other electronics companies also tolerated exploitation of workers by suppliers. Indeed, Apple arguably was one of the better companies; it established a code of conduct, demanded annual reports from its suppliers, and inspected their operations periodically.

Nevertheless, Foxconn's wages, labor conditions, and dormitory-style living conditions were so poor that in the years 2009–2011 fourteen workers committed suicide by jumping from the tops of Foxconn buildings. The rural migrants who worked in such factories were not only putting in long hours and living crammed together in corporate dormitories; they also were suffering because their real wages scarcely changed between 2000 and 2008, when China's real GDP per capita doubled. Chinese workers had known real wage growth during the 1980s and the early 1990s. According to Yasheng Huang, a professor at MIT's Sloan School of Management, "Some in the media have questioned the sanity of those workers at the electronics company Foxconn who committed suicide. But maybe these workers knew far more about the divergence between GDP and personal income than the media commentators."[45] In 2011, in response to continuing protests, the company raised wages somewhat, but it also announced that it would install robots to do many routine jobs.[46] Protests continued, and early in 2012 "150 Chinese workers at Foxconn . . . threatened to commit suicide by leaping from their factory' roof in protest at their working conditions." (See figure 9.2.) "The assembly line ran very fast," one worker complained, "and after just one morning we all had blisters and the skin on our hands was black. The factory was also really choked with dust and no one could bear it."[47] Apple had been informed of such conditions by outside monitors and knew from its own audits that Foxconn violated its code of conduct frequently. Yet the violations persisted. In 2011, when Apple made profits of $26 billion on revenue of $108 billion, poorly paid workers at Foxconn sometimes put in 72 hours a week.[48]

In every month of 2011, 5 percent of the 24,000 workers at Foxconn's largest plant quit. Moreover, it wasn't the only Chinese factory facing strikes and protests. "At Honda car plants in the country's southeast . . . workers went on strike to demand higher wages and the right to form their own unions."[49] These protests spread to other factories. In 2009 and 2010, Chinese workers in the highly industrialized province of Guangdong received wage increases of 20–30 percent.[50] In 2011 and 2012, Chinese companies were finding it difficult to recruit more workers from the countryside. One reason for this was the high cost of living in China's cities; another was the success of the one-child-per-family policy. Between 2005 and 2011 the number of young people entering the labor force fell by 20 percent. By 2012 Foxconn was forced to raise wages between 16 and 25 percent to attract replacements for workers who had quit.[51]

In the United States, many of the assembly-line jobs that remained were at factories where work was organized in a manner inspired by consultants with expertise in lean production. Such factories tended to have an egalitarian tone, with no reserved parking spaces, a single cafeteria for all employees, similar uniforms for all assembly workers, and a management style calculated to elicit cooperation. How did workers respond to these Japanese-inspired innovations? At first, not very well. In 1988, when US companies were somewhat unsuccessfully trying to adopt lean production, some critics called it "management-by-stress."[52] "In the early phases of lean production," the labor historian Kim Moody observes, "much was written about worker 'empowerment,' multi-skilling, and job satisfaction," but "lean production was increasingly seen by workers as an exhausting and unhealthy system." They complained of "standardizing tasks, tightening work cycles, reducing

FIGURE 9.2
Assembly-line workers threatening to commit suicide by jumping off the roof of the Foxconn factory in China, January 2012

relief time, [and] wringing 'unworked' seconds from each minute."[53] Workers hadn't liked the old assembly line, but it was familiar to them. The transition to multi-skilled teamwork undermined a system of wages and benefits that unions had fought to achieve over generations. American workers were also accustomed to work stoppages and strikes, which were rare in Japanese factories. Toyota, Honda, and other operators of "transplants" sought with some success to avoid confrontations and to negotiate disputes in the context of each individual plant, resisting the idea of company-wide solutions. They opposed unions. In the 1980s and the early 1990s almost none of their plants were unionized, and all paid less than US automakers.

Nevertheless, some workers were hopeful when first hired to work at a new Japanese-inspired factory. For example, a plant in Ontario jointly operated by General Motors and Suzuki seemed to offer a pleasant environment, empowerment, and a cooperative relationship with management. However, workers' enthusiasm faded during the plant's first two years, and they concluded that it was "just another car factory."[54] In 1992 they went on strike for five weeks and forced management to allow them to unionize. It should be noted, however, that GM was not a leader in adopting lean production,

lagging behind Ford precisely in these years. The problems at the GM Ontario plant arguably were less due to Japanese methods than to failure to
incorporate them. A survey of workers' resistance to changes in production
at a number of factories concluded that "where adversarial relations exist, lean production principles diffuse more slowly and partially." Workers'
distrust accounted for "a relatively slow rate of diffusion of lean production
principles within existing U.S. plants."[55]

At factories where lean production was more successful there were still
problems, however. The radical compression of work space that came with
lean production was accompanied by reductions in the workforce. One
union official commented: "You see empty space and you don't see it filled,
and the way empty space affects our members is as a constant daily reminder
that their space could be next." Lean production sped up the pace, eliminating small pauses and breathing room in the rhythms of work. As one
Canadian assembly-line worker put it, "it is a real drive to cut any waste in
the system, and I think they do this to the point where the workers are basi-
cally running ragged for the full eight hours of the day. . . . It really takes a
toll on your body. . . ."[56] Before lean production, some jobs could be done
sitting down. Under lean production, many workers stand for the entire
shift, moving constantly as they perform multiple tasks. Accordingly, the
ideal worker for lean production should be healthy, agile, flexible, and able
to repeat movements for hours with little time to change position, stretch,
or relax.

Such work leads to repetitive strain and sometimes to permanent im-
pairment. Typical injuries include "tenosynovitis, tendinitis, carpal tunnel
syndrome, epicondylitis, bursitis, occupational back disease, thoracic outlet
syndrome, and white finger disease, each of which describes a different
form of damage to muscles, tendons, and nerves of the hands, arms, shoul-
ders, neck, feet, and legs."[57] After lean production was introduced at one
GM plant, half of the workers reported they worked in pain at least some
of the time, and 40 percent said they were continually forced to work in
awkward positions.[58] A participant-observer at an Indiana Subaru plant reported that roughly half of the workers on her team had repetitive strain
injuries.[59] In a survey of more than 2,100 workers in a Michigan Mazda
plant, three out of four agreed with the statement "I will likely be injured
or worn out before I retire."[60] Lean production often harms the flexible
bodies that it demands.

From the corporation's viewpoint, however, lean production is not about workers' bodies but about efficiency. One manager put it this way: "As you reduce space you can load up people's time and all of the small informal ways that we had of getting micro-breaks or pauses from repetitive action are now gone and so our work effort is more pure work effort."[61] Managers who embrace lean production tend to see workers as machines that can be disciplined to labor without short breaks. Unions might have protected workers against strain and stress, but many lean companies, notably the Japanese "transplants," are non-union, and therefore workers have little protection. In theory, being a member of a team protects each individual. But the labor historian Steve Babson found at a Mazda transplant in Michigan that teams existed "primarily as a rhetorical device," and that team leaders didn't represent their workers or the union but management.[62] Similarly, to the limited extent that lean production was introduced into Mexico in the 1990s, it was often a top-down imposition, sometimes called "*kaizen* from above."[63] In such cases, managers tinkered with the production system but received little input from workers and were hampered by high absenteeism and worker turnover. Low wages and a poorly educated workforce are not conducive to lean production.

American unions resisted the lean production system for a decade or more, notably at General Motors. In June 1998, 5,800 workers struck at a plant in Flint that made components for many vehicles, and they soon brought most of the corporation to a halt. GM had adopted just-in-time delivery, and its small inventories quickly ran out. In July, as the strike rippled through the entire corporation and its suppliers, production dropped to less than 10 percent of what it had been the previous July. All but two of GM's 29 US factories shut down or drastically scaled back production, and 193,000 workers were laid off. Including GM suppliers, by the end of the month 137 factories shut down. Government economists calculated that the US economy as a whole was 1 percent smaller for the year as a result of the Flint strike.[64] It showed that a union in control of one choke point could shut down a company. But this labor victory also signaled the failure of GM and the unions to unite and face the Japanese challenge. GM achieved a better working relationship with the United Auto Workers in 2000, when they signed a comprehensive pact. Nevertheless, as Bennett Harrison put it in a widely cited book, after corporations made the transition they often were "lean and mean."[65]

At the same time that lean production was being introduced, computers were being integrated into assembly-line work. The visions of automation that Norbert Wiener and Kurt Vonnegut had explored in the early 1950s were becoming reality. Computers no longer merely drove particular machine tools or monitored inventory. Overarching systems used cameras, scanners, and bar codes to track the movement of all parts and operations. As early as 1983, at Chrysler's newly built plant in Windsor, Ontario, 97 percent of the 3,800 welds each vehicle required were made by 112 robots. The assembly line in the Windsor plant was monitored and controlled by computers at 1,837 points. The following year, Chrysler opened "an even more fully integrated in-line-sequenced plant" that used robots, lasers, and cameras to "inspect 350 points on the car bodies passing through assembly."[66] Not to be outdone, GM had 250 robots at its Buick City, opened in 1986. The development of microprocessors enabled "flexible robotics" that could manufacture several models on one line. By the late 1980s, analysts were predicting that these developments would cause at least one-third of all assembly-line jobs to disappear.[67]

Toyota generally took a cautious approach to introducing robots,[68] but it adopted robot welders as soon as they were flexible enough to work within its systems. Human beings were being replaced by robots in other job areas too, notably the stamping of body panels and the painting of completed bodies. In 2010 there were more than a million multi-purpose robots in operation worldwide. Japan, with 285,000 such robots, had the most, followed by North America (168,000), Germany (148,000), South Korea (101,000), Italy (62,000), and China (52,000).[69] In the world as a whole, for every 200 human beings in manufacturing there was one robot, but they weren't distributed evenly. The Japanese auto industry "employed" one robot for every seven people, the German auto industry one for every nine. The leading buyers of robots in 2010 were automotive corporations (33,000) and electronics companies (31,000). And 50,000 more robots were sold to manufacturers of plastics, rubber, chemicals, and food. The average "life span" of such a robot was 12 years.[70] American, Japanese, and German firms emerged as the leading manufacturers of robots. The German firm KUKA, which sold robots to BMW, Volkswagen, Ford, GM, and many other car manufacturers, had products that could perform a wide range of tasks, from delicate movements to welding to lifting heavy objects, such as motors, for precision placement.

Yet workers with highly developed skills were still needed. A mathematics teacher studied the transformed workplace and found that "spatial and geometric reasoning and problem-solving" remained essential. Workers had to translate two-dimensional drawings into three-dimensional objects, and at times they had to adjust machines and computer codes to do so. The parts produced had to be measured frequently to ensure that they met stringent standards. At times, workers had to use trigonometry "to locate points at fixed angles and distances from known points," a task that became more demanding when "blueprints lack these locations." Missing coordinates had to be supplied so that dimensions could be calculated. Even after the entire set-up was right, during production the dimensions of parts still had to be continually measured. Cutting and drilling are dynamic processes involving powerful machines, and slight slippage or "movement is inevitable, so regular checks and adjustments are necessary."[71] Computerization by no means reduced the machinist to an automaton. The job demanded three-dimensional visualization, geometry, trigonometry, and measurement (in both the English and the metric system), as well as adjusting and fine-tuning the machines.

Likewise, an analyst who studied production of color television screens at ten factories in 1999 found "a wide gap between theory and practice. What is specified by engineers and what actually happens on the shop floor may differ considerably." Engineers alone couldn't solve all the problems, because they lacked the tacit knowledge of those on the shop floor, and factories were more successful if they gave workers primary responsibility for trouble-shooting. However, the best solutions emerged at plants (notably in Japan) where workers and engineers pooled their expertise and worked together on "chronic process problems."[72] In short, as assembly-line work moved offshore, the blue-collar jobs that remained required higher levels of education and skill.

White-collar employment was also being re-engineered and computerized. In 1995 the American Management Association published a book for its members that defined white-collar work as "the invisible assembly line."[73] It argued that computerized systems revealed the hidden linkages between the various departments of a firm. The keys to increasing the flow of work were improving skill in processing information and moving that information rapidly—for example, from sales to consumer credit checks to production.

On this "invisible assembly line," the ideal knowledge worker took "ownership" of projects and made decisions on the basis of what the corporation was trying to achieve.[74]

This was the managerial perspective on speeding up white-collar work, but employees often experienced computerization as job elimination. For example, when retailers introduced the use of scanners and bar codes to speed up inventory, re-ordering, and cashier work, they downsized. The merchandising division of Sears fired 50,000 people in 1993, even as its sales rose 14 percent.[75] Walmart began to send its sales figures automatically to suppliers, so that without any human intermediaries Procter & Gamble's production lines knew exactly how much toothpaste and soap had to be replaced every day. IBM reorganized its credit division, which vetted customers' requests for financing. Before re-engineering, credit checks, decision making, and preparing forms took seven days. Management found that the actual processing time was only 90 minutes, but forms took time to move from one office to the next and sat in piles on each desk. After the flow of work was reorganized and computerized, the seven days were reduced to four hours, with forms transferred electronically rather than sent as letters or files.[76] In many companies, secretaries were fired, or secretaries who left weren't replaced, and mid-level executives were given personal computers and printers. Insurance companies integrated policy writing into computer software, so that an agent only had to add the customer's name and personal data and the kind of coverage desired, then print out a contract. In other businesses, online sales eliminated even the brief involvement of salesmen, abolishing more jobs. Re-engineering made corporations more profitable, but many white-collar jobs disappeared, and those who remained felt less secure.

Nevertheless, during the 1990s overall employment grew both in Europe and in the United States. Many of the new positions were rationalized and subjected to work-flow control through computerization. Although Frederick Winslow Taylor's scientific management and the notion of "one best way" to do each task were often at the root of these changes, the preferred term in the 1990s was "re-engineering." The link between Taylor and the standardization and routinization of white-collar work was William Henry Leffingwell. Though not even indexed in *The Invisible Assembly Line*, he developed Taylor's ideas in *Scientific Office Management* (1917) and other publications.[77] Leffingwell demonstrated that such matters as handling mail orders could be reorganized to double output, and argued that better-designed forms could be filled out more quickly. At the time, much white-collar work remained beyond the reach of systemization and continuous scrutiny. But the idea of reorganizing office work appealed to management, and the new profession made incremental advances that the computer accelerated. By the 1990s, the vision of reorganizing and deskilling white-collar work to resemble an assembly line seemed within reach.[78] Computer software provided scripts and routines for workers to follow when dealing with insurance claims, fielding customers' complaints, or filling orders. Some of the knowledge that a white-collar specialist once possessed, including mathematical calculations, could be distilled into a software program. Such programs made it possible for corporations to hire people with little training or experience to work in phone centers and back offices, churning out results. A computerized system, one manager explained, "requires less thought, judgment, and manual intervention."[79] Such managers assumed that white-collar work ought to be organized on the model of an assembly line of the 1950s.

Using computers, managers could keep detailed records of how many customers or claims each employee processed, and could calculate how many minutes and keystrokes the employee needed to do it. At call centers, companies established the "average talk time" (ATT) that it should take to deal with a customer, which was typically between 90 and 150 seconds. They monitored employees to see if they worked fast enough. As with the classic Ford assembly line, management focused on throughput more than quality. A study of a call center helping customers who had problems with Xerox copying machines found that the staffers were often unable to translate customers' complaints, stated in everyday language, into the engineering terminology of the software program.[80] The purpose of the help center was to minimize the high cost of sending out repairmen, but staffers often weren't able to diagnose the problems. Moreover, the solutions they did find couldn't be added to the database. Consultants recommended that the company translate the software into lay language and permit staffers to integrate their solutions into the system. But managers rejected these suggestions and instead redoubled their emphasis on top-down controls.

Such managers saw the classic assembly line as a way to organize work that would simplify each job to a routine and drive workers to repeat their task more quickly. In lean production, in contrast, managers expect workers to participate in defining the work and to improve the solutions available to customers. The call centers that imposed traditional assembly-line organization on white-collar work often relocated abroad. American credit card companies established centers in the Caribbean, and British telephone customers found themselves talking to help-desk people in India. American Express, J. P. Morgan Chase, and Standard Chartered Bank sent 13,000 back-office jobs to India.[81] Not only had production been disconnected from consumption; sales were being disconnected from service.

The profits made from exporting jobs and from computerizing white-collar work flowed not to workers but to managers. In the 1970s, the typical executive made 42 times the wages of the average worker. That might seem a large differential, but in the following decades executive compensation skyrocketed. "By 2000 in America," according to the economist Joseph Stiglitz, "CEOs were getting more than 500 times the wages of the average employee."[82] Moreover, workers' benefits declined during these years. The analyst Simon Head from the Rothermere Institute at Oxford found that "between 1995 and 2000," at a time when chief executive pay was rising 25 percent per year, the worker's average annual increase was only "0.7 percent . . . when the impact of declining benefits was factored in."[83] Yet these were the best five years for American workers between 1973 and 2000. After then, jobs began to disappear rapidly. Between 2000 and 2008, employment in motor vehicle manufacturing, including parts suppliers, fell from 1,315,000 to 880,000.[84] Many more workers lost their jobs during the recession that began in 2008[85] and led to the bankruptcy of both General Motors and Chrysler in 2009. When GM and Chrysler re-emerged, many plants had closed and whole lines of business had been discontinued or sold off. In 1914 Henry Ford knew that high wages drove a consumer economy. But corporations broke the social contract that had been established with labor during the first seven decades of the twentieth century. Japanese-inspired plants hired fewer workers, paid them less, and provided fewer benefits than Detroit long had. When Toyota created 20,000 American jobs,[86] a larger number of jobs disappeared elsewhere.

Much as workers professed to hate the assembly line, it had been naturalized as the best way to work efficiently, even in volunteer work. For example, in 2011 in Minneapolis 1,000 volunteers produced 200,000 "Mobile Packs" to feed poor children in the Philippines and in Haiti.[87] Every Christmas season, in all parts of the United States, hundreds of churches and charitable organizations set up temporary lines to fill bags with food and presents for the needy. Usually the volunteers decide spontaneously to organize the work as an assembly line. The typical charity line may not meet all the formal criteria for an assembly line, but it is a sequenced division of labor that fills boxes or grocery bags moved along counters or tables. When demand for charity increased during the economic crisis that began in 2008, informal assembly lines had to speed up. Toyota's System Support Center in Cincinnati stepped in with a program to help non-profits "implement the 'lean' manufacturing techniques" developed for automobile manufacturing. Toyota sped up the charity lines by 50 percent.[88] No doubt some of the beneficiaries of these lean charity lines had lost their jobs to lean production.

The assembly line's use in volunteer charity work illustrates how it had become a "general purpose technology" (GPT). The economic historians Timothy Breshahan and Manuel Trajtenberg introduced this concept, which became common in the late 1990s.[89] A GPT, such as the steam engine, the internal combustion engine, or the Internet, has a widespread effect on all aspects of the economic system.[90] GPTs differ from niche technologies in having many uses, considerable scope for improvement, many distinct applications, and strong complementarities with other technologies. A GPT has a measurable effect on the economy, but its adoption is by no means instantaneous. It may take 20 years to be absorbed and developed. The assembly line fits this definition well. The first assembly line at Highland Park radically improved productivity, yet it had considerable scope for improvement. It had uses in a wide range of industries, and it had strong complementarities with other technologies. The efficiency gains and the higher wages to which it led spread from automobile factories to many other industries.

Furthermore, as GPT theory postulates, improvements in the assembly line continued. Recently it has been adapted to "wide sourcing," a practice in which tasks are broken down into small parts and then sent out over the Internet to people willing to do "microtasks" for a piece rate. This idea "was pioneered by the Mechanical Turk service, introduced by Amazon.com in 2005. Mechanical Turk resembles an online bulletin board. Businesses post income-earning opportunities, with rewards for each task completed. Turkers, as the independent contractors are informally called, choose a task they like and are qualified for."[91] It became possible to subdivide work, distribute it worldwide, and track every operation. In this system, workers have no idea what the larger project is, and typically they are paid two or three cents for each microtask. Many microtasks are expected to take only 2 seconds each, which means that 14,400 iterations of such a task can be performed in an eight-hour day. On such a virtual assembly line, it is hard to earn as much as the minimum hourly wage paid in the United States.

Computers also facilitated "mass customization." The classic assembly line produced identical things, but consumers increasingly yearned for variety and individuality. Computerized assembly lines made it easier to minister to this desire by delivering more varied products. "Mass customization" permitted any customer to order an exact combination of colors, components, and options, whether for a new computer or a new vehicle. At least in theory, this had already been achieved by 2002, yet in that year only 6 percent of American cars were made to order. In contrast, 60 percent or more of Japanese and German consumers bought cars that way.[92] The US couldn't convert fully to lean production unless consumers changed their purchasing habits. For generations they had been accustomed to visiting automobile dealerships, looking for a car that caught their fancy and that they could drive away almost immediately. Ordering a car and waiting for weeks while it was manufactured had less appeal than the instant gratification of test-driving and buying one on the spot. As a result, US automobile production was still "pushed" to the consumer far more than it was pulled by orders. From labor's point of view, the growth of "mass customization" could create jobs, for when consumers want products built to individual specifications workers have a more important role in final assembly.

Despite the loss of millions of jobs to *maquiladoras* and other factories abroad, the value of US industrial production has been rising since 2000. The reason for the increase is that everyday practice on assembly lines has changed enormously since the assembly line was invented at Highland Park. High-tech manufacturing requires skilled workers, a strong educational system, and a reliable infrastructure (including electricity, highways, and Internet service). Both in the United States and abroad, work is increasingly divided between low-skill jobs that cannot profitably be automated and high-skill jobs that require education and then training. For the first seventy years of the assembly line, and especially after the successful unionization drives of the 1930s, skilled workers complained that their expertise was becoming irrelevant while semi-skilled work was better rewarded than ever before. Until the 1970s, rising productivity lifted almost all workers' wages in mass-production industries. In more recent decades, however, the labor force has come to be divided into the semi-skilled (whose jobs are disappearing) and the skilled (who command considerably higher wages). The new assembly lines have raised productivity and have kept the United States competitive, but it seems that mass-production industries will never again employ the majority of American blue-collar workers.

In 1979 the American auto manufacturers employed nearly 1.1 million people, General Motors accounting for nearly half of those jobs.[93] By 2005, GM employed only 125,000, and by 2012 only half that.[94] Lean production, automation, and outsourcing have affected other mass-production manufacturers similarly. Nor is the process complete. In the 2010–2011 edition of its Career Guide to Industries, the US Bureau of Labor Standards estimated that between 2008 and 2018 one-sixth of the remaining assembly-line jobs would disappear. The standards for new hires will also rise, as "manufacturers increasingly emphasize continuing education and cross-train" workers so they can be multi-skilled members of teams.[95]

Alternatives to jobs in the auto industry seldom are in manufacturing. In 2011 the largest employer in the United States was Walmart, with 2.1 million employees—more than the number of people employed by all US automobile manufacturers and suppliers combined. Walmart, Target, and other warehouse stores are, in a very real sense, outcomes of the assembly line, for they sell mass-produced goods almost exclusively. But these companies don't pay high wages. Walmart's pay scale and benefits are inferior to what the UAW negotiated in the 1960s and the 1970s. Labor profits less from the assembly line in 2013 than it did in 1963. As Gramsci predicted, wages fell after the assembly line was "generalized and defused."[96] Henry Ford had used productivity increases to double wages to $5 a day and to shorten hours, thereby boosting the demand for more consumer goods and giving workers more leisure time in which to enjoy them. In striking contrast, the American auto companies and the UAW negotiated lower wages for workers who started after 2007. Those hired before that year received $29 an hour; those hired afterward got only $16–$19 an hour.[97]

At the centennial of the assembly line, American workers had longer working hours, lower wages, and worse benefits than Western European workers. In 1950, the United States regarded Europe as an inexpensive labor market. In 2010, BMW found a "cheap labor platform in America."[98] At its South Carolina factory, BMW paid American workers only about half as much as it paid their European peers. Moreover, the vehicle they made, the X3, was too expensive for most American consumers, with a sticker price that ranged from $37,000 to $63,000. Many of the X3s made in Spartanburg were exported.

Fears of technological unemployment had surfaced during the late 1920s, had haunted the Great Depression, and had reappeared in the wake of early automation during the 1950s. But since 1990 these fears have proved all too accurate. In the 1920s Americans expected mass production to enhance worker's lives. In the 1950s they were told to expect mass leisure and early retirement based on automation. Instead, productivity gains and outsourcing wiped out millions of blue-collar jobs, and after 2008 anyone who was semi-skilled faced the prospect of earning less than his or her parents had.

Returning factory jobs to the United States became a theme in the 2012 presidential campaign. "No American company should be able to avoid paying its fair share of taxes by moving jobs and profits overseas,"[99] President Barack Obama declared in February 2012. He wanted every multi-national company to pay a minimum tax that could be used to lower taxes for companies that created jobs inside the US rather than exporting them. Rick Santorum, a former senator running in the Republican primaries, had the same goal, but a different solution. He proposed to eliminate corporate taxes altogether, making the US more attractive to investors. Where the $1.3 trillion in lost revenue would come from wasn't clear, however.

A few high-tech companies have kept most of their manufacturing inside the United States. Notably, Intel continued to design and manufacture computer chips primarily at ten locations inside the United States. Likewise, Sea-Micro decided to build a new factory producing servers in Santa Clara, California. Furthermore, some manufacturing jobs were coming home. In 2012, General Motors closed a plant in Mexico and opened a new $244 million factory in Baltimore to make motors for its new electric cars.[100] State and federal agencies promoted such "in-sourcing" with subsidies. GM invested a little more than half of the money needed to build its new Baltimore plant; the rest of the funding came from a grant from the Department of Energy ($106 million) and small grants from the state of Maryland and the city of Baltimore. But government funding can only partly account for the trend toward "in-sourcing." Analysts also noted a tendency to move electronics manufacturing units back to the US, particularly when it came to making complex products in low volume (notably in the aerospace and medical fields). In 2010 and 2011, more than thirty mid-size manufacturing plants moved back to the US from Asia.[101] They were returning because the cheap labor in Asia isn't as cheap as it once was, because there are clear advantages to manufacturing close to the home office and close to American customers, because the cost of transportation is rising as a result of worldwide energy shortages, and because the Chinese currency is expected to appreciate. In addition, there are technical advantages to being in the Silicon Valley area. More than 250 electronics manufacturers lie within 40 miles of San Jose.

These trends benefit the American economy, but not many jobs will be created. In Baltimore, General Motors hired only 189 new workers to build motors in its new plant, where much of the work was automated. In effect, it cost $1.29 million to create each of the new jobs. In 2011, when GM sold 9,025 million vehicles and regained its position as the largest automobile manufacturer in the world, its profits amounted to $7.6 billion. Its largest market was in China, where it sold 2,547,000 vehicles. In its lean, computerized, and automated North American factories, GM employed not half a million blue-collar workers but 47,500, who accounted for only one-fourth of its worldwide workforce. Each US worker received a $7,000 profit-sharing check—something few of them could have imagined in 2009, when GM went bankrupt.[102] GM's swift turnaround suggests that there is a profitable future for high-tech assembly lines inside the United States. The problem is to find employment for the rest of the displaced blue-collar workers.

Remember that it is precisely in times like these, in moments of trial and moments of hardship, that Americans rediscover the ingenuity and resilience that makes us who we are; that made the auto industry what it once was and what it will be again; that sent those first mass-produced cars rolling off the assembly lines; that built an arsenal of democracy that propelled America to victory in the Second World War; and that powered our economic prowess in the first American century.

—Barack Obama, University of Maryland, March 30, 2009[1]

On the centenary of the assembly line, Detroit is the appropriate place to think about what it means. Ford's old Piquette Avenue plant, where the Model T was invented, still stands, with a plaque outside. Ford's Highland Park plant, where the first assembly line was set up, also still remains. Indeed, there are huge empty factories all over Detroit, and many people lament the city's decline.[2] Books have been published with such titles as *Lost Detroit*, *The Ruins of Detroit*, and *Detroit Disassembled*, each containing magnificent color photographs of windowless factories, dank water-stained theaters, decaying mansions, weedy vacant lots, moss-grown offices, abandoned hotels, crumbling public schools, and other scenes of urban collapse. The devastation is visually compelling, and it is tempting to conclude that the bustling city that was Detroit between 1913 and 1973 was the visual correlate of the classic assembly line, and that today's depopulated spaces are results of lean production and automation. Yet on inspection this equation breaks down, because it doesn't take into account the effects of racial violence,[3] the exporting of jobs overseas, or the de-centralization of car production. It would

FIGURE 1 0. 1
Abandoned building at River Rouge plant, 2011. Photograph by David E. Nye.

be more accurate to say that Detroit exemplifies what Joseph Schumpeter called the "creative destruction" of capitalism.

Paul Clemens devoted a book (titled *Punching Out*) to the fate of Detroit's Budd factory, which had made automobile parts since 1919. That factory was disassembled piece by piece, and the giant stamping machines were shipped to Brazil and Mexico. The largest of the machines from the old Budd factory now stamp out parts for Chrysler in Mexico.[4] Back in Detroit, the abandoned Budd building stood alongside a Chrysler factory.

Yet the automobile companies haven't disappeared from Detroit, even if many factories have been closed and disassembled. General Motors and Chrysler went into Chapter 11 bankruptcy protection in 2009 but soon returned to profitability. In 2012, along with Ford, they were expanding production. The story of Detroit is not the same as that of the assembly line, which has become international and which in a new form is more productive than ever.

Imagine that the workers of 1913 could visit the Ford Focus Michigan Avenue plant that opened on the outskirts of Detroit at the beginning of 2011. They would see the five phases of automobile manufacturing they knew: casting and drilling engine blocks, stamping panels for the car's body, welding the panels together, painting the body, and final assembly. Yet how each of these things is done has changed. The number of people on the factory floor has decreased, and the whole system is linked together in multiple ways by computer systems.

With nearly identical Focus plants around the world, Ford saves money through bulk purchase of machine tools and robots. The Focus is also made in Germany, and the German factory closely resembles the one in Detroit. Fully 85 percent of all the parts are identical no matter where the cars are made. Variations in national regulations account for the remaining differences. The job classifications in the factories are not identical, but there are fewer than before. This increasing uniformity is reminiscent of Henry Ford's attempts to manufacture the Model T in the same form everywhere. But today Ford executives realize that the Focus is considered a small car in the United States, a medium-size one in Europe, and a large one in some emerging markets. It therefore must be marketed differently in each context.

The new Focus was created by designers working with engineers and experienced workers ("product specialists") who looked at the work process to see where problems might arise. Is a part expensive to manufacture or likely to malfunction? Could a man get his hand into a place to install a part? As such questions were dealt with, the workers and engineers signed off on each design and each change. Production engineers then laid out a virtual assembly line where production could be simulated, problems anticipated, and alterations made. Only after the virtual line was debugged did construction of the actual one begin, in a factory across the street from where the earlier Focus was made. Building the new line from scratch took only 11 weeks.

Engines for the new Focuses are made in a separate building. Jobs in the engine department were already being deskilled in Henry Ford's day. At the River Rouge plant in 1935, an eight-spindle boring machine that made sixteen valve and pushrod holes in the V-8 engine blocks required only one operator. Such work was further automated in the late 1940s and the early 1950s. But once an engine block is drilled, skilled men are still needed for much of the remaining engine work, such as installing valves, crankshafts, and pushrods and breaking in and testing the new engines. Though machines have taken over much of the engine and drive-train work, human beings are still required.

Few workers are needed in the 280,000-square-foot building where steel blanks are transformed into doors, roofs, hoods, and panels. In the early days of automobiles many of their parts were forged, but by the 1920s forging was replaced with stamping wherever that was practicable. Photographs from the interwar era show men feeding in blanks, taking out the newly stamped parts, and putting them on conveyors.[5] In 2011 workers are no longer needed to feed the two gigantic 4,500-ton presses and the many smaller presses nearby. Laser-guided electric vehicles deliver flat steel blanks to them. The blanks are automatically fed in, and each press closes with a mighty crunch to turn out intricately shaped and curved panels. The stamping department needs only a few skilled men to keep the automatic system running. Some panels are also made by hydroforming (a process, invented in the 1950s, that uses high-pressure fluids to force metal sheets to conform to a die). At first used only for specialized cars, Ford began to use hydroforming in 1994 to produce parts for its Contour and Mystique models. Like stamping, hydroforming is highly automated.

The panels are sent to the Body Shop, where 500 robots make 4,000 precise welds, with little sparking. The Bureau of Labor Statistics notes that robots now perform the majority of industrial welding. Human welders and machinists only produce batches of parts to fill small orders. Likewise, tool and die makers maintain and repair machine tools, overhead conveyors, and the like. This is highly paid, skilled work. But the huge workforce once needed in the Body Shop has disappeared. In 1913 more than half of a car's body was made out of wood, and it was built much as a carriage would be. Ford's competitors Hupmobile, Dodge, and General Motors adopted all-steel bodies in the 1920s. But for decades men bolted and/or welded the bodies together. In 2011, however, I saw only two workers. They placed the frame for the left side of a car in a rack and stepped back while robots welded several smaller parts to it, then lifted it up and rotated it into position to be joined to another panel. Next, the two workers placed the frame for the right side of the car in position, and it too was welded and passed down the automated line. No other workers were involved as the many parts were added until a complete car body emerged less than an hour later. The buzzing sounds of welding punctuated the humming of electric motors as enormous robots delicately flipped each body over or turned it around so that other robots could attach more pieces. The steel panels are cut to extremely precise dimensions, making possible a tight, rigid body that is strong enough to withstand a rollover accident. Because the precise edges fit snugly together, welding leaves few rough spots that could create problems for the painting plant, where it is sent next.

For many decades, car bodies needed a great deal of human attention before and during painting. In 1937 bodies were rustproofed, covered with "many coats of primer, putty glaze, filler or ground coats," wet sanded, dried, and finally given a sealer coat. Back then, to achieve a lustrous finish, workers buffed each car, using "lambs wool attached to polishing discs revolving at high speed," and hand rubbed them with cheesecloth. Even the hand-rubbed finish wasn't final. After the bodies were trimmed, additional polishing was done during later stages of assembly, "right up to the final O.K. service inspection."[6] Today, most polishing jobs have been automated.

Painting the Ford Focus is also highly automated, whereas the earliest Model Ts were painted with brushes. Spray painting, adopted in the 1920s, was a dangerous and dirty job. As late as the early 1930s painters didn't wear masks.[7] Because the body of a Model T contained so much wood, high heat in the drying tunnels wasn't desirable, and each coat took hours to dry. Painting was a bottleneck in production until the late 1930s, when Ford began to use infrared light to reduce drying times from hours to minutes. In the same years, "synthetic resin enamels took the place of the early varnishes

FIGURE 10.2
Robots lowering the roof of a Ford Focus into place and welding body panels together at Ford's Michigan Avenue plant, May 2011. Photograph by David E. Nye.

and lacquers, and an endless variety of colors was possible."[8] Even in the 1970s there were still painting jobs on assembly lines, and the paints were hard on the lungs. Because of the health risks involved, painting was one of the first jobs to be automated. In 2011, robots gently immerse each vehicle in a pool of undercoating, and shortly afterward other robots apply a base coat, then two tinted clear coats. Spraying multiple coats without waiting for complete drying is a new Ford process that eliminates the cost of repeatedly drying a body in heat tunnels.

The painted Focus bodies move over a covered bridge to the upper level of the Final Assembly Building, which covers an area as large as 22 football fields. As the bodies drop down one story, they swing into position over another line carrying their matching drive trains. Workers have long called the precise lowering of the body on to the drive train the "marriage" that creates a vehicle. The linkage once required four men to line up the drive train with the body as it was slowly dropped into position and bolted fast. Today the "marriage" takes place automatically, with no witnesses. This is a remarkable example of automation, for the mix of different bodies on the overhead line must perfectly match the sequence of drive trains on the lower line.

FIGURE 10.3
Power trains (below) about to be "married" with painted car bodies (above) just before final assembly, Michigan Avenue plant, May 2011. Photograph by David E. Nye.

Next the doors are removed and hung on parallel lines that run along beside the main car assembly line. This avoids scratching the doors and makes the body more accessible to the workers who transform it from a shell into a comfortable, fully appointed vehicle. They install the electric wiring, cover it with carpeting and upholstery, add the dashboard, the seats, the windshield and the rear window, the radio, and other electronic equipment, and mount various components under the hood. Workers still have roughly one minute for each task, but there are many more parts in each car than in 1913. The line also looks far different. Instead of pulling the car along a raised track, as was done for decades, an entire section of the floor slowly slides along. Workers casually step on or off this moving platform, which is flush with the floor and carries workers as well as the vehicle itself. The traditional lines used from the 1920s to the 1950s forced workers to stretch, crawl, stoop, and otherwise accommodate themselves to the fixed height of the cars passing by. But since every installation cannot best be done at the same height, the car is now lifted or lowered automatically to the most convenient position for each worker and each job. Workers set the ideal height for their station. As a vehicle approaches, a device that resembles a giant accordion under each car automatically inflates or deflates, raising or lowering it as required.

Back in 1913, Model Ts were all the same shape, size, and color, and their identicalness was central to the concept of mass production. But today's Focuses vary a great deal. The plant has two different model platforms and can assemble five different models, each in a wide range of colors. A red five-door hatchback may follow a white four-door sedan. A newer factory in Louisville produces eight different models on three platforms.[9] Some parts are used in all models, but many differ from one car to the next. Even the side mirrors can vary. How do workers know what parts to select as the cars come along, one every minute? A sheet of paper attached above the left front wheel well specifies that car's precise "DNA." (See figure 10.6.) It lists the components that vary by model and the options that a customer

FIGURE 10.4
A Cadillac assembly line in 1927. Courtesy Photographic Department, Cleveland Public Library.

FIGURE 10.5
The "apron" containing components hangs in front of a vehicle. Beneath it an accordion-like device expands or contracts to adjust the height of the entire car for the best position to do each task on the Focus line at Ford's Michigan Avenue plant. Photograph by David E. Nye, May 2011.

has selected. The variety of the cars coming off the line is staggering. Henry Ford made his fortune on identical Model Ts, but today cars can be built with up to half a million possible variations.

Using bar codes, a software system tracks the movement and installation of every part. Each can be located at any time, even after they have been assembled into complete cars that await shipment. If quality-control inspectors discover a certain batch of parts are defective, all of the cars that contain them can be located instantly and electronically locked. After that, they literally cannot be shipped—the plant gate will not open for such a vehicle—until the part has been replaced or repaired. It is unlikely that altogether wrong

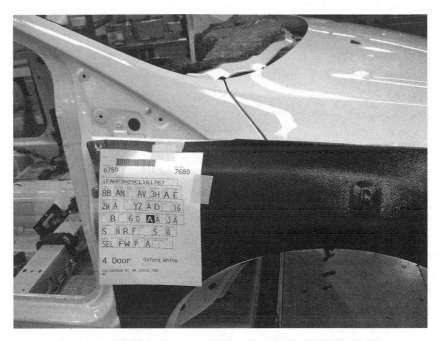

FIGURE 10.6
The "DNA sheet" above the right front wheel of a car on the assembly line of the
Michigan Avenue plant. Photograph by David E. Nye, May 2011.

parts will be installed, however, because as each vehicle goes down the line
the components required hang right in front of it, in what looks like a giant
apron covered with pockets. The man or woman who installs any non-
standard part will find it in the apron, and it should correspond to what is
called for on the car's "DNA sheet." Moreover, digital cameras periodically
scan the work and check what is installed against what is called for. At the
end of the line, the doors, which meanwhile have been fitted with windows,
locks, upholstery, and other parts, are reinstalled. The completed car moves
into a final inspection area, where more cameras and inspectors examine it
under specially designed lighting that reveals even tiny flaws in the finish.
Once approved, it is fueled, started, tested, and made ready for shipment.

Five months after the new Focus line commenced operation, progress
from steel blanks to a completed car took 20 hours. That speed would have
seemed miraculous in 1975, much less in 1913, yet it will doubtless improve. The earlier Ford Taurus, toward the end of its production run, took
only 14 hours. The new factory needs just 3,000 workers and managers, on

two shifts, to produce 300,000 cars a year, roughly 100 for every employee. In 1913, Ford needed 13,000 people to make 260,000 cars each year, or 20 per employee. But such comparisons are complicated. Parts made elsewhere represent human labor that must be counted. In 1913 Highland Park got parts from nearby suppliers. At the Focus plant, 40 or more containers arrive every day, full of parts from all over the world. Further complicating the comparison are the hundreds of robots that do the jobs that in 1913 were done by human beings. Building and maintaining these robots also took thousands of hours of labor. Finally, Highland Park made a much simpler car, in only one version, whereas the new plant produces thousands of variants of several models on multiple platforms.

It is difficult to construct a statistic that takes all these factors into account, but one can grasp the scale of the change. In 1914 the Ford assembly line produced 30 times as many cars per worker as the nearby craft-based Packard factory that Frederick Winslow Taylor had organized. This appears to be a 3,000 percent increase in productivity. But the Packard was more luxurious and roughly three times as expensive as the Model T, so perhaps the productivity increase should be reduced somewhat. On the other hand, after 1914, Ford made incremental improvements every year, slashing Model T assembly time from 966 man-hours in 1912 to 228 man-hours in 1923.[10] This was a further improvement of 400 percent. During the next half century, up to 1973, overall productivity doubled, albeit in small increments of a few percentage points each year. Then Toyota's lean methods further doubled the 1973 productivity level. When Detroit caught up with the Japanese in the 1990s, therefore, the assembly line was perhaps four times as efficient as it had been in circa 1923 and vastly more efficient than when first introduced. Moreover, since the 1990s productivity continued to rise as robots replaced many workers. The whole transformation is even more impressive when compared with craft methods used at the Taylorized Packard plant in 1912. If the Michigan Avenue Focus plant reverted to that form of craft production, its 3,000 workers could make only 2,000 Focuses a year, instead of 300,000.

In 2011 many different vehicles came down a single line, and workers no longer had just one job. They worked on teams who were collectively responsible for one section of the line. Quality control, once focused near the end of each of the five phases of production, now is continual. There are no large inventories; instead there is just-in-time delivery. The whole system is

tied together by computers that record the movements of parts from shipment to arrival to installation. There are four generations of computers,
each with different software. The programming contains 9.5 million lines
of code and is outsourced to Microsoft, which also is responsible for testing and trouble shooting. Computers steer the many robots and automatic
machines that make the panels, weld them into bodies, and paint them. But
workers remain numerous in final assembly, even if pre-assembly of whole
units such as the dashboard has reduced the number of parts added on the
line. Toyota, Ford, and other manufacturers have found that automation still
has its limits, and the newest factories have more workers on final assembly
than those of a few years earlier. Reducing the fixed expense for robots and
automation gives manufacturing more flexibility. For many jobs, human
beings remain more adaptable than machines.[11] Moreover, labor is only 15
percent of the direct cost of making the car. The rest of the costs are in the
plant, in machinery, in transportation, in materials, in design, in testing, and
in marketing.

Relative to 1913, managers have less influence over their factories, because they too are working within guidelines established by the computerized system. A manager has less scope because the robots, the tracking
of parts, the automatic quality-control checks, and the organization of the
work are not so much a hierarchy he commands as a system that he monitors
and maintains. The vast system is tightly linked together, and the manager's
job is to keep it running according to standards that to a considerable degree
are built in. Workers likewise have limited scope for decision making, even
if they now work in teams. Their work is evaluated automatically. If they
install the wrong part or put the right one in incorrectly, the problem is soon
exposed. The individual, whether manager or worker, matters less because
computers so thoroughly tie the whole together. On a 1913 assembly line,
workers felt diminished because the jobs were repetitive and interchangeable. After lean production was introduced, teamwork became the norm. A
worker had to master more than one skill, and each task required continual
adjustment to the different models coming down the line. This made work
more interesting, but it also eliminated brief respites from pressure. Overall, the post-lean-production computerized assembly-line factory needs only
3,000 workers to produce as many cars as 15,000 classic assembly-line workers could produce in 1913. Moreover, the cars coming out of the factory are
more varied and far more complex than the Model T.

A factory tour explains how cars are currently made, but it doesn't reveal what it is like to work there or explain the assembly line itself, which has become far more than the means to this single end. Because the assembly line has become intertwined with many aspects of American society, including leisure and consumption as well as work, its meaning has become almost ungraspable in its multiple forms and varied effects. In *Capitalism and Material Life* the great French historian Fernand Braudel noted that societies are often slow to understand new techniques or to develop practical applications of discoveries. Technology, he concluded, "is only an instrument," and "man does not always know how to use it."[12] We are still learning how best to use the assembly line, and we are still trying to understand its long-term implications. To grasp its larger trajectory, it is helpful to see how it has been understood during the last century. There appear to be three kinds of stories.

Perhaps the best known of these stories today depicts the classic Ford assembly line as a harsh and unremitting taskmaster. In *The Gravedigger's Daughter* Joyce Carol Oates described a woman working on an assembly line in upstate New York. The noise "lulled her into a trance," and "her teeth rattled from the conveyor belt vibrations." She was "unable to turn her attention away from the strops of tubing on the rubber belt moving jerkily along and always faster than you wanted." She was constantly in danger of having her hand "hooked by the stamping machine and half the fingers smashed."[13] The temperature in the plant rose to 110°F in the summer, and the heat was almost unbearable because she had to wear goggles, a heavy safety apron, and work shoes with reinforced toes.[14] Few such jobs now exist in the United States, and the description of the stamping machine would be more accurate for 1933 than for 2013.

In *Brazil* John Updike described a new factory as "a great, hard-hearted machine." It was "a giant shed whose northern end, like a hungry mouth, took in Volkswagen parts, and whose southern end, like a tireless anus, emitted the completed [Volkswagens]." Inside, "beneath a heaven consisting of a flat steel roof," the men are deafened by "the racket of assembly . . . so incessant and loud" that the protagonist "feared he would lose not only his ear for *forro* music but all capacity for the enjoyment of life. The machines made machines of men."[15] Like Oates, Updike imagined an assembly line that scarcely existed any more inside the United States. However eloquent, their work harked back to the social realism of the 1930s.

It seemed that for most American authors, the assembly line long remained that of Henry Ford. In *Middlesex*, Jeffrey Eugenides described Ford's River Rouge plant in 1922. It was "that massive, forbidding, awe-inspiring complex we saw from the highway, that controlled Vesuvius of chutes, tubes, ladders, catwalks, fire, and smoke, known, like a plague or a monarch, only by a color: 'The Rouge.'"[16] For an employee going to work there each day, the factory is first distant clouds of smoke, then a chemical smell, then "a fortress of dark brick," and finally clamoring, tangled, converging assembly lines that stretch beyond the factory to the mines and forests where they suck raw materials out of the earth. "Historical fact: people stopped being human in 1913. That was the year Henry Ford put his cars on rollers and made his workers adopt the speed of the assembly line."[17] In such passages the assembly line seems a dehumanizing force imposed on society. In cinema, too, the assembly line has been typically part of an oppressive or authoritarian regime, from Pink Floyd's rock opera *The Wall* to the 1999 movie *The Matrix*. Likewise, the labor depicted in Lars von Trier's 2000 film *Dancer in the Dark* reprises earlier visualizations of the factory.[18] The actual assembly lines of 2013 are almost never represented in film, in literature, or in popular culture.

This oppressive assembly line story, in which an isolated worker does the same task repeatedly, became the most common description of mass production in the 1930s, and it has become the story taken for granted by many people. Yet it is typical of the last in the cycle of stories about new technologies. Each new machine—for example, the railroad, the airplane, the television, or the assembly line—passes through a characteristic cycle of public responses: celebration, adoption, naturalization, complaint, and resignation. After an initial celebration, a technology's utopian sheen begins to wear off. The technology is adopted and woven into everyday life, and it becomes "natural." It is taken for granted. In the United States the assembly line was celebrated for a decade after 1913, and rapidly adopted. It was naturalized by the end of the 1920s. In the next stage, the once utopian machine or system begins to seem a problem or a necessary evil. Americans had a mania for their new railways in the 1830s, but by the 1880s railways were commonplace and were attacked by reformers as monopolistic concentrations of power.[19] Americans yearned for an alternative mode of transportation. They readily embraced the automobile, and the passenger railroads went into a long decline. Similarly, by the 1960s and especially in the 1970s the assembly line had become familiar but unloved. It was denounced for abolishing individuality, for wastefully mass-producing, and for worsening the environmental crisis. In the last decades of the twentieth century, consultants and managers promoted lean production and mass customization as superior alternatives. But lean production systems were still assembly lines, and the public's enthusiasm for them was short-lived.

Americans had evinced much more excitement about the assembly line when it had first appeared, in 1913. In that early story it seemed the culmination of a century of American industrial development. In this perspective, the original Ford line came together quickly between 1907 and 1913 because all the elements needed to construct it had been developed during preceding generations. In the late 1890s reliable electric motors became available. Their use increased rapidly, making possible flexible factory layouts with the machines no longer tethered to long overhead drive shafts. New forms of production became possible, synthesizing techniques developed earlier in slaughterhouses, canneries, clock factories, bicycle plants, armories, and elsewhere. The assembly line was also predicated on the idea of making fully interchangeable metal parts, something that had been achieved in the course of the nineteenth century. The assembly line was understood as the triumphant conclusion to a story that began with Oliver Evans' eighteenth-century automatic flour mill. This rapid industrial evolution became a central American story during the early years of the Cold War, when it was used to define the United States as a nation of democratic tinkerers.

In this story the assembly line was the engine of a widely shared prosperity. The Ford Motor Company conceivably might have tried to keep its details a secret, but instead it set up a moving line at the San Francisco Exposition in 1915, and it welcomed both competitors and millions of visitors to Highland Park to see the line there in operation. For some the vast factory seemed a sublime man-made landscape as deeply moving as Niagara Falls and other wonders of nature.[20] To explain his new system in detail, Henry Ford collaborated with the authors of *Ford Methods and Ford Shops*. The company also made educational films about its methods and distributed them free to movie theaters. The system pioneered at Highland Park spread rapidly to all parts of the country, where it was used to produce millions of new appliances, bicycles, bathtubs, lawnmowers, gadgets, and home furnishings that increased the level of the average American's material culture. The higher wages paid in the 1920s further contributed to this view of the assembly line as the agent of progress. Mass production apparently guaranteed a higher standard of living for everyone. It underlay the world's fairs in Chicago (1933) and New York (1939), as well as the "People's Capitalism" public-relations campaign of the 1950s, and it remains an important part of corporate advertising and political discourse.

This progressive story also emphasized how the assembly line enhanced the global leadership of the United States. Ford and General Motors early built factories overseas, enabling foreign engineers and consumers to see mass production in action. The assembly line quickly became known throughout the industrialized world. Franklin D. Roosevelt embellished this story with the notions that the assembly line was democratic in origin and that it ensured victory in World War II. Later the Marshall Plan and other Cold War programs sought to convert the Free World to mass production. It was argued that the assembly line would defeat the Communist Party line. Bill Clinton retold this story in capsule form in a 1999 speech:

Here in Detroit nearly a century ago, as all of you know better than me, Henry Ford set history in motion with the very first assembly line. He built not only a Model T but also a new model for the way America would do business for quite a long while. He said he was looking for leaders and thinkers and workers with, I quote, 'an infinite capacity to not know what can't be done.' People like that came together in Detroit and all across America; they forged America's transition from farm to factory. Detroit led the way, and America led the world.[21]

When Barack Obama spoke at the University of Maryland a decade later, he also used this narrative:

Remember that it is precisely in times like these, in moments of trial and moments of hardship, that Americans rediscover the ingenuity and resilience that makes us who we are; that made the auto industry what it once was and what it will be again; that sent those first mass-produced cars rolling off the assembly lines; that built an arsenal of democracy that propelled America to victory in the Second World War; and that powered our economic prowess in the first American century.[22]

While the triumphant story of democratic progress remained a staple of presidential rhetoric about the assembly line, the critical counter narrative argued that the assembly line was not exclusively American, nor was it necessarily the hallmark of democracy. Lenin and Hitler also embraced it, and it could be found in some of the Nazis' concentration camps. The counternarrative presented the assembly line much as Oates, Updike, and Eugenides did: as an inexorable force that crushes the individual and threatens humanity with dull repetition and standardization. In these stories the assembly line levels downward to mediocrity and conformity. It seemed that mass production erased cultural differences. Many argued that industrial technologies were homogenizing people, places, and products, making them interchangeable. Lewis Mumford, Jacques Ellul, Theodore Roszak, and many others argued that because technical systems had become more complex and interlinked, human beings had become dependent upon the machine and were being forced to adjust to its demands. Mass-production technologies apparently shaped the personality and dominated mental habits. The Beat poets and the Counterculture also attacked the cultural conformity of a mass society. Other critics, such as Vance Packard, disparaged the wastefulness of an assembly-line culture, a theme later taken up by environmentalists. Later still, post-modernists saw the assembly line as a central technology in the compression of space and the subdivision of time, and in the promotion of a culture that idealized the copy—indeed, a culture in which there were no longer any originals. Neo-Marxists were particularly scathing in making the case,[23] and supposed that society passed through unavoidable stages of increasing regimentation, labeled "Taylorism" and "Fordism." Each of these critical narratives presented the assembly line as exploitative, predictable, and unavoidable.

A third group of stories argued, in contrast, that the assembly line's effects were unforeseeable and unintended. Certainly the US government didn't invite Japanese engineers to tour its factories in the 1950s with the expectation that they would invent a superior production system, challenge Detroit, and invade the American market. More broadly, Henry Ford had expected the assembly line to underwrite high wages so workers would be able to buy the consumer goods they manufactured. The high-wage policy was further reinforced after unionization, and from the 1950s until the early 1970s the UAW improved the yearly income and the benefits of its members. Auto workers set a standard of compensation for American society as a whole. But after the mid 1970s, wages didn't kept pace with productivity. By 2012, millions of Americans worked longer hours for lower wages than their German, Swedish or Dutch counterparts. Even so, American corporations moved many jobs to other countries. This third narrative of the assembly line found its visual equivalent in photographs of abandoned factories and the decaying cores of industrial cities such as Detroit, Cleveland, and Buffalo. Even parts of Ford's famous River Rouge plant have been abandoned.

(See figure 10.1.) Such images suggest an ironic story in which the assembly line's promises of prosperity weren't realized. Productivity increased, but jobs disappeared, wages stagnated, factories were closed, and communities in the "Rust Belt" withered.

These conflicting narratives suggest how hard it is to achieve a clear perspective on the assembly line. Early commentators thought it was something completely new, when in fact the assembly line was to a considerable degree a combination of earlier practices. Likewise, many reporters and much of the general public mistakenly focused on the moving belt and saw that as the central innovation.[24] Quite a wide range of observers were confused about what the assembly line meant. Between 1914 and 1920 many American socialists welcomed Henry Ford's innovation and saw him as a maverick businessman on the side of the workers. In contrast, some businessmen attacked Ford's high-wage policy and worried that it would create serious economic problems. Ford himself thought the assembly-line factory could be exported with minimal changes to the rest of the world, but cultural differences made technology transfer partial and difficult. The Russians lacked industrial management skills, an educated workforce, and a consumer culture. The British wanted more worker autonomy on the factory floor, smaller cars, and right-hand drive. The French wanted a greater variety of cars. The Germans resisted deskilling of workers and often couldn't make the enormous investments an assembly-line factory required.

Some version of the assembly line did emerge in each of these countries, but in none of them was it established as thoroughly as in Detroit. Nevertheless, many Europeans persisted in seeing "Fordism" as a stage in history, and the Frankfurt School viewed mass production as the destroyer of cultural values, leveling differences and creating a banal world of repetition. Such critiques also became common in the United States by the 1950s. Yet, in fact, as mass consumption grew differences flourished. In the 1920s, telephones, like the Model T, were identical and black. But as the telephone became universal, its design metamorphosed into thousands of variations. Likewise, the owners of houses in Levittown transformed their once-identical houses year by year until each one was unique. A century after the assembly line emerged, the car makers provided consumers with millions of model variations to choose between.

These developments were difficult to foresee, however. For decades after World War II the "Big Three" (GM, Ford, and Chrysler) believed that they would soon manufacture in automated factories. Yet by the mid 1970s, 99 percent of the workforce was still flesh and blood, with only a few thousand robots. Meanwhile, factory efficiency had stagnated relative to Japan. In part because American manufacturers had led the world in efficiency for generations, it took them decades to understand the superiority of lean production. Japanese firms didn't buy as many expensive, specialized machines. Rather, they cut waste and engaged creatively with their workers. Like Europeans in the 1920s, many American firms at first proved to be poor recipients of technological transfer. Some claimed that the Japanese methods could work only in a homogeneous culture that didn't value individualism. American automakers were slow to learn lean production, and they lost market share because they thought they could select one or another element of the system rather than make a comprehensive change. American unions made the transition to lean production more difficult, because they helped to create and protect a byzantine system of job classifications that thwarted innovations in the production process. The traditional assembly line could survive only as long as it was more efficient and made better products than foreign competitors. In fact, American workers knew how to be far more efficient, but they hoarded the time they saved and only grudgingly contributed it to more efficient overall production, in stark contrast to how Japanese managers and workers built cooperation into their systems. American managers and workers had become path-dependent, holding on to the classic assembly line that had served them well from 1913 until 1973.

Many ordinary Americans also got it wrong. From the late 1920s through the 1930s, during the postwar period, and again in the 1990s, they feared that mass production meant technological unemployment. Instead, as the assembly line raised productivity, it facilitated the shift to a white-collar service economy. But the assembly line wasn't used to reduce working hours for all. It didn't usher in the age of early retirement and unprecedented leisure that had been confidently predicted in the early years of the Cold War. Instead, the pace and the hours of work increased. Ford's $5 day had helped workers to become consumers, but after 1975, as productivity rose, corporations used profits to pay dividends and raise executive salaries. Class differences increased in the United States after 1990, contradicting the Cold War expectation that mass production leveled class differences and distributed abundance. The Department of State had believed it could promote democracy by exporting technologies of mass production. The Marshall Plan did help to improve the productivity of Western Europe, which already had democratic traditions. But Asian nations offer a less clear-cut case. Are they using mass production to build economic and political democracy? The jury is still out.

Some form of the assembly line lies at the heart of most contemporary production. It has become a ubiquitous expectation that modern factories will standardize parts, subdivide work, ensure precise timing and sequencing of tasks, transfer heavy labor to machines, and seamlessly coordinate the flow of production. For a century, it has been found that efficiency can keep improving. Geographical constraints on production have also been largely abolished. All sorts of work can be performed in widely dispersed locations and yet be part of a single process. The operation of the global assembly line also embodies the idea of acceleration, which has been woven deeply into consciousness. Producers expect continual efficiency improvements, consumers think it natural to own ever more goods, and people generally expect to multi-task and to pack more experiences into less time.

These expectations have created worldwide pressure for continual acceleration in the pace of living. As a result, the increasing production of assembly lines has become inseparable from the ecological problems of resource depletion and global warming. From an environmental perspective, the assembly line can seem apocalyptic, because it churns out consumer goods and threatens to exhaust the earth's resources. Thus, its success can also be seen as a story of environmental decline. In 1913 few imagined a future with global warming, oil shortages, and unsustainable demands for the earth's resources. Can the assembly line instead become part of an environmentally sustainable system? Can it be placed at the center of a new, fourth story about sustainability and recycling?

Manufacturers have begun to respond to environmental concerns by polluting less and by building "green factories." Factory tours that once emphasized speed and efficiency now also highlight recycling and sustainability. It has become good public relations to reduce a company's carbon footprint. Ford managed this at its Dagenhem engine assembly plant on the banks of the Thames outside London by installing three giant wind turbines. They produce 11.4 million kilowatt-hours, enough for all the factory's needs.[25] That wasn't a new concern. In the 1920s and the 1930s, Henry Ford worried about the long-term environmental implications of the assembly line.

He recognized that demands on natural resources would lead to shortages, and he looked for ways to use renewable materials, such as soybeans and wood, in making automobiles. Ford encouraged what was then called "chemurgy," a proto-environmental movement that found industrial uses for farm products.[26]

In 2000, William Clay Ford, great-grandson of the founder, decided to spend $2 billion rebuilding the River Rouge factory with the environment and lean manufacturing in mind. It is a flexible factory with three assembly lines that can produce nine different models. It has a living green roof that covers 15 acres and greatly reduces water runoff as well as providing insulation. (See figure 10.7.) The parking lots were also redesigned to absorb rain rather than shed it as runoff, and the site allows water to percolate slowly through marshy areas before entering the Rouge River. The soil was full of industrial chemicals, but carefully selected plantings are neutralizing or breaking down the toxic substances. The plantings were cheaper than replacing tons of soil, and they beautified the grounds. Furthermore, a wetland area costs millions of dollars less than building new storm sewers. Inside, the rebuilt factory has abundant natural light and many energy-saving features.[27] Ford hired Harley Ellis Devereaux to design a Visitor Center that in 2009 earned LEED gold certification. Like the Rouge factory next door, it has a green roof.[28] Ford also won the first Green Car Award in 2006, for its Mercury Mariner. Moreover, in 2012 an all-electric Focus was available.

General Motors was also interested in becoming a green company. It won the Green Car Award in 2008 for its Chevrolet Tahoe Hybrid, a large vehicle often used by police and fire departments, and in 2012 the Chevrolet Volt was one of the highest-rated hybrid cars.[29] A GM factory in Lansing was awarded a gold certificate by the United States Green Building Council.[30] One-fourth of all the materials used to build it had been recycled. Each year it consumes 4 million fewer gallons of water and 3 million fewer kilowatt-hours of electricity than a conventional facility of the same size. Its white polymer roof absorbs little heat in summer. Moreover, half of the entire site was left undeveloped as a nature preserve. Volkswagen sought the same distinction for its new Chattanooga factory, which began production in 2011. It had extra wall insulation and a white reflective roof, and it too minimized the use of water and electricity. Volkswagen adopted the slogan "Green city, green plant, green car."[31] Its Jetta was the American "green car of the year" in 2009. In short, at Ford, at GM, at VW, and at other companies green

FIGURE 10.7
The green roof on the remodeled portion of the River Rouge plant, May 2011.
Photograph by David E. Nye.

manufacturing is considered both a good marketing strategy and a way to save operating costs.[32]

However, there is a contradiction between green manufacturing and many aspects of the automobile industry. Planned obsolescence is not an inherently ecological practice. Large cars, SUVs, and trucks are wasteful, even if the vehicles are disassembled at the end of their useful lives and recycled. The assembly line is not the ideal instrument with which to promote frugality or minimize consumption. Likewise, the globalization of production relies on enormous energy use for the transportation of both components and finished goods. The assembly line was hardly developed as a mechanism for sustainability, and to make it into one requires new cultural practices.

Some new ideas have begun to emerge. The architect in charge of the makeover of the River Rouge plant, William McDonough, became an international spokesperson for integrating product recycling into the system of production. In 2002 he co-authored *From Cradle to Cradle*, a book that made the case for improving productivity by planning for reuse at every step in the manufacturing process.[33] "Building a truly sustainable automobile indus-try," McDonough asserted, "means developing closed-loop systems for the manufacturing and re-utilization of auto parts. In Europe, the End-of-Life Vehicle Directive [passed by the EU in September 2000] makes manufac-turers responsible for automotive materials, pushing companies to design for disassembly and effective resource recovery. Cradle-to-cradle systems, in which materials either go back to industry or safely back to the soil, are built for effective resource recovery."[34] In Germany, for example, any mo-tor vehicle that has been registered in the EU for at least a month before disposal can be turned in for free disassembly and shredding.[35] By 2006, three-fourths of all vehicles were being recycled in this way, and the EU mandated further improvements.

Such practices are better than simply junking old cars, but they aren't good enough. They reduce waste, but the materials recycled are degraded in quality and purity. A car shredder mixes together high-grade steel, cop-per, and other metals. When smelted, this yields a lower-grade product that can't be used to make new car bodies. To avoid such "down-cycling," McDonough develops products that can truly be recycled. He advocates thinking about industrial production as part of a "technical metabolism" that "can be designed to mirror natural nutrient cycles; it's a closed-loop system in which valuable, high-tech synthetics and mineral resources circulate in an endless cycle of production, recovery and remanufacture." Society needs disassembly lines that recover materials without degrading them for reuse in new products.[36] In its best form, the "technical metabolism" mirrors biolog-ical metabolism and is powered by wind and solar energy.[37] The goal is not to minimize harm but to maximize environmental benefits. "The health of the site is measured not in terms of meeting minimum government-imposed standards but with respect to things like the number of earthworms per cubic foot of soil, the diversity of birds and insects on the land and of aquatic spe-cies in a nearby river, and the attractiveness of the site to local residents."[38] Reconceiving every assembly line as part of a larger technical metabolism can be linked to lean production's emphasis on eliminating waste. However, at the centennial of the assembly line, "technical metabolism" remains more a metaphor than a working model of a sustainable industrial economy. To achieve that goal will require new kinds of factories, new corporate values, and new forms of consumption. Environmentally sustainable production can flourish if consumers support recycling rather than throw old products away. The assembly line will have to be reconceived as far more than a physical arrangement of machines. It is at the center of an entire cultural system that stretches far beyond the factory gates, including farms, iron and copper mines, rubber plantations, transportation networks, energy systems, steel mills, parts suppliers, the factory itself, banks, repair shops, recycling programs, and landfills. If misused, the assembly line only appears to guarantee a cornucopia of goods; in fact it becomes a sorcerer's apprentice, rolling out disposable goods that choke landfills.

Braudel's conclusion remains sound. We are still learning how best to use the assembly line. Indeed, the many narratives about it are all being acted out simultaneously. In 2013 Americans are using the assembly line both to enrich and to impoverish, both to create and to eliminate jobs, both to build arsenals and to make consumer goods, and both to diminish and to increase class differences. Some factories have closed forever, others have moved to Latin America or Asia, and still others remain competitive in Europe and the United States by combining lean production and automation. Many of the products of assembly lines fill vast landfills, but many also are taken apart and recycled. At the assembly line's centenary, its overall trajectory remains uncertain, and its forms are still emerging. To one generation the railroad or the electrical system or the assembly line seems to herald a utopian future, but later the same technology is attacked as a despicable monopoly, an inhumane system, or an environmental calamity. The assembly line was welcomed with lavish praise just after 1913 but since has often been excoriated. Even with a century's hindsight, we are still grappling with what it has meant and what it still portends.

Yet some conclusions can be drawn. The assembly line wasn't a planned development; rather, it emerged in 1913 from a dynamic situation. People with many different technical backgrounds were hired by a rapidly expanding company. Together they sought ways to improve productivity, and when they moved into a new, spacious factory in 1910, they pooled their ideas and drew on their varied work experiences to create a new method of production. It is quite telling that Ford's executives didn't even have a name for the assembly line at first, and that the term "assembly line" was little used even in the technical press in 1913 and 1914. The Ford executives' innovation wasn't a research-and-development goal, nor was it first developed as a theory and then put into practice. Rather, it emerged in a company that was distinctly un-bureaucratic, that encouraged managers to experiment, and that didn't have rigid walls between its departments. Moreover, many of these generalizations also apply to the Japanese automobile industry when it developed the new methods that were later to be called "lean production."

Both the Ford team of 1910–1914 and the Toyota team of the 1950s were tinkering with and improving their systems of production in order to meet rapidly rising demand. Both achieved startling results even though, as Takahiro Fujimoto concluded, "the Japanese had no idea—in any systemic, big-picture sense—what they were doing."[39] This remark should not be taken to mean that they were just lucky. Rather, these were brilliant engineers who learned by going where they had to go, in an exploratory process familiar to artists and inventors but foreign to the mindset of planners and bureaucrats. Had the employees at either Ford or Toyota applied for a grant, claiming to be able to more than double factory productivity using already existing technologies, no doubt their claim would have been rejected as unlikely or even absurd. (How could the thousands of others working in the same industry not have seen the opportunity?) But rather than make extravagant claims beforehand, they worked together to see what was possible. The history of the assembly line, both its invention and reinvention, suggests that fundamental transformations are unpredictable. They can emerge unexpectedly when talented people are given time, resources, and opportunities to experiment.[40]

Once a new technological process or system exists, observers can see how pre-existing techniques, ideas, machines, and processes contributed to its emergence. In retrospect, a major innovation often seems obvious. History appears to move logically from Oliver Evans' mill to Eli Whitney's early efforts to manufacture guns with interchangeable parts to the mass production of clocks and sewing machines. The story seems to lead inexorably toward Highland Park and the assembly line of 1913. In retrospect the assembly line begins to look inevitable, but it is important to understand that it was not. Prototypes of the assembly line emerged briefly in Sweden and in France before 1800, but neither was developed.[41] And the assembly line might not have developed in Detroit in 1913 either. Craft production was profitable and could have continued. American automobile factories of the 1920s might have resembled their European counterparts, and American cities might have remained more densely populated, with greater reliance on mass transit and bicycles.

The difficulties of technology transfer also suggest that major innovations are hardly inevitable. Ford and General Motors invested enormous sums in

European expansion programs, and European automakers repeatedly sent teams to Detroit to study the automobile plants there. But technological transfer proved slow and often difficult, and in no case did it result in a European factory that functioned just like an American plant. The assembly line, like any other technology, is not an abstract concept but a process embedded in culture. The United States of 1913 was a large market with a rapidly growing middle class. There were millions of potential customers for identical, inexpensive, mass-produced automobiles. The same wasn't true of any nation in Europe, whose automobile makers couldn't reap all the benefits of the Ford system. Their production runs had to be smaller, and their customers demanded a more differentiated line of vehicles. Furthermore, protectionist tariffs balkanized the European market. Ford and General Motors would have preferred to have just a few large factories that manufactured cars for all of Europe. However, they were forced to establish separate national plants and to develop somewhat different models for each market, which made their European cars more expensive than those they produced in the United States. If American companies often found it difficult to adjust their mass-production systems to European conditions, Austin, Renault, Citroën, Fiat, Opel, and other European manufacturers adopted the assembly line slowly and selectively during the interwar years. Cultural differences—national, economic, managerial, and industrial—obstructed full transfer of the classic assembly line.

Half a century later, technology transfer proved difficult for Americans when they were confronted with new forms of Japanese manufacturing. Toyota, Honda, and Nissan were already outcompeting Detroit in the 1970s, but it took more than two decades for the American firms to understand and adopt their new practices. Like the Europeans between 1910 and 1930, US engineers and managers made many journeys to study the competition. They engaged in joint ventures, and they tried to adopt new ideas selectively. But technology transfer was slow between 1975 and 1985, because it met resistance from labor unions, suppliers, and management itself. GM's Saturn Division ultimately failed, even though it was backed by GM's president. The Saturn Division had its own factory, and it had streamlined its labor system with entirely new contracts with the UAW. But it failed to spearhead a transformation, and GM lost a considerable share of the automobile market before achieving the efficiencies of lean production at the end of the 1990s. Ford made the change more quickly, but still required about 15 years. Technology transfer is difficult, because it is never merely a technical change. It is always a complex social transaction. This cultural resistance is due in part to what historical economists call "path dependency" inside each firm, and in part to what historians of technology call the "technological momentum" of the entire ensemble of institutions and practices that surround any successful, large system, such as a centralized electrical grid, a railroad network, or the assembly-line system of production.

The generalizations that emerge from the history of the assembly line are interrelated. The technological momentum of existing systems encourages small, incremental changes, but otherwise reinforces the status quo and resistance to the introduction of alternative systems. A fundamental change in the production system isn't likely to emerge in older industries that have long-established methods (or strong path dependency) and stable markets. Technological innovation is more likely in new industries—such as the American auto industry circa 1913 or the Japan auto industry circa 1955—in which strong demand puts a premium on innovation, especially if rapid expansion of the firm brings in new people with a variety of backgrounds. In such companies one is more likely to see the sudden emergence of what Joel Mokyr has called "a macroinvention"—that is, "an invention without clear-cut parentage, representing a clear break from previous technique."[42]

Detroit was the specific location where this particular macroinvention emerged, but today it can be found everywhere. Continually adapted to new products, cultural geographies, and markets, it has become a ubiquitous general purpose technology. In the United States, it is woven deeply into consciousness, and seems a "natural" way to organize work or to structure the built environment. Americans learned to assemble what they need from services along their highways (some of which they called beltways), to assemble meals in cafeterias, to modularize their education into interchangeable credit courses, and to desire identical mass-produced goods. By embracing the assembly line, Americans also adopted the acceleration of production and its corollary, intensified consumption, which logically also required high wages. Henry Ford understood these relationships in 1913, which is one reason why as soon as the assembly line was up and running he announced the $5 day. For the next two generations, with the notable exception of the Great Depression, production, consumption, and wages all rose together. Millions of blue-collar Americans more than doubled their real wages, and became homeowners. But this economic order began to unravel during the energy crisis and the recession of the 1970s, exacerbated by competition from Europe and from Japan. The real wages of assembly-line workers stopped growing, and blue-collar America shrank as jobs were exported to Latin America and Asia, or were eliminated through lean production, or were automated out of existence. General Motors, Chrysler, and Ford had once directly employed more than a million men and women, with millions more working for their suppliers. But by 2012 the "Big Three" no longer played such a large part in the national economy. More than 80 percent of their workforce was gone, and workers hired after 2007 were paid less in real terms than those hired in 1973.

Despite this enormous loss of manufacturing jobs, Americans still expected to enjoy a cornucopia of assembly-line goods. But in 2013, with supplies of gasoline uncertain amid the threat of global warming, it was time to revise America's understanding of the assembly line. Accelerated production no longer assured higher wages and better living standards. In practice, the assembly line hadn't broken down the divisions between classes and ushered in an egalitarian "people's democracy," but rather had been used to widen the gulf between workers and managers. Nor, as the suicidal workers at Foxconn reminded the world, was exporting mass production certain to produce economic equality or political democracy abroad.

In 2013 Americans struggled to hold on to the form of life that they had created through the assembly line, the high wages it once paid, and the cornucopia of goods it produced. What had become an assembly-line way of life ran ever faster as people worked longer hours, and commuted in ever more automobiles back to homes full of mass-produced appliances, gadgets, and toys. Their children could scarcely imagine another existence, because the lifeworld of mass production had existed for a century. Americans accepted mass production as though it were part of the natural order, with its subdivision of work, its interchangeable parts, and its organization of everyday life in terms of efficiency and productivity. Year after year they expected higher wages, more consumer goods, and a general acceleration of experience. By 2013, however, this was an outdated and unsustainable economic order. The classic assembly line had been based on a large semiskilled working class, not on robots and outsourcing. It assumed unlimited raw materials, not an expanding world population that competed for finite resources. In 2013 it was time to reinvent both production and consumption and construct a greener assembly-line America.

NOTES

CHAPTER 1

1. Quoted in *American Superiority at the World's Fair*, ed. Rodgers, 99.

2. Fitch, "The Rise of the Mechanical Ideal," in *Magazine of American History* (1884), 516–527.

3. Basalla, *The Evolution of Technology*.

4. Ibid., 24.

5. Ibid., 218.

6. Kouwenhoven, *Made in America*, 16–18.

7. Boardman, *America and the Americans*, 26,

8. From *American Superiority at the World's Fair*, ed. Rodgers, 99. Mick Gidley first drew this passage to my attention.

9. Nye, *America as Second Creation*, 21–42. For a photographic essay on the grid, see Corner and MacLean, *Taking Measures Across the American Landscape*.

10. On colonial land patterns, see Stilgoe, *Common Landscape of America, 1580–1845*.

11. Fisher, *Still the New World*, 47.

12. Blondheim, *News over the Wires.*

13. Cronon, *Nature's Metropolis*, 120–124.

14. O'Malley, *Keeping Watch*, 99–144.

15. Levasseur, "The Concentration of Industry and Machinery in the United States," 18–19, 21–24.

16. Basalla, 188.

17. Doolittle, *The Romance of the Automobile Industry.* 317, 319. Cited in Casey, The Driving Machine, 42–43.

18. Haworth, "Focal Things and Focal Practices," 59.

19. Mitchem, "Of Character and Technology," 144.

20. Ibid., 146.

21. Lubar, "Machine Politics," 208.

22. On the Chrysler exhibit, see *Official Guide Book, New York World's Fair* and Nye, "Yesterday's Ritual Tomorrow."

23. For a discussion of how this manifests itself in tourism, see Nye, *Narratives and Spaces*, 13–24.

24. On Native Americans and time, see Waters, *Pumpkin Seed Point*, 100–111.

25. Thoreau, "Walking."

26. Ford's interest in Emerson and Thoreau developed after 1901. See Ford Archives, Oral History Collection, "The Reminiscences of Oliver E. Barthel," 71 and "The Reminiscences of Harold M. Cordell," 93. Ford's personal copy of Emerson's essays is with his personal notebooks (accession 1, box 14). See also Burroughs, *John Burroughs Talks*, 326.

CHAPTER 2

1. Reminiscences of Richard Kroll, October 1953, Oral History Collection, Ford Motor Company Archives.

2. Ibid.

3. Olson and Cabadas, *The American Auto Factory*, 20.

4. Reminiscences of Max Wollering, Ford Motor Company Archives. See also Lewchuk, *American Technology and the British Vehicle Industry*, 47–49 and passim.

5. Rae, *American Automobile Manufacturers*, 104.

6. Wallace, *The Social Context of Invention*, 3.

7. Arms, "From disassembly to assembly."

8. Giedion, *Mechanization Takes Command*, 87–90.

9. Barbieri-Low, "The Organization of Imperial Workshops During the Han Dynasty," iii.

10. Ibid., 333.

11. Biggs, *The Rational Factory*, 17.

12. Friedel, *A Culture of Improvement*, 471.

13. Hounshell, *From the American System to Mass Production, 1800–1932*.

14. Ibid., 151.

15. Duboff, *Electric Power in American Manufacturing, 1889–1958*, 82.

16. Reminiscences of George Brown, volume 1, Ford Motor Company Archives, accession 65, 75.

17. On Ford's managers, see Hounshell, 220–228, 239–241.

18. Kroll, 15–16.

19. Reminiscences of Mr. William C. Klann, Ford Motor Company Archives, October 1955, 40–43.

20. Ibid., 44–45.

21. Hounshell, 254.

22. Hounshell, 248–249.

23. Adam Smith, *The Wealth of Nations*, book 1, chapter 1.

24. Ibid.

25. Reminiscences of Anthony Harff, Ford Motor Company Archives, accession 65, 18.

26. Ibid., 19.

27. Walker and Guest, *The Man on the Assembly Line*, 12.

28. Harff, 29–30.

29. Ford, *My Life and Work*, 108.

30. Alder, "Innovation and Amnesia," 297, 301–302.

31. Smith, "Eli Whitney and the American System of Manufacturing."

32. Williams, Haslam, and Williams, "Ford versus 'Fordism,'" 225.

33. Woodhouse, "Electrical Driving of Textile Machinery," *Cassier's* 38 (1910), May, 30.

34. Biggs, 123–125. For more on Ford factory architecture, see Ling, *America and the Automobile*, 127–167.

35. Williams, Haslam, and Williams, "The Myth of the Line," 74.

36. Ibid., 74.

37. Ibid., 76.

38. Nye, *The Invented Self*, 66–70.

39. Williams et al., "Ford versus 'Fordism,'" 199.

40. Barclay, *Ford Production Methods*, 205.

41. Franz, *Tinkering*, 74–102. See also Kline, *Consumers in the Country*, 55–86.

42. To place the assembly line in the larger context of changes in industrial scale at this time, see Friedel, 449–478.

43. Klann, 56. Klann's reminiscences are quite good for the details of what happened (32–85), but his chronology is not entirely reliable.

44. Reminiscences of George Brown, volume 1, Ford Motor Company Archives, accession 65, 88–89.

45. Biggs, 118–136.

46. For more on factory design, see Lewis, "Redesigning the Workplace," 666.

47. Raff and Summers, "Did Henry Ford Pay Efficiency Wages?" S75.

48. McCarthy, "Henry Ford, Industrial Ecologist or Industrial Conservationist?" 57.

49. Casey, *The Model T*, 74.

50. Kroll, 35.

51. Aitken, *Taylorism at Watertown Arsenal*; Noble, *America by Design*, 268–271; Haber, *Efficiency and Uplift*.

52. Nevins and Hill, *Ford*, 474.

53. Raff, "Productivity Growth at Ford in the Coming of Mass Production," 183.

54. See Alder, 297.

55. Ibid., 310.

CHAPTER 3

1. Filene, *Successful Living in this Machine Age*, 1931

2. Lewis, *The Public Image of Henry Ford*, 54.

3. "America's Future in Light of the Past," *Literary Digest* XI (1895), no. 23, 668.

4. Mulhall, "The Increase of Wealth," 78–85.

5. Thurston, "Our Progress in Mechanical Engineering," 7–8.

6. Thurston, "The Trend of National Progress," 310.

7. Wright, *The Industrial Evolution of the United States*, 345–351.

8. Arnold, "Ford's Methods and Ford Shops," 858.

9. "Huge Ford Assembly Plant at Highland Park, Detroit, Is a Wonderful Place to See," *Los Angeles Times*, March 24, 1918.

10. The search engine of the *New York Times* returns "High Motor Value at Low Prices Attained in Quantity Production" (January 7, 1923) as the first story in which the term "assembly line" appears.

11. Jones, ed., *Engineering Encyclopedia*, volume 2, 1001–1002.

12. Beniger, *The Control Revolution*, 246.

13. Boorstin, *The Americans*, 343.

14. Nye, *Consuming Power*, 118–119.

15. Boorstin, 343.

16. Strasser, *Satisfaction Guaranteed*, 112–113.

17. Marchand, *Creating the Corporate Soul*, 256 258.

18. Nye, *American Technological Sublime*, 129.

19. Arnold and Faurote, *Ford Methods and the Ford Shops*.

20. Littmann, "The Production of Goodwill," 80.

21. Lewis, *The Public Image of Henry Ford*, 54.

22. Paul Lowry, "Men Swarm Like Bees in the Ford Factory," *Los Angeles Times*, February 4, 1923.

23. Lewis, 55.

24. Fuessle, *Gold Shod*, 77.

25. Nye, *American Technological Sublime*, 36–41, 60–61

26. Conrad, *Temper*, 82.

27. Ibid., 300.

28. Rubenstein, *Making and Selling Cars*, 61.

29. William F. Verner, personal notebook from 1919 to 1920, Henry Ford Archives, accession 521.

30. Logan Miller, *Reminiscences*, 14–15. Owen Bombard Oral History Collection, Henry Ford Archives.

31. Littmann, "The Production of Goodwill," 77.

32. Cited in Lewis, 161. There are hundreds of clippings in a similar vein, from the popular press in clipbooks 23–71 (held at the Henry Ford Archives).

33. Ford and Crowther, *My Life and Work*.

34. Bray, *Guide to the Ford Film Collection in the National Archives*, 58, 75–77, 83–92.

35. Ford Archives accession 572, box 1, folder 1.2.

36. Marchand, *Creating the Corporate Soul*, 272.

37. "Motor Cars for Everybody," *New York Times*, August 2, 1916; "Ford Sets Output Record," *New York Times*, August 27, 1921.

38. Tedlow, *New and Improved*, 152–153.

39. Cited in Boorstin, *The Americans*, 554.

40. Nye, *Electrifying America*, 268.

41. See http://www.historysanjose.org/cannerylife/through-the-years/1917-1966/mechanization/index.html

42. Silas Bent, "Baking Evolves into Big Business," *New York Times*, November 30, 1924.

43. "Rotary Milking Machine Brings Factory Methods to the Farm," *Science News Letter*, November 22, 1930, 325.

44. U.S. Department of Commerce, *Fifteenth Census of the United States, Report on Manufacturing*, Volume 2, Washington DC, 1933, 1189–1190,1221. The statistics in this report are from 1929.

45. Ibid., 1224.

46. Measured in wages paid, value of products, and horsepower employed in the shops, the railroad car and locomotive business grew by at least 300 percent between 1900 and 1930. That the railroads themselves were unprofitable was another matter. Ibid., 1209.

47. Ibid., 1223.

48. Peterson, *American Automobile Workers, 1900–1933*, 47.

49. *Fifteenth Census*, 13.

50. Ibid., 13.

51. Arthur A. Stuart, "It's Here—The All-Steel House," *Popular Science Monthly*, November 1928, 33–35, 155.

52. Evans Clark, "Mass Production Solving Housing Problem," *New York Times*, January 25, 1923.

53. See National Building Museum website (http://designingtomorrow.wordpress.com).

54. Williams, "The World's Got to Have Me!" 449.

55. Ibid., 450.

56. Ibid., 454.

57. Long, "Motor Transport and Our Radial Frontier," 109.

58. Ibid., 118.

59. Summarized in Allen, *Only Yesterday*, 141.

60. Christy Borth, "The Automobile in Popular Song," pamphlet distributed at 43rd National Automobile Show, October 1960, 15. Copy in Benson Ford Library.

61. "London Concerts," *Musical Times*, October 1, 1929, 931.

62. Bobbitt, *The Curriculum*, 11, 15.

63. Strangely, Bobbitt has been called an enthusiast for Taylorism, yet he criticized the Taylor system. If anything, his theories would seem to anticipate lean production.

64. Sayre, "American Vernacular," 314–315.

65. Ibid., 315.

66. The 1924 film version of *Ballet mécanique* can be seen at http://www.youtube.com.

67. Bijsterveld, *Mechanical Sound*, 148–149.

68. McCarren, *Dancing Machines*.

69. Kracauer, *The Mass Ornament*.

70. Ibid., 77.

71. After World War II synchronized swimming gradually spread to the rest of the world, becoming an Olympic event in 1984.

72. Cited in Lucic, *Charles Sheeler and the Cult of the Machine*, 92.

73. Cited in Rubin, "A Convergence of Vision," 208.

74. Eugene Jolas, "The Industrial Mythos," *transition* 12 (November 1929), 123.

75. Cited in Corwin, "Picturing Efficiency," 154, 156.

76. Filene, "Mass Production Makes a Better World."

77. Berkley, *The Filenes*, 188.

78. Filene, *Successful Living in this Machine Age*.

79. Filene, *Speaking of Change*, 279.

80. Tauranac, *The Empire State Building*, 205.

81. "Tallest Tower Built in Less Than a Year," *New York Times*, May 2, 1931. See also Tauranac, 215.

82. Douglas Haskell, "A Temple of Jehu," *The Nation*, May 27, 1931, 590.

83. Loeb, *Life in a Technocracy*, 12, 61, passim.

84. Schrenk, "'Industry Applied,'" 31.

85. *Official Guide: Book of the Fair, 1933*, 51.

86. Marchand, *Creating the Corporate Soul*, 271–272.

87. *Machine Art: March 6 to April 30, 1934*, exhibition catalog, Museum of Modern Art, 1934.

CHAPTER 4

1. Cited in Casey, *The Model T*, 33.

2. Rodgers, *Atlantic Crossings*, 367.

3. Fridenson, "Ford as a Model for French Car Makers, 1911–1939," 126–127. On Fiat and Italian adoption of the assembly line, see Bigazzi, "Gli operai della catena di montaggio," 895–949.

4. Lewis, *The Public Image of Henry Ford*, 53.

5. Lewchuk, "Fordist Technology and Britain," 19.

6. Lewis, 129.

7. Ibid., 131.

8. Cohen, "The Modernization of Production in the French Automobile Industry between the Wars," 760.

9. Ibid., 761–770.

10. McNeill, *The Pursuit of Power*, 232–236, 330–331, 355, 358–359.

11. Ford Archives, accession 572, box 1, folder 1.19. See also Darwin S. Hatch, "A Motor Year Revamped by War," *Motor Age* 32, no. 26 (December 27, 1917), 5–11.

12. Wilkins, *American Business Abroad*, 61.

13. Cited in ibid., 77.

14. Cohen, 759.

15. Wilkins, 80.

16. Fridenson, 135.

17. McLeod, "Architecture or Revolution," 135.

18. Ibid., 136–137.

19. Kuisel, *Ernest Mercier, French Technocrat*, 45–88.

20. McLeod, 141–142.

21. Maier, "Between Taylorism and Technocracy," 58.

22. Ibid., 61.

23. See Paul Devinat, *Scientific Management in Europe*. International Labour Office, 1927, esp. preface and p. 63. For more on Filene, see chapter 2.

24. "Japan Gets Ford Assembly Line," *Graham Guardian*, January 14, 1921.

25. Tolliday, "The Origins of Ford of Europe," 154.

26. Ibid., 153.

27. Sørensen et al., "Ford Denmark and the Scandinavian Market."

28. "European Deliveries, Profits, 1930, 1931," accession 572, box 17, folder 11.14, Ford Archives. Profits weren't a simple function of net sales. Holland and Belgium each sold one-third fewer cars and trucks than Denmark, yet made a slightly larger profit.

29. Ibid., 158–159.

30. Casey, *The Model T*, 71–72.

31. Sigfried, *The United States Today*, 196.

32. Pells, *Not Like Us*, 11.

33. Sam A. Lewisohn, quoted in "Found Europe Avid of American Ideas," *New York Times*, June 19, 1926.

34. Foreman-Peck, "The American Challenge of the Twenties," 868.

35. Lewchuk, 155–157.

36. Reminiscences of Mr. William C. Klann, Ford Motor Company Archives, October 1953, 174.

37. Tolliday, "The Rise of Ford in Britain," 15–16.

38. *New York Times*, November 13, 1928 (typed copy preserved in Ford Archives, accession 572, box 17, folder 11.15).

39. Charles Sorensen to Henry Ford, August 16, 1929, Ford Archives, accession 572, box 17, folder 11.14.

40. Ralph Roberts, letter to Charles Sorensen, August 6, 1930, 2. In Ford Archives, accession 572, box 17, folder 11.12.2.

41. Wilkins, 239–241, 246.

42. Batchelor, *Henry Ford*, 75–76.

43. Tolliday, "Management and Labour in Britain."

44. Lewchuk, *American Technology and the British Vehicle Industry.*

45. Keene, "Production—A Dream Come True," 31.

46. Shpotov, "Ford in Russia," 506–508.

47. See Hellebust, "Aleksei Gastev and the Metallization of the Revolutionary Body," 500–518.

48. Hughes, *American Genesis.*

49. Julius Hammer, letter to Henry Ford, June 1, 1923, Henry Ford Archives, accession 572, box 17, folder 11.14, 2.

50. Shpotov, 512.

51. McCauley, "Production Literature and the Industrial Imagination," 448.

52. Ibid., 449–450.

53. Ibid., 462.

54. Shpotov, 521–523.

55. Farber, *Sloan Rules*, 144–145.

56. "Agreement, May 1929 between the Ford Motor Company and the Supreme Council of National Economy," accession 572, box 17, folder 11.14, Ford Archives.

57. Shpotov, 517.

58. Hughes, 271–272.

59. Cohen, "The Soviet Fordson," 549.

60. Shearer, *Industry, State and Society in Stalin's Russia, 1926–1934.*

61. Kotkin, "Modern Times," 117.

62. Cohen, "The Soviet Fordson," 552–553.

63. Shearer, "The Reichskuratorium für Wirtschaftlichkeit," 569–602.

64. Ibid., 578.

65. Hughes, 288.

66. Kottgen, *Das wirtschaftliche Amerika*, Berlin, 1925.

67. Cited in Casey, *The Model T*, 33.

68. Shearer, "Talking about Efficiency."

69. Batchelor, 78.

70. Nolan, *Visions of Modernity*, 73.

71. Ibid., 74.

72. Ibid., 75.

73. Ibid., 76.

74. J. Ronald Shearer, "The Reichskuratorium," 601.

75. Correspondence to and from Perry and Sorensen, 1930, accession 572, box 16, folder 1, Ford Archives. Germany imposed heavy duties on the import of machine tools, leading to questions about how many Ford wanted to import.

76. Thomes, "Searching for Identity, Ford Motor Company in the German Market, 1903–2003," 158

77. "Memorandum," 17, signed "Albert," accession 572, box 16, folder 3, "Germany" Ford Archives. Presumably this was written by Dr. Albert.

78. Wilkins, 235.

79. Letter from J. Steppacher to Leibold, July 13, 1932, accession 572, box 16, folder 3, Ford Archives.

80. Letter to Ford Motor Company dated June 9, 1933, accession 572, box 16, folder 3, Ford Archives. It is significant that this letter wasn't addressed to a person and takes a rather impersonal tone.

81. Letter to Edsel Ford dated June 15, 1933, carbon copy with no signature, accession 572, box 16, folder 3, Ford Archives.

82. Letter from Perry to Sorensen, December 19, 1933, accession 572, box 16, folder 3, Ford Archives.

83. Letter to Leibold, April 26, 1934, last page and signature missing, accession 572, box 16, folder 3, Ford Archives. "Mr. Ford has only to [*sic*] ways to choose with his German plant: To close down or go ahead in a real Ford way, that means in a big way."

84. Carbon copy of a letter to Percival Perry from Detroit, September 24, 1934, accession 572, box 16, folder 4 "Germany."

85. Thomes, 158–160.

86. Spode, "Fordism, Mass Tourism and the Third Reich," 133, 135.

87. Homburg, *Rationalisierung und Industriearbeit*.

88. Rabinbach, "The Aesthetics of Production in the Third Reich," 43–74.

89. Allen, "Flexible Production in Ravensbrück," 201.

90. Maier, "Between Taylorism and Technocracy," 28–29.

91. Sigfried, *The United States Today*.

92. Ibid., 182, 180.

93. Duhamel, *America the Menace*.

94. Kuisel, *Seducing the French*, 2.

95. Aron and Dandieu, *Le Cancer américain*.

96. See Armus, *French Anti-Americanism (1930–1948)*, which is in part a critique of Mathy, *Extrême Occident*.

97. Roger and Bowman, *The American Enemy*, 274, 278–279.

98. Evans, "Jean Patou's American Mannequins," 247, 249, 259, 260.

99. Celine, *Journey to the End of the Night*, 223–224.

100. Kroes, "Americanization and Anti-Americanism," 506.

101. Stead, *The Americanization of the World; or, The Trend of the Twentieth Century*.

102. Lawrence, *Studies in Classic American Literature*, 9.

103. Huxley, *Brave New World*.

104. Sombart, *Why Is There No Socialism in the United States?*

105. Cited in Kroes, 21.

106. Nolan, 114.

107. Ibid., 119.

108. Toller, "Ford Through German Eyes," 108–109.

109. On the plot, see Boon, "Narrative Voices in *A Nous la Liberté*," 514–519.

110. "Vocational Guidance and its Physiology: 'Taylorism' and 'Fordism' Are Called Failures in Europe," *New York Times*, May 10, 1927.

111. Gramsci, "Americanism and Fordism," 310.

112. Ibid., 312.

113. Batchelor, 79–80.

114. International Directory of Company Histories, volume 1, 161.

115. Letter dated October 11, 1929, accession 572, box 17, folder 11.14, Ford Archives.

116. "Memorandum on the present situation of Ford Italiana S.A. and plans for the further conduct of Ford business in Italy," accession 572, box 17, folder 11.14, Ford Archives.

117. Letter dated February 21, 1934, accession 572, box 17, folder 11.14, Ford Archives.

118. Report of the Board of Directors of Ford S.A.F., accession 572, box 16, folder 11.14 (France).

119. Ford Motor Company AG Cologne, Germany, "Manager's Report to Directors—Fourth Quarter 1935," 3, accession 572, box 16, folder 11.14. 4 (Germany).

120. Dubriel, *Robots or Men? A French workman's Experience in American Industry*, 138–149. On Dubreuil, see Person, "Man and Machine," 88.

121. Jay, *The Dialectical Imagination*, 216.

122. Cited in Jay, 213–214.

123. Benjamin, *Illuminations*, 224.

124. Ford Archives, accession 572, box 17, folder "Europe, 1930s." This folder contains statements of profits and losses for every major city and factory in Europe, as well as aggregate figures.

125. Lewchuk, *American Technology and the British Vehicle Industry*, 188.

CHAPTER 5

1. "Will Rogers Says" (syndicated column), *Gettysburg Times*, December 31, 1930.

2. Peterson, 52–53.

3. "The Ford Melon for Labor," *Literary Digest*, January 17, 1914, 95; "Profit Sharing or Largesse?" *The Nation* January 15, 1914, 51–52; "Probing the Ford Labor Melon," *Literary Digest*, January 24, 1914, 144.

4. "Beadle Speaks Up for Henry Ford," *Detroit Free Press*, February 16, 1914. Ford clipping files, accession 13, volume 5, Ford Archives.

5. "Ford Plan Victor in Heated Debate," *Cleveland Leader*, February 27, 1914. Ford clipping files, accession 13, volume 5, Ford Archives.

6. "Ford Plan Subject of Lively Debate," *Columbus Journal*, March 9, 1914. Ford clipping files, accession 13, volume 5, Ford Archives.

7. "Ford forced the Rich to Blush," *New York Tribune*, March 9, 1914. Ford clipping files, accession 13, volume 5, Ford Archives.

8. More stories about this debate can be found in accession 13, volume 5, Ford Archives.

9. O'Hare, reprinted in Roediger, "Americanism and Fordism—American Style," 252.

10. Reed, "Why They Hate Ford," 11–12; "Industry's Miracle Maker," *Metropolitan* 45, October 1916, 64–68.

11. Slichter, *The Turnover of Factory Labor*; Brissenden and Franket, *Labor Turnover in Industry*.

12. Raff and Summers, "Did Henry Ford Pay Efficiency Wages?" S63–S64.

13. Slichter, 233.

14. Cited in Meyer, 44.

15. Ibid., 40.

16. Ibid., 40.

17. Madison, "My Seven Years of Automotive Servitude," 19.

18. Ibid., 15.

19. Goodrich, "Power and the Worker," 97–98.

20. Koritz, "Drama and the Rhythm of Work in the 1920s," 554.

21. Lynd and Lynd, *Middletown*, 41.

22. O'Neill, *The Hairy Ape*, 147.

23. Cited in Koritz, 556.

24. Ibid., 556.

25. Cited in ibid., 558.

26. Sherwood Anderson, "A Great Factory," 52.

27. Anderson, *Poor White*, 343–344.

28. Woirol, *The Technological Unemployment and Structural Unemployment Debates*, 25.

29. Say, *A Treatise on Political Economy*.

30. Rotunda & Plant Visitors Attendance Statistics, 1924–1964, accession 1222, Ford Archives.

31. Chase, *The Tragedy of Waste*; *Men and Machines*; *The Nemesis of American Business*; *The Economy of Abundance*.

32. Cited in Bix, 123.

33. Dreiser, *Tragic America*, 195.

34. Bix, 127.

35. Cited in ibid., 131.

36. "Will Rogers Says" (syndicated column), *Gettysburg Times*, December 31, 1930.

37. Chandler, *Scale and Scope*, 208.

38. Sward, *The Legend of Henry Ford*, 344–345.

39. Ibid., 351–354.

40. Anderson, "Lift Up Thine Eyes," 162–163.

41. Wilson, "Detroit Motors," *The New Republic*.

42. Dos Passos, *The Big Money*, 50.

43. Ibid., 55.

44. Conroy, *The Disinherited*.

45. Cited in Congdon, *The Thirties*, 479.

46. Both cited in Edsforth et al., "The Speedup," 41–42.

47. Richards, "On the Assembly Line," 424–428.

48. Lynch, "Some Expectations of the Workers," 110.

49. Steele, *Conveyor*, 80–81.

50. Smitter, *F.O.B. Detroit*, 121–122.

51. Ibid., 122.

52. Dinnerstein, *Swinging the Machine*, 11.

53. Ibid., 56.

54. Ibid., 221–222.

55. Cited in ibid., 223.

56. Hooker, *Life in the Shadows of the Crystal Palace, 1910–1927*, 55.

57. Meier and Rudwick, *Black Detroit and the Rise of the UAW*, 16–17, 24–25.

58. Brody, *Nobody Starves*.

59. Steele, *Conveyor*, 92.

60. Smitter, 72. See also Albert Maltz, *The Underground Stream*.

61. Chaplin, *My Autobiography*, 377–378.

62. Rivera, *Portrait of America*, 17.

63. Downs, *Diego Rivera*, 168–169.

64. Quoted in *Art Digest VII*, April 15, 1933, 2.

65. Downs, review of *The Mexican Muralists in the United States*, 50.

66. "Radicals: Anti-Ford," *Time*, June 16, 1925.

67. Leonard, *The Tragedy of Henry Ford*, 11.

68. Zieger and Gall, *American Workers, American Unions*, 50.

69. Meyer, "Rough Manhood," 127.

70. Rauchenbush, *Fordism*, 34.

71. Ibid., 35.

72. *Life*, January 19, 1937, 10.

73. Maurice Sugar, "Sit Down," in Lomax, Guthrie, and Seeger, *Hard Hitting Songs for Hard-Hit People*, 245.

74. Fine, *Sit-Down*, 193–197.

75. For a brief contemporary account, see Stolberg, *The Story of the CIO*, 166–169.

76. Gilliland and Beck, "Oh, Mr. Sloan," in Lomax, Guthrie, and Seeger, 243.

77. Bob Stinson, "The Sit Down," in Terkel, *Hard Times*, 156–161.

78. Fine, 301.

79. Farber, *Sloan Rules*, 199.

80. Congdon, *The Thirties,* 478.

81. Reprinted in Lomax, Guthrie, and Seeger, 249.

82. Bryan, *Rouge*, 218.

83. Marchand, *Creating the Corporate Soul*, 283–291.

84. Marchand, "*Life* Comes to Corporate Headquarters," 133.

85. Nye, *Image Worlds*, 71–90.

86. Marchand, 291–295.

87. Meikle, *Twentieth Century Limited*, 200–209.

88. Letter and enclosures from Donald H. Long to H. G. McCoy, Detroit, General Correspondence and press releases, Ford Archives, accession 56, Fred L. Black files, box 1.

89. General correspondence and press releases, Ford Archives, accession 56, Fred L. Black files, box 1.

90. Letter from Edward Mabley in Teague office to Donald Long, N. W. Ayer & Son, December 9, 1938, Ford Archives, accession 56, Fred L. Black files, box 1.

91. Lewis, *The Public Image of Henry Ford*, 306–307.

92. Rotunda & Plant Visitors Attendance Statistics, 1924–1964, accession 1222, Ford Archives.

93. General correspondence and press releases, Ford Archives, accession 56, Fred L. Black files, box 1.

94. Marchand, 299–301.

95. Quoted in ibid., 301.

CHAPTER 6

1. Cited in Haddow, *Pavilions of Plenty*, 22.

2. Franklin D. Roosevelt, "Radio Address," November 4, 1938 (available at http://www.presidency.ucsb.edu).

3. Franklin D. Roosevelt, "Message to Congress on the St. Lawrence Seaway and Power Project," June 2, 1941, "Fireside Chat," December 9, 1941, and "Greeting to the U.S. Chamber of Commerce," April 26, 1943 (available at http://www.presidency.ucsb.edu).

4. Lyrics available at http://www.loc.gov.

5. Kimble and Olson, "Visual Rhetoric Representing Rosie the Riveter," 533–570.

6. *Life*, August 19, 1940, 37–48.

7. *Time*, March 23, 1942.

8. Ibid.

9. Pursell, "The Technology of Production," 61.

10. Lewis, *The Public Image of Henry Ford*, 348–353.

11. Borth, *Masters of Mass Production*, 237.

12. Zeitlin, "Flexibility and Mass Production at War," 46–79.

13. Ibid., 54.

14. Ibid., 72–73.

15. Allen, "Flexible Production in Ravensbrück," 182–217. See also Allen, *The Business of Genocide*, 74–77 and passim.

16. Zeitlin, 58–59.

17. Pursell, 61.

18. Muther, *Production Line Technique*, 116.

19. Ibid., 74.

20. Ibid., 115.

21. Ibid., 76.

22. Ibid., 40.

23. Ibid., 40.

24. Full-page advertisement, *Popular Science*, August 1941, 2.

25. Borth, *Masters of Mass Production*, 19.

26. Cited in ibid., 280.

27. Burlingame, *Engines of Democracy*, 535, 397.

28. Ibid., 398.

29. Ibid., 535, 387, 398.

30. Teague, *Land of Plenty*.

31. Fehér, Heller, and Márkus, *Dictatorship Over Needs*.

32. Kotkin, "Modern Times," 160.

33. Zeitlin, 74.

34. *International Directory of Company Histories*, volume 1, 206.

35. Henry Ford II and Graeme Howard, "Report on European Trip, February–March, 1948, submitted April 5, 1948. Accession 1353, Ford Archives, ii.

36. Ibid., 16–17.

37. Ibid., 24.

38. Ibid., Conclusion.

39. White, *The American Century*, 204.

40. *International Directory of Company Histories*, volume 1, 161.

41. Cited in Haddow, *Pavilions of Plenty*, 22.

42. *International Directory of Company Histories*, volume 1, 161.

43. Haddow, 24.

44. Ibid., 22.

45. Elwood, *Rebuilding Europe*, 64.

46. Yarrow, "Selling a New Vision of America to the World," 12.

47. Eisenhower spoke to the national convention of junior chambers of commerce.

48. Elwood, 219.

49. Jones, *Forcing the Factory of the Future*, 51–75.

50. Ibid., 55–70.

51. *International Directory of Company Histories*, volume 1, 188.

52. Ibid., 189.

53. Bruckberger, *Image of America*, 196.

54. Roger William Riis, "Guided Tours to New Ideas," *Nation's Business*, May 1950, 48.

55. Partner, *Assembled in Japan*, 61–66.

56. Riis, 48.

57. Ole Bech-Petersen, Encounters, 207.

58. Riis, 50.

59. Ritzer, *The McDonaldization of Society*.

60. de Grazia, *Irresistible Empire*. She also contributed to *Selling Modernity: Advertising in Twentieth-Century Germany*.

61. Rydell and Kroes, *Buffalo Bill in Bologna*.

62. White, *The American Century*, 164.

63. Barry Eichengreen, "The European Economy Since 1945," *New York Times*, March 25, 2007. Excerpted from Eichengreen, *The European Economy since 1945*.

64. Ibid.

65. http://www.boardgameswiki.com/index.php?title=Assembly_Line%28SANDR 1953%29

66. Nye, *American Technological Sublime*.

67. Hunter, *Steamboats on Western Rivers*.

68. Kouwenhoven, *Made in America*, 20–42, passim.

69. Blair, *Modular America*.

70. Cited in Hixson, *Parting the Curtain*, 133.

71. "People's Capitalism," cited in Haddow, 51–52.

72. "Eisenhower Pays a Visit to Exhibit on Capitalism," *Los Angeles Times*, February 14, 1956.

73. "Eisenhower Visits Capitalism Show; Suggests Changes in Exhibit to Be Sent Overseas to Combat Red Falsehoods," *New York Times*, February 14, 1956.

74. "U.S. Exhibit Ready to Vie with Reds," *New York Times*, August 19, 1956. On the "People's Capitalism" campaign, see Belmonte, "Modernization and US Overseas Propaganda," 119–122.

75. Potter, *People of Plenty*, 102.

76. *Wall Street Journal*, May 13, 1957.

77. Perlo, "'People's Capitalism' and Stock Ownership," 335.

78. Frank, *The Americans*.

79. Letter from Robert Frank to Mary Frank, cited in Brinkley, *Wheels for the World*, 593.

80. Rubenstein, *Making and Selling Cars*, 154.

81. Ibid., 153–154.

82. Rotunda & Plant Visitors Attendance Statistics, 1924–1964, accession 1222, Ford Archives.

83. Schor, *The Overworked American*, 66–67.

84. Cited in ibid., 65.

85. Gorer, *The American People*, 142–143.

86. Chinoy, *Automobile Workers and the American Dream*, 34.

87. Ibid., 70.

88. Ibid., 71.

89. Ibid., 36–37, 62.

90. Ibid., 127.

91. Swados, "Myth of the Happy Worker," 114.

92. Swados, *On the Line*.

93. Ibid., 76.

94. Ibid., 75.

95. Giles Slade, *Made to Break*, 45.

96. Cited in Flink, *The Automobile Age*, 287.

97. Walter Holbrook, "Assembly-Line Cities," *Popular Science*, August 1941, 96–99.

98. Sarah Jo Peterson, "The Politics of Land Use and Housing in World War II Michigan," 5–6.

99. Images of the Dymaxion House can be seen at http://www.hfmgv.org.

100. William Gordon purchased two prototypes and had one of them inserted into the side of his family's home, where it remained until the Henry Ford Museum bought and restored it.

101. On Fuller's housing ideas, see Nye, "Energy in the Thought and Design of F. Buckminster Fuller."

102. Jackson, *Crabgrass Frontier*, 234–238.

103. Riesman, "The Suburban Sadness."

104. Ditto and Stern, *Eichler Homes*.

105. See Hines, *Richard Neutra and the Search for Modern Architecture*, 273, 279.

106. "Improving Homes a New Specialty," *New York Times*, June 7, 1959.

107. Rebroadcast in the TV special *The Best of Gleason*, June 8, 1988.

108. Bergson, *Laughter*, 11. I thank Leo Marx for drawing my attention to this essay.

109. Faunce, Hardin, and Jacobson, "Automation and the Employee," 63.

110. Simpson, "Bureaucracy, Standardization, and Liberal Arts," 129, 130.

111. Ibid., 131.

112. On the Frankfurt School, see Jay, *The Dialectical Imagination*.

113. Riesman, *The Lonely Crowd*.

114. However, see Nye, "Technology and the Production of Difference," 597–619.

115. Riesman, "The Nylon War," 71.

116. Riis, 49.

117. Cited in Haddow, 217. For more on the Moscow exhibition, see Sandeen, *Picturing an Exhibition*, 136.

CHAPTER 7

1. John Steinbeck, *Travels with Charley*, 97.

2. Williamson, *The Humanoids*.

3. Vonnegut, *Player Piano*, 15.

4. Philip K. Dick, "Autofac," *Galaxy*, November 1955.

5. Mumford, *The Myth of the Machine*, 176.

6. Ferguson, *Oliver Evans*, 13–32.

7. Burlingame, *Engines of Democracy*, 398.

8. Bright, *Automation and Management*, 5.

9. "The Automatic Factory," *Fortune*, November 1946.

10. LeGrand, "Ford Handles by Automation," 107–122.

11. Wiener, *The Human Use of Human Beings*. Also see Diebold, *Automation*.

12. Wiener, 155–156.

13. Ibid., 154–159.

14. Ibid., 162.

15. See Noble, *Forces of Production*, 75.

16. Waldemar Kaempffert, "Walter Reuther's Fears of Automation Stir New Interest in Factory of the Future," *New York Times*, December 12, 1954.

17. Ashburn, "Detroit Automation," 22.

18. Ibid., 25.

19. Meyer, "An Economic Frankenstein," UAW Workers' Responses to Automation at the Ford Brook Park Plant in the 1950s," 55–56, 75–76.

20. Noble, 150–151.

21. Cited in Nye, *Technology Matters*, 121.

22. Noble, chapters 1 and 2.

23. William Freeman, "Automation Aims at New Freedom," *New York Times*, January 3, 1955.

24. Buckingham, "The Great Unemployment Controversy," 49.

25. Ibid., 50–52.

26. "Automation Job Impact: Good? Bad?" *Los Angeles Times*, April 16, 1961.

27. "Automation Gives Schools Problem," *New York Times*, April 9, 1963.

28. Remark by Frank B. Powers, "G.E. Head Depicts Automation Gain," *New York Times*, October 27, 1955.

29. Bix, *Inventing Ourselves Out of Jobs?* 261.

30. Cited in Meyer, "'An Economic Frankenstein,'" 73.

31. Ibid., 73.

32. Wayne Johnson and Howard Gingold, "Automation: Portent of a Second Industrial Revolution," *Los Angeles Times*, September 9, 1957.

33. http://www.presidency.ucsb.edu/ws/index.php?pid=10434&st=automation&st1=#ixzz1QS9aPhwe

34. http://www.presidency.ucsb.edu/ws/index.php?pid=11338&st=automation&st1=#ixzz1QSCGjDEu

35. "Automation Aims at New Freedom" *New York Times*, January 3, 1955; "G.E. Head Depicts Automation Gain," *New York Times*, October 27, 1955.

36. Edward R. Murrow, "Automation—Weal or Woe?" *See It Now*, CBS, June 9, 1957.

37. http://www.presidency.ucsb.edu/ws/index.php?pid=29602&st=automation&st1=#ixzz1QSDlcadb

38. Arthur J. Goldberg, "Challenge of 'Industrial Revolution II,'" *New York Times Magazine*, April 2, 1961.

39. Ibid.

40. Nate Polowetzky, "Automation Job Impact: Good? Bad? *Los Angeles Times*, April 16, 1961.

41. Elmer J. Holland, cited in ibid.

42. Reuther, cited in ibid.

43. Buckingham, 52.

44. Cited in Bix, 258.

45. George G. Kirstein, "The Manpower Revolution," *The Nation*, February 10, 1964.

46. Peter Drucker, "Automation Is Not the Villain," *New York Times Magazine*, January 10, 1965.

47. "Fallacies and Facts About Automation," *New York Times Magazine*, April 7, 1963.

48. *Official Guide, New York World's Fair, 1964/1965*, 1, 53, 204, passim. See also Bix, 266.

49. Ibid., 257.

50. See Brody, *Workers in Industrial America*, 222–228.

51. Frum, *How We Got Here*, 21.

52. Garson, "Automobile Workers and the Radical Dream," 165, 172, passim.

53. A. C. Ward, cited in Steiner, "The Diversity of American Fiction," 860.

54. Macdonald, "A Theory of Mass Culture," 8–9, passim.

55. van den Haag, "Notes on American Popular Culture," 65–66.

56. Ibid., 65.

57. "Better Use of Teacher Competencies" (editorial, National Institute of Health), quoted in *Journal of Teacher Education*, July 1956, 149–150.

58. Miller, "Radio and Propaganda," 69.

59. Steinbeck, *Travels with Charley*, 97.

60. Steinbeck, *The Grapes of Wrath*, 48–49.

61. Lederer, *A Nation of Sheep*.

62. Melosi, *Garbage in the Cities*, 190–191; J. R. McNeil, *Something New Under the Sun*, 288.

63. Steinberg, *Down to Earth*, 231.

64. Marx, *Capital*, 187.

65. http://www.youtube.com/watch?v=_HyaL1Y_Ibc

66. Smith, *Dancing in the Street*, 127–130. Quotation from Ann Fleming, "Motown Memories," *The Guardian*, June 25, 2009.

67. Brinkley, *Wheels for the World*, 617.

68. Pursell, *Technology in Postwar America*, 89–91.

69. Ellul, *The Technological Society*.

70. Ibid., 429.

71. Allen Ginsberg, *Howl and Other Poems*, 22.

72. Ibid., "America."

73. Mumford, 183.

74. Ibid., 183.

75. Savio's speech is available at http://www.narhist.ewu.edu.

76. Kesey, *One Flew Over the Cuckoo's Nest*.

77. Malvina Reynolds, "Little Boxes," RCA Victor, 1962.

78. Mumford, 177–178.

79. Turner, *From Counterculture to Cyberculture*, 78.

80. Ibid., 79.

81. Roszak, *The Making of a Counter Culture*, 12.

82. Reich, *The Greening of America*, 157.

83. Aronowitz, *False Promises*, 21, 34.

84. Fink, *The Automobile Age*, 346–347.

85. Early DRUM publications can be found at http://libcom.org.

86. Zangrando and Zangrando, "Black Protest," 141–159.

87. Denby, *Indignant Heart*, 262–264.

88. Katznelson "Participation and Political Buffers in Urban America," 470.

89. Cited in Aronowitz, 34.

90. Ibid., 26.

91. Cited in Meyer, "The Degradation of Work Revisited."

92. Aronowitz, 33–34.

93. Quoted in Sandler, "You Can Sell Your Body But Not Your Mind," 172.

94. Ibid., 173.

95. Ibid., 174.

96. Ibid., 176.

97. Ibid., 181–188.

98. Interview with John Rohrkemper, December 22, 1981, East Lansing; Dewhurst, "The Arts of Working: Manipulating the Urban Work Environment," 192–202.

99. Ibid., 195.

100. Lyrics available at http://www.hit-country-music-lyrics.com.

101. This strike was featured in *Made in Dagenham* (BBC Films and UK Film Council, 2010).

102. Linhart, *The Assembly Line*, 21–39.

103. Ibid., 38.

104. Ibid., 56.

105. Ibid., 40.

106. Louis Malle, *Humain, Trop Humain*, Nouvelles Éditions de Films, 1974.

107. Staudenmaier, review of Linhart, 503.

108. Walker and Guest, *The Man on the Assembly Line*, 79–80.

109. Wood, ed., *The Transformation of Work*, chapter 8.

110. On the Swedish alternatives, see Berggren, *Alternatives to Lean Production*.

111. Fressenet, "'Reflective Production,'" 107.

112. Dunford, "Toward a Post-Fordist Order?" 194.

113. Janice C. Simpson, "The Robot Revolution," *Time*, December 8, 1980.

CHAPTER 8

1. Fujimoto, *Competing to Be Really, Really Good*, 65.

2. Fujimoto, *The Evolution of a Manufacturing System at Toyota*, 27.

3. James Skurowiecki, "Hong Kong Hooey," *The New Yorker*, November 17, 2003.

4. Ibid., 63.

5. Drucker, *Post-Capitalist Society*, 68–69.

6. Mishel, Bernstein, and Shierholz, *The State of Working America*, 361; Shimokawa, "Comparing Productivity of the Japanese and US automobile industries," 8–56.

7. Mishel et al., 365.

8. Flink, *The Automobile Age*, 344.

9. Abo, "Japanese Motor Vehicle Technologies Abroad in the 1980s," 170.

10. Kendrick and Grossman, *Productivity in the United States*, 158.

11. David Nyhan, "Report from the Assembly Line," *Boston Globe*, February 7, 1982, 1.

12. http://www.allcountries.org/uscensus/1279_motor_vehicle_factory_sales_and_retail.html

13. Utterback, *Mastering the Dynamics of Innovation*, 145–166.

14. Even IBM, the largest computer corporation and also the manufacturer of a profitable line of electric typewriters, was slow to enter the market for personal computers. Despite early success, IBM ultimately stopped making such computers.

15. David, "Clio and the Economics of QWERTY," 1–17.

16. These returns include both profits and lowered transaction costs. North, "Institutions," 109.

17. Abernathy, *The Productivity Dilemma*.

18. Benner and Tushman, "Exploitation, Exploration, and Process Management," 239.

19. The classic work remains Kuhn, *The Structure of Scientific Revolutions*.

20. Freyssenet, "Intersecting Trajectories and Model Changes," 12.

21. On these two systems, see Boyer and Freyssenet, *The Productive Models*, 77–100.

22. Dohse, Jürgens, and Malsch, "From 'Fordism' to 'Toyotaism'?" 118.

23. Greatly simplified from Lecher and Welsch, *Japan-Mythos und Wirklichkeit*.

24. On Benedict, see Geertz, *Works and Lives*, 85.

25. Ingrassia and White, *Comeback*, 280.

26. Fujimoto, *Competing to Be Really, Really Good*, 65.

27. Fujimoto, *The Evolution of a Manufacturing System at Toyota*, 48–49.

28. Ibid., 34.

29. See Cusumano, *The Japanese Automobile Industry*.

30. Wada and Shiba, "The Evolution of the 'Japanese Production System,'" 325.

31. On the Hawthorne experiments, see Roethlisberger and Dickson, *Management and the Worker*.

32. The conclusions from these experiments were later challenged by Franke and Kaul in "The Hawthorne Experiments."

33. Shimokawa and Fujimoto, "How It All Began: An Interview with Taiichi Ohno," in Shimokawa and Fujimoto, *The Birth of Lean*, 9–10.

34. Deming, *Out of the Crisis*, 49, 487.

35. Tsutsui, "W. Edwards Deming and the Origins of Quality Control in Japan," 295–325. Tsutsui debunks Deming's role by emphasizing that a small core of specialists in Japan already knew about quality control before he came, by noting that

Deming didn't bring new ideas to the classroom, and by emphasizing how the Japanese evolved away from his approach. However, he doesn't deny Deming's generosity, his teaching ability, or his inspirational role.

36. On Deming in Japan, see Gabor, *The Man Who Discovered Quality*, 69–98.

37. Deming, *Out of the Crisis*, 490–491.

38. Wada and Shiba, 333.

39. Ibid., 334.

40. Ibid., 333.

41. Adams and Butler, *Manufacturing the Future*, 207.

42. Feigenbaum, *Total Quality Control*.

43. See, for example, Juran and Gryna, *Quality Planning and Analysis*.

44. Tsutsui, 318.

45. Deming, *Out of the Crisis*, 486–491.

46. Fujimoto, *The Evolution of a Manufacturing System at Toyota*, 32.

47. Cited in ibid., 61.

48. Ibid., 59.

49. Ibid., 50.

50. Ibid., 71.

51. Ibid., 42.

52. Ibid., 44.

53. Shimokawa, "Introduction," in Shimokawa and Fujimoto, *The Birth of Lean*, 9, xiv.

54. Ingrassia and White, *Comeback*, 167.

55. Shimokawa, "Introduction," xiv.

56. Ohno, "How the Toyota Production System was Created," 133.

57. Herod, "Implications of Just-in-Time Production for Union Strategy," 523.

58. McKinsey & Company, *Lessons from the US Automobile Industry*, 83.

59. Chalmers, *Industrial Relations in Japan*, 51, 56, passim.

60. Partner, *Assembled in Japan*, 209.

61. On *kaizen* in the United States, see Ortiz, *Kaizen Assembly*.

62. Ibid., 222–225.

63. Chandler, *The Visible Hand*, chapters 8–11.

64. Rubenstein, *Making and Selling Cars*, 38.

65. "Three models on one assembly line," *American Machinist* 71 (November 28, 1929), 881.

66. Monden, "What Makes the Toyota System Really Tick?"

67. "The Blue Collar Worker's Lowdown Blues," *Time*, November 9, 1970.

68. Adler, "Democratic Taylorism," 212–213.

69. Thanks to John-Erik Bigbie for pointing out this contrast.

70. Ingrassia and White, *Comeback*, 58–59; John Shook, interview with Lou Farinola, March 3, 2009 (http://www.lean.org/shook/).

71. Abo, "Japanese Motor Vehicle Technologies Abroad in the 1980s," 175–178.

72. Kenney and Florida, *Beyond Mass Production*, 96.

73. On the influence of "Japanese transplants" on American parts suppliers, see Cosumano, "Supplier Relations and Management," 563–588.

74. *Gung Ho*, Paramount Pictures, 1986.

75. Abo, *Hybrid Factory*, 251.

76. Abo, "Japanese Motor Vehicle Technologies Abroad in the 1980s," 186–187.

77. Ibid., 188.

78. Utterback, *Mastering the Dynamics of Innovation*, 192–194.

79. Ibid., 194.

80. Ibid., 160.

81. Ibid., 98.

82. Ibid., 96.

83. Gabor, 8–9.

84. McKinsey & Company, *Lessons from the US Automobile Industry*, chapter 2 ("How the Big Three Learned, Adopted, and Diffused Lean Production"), 78.

85. Milkman, *Farewell to the Factory*, 148.

86. Ibid., 7–8, 149–150.

87. Ibid., 67.

88. Karp, "Manufacturing Genius."

89. Hoogvelt and Yuasa, "Going Lean or Going Native?" 288.

90. http://www.newyorker.com/archive/2003/11/17/031117ta_talk_surowiecki

91. Cited in Heale, "Anatomy of a Scare," 23.

92. David Boaz, "Yellow Peril Reinfects America: U.S. Hostility Turns to Japan," *Wall Street Journal*, April 7, 1989. See also Lyman, "The 'Yellow Peril' Mystique," 683–747.

93. Crichton, *Rising Sun*.

94. Hamper, *Rivethead*.

95. Krafcik, "Triumph of the Lean Production System," 161.

96. Womack et al., *The Machine That Changed the World*, 92.

97. Ibid., 225.

98. Kenney and Florida, *Beyond Mass Production*.

99. Lynn, "Unmade in America," 33–35.

100. Kinni, *America's Best*, 372–373.

101. Ibid., 379.

102. Ibid., 368–369.

103. See Kochan, Lansbury, and MacDuffie, *After Lean Production*.

104. McKinsey & Company, *Lessons from the US Automobile Industry*, 81.

105. Shook, interview with Farinola.

106. Rubenstein, *Making and Selling Cars*, 48–49.

107. Levine, "Staying Power," 10.

108. Levine, *What Work Is*.

109. McGraw, "Historians in the Streets," 293, 296.

110. "Detroit's Population Crashes," *Wall Street Journal*, March 23, 2011.

111. Levine, *A Walk with Tom Jefferson*.

112. Shimokawa, *Japan and the Global Automotive Industry*, 58, 100–101.

113. Ibid., 102.

CHAPTER 9

1. Charles Duhigg and Keith Bradsher, "How US Lost Out on iPhone Work," *New York Times*, January 21, 2012.

2. Rubenstein, *Making and Selling Cars*, 155.

3. Bruce Springsteen, *Darkness on the Edge of Town* (Columbia, 1978).

4. Harry Chapin, *Legends of the Lost and Found: New Greatest Stories Live* (Elektra, 1979).

5. Billy Joel, *The Nylon Curtain* (Columbia, 1982).

6. Bluestone and Harrison, *The Deindustrialization of America*.

7. McKersie and Sengenberger, *Job Losses in Major Industries*.

8. Schor, *The Overworked American*, 45.

9. Ibid., 81.

10. Ibid., 29.

11. http://www.bls.gov/iag/tgs/iagauto.htm

12. OECD, "Average Hours Actually Worked per Worker, 2000–2010" (http://stats.oecd.org).

13. http://www.bls.gov/news.release/prin.t02.htm

14. Davidson, "Making It in America."

15. US Department of Labor, Bureau of Labor Statistics.

16. Ehrenreich and Fuentes, "Life on the Global Assembly Line."

17. *The Global Assembly Line* (New Day Films, 1986).

18. John Walton, review of *The Global Assembly Line*, *Contemporary Sociology* 16 (1987), no. 2: 261–263.

19. Hu-Dehart, "Globalization and Its Discontents," 247.

20. Reese, "Nimble Fingers," 46.

21. Bei Bao et al., *A Splintered Mirror*, 43–44.

22. Sloan and Schroder, "Beyond Cross-Cultural Psychology," 139.

23. "Long, Hard Days at Pennies an Hour," *Business Week*, October 31, 1988, 46–47.

24. Shaiken, "Motown Blues," 56.

25. Dudley, *The End of the Line*.

26. Adler, *Mollie's Job*.

27. Rifkin, *The End of Work*, 138.

28. Livingston, "Murder in Juarez," 59–76.

29. Shaiken, "Motown Blues," 54.

30. Shaiken, "Lean Production in a Mexican Context," 251–253.

31. Hu-Dehart, 246.

32. Schoenberger, *Levi's Children*, 61–67.

33. Snyder, *Fugitive Denim*, 251–262.

34. Klein, *No Logo*, 1999.

35. Armbruster-Sandoval, *Globalization and Cross-Border Solidarity in the Americas.*

36. For example, the suicides at Apple's major supplier weren't mentioned at Apple's February 2012 shareholder meeting. See David Streitfeld, "At Apple Conclave, Nothing But Good News," *New York Times*, February 24, 2012.

37. Shaiken, "Lean Production in a Mexican Context," 248.

38. See, for example, Ford, *The Lights in the Tunnel*, 128–129.

39. Wilson, "GM, Lear Make History in Brazil."

40. Rothstein, "Economic Development Policymaking Down the Global Commodity Chain," 49–69.

41. Hu-Dehart, 248.

42. Charles Duhigg and Keith Bradsher, "How US Lost Out on iPhone Work," *New York Times*, January 21, 2012. Apple's market value was $469 billion. Charles Duhigg and Nick Wingfield, "Apple Asks Outside Group to Inspect Factories," *New York Times*, February 14, 2012.

43. Duhigg and Bradsher, "How US Lost Out."

44. Charles Duhigg and David Barboza, "In China, Human Costs Are Built Into an iPad," *New York Times*, January 25, 2012.

45. Huang, "Rethinking the Beijing Consensus," 11.

46. "Foxconn Pledges No Layoffs in 2012 as It Adds 300,000 Robots to Assembly Line," at http://news.xinhuanet.com.

47. Malcolm Moore, "'Mass Suicide' Protest at Apple Manufacturer Foxconn factory," *The Telegraph*, January 17, 2012.

48. As reported by Apple to Securities and Exchange Commission (http://www. apple.com/pr/library/2011/10/18Apple-Reports-Fourth-Quarter-Results.html).

49. Cunningham and Wasserstrom, "Interpreting Protest in Modern China," 13.

50. Robinson, "The China Road," 53.

51. Michelle Dammon Loyalka, "Chinese Labor, Cheap No More," *New York Times*, February 17, 2012; "Supply of Rural Workers in Chinese Cities Gets Smaller," *China Post*, January 17, 2011.

52. Parker and Slaughter, "Choosing Sides," 5.

53. Moody, "American Labor in International Lean Production."

54. Rinehart, Huxley, and Robertson, *Just Another Car Factory*.

55. Kochan, Lansbury, and MacDuffie, *After Lean Production*, 307.

56. Leslie and Butz, "'GM Suicide,'" 360–378.

57. Ibid., 369.

58. Ibid., 368.

59. Graham, "Subaru-Isuzu: Worker Response in a Nonunion Japanese Transplant," 200.

60. Babson, "Whose Team?" 241.

61. Leslie and Butz, 364.

62. Babson, "Whose Team?" 237.

63. Helper, "Can *Maquilas* Be Lean?" 271.

64. Herod, "Implications of Just in Time Production for Union Strategy," 527.

65. Harrison, *Lean and Mean*.

66. Flink, *The Automobile Age*, 399–400.

67. Ibid., 401.

68. Liker, *The Toyota Way*, 166–168.

69. Statistics from International Federation of Robotics (http://www.ifr.org).

70. Statistics from "World Robotics—Industrial Robots 2011" (http://www.worldrobotics.org).

71. Smith, "Preparing Students for Modern Work," 254–258.

72. Khurana, "Managing Complex Production Processes," 85–97.

73. Stamp, *The Invisible Assembly Line*, vii, 151, passim.

74. Ibid., 151.

75. Ibid., 153.

76. Rifkin, 102–103.

77. Leffingwell, *Scientific Office Management*.

78. Head, *The New Ruthless Economy*, 67.

79. Quoted in Zuboff, *In the Age of the Smart Machine*, 157.

80. Head, 104.

81. Nye, *Technology Matters*, 129–130.

82. Stiglitz, *The Roaring Nineties*, 124.

83. Head, 3.

84. Michaela D. Platzer and Glennon J. Harrison, "The US Automotive Industry: National and State Trends in Manufacturing Employment," Federal Publications Paper 666, 8-3-2009, 11–12.

85. Mishel, Bernstein and Shierholz, *The State of Working America*, 134.

86. Maynard, *The End of Detroit*, 308.

87. Dan Moran, "Volunteers Make Food Packs for Starving Children," *Chicago Sun-Times*, December 5, 2011.

88. "Toyota Makes Food Baskets" (http://news.cincinnati.com).

89. Bresnahan and Trajtenberg, "General Purpose Technologies."

90. Rosenberg and Trajtenberg, "A General Purpose Technology at Work."

91. Randall Stross, "When the Assembly Line Moves Online," *New York Times*, October 30, 2010.

92. Holweg and Pil, *The Second Century*, 6.

93. Christopher J. Singleton, "Auto Industry Jobs in the 1980s," *Monthly Labor Review* 115 (1992), no. 2, 19–20.

94. Danny Hakim, "G.M. Will Reduce Hourly Workers in U.S. by 25,000," *New York Times*, June 8, 2005.

95. Bureau of Labor Statistics, Career Guide to Industries, 2010–2011 Edition, Motor Vehicles and Parts Manufacturing (http://www.bls.gov).

96. Gramsci, "Americanism and Fordism," 310.

97. Nick Bunkey, "Group Predicts 28 Percent Gain in Carmaking Jobs by 2015," *New York Times*, November 29, 2011.

98. "German Carmaker Finds Cheap Labor Platform in America," *World Socialist Web Site* (http://www.wsws.org).

99. "Inquirer Editorial: Outsourcing Targeted," *Philadelphia Inquirer*, February 19, 2012.

100. Lorraine Mirabella, "New GM Plant Will Bring Jobs from Mexico to Baltimore," *Baltimore Sun*, February 16, 2012.

101. Cade Metz, "As Apple Toils in China, Others Make It in America," wired.com.

102. "GM Books Record Annual Profit; Union Workers Due $7,000," *USA Today*, February 16, 2012.

CHAPTER 10

1. Barack Obama, speech at University of Maryland, March 30, 2009, American Presidency Project, University of Santa Barbara (http://www.presidency.ucsb.edu).

2. Austin and Doerr, *Lost Detroit*; Marchand and Mefre, *The Ruins of Detroit*; Levine and Moore, *Detroit Disassembled*.

3. Sugrue, *The Origins of the Urban Crisis*, 1996.

4. Clemens, *Punching Out*, 258.

5. Bryan, *Rouge*, 126.

6. See "Body Polishing, Chrysler Corporation," Notes on the back of photograph W354794_1, Baker Library, Harvard Business School

7. Bryan, 172–173.

8. Ibid., 172.

9. Information in the following paragraphs based on a tour of the Ford Focus plant outside Detroit on May 19, 2011, including an hour-long conversation with Jim Tetreault, Ford's Vice President for North American Manufacturing.

10. Martin La Fever, "Workers, Machinery, and Productivity in the Automobile Industry," *Monthly Labor Review* 19 (October 1924), 738.

11. Jeffrey K. Liker, "Toyota's latest processes have less automation and more people," *Times of India*, February 6, 2012.

12. Braudel, *Capitalism and Material Life*, 274.

13. Oates, *The Gravedigger's Daughter*, 3.

14. Ibid., 10.

15. Updike, *Brazil*, 83.

16. Eugenides, *Middlesex*, 93.

17. Ibid., 95.

18. *Dancer in the Dark* (Zentropa Film, 2000).

19. Nye, *America as Second Creation*, 175–203.

20. Nye, *American Technological Sublime*, 129–139.

21. http://www.presidency.ucsb.edu/ws/index.php?pid=56834&st=assembly+line &st1=#ixzz1QBOezcQ 4

22. http://www.presidency.ucsb.edu/ws/index.php?pid=85927&st=assembly+line &st1=#ixzz1QBWOt5MW

23. Lederer, *A Nation of Sheep*. For a Marxist version of this argument, see Ewen, *Captains of Consciousness*.

24. In fact, "Model T output increased at a higher rate *before* the advent of the assembly line than after, while the price decreases before and after the line were quite similar. Before 1913, the keys to expanding production and reducing prices were efficient handling of materials, the sequential arrangement of machine tools, the use of fully interchangeable parts, the employment of single-purpose machines, and a highly developed station assembly system." Casey, 51.

25. Kristy Hessman, "Wind Power Drives Ford's UK Plant" (http://www.earthtech-ling.com).

26. Nye, *Henry Ford*, 80. Ford's laboratories found many uses for soybeans, including a paint used on cars and a plastic that was used for the entire body of a prototype car in 1941. See Watts, *The People's Tycoon*, 483–485.

27. K. Naughton, "Growing a Green Plant," *Newsweek*, November 13, 2000, 58–60.

28. *Design News*, October 1, 2009, 11.

29. http://usnews.rankingsandreviews.com/cars-trucks/Chevrolet_Volt/

30. Suzanne Ashe, "GM's Lansing, Mich., plant meets Energy Star standards," CNET, December 6, 2011 (http://reviews.cnet.com).

31. "VW Goes Green," *Chattanooga Times Free Press*, March 21, 2010.

32. Shaiken, ""Motown Blues: What Next for Detroit?," 51. GM, Ford, and Chrysler moved more slowly to make green cars than to build green factories. They profited from selling light trucks and SUVs. While making a $10,000 profit on each SUV,

they were willing to lose market share for conventional cars, profits on which were closer to $1,000.

33. McDonough and Braungart, *Cradle to Cradle*.

34. William McDonough and Michael Braungart, "Restoring the Industrial Landscape," at http://www.mcdonough.com.

35. US Environmental Protection Agency, "Recycling and Reuse: End-of-Life Vehicles and Producer Responsibility," at http://www.epa.gov.

36. McDonough and Braungart, 164–165.

37. Ibid., 165.

38. Ibid., 162.

39. Fujimoto, *Competing to Be Really, Really Good*, 65.

40. Nye, *Technology Matters*, 35–47.

41. Alder, "Innovation and Amnesia."

42. Mokyr, *The Lever of Riches*, 290.

BIBLIOGRAPHY

A complete bibliography of popular and scholarly writings about the assembly line would more than fill a volume this size. The following list contains only scholarly books and articles that are cited in the text. References to newspapers, magazines, websites, films, and primary source materials are given in the notes. In lieu of a longer bibliography, I want to explain briefly my view of this literature.

My methodological assumptions are laid out in the first four chapters of *Technology Matters* (2006) and in the introductions to *Narratives and Spaces* (1997) and *Electrifying America* (1990). Briefly, I hold that machines are not deterministic, and that what feels like determinism is better understood as the technological momentum of well-established systems of machines that were put in place in earlier generations. I have found that over time both specialists and ordinary citizens find technological systems such as the assembly line increasingly "natural." Yet they are profoundly cultural, and adoption (or transfer) of new technologies is often difficult and in most cases takes many years. The meanings given to a technological system change over time—often quite radically, as in the case of the assembly line.

As a historical subject, the assembly line has been a source of conflict. Writers have approached it from contradictory perspectives and without sharing the same nomenclature, focus, or periodization. Roughly speaking, there are business, labor, Marxist, and technological historians who write on this subject, and all of them have made valuable contributions. Their works develop, respectively, the points of view of corporate leaders, workers, radicals, and engineers. In addition, the cultural consequences of the assembly line are examined in histories of consumption.

Business and economic historians study the assembly line primarily from the point of view of management. They are interested in productivity, innovation, competition, and technology transfer. They tend to focus on corporate strategy, organizational structure, leadership, and competition between firms. Business historians see entrepreneurs as agents of historical change who select from a range of technologies, only one of which is the assembly line, in order to gain market share and profits. Mass production is important to them, but so are changes in corporate organization, mergers, marketing strategies, branding, industrial design, inventions, and research and development. In short, for a business historian the assembly line is just one of an ensemble of topics, and not always the most important one.

Labor historians tend to emphasize the historical agency of workers, and focus far less on managers. They are interested in workers' rights, wages, and welfare. When dealing with the assembly line they often write about alienation, the deskilling of labor, struggles for control of production on the shop floor, and strikes. Their larger focus is on achieving industrial democracy and on gaining a fair share of profits for the worker including adequate health care and a standard of living that keeps pace with improvements in productivity.

Marxist historiography offers a related but not identical perspective. It treats the assembly line as the central element in a historical stage of development, usually called "Fordism," that comes just after (and often is discussed together with) "Taylorism." The larger question for Marxists is commonly that of how changes in production are related to changes in social and political power. Marxists seldom write from the perspective of the boardroom. For much of the twentieth century they discussed "late capitalism" as a system riddled with internal contradictions that eventually would collapse, and they long assumed that some form of socialism would replace it. Marxists tend to see history as a series of historical stages, and "Fordism" as a decisive, irreversible, change. In addition, during the 1920s and the 1930s, revisions of Marxism were developed, notably by such scholars as Max Horkheimer, Walter Benjamin, and Antonio Gramsci who focused more on the superstructure of culture. They had considerable influence in the second half of the twentieth century, both in Europe and in the United States.

Marxist and labor historians overlap and share a common language that usually is not much used by historians of technology. The latter typically reject the view that the assembly line represents a distinct historical stage of development and accordingly do not have much use for the term "Fordism." That term was coined in the 1920s in Europe and was widely used in the United States only after about 1970.

Historians of technology see the assembly line as the culmination of a long series of changes in production. Successful firms didn't always adopt it. Historians of technology combine the manager's, the worker's, the engineer's, and the consumer's point of view, selecting among them on the basis of the problem being examined. They often focus on the invention and the early uses of the assembly line more than on its subsequent development. While they share some of the interests of business, labor, and Marxist historians, they are specifically concerned with the layout of factories, work routines, changes in machine design, the discovery of new techniques, and how this knowledge is preserved and transferred. Their larger questions are about how people use new technologies to effect changes in social organization, both inside and outside the factory, and how technologies are used to modify everyday life.

As if these differences among historians weren't enough, popular writers, literary critics, and novelists from the 1910s on have often assumed that the assembly line was deeply implicated in their discussions of "the machine," "mechanization," "the second industrial revolution," and "automation." The thrust of much of this popular argument has been deterministic: "the machine" was taking us somewhere, whether we liked it or not. I do not subscribe to such views.

Given the many approaches to the assembly line, this book could easily have fallen into a quagmire of methodological wrangling. I have not seen it as my task to comment continually on my sources' varying methods and assumptions. Such bibliographic discussions would be of interest to specialists but not to the general readers this book addresses. I have sought to distill the insights I found in this vast literature in order to tell a broad story in accessible language. This story has room in it for workers, managers, engineers, consumers, corporations, and nation-states. It also takes account of the perceptions of the assembly line expressed in fiction, film, painting, photography, and popular music. My intent has been to write an interdisciplinary and technically accurate cultural history that rejects determinism and other easy explanations of the assembly line.

WORKS CITED

Abernathy, William. *The Productivity Dilemma: Roadblock to Innovation in the Automobile Industry*. Johns Hopkins University Press, 1978.

Abo, Tetsuo. "Japanese Motor Vehicle Technologies Abroad in the 1980s." In *The Transfer of International Technology*, ed. David J. Jeremy. Elgar, 1992.

Abo, Tetsuo. *Hybrid Factory: Japanese Production Systems in the United States*. Oxford University Press, 1994.

Adams, Stephen B., and Orville R. Butler. *Manufacturing the Future: A History of Western Electric*. Cambridge University Press, 1999.

Adler, Paul. "Democratic Taylorism: The Toyota Production System at NUMMI." In *Lean Work: Empowerment and Exploitation in the Global Auto Industry*, ed. Steve Babson. Wayne State University Press, 1995.

Adler, William. *Mollie's Job: A Story of Life and Work on the Global Assembly Line*. Scribner, 2001.

Aitken, Hugh. *Taylorism at Watertown Arsenal*. Harvard University Press, 1960.

Alder, Ken. "Innovation and Amnesia: Engineering Rationality and the Fate of Interchangeable Parts Manufacture in France." *Technology and Culture* 38 (1997), no. 2, 273–311.

Aldridge, John W. *Talents and Technicians: Literary Chic and the New Assembly-Line Fiction*. Scribner, 1992.

Allen, Frederick Lewis. *Only Yesterday*. Harper & Row, 1931.

Allen, Michael Thad. "Flexible Production in Ravensbrück." *Past and Present* 165 (1999), November, 182–217.

Allen, Michael Thad. *The Business of Genocide*. University of North Carolina Press, 2002.

Anderson, Sherwood. "Lift Up Thine Eyes." *The Nation*, May 28, 1930.

Anderson, Sherwood. "A Great Factory: Problems and Attitudes in Life and Industry Considered from a Workman's Angle." *Vanity Fair* 27 (1926), November.

Anderson, Sherwood. *Poor White*. Viking, 1966 (reprint of 1920 edition).

Armbruster-Sandoval, Ralph. *Globalization and Cross-Border Solidarity in the Americas: The Anti-Sweatshop Movement and the Struggle for Social Justice*. Routledge, 2005.

Arms, Richard G. "From Disassembly to Assembly: Cincinnati: The Birthplace of Mass-Production." *Bulletin of the Historical and Philosophical Society of Ohio* 17 (1959), no. 3, 195–203.

Armus, Seth D. *French Anti-Americanism (1930–1948): Critical Moments in a Complex History*. Lexington Books, 2007.

Arnold, Horace L., and Fay L. Faurote. *Ford Methods and the Ford Shops*. Engineering Magazine Company, 1915.

Arnold, Harold L. "Ford Methods and Ford Shops." *Engineering Magazine* 47 (1914), 163–171, 370–376, 491–497.

Aron, Robert, and Arnaud Dandieu. *Le Cancer américain*. Rieder, 1931.

Aronowitz, Stanley. *False Promises: The Shaping of American Working Class Consciousness*. McGraw-Hill, 1973.

Ashburn, Anderson. "Detroit Automation." *Annals of the American Academy of Political and Social Science* 340 (1962), no. 1, 21–28.

Austin, Dan, and Sean Doerr. *Lost Detroit: Stories Behind the Motor City's Majestic Ruins*. History Press, 2010.

Babson, Steve, ed. *Lean Work: Empowerment and Exploitation in the Global Auto Industry*. Wayne State University Press, 1995.

Babson, Steve. "Whose Team? Lean Production at Mazda, USA." In *Lean Work*, ed. Babson. Wayne State University Press, 1995.

Bank Downs, Linda. Review of *The Mexican Muralists in the United States*. *Archives of American Art Journal* 29 (1989), no. 1/2, 50.

Bank Downs, Linda. *Diego Rivera: The Detroit Industry Murals*. Norton, 1999.

Barbieri-Low, Anthony Jerome. The Organization of Imperial Workshops During the Han Dynasty. PhD dissertation, Princeton University, 2001.

Barclay, Hartley W. *Ford Production Methods*. Harper, 1936.

Basalla, George. *The Evolution of Technology*. Cambridge University Press, 1988.

Batchelor, Ray. *Henry Ford: Mass Production, Modernism and Design*. Manchester University Press, 1994.

Bech-Petersen, Ole. Encounters: Danish Literary Travel in the United States. PhD dissertation, University of Southern Denmark, 2000.

Bei Bao, Duo Duo, Gu Cheng, Jiang He, Mang Ke, Shu Ting, and Yang Lian. *A Splintered Mirror: Chinese Poetry From the Democracy Movement*. North Point, 1991.

Belmonte, Laura. "Modernization and US Overseas Propaganda." In *Staging Growth: Modernization, Development, and the Global Cold War*, ed. David C. Engerman et al. University of Massachusetts Press, 2003.

Beniger, James R. *The Control Revolution: Technological and Economic Origins of the Information Society*. Harvard University Press, 1986.

Benjamin, Walter. *Illuminations*. Schocken, 1969.

Benner, Mary J., and Michael L. Tushman. "Exploitation, Exploration, and Process Management: The Productivity Dilemma Revisited." *Academy of Management Review* 28 (2003), no. 2, 238–256.

Berggren, Christian. *Alternatives to Lean Production*. Cornell University Press, 1993.

Bergson, Henri. *Laughter: An Essay on the Comic*. Macmillan, 1911.

Berkley, George F. *The Filenes*. International Pocket Library, 1998.

Bigazzi, Duccio. "Gli operai della catena di montaggio: la Fiat 1922–1943." In Anno XX—La classe operaia durante il fascismo *Annali della Fondazione Giangiacomo Feltrinelli* 1981), 895–949.

Biggs, Lindy. *The Rational Factory: Architecture, Technology and Work in America's Age of Mass Production*. Johns Hopkins University Press, 1996.

Bijsterveld, Karin. *Mechanical Sound: Technology, Culture, and Public Problems of Noise in the Twentieth Century*. MIT Press, 2008.

Bix, Amy Sue. *Inventing Ourselves Out of Jobs? America's Debate over Technological Unemployment, 1929–1981*. Johns Hopkins University Press, 2000.

Blair, John. *Modular America*. Greenwood, 1988.

Blondheim, Menahem. *News over the Wires: The Telegraph and the Flow of Public Information in America, 1844–1897*. Harvard University Press, 1994.

Bluestone, Barry, and Bennett Harrison. *The Deindustrialization of America: Plant Closings, Community Abandonment, and the Dismantling of Basic Industry*. Basic Books, 1982.

Boardman, James. *America and the Americans*. Longman, Rees, Orme, Brown, Green & Longman, 1833.

Bobbitt, Franklin. *The Curriculum*. Houghton Mifflin, 1918.

Bonig, Jürgen. "Technik und Rationalisierung in Deutschland zur Zeit der Weimarer Republik." In *Technik-Geschichte*, ed. Ulrich Troitzsch and Gabriele Wohlauf. Suhrkamp, 1980.

Bonin, Hubert, Yannick Lung, and Steven Tolliday, eds. *Ford: The European History, 1903–2003*. Éditions P.L.A.G.E., 2003.

Boon, Jean-Pierre. "Narrative Voices in *A Nous la Liberté*." *French Review* 55 (1982), no. 4, 514–519.

Boorstin, Daniel. *The Americans: The Democratic Experience*. Random House, 1973.

Borth, Christy. *Masters of Mass Production*. Bobbs-Merrill, 1945.

Borth, Christy. The Automobile in Popular Song. Pamphlet distributed at 43rd National Automobile Show, Detroit, 1960. Copy in Benson Ford Library, Dearborn.

Boyer, Robert, and Michel Freyssenet. *The Productive Models: The Conditions of Profitability*. Palgrave Macmillan, 2002.

Braudel, Fernard. *Capitalism and Material Life*. Harper, 1973.

Bray, Mayfield. *Guide to the Ford Film Collection in the National Archives*. National Archives, 1970.

Bresnahan, Timothy F., and Manuel Trajtenberg. "General Purpose Technologies: 'Engines of Growth?" *Journal of Econometrics* 65 (1995), no. 1, 83–108.

Bright, James R. *Automation and Management*. Graduate School of Business Administration, Harvard University, 1958.

Brinkley, Douglas. *Wheels for the World*. Viking, 2003.

Brissenden, Paul F., and Eli Franket. *Labor Turnover in Industry: A Statistical Analysis*. Macmillan, 1922.

Brody, Catharine. *Nobody Starves*. Longmans, Green, 1932.

Brody, David. *Workers in Industrial America*. Oxford University Press, 1980.

Bruckberger, R. L. *Image of America*. Viking, 1959.

Bryan, Ford R. *Rouge: Pictured in Its Prime*. Wayne State University Press, 2003.

Buckingham, Walter. "The Great Unemployment Controversy." *Annals of the American Academy of Political and Social Science* 340 (1962), March, 46–52.

Burlingame, Roger. *Engines of Democracy*. Scribner, 1940.

Burroughs, John. *John Burroughs Talks*. Houghton Mifflin, 1922.

Casey, Robert. *The Model T: A Centennial History*. Johns Hopkins University Press, 2003.

Casey, Roger N. The Driving Machine: Automobility and American Literature. PhD dissertation, Florida State University, 1991.

Céline, Louis-Ferdinand. *Journey to the End of the Night*. Viking, 1964.

Chalmers, Norma J. *Industrial Relations in Japan: The Peripheral Workforce*. Routledge, 1989.

Chandler, Alfred D. *Scale and Scope*. Harvard University Press, 1990.

Chandler, Alfred D. *The Visible Hand*. Harvard University Press, 1977.

Chaplin, Charles. *My Autobiography*. Simon and Schuster, 1964.

Chase, Stuart. *The Tragedy of Waste*. Macmillan, 1925.

Chase, Stuart. *Men and Machines*. Macmillan, 1929.

Chase, Stuart. *The Nemesis of American Business*. Macmillan, 1931.

Chase, Stuart. *The Economy of Abundance*. Macmillan, 1934.

Chinoy, Ely. *Automobile Workers and the American Dream*. Beacon, 1965 (reprint of 1955 Random House edition).

Clemens, Paul. *Punching Out: One Year in a Closing Auto Plant*. Doubleday, 2011.

Cohen, Yves. "The Modernization of Production in the French Automobile Industry between the Wars: A Photographic Essay." *Business History Review* 65 (1991), 754–780.

Cohen, Yves. "The Soviet Fordson, Between the Politics of Stalin and the Philosophy of Ford, 1924–1932." In *Ford: The European History, 1903–2003*, ed. Hubert Bonin, Yannick Lung, and Steven Tolliday. Éditions P.L.A.G.E., 2003.

Congdon, Don. *The Thirties; A Time to Remember*. Simon and Schuster, 1962.

Conrad, Lawrence H. *Temper*. Dodd, Mead, 1924.

Corner, James, and Alex S. MacLean. *Taking Measures Across the American Landscape*. Yale University Press, 1996.

Corwin, Sharon. "Picturing Efficiency: Precisionism, Scientific Management, and the Effacement of Labor." *Representations* 84 (2003), autumn, 138–165.

Crichton, Michael. *Rising Sun*. Ballantine Books, 1992.

Cronon, William. *Nature's Metropolis: Chicago and the Great West*. Norton, 1991.

Cunningham, Maura Elizabeth, and Jeffery N. Wasserstrom. "Interpreting Protest in Modern China." *Dissent*, winter 2011, 13–18.

Cusumano, Michael A. *The Japanese Automobile Industry: Technology and Management at Nissan and Toyota*. Harvard University Press, 1985.

Cusumano, Michael A. "Supplier Relations and Management: A Survey of Japanese, Japanese-Transplant, and U.S. Auto Plants." *Strategic Management Journal* 12 (1991), no. 8, 563–588.

David, Paul A. "Clio and the Economics of QWERTY." *American Economic Review* 75 (1985), May, 332–337.

Davidson, Adam. "Making It in America." *Atlantic Monthly*, January–February, 2012.

de Grazia, Victoria. *Irresistible Empire: America's Advance through Twentieth-Century Europe*. Harvard University Press, 2005.

Deming, W. Edwards. *Out of the Crisis*. MIT Press, 2000.

Denby, Charles. *Indignant Heart: A Black Worker's Journal*. Wayne State University Press, 1989.

Devinat, Paul. *Scientific Management in Europe*. International Labour Office, 1927.

Dewhurst, C. Kurt. "The Arts of Working: Manipulating the Urban Work Environment." *Western Folklore* 43 (1984), no. 3, 192–202.

Dick, Philip K. "Autofac." *Galaxy*, November 1955.

Diebold, John. *Automation: The Advent of the Automatic Factory*. Van Nostrand, 1952.

Dinnerstein, Joel. *Swinging the Machine*. University of Minnesota Press, 2003.

Ditto, Jerry, and Lanning Stern. *Eichler Homes: Design for Living*. Chronicle Books, 1995.

Dohse, Knuth, Ulrich Jürgens, and Thomas Malsch. "From 'Fordism' to 'Toyotaism'? The Social Organization of the Labor Process in the Japanese Automobile Industry." *Politics Society* 14 (1985), 115–146.

Doolittle, James Rood. *The Romance of the Automobile Industry*. Klebold, 1916.

Dos Passos, John. *The Big Money*. In *U.S.A.* Random House, 1937.

Dreiser, Theodore. *Tragic America*. Liveright, 1931.

Drucker, Peter F. "Automation Is Not the Villain." *New York Times Magazine*, January 10, 1965.

Drucker, Peter F. *Post-Capitalist Society*. HarperBusiness, 1993.

Duboff, Richard B. *Electric Power in American Manufacturing, 1889–1958*. Arno, 1979.

Dubreuil, Hyacinthe. *Robots or Men? A French Workman's Experience in American Industry.* Harper & Row, 1930.

Dudley, Kathryn Marie. *The End of the Line: Lost Jobs, New Lives in Postindustrial America.* University of Chicago Press, 1994.

Duhamel, Georges. *America the Menace: Scenes from the Life of the Future.* Houghton Mifflin, 1931.

Dunford, Mark. "Toward a Post-Fordist Order?" *Review of International Political Economy* 2 (1995), no. 1, 185–204.

Edsforth, Ronald, and Robert Asher. "The Speedup: The Focal Point of Worker's Grievances, 1919–1941." In *Autowork*, ed. Robert Asher and Ronald Edsforth. State University of New York Press, 1995.

Ehrenreich, Barbara, and Annette Fuentes. "Life on the Global Assembly Line." *Ms.,* January 1981, 53–71.

Eichengreen, Barry. *The European Economy since 1945.* Princeton University Press, 2006.

Ellul, Jacques. *The Technological Society.* Knopf, 1964.

Elwood, David. *Rebuilding Europe: Western Europe, America, and Postwar Reconstruction.* Longman, 1992.

Eugenides, Jeffrey. *Middlesex.* Bloomsbury, 2002.

Evans, Caroline. "Jean Patou's American Mannequins: Early Fashion Shows and Modernism." *Modernism/Modernity* 15 (2008), no. 2, 247–260.

Ewen, Stuart. *Captains of Consciousness: Advertising and the Social Roots of the Consumer Culture.* McGraw-Hill, 1975.

Farber, David. *Sloan Rules: Alfred P. Sloan and the Triumph of General Motors.* University of Chicago Press, 2002.

Faunce, William A., Einar Hardin, and Eugene H. Jacobson. "Automation and the Employee." *Annals of the American Academy of Political and Social Science* 340 (1962), March, 60–68.

Fehér, Ferenc, Agnes Heller, and György Márkus. *Dictatorship over Needs.* Oxford University Press, 1983.

Feigenbaum, Armand V. *Total Quality Control: Engineering and Management.* McGraw Hill, 1961.

Ferguson, Eugene S. *Oliver Evans: Inventive Genius of the American Industrial Revolution.* Hagley Museum, 1980.

Filene, Edward A. "Mass Production Makes a Better World." *Atlantic Monthly*, May 1929, 629–637.

Filene, Edward A. *Successful Living in This Machine Age*. Simon & Schuster, 1931.

Filene, Edward A. *Speaking of Change: A Selection of Speeches and Articles*. National Home Library Foundation, 1939.

Fine, Sidney. *Sit-Down*. University of Michigan Press, 1969.

Fisher, Philip. *Still the New World: American Literature in a Culture of Creative Destruction*. Harvard University Press, 1999.

Fitch, Charles. "The Rise of the Mechanical Ideal." *Magazine of American History* 11(1884), 516–527.

Flink, James J. *The Automobile Age*. MIT Press, 1988.

Ford, Henry, with Samuel Crowther. *My Life and Work*. Heinemann, 1922.

Ford, Martin. *The Lights in the Tunnel*. Acculant, 2009.

Foreman-Peck, James. "The American Challenge of the Twenties." *Journal of Economic History* 42 (1982), 865–881.

Frank, Robert. *The Americans*. Grove, 1959.

Franke, Richard Herbert, and James D. Kaul. "The Hawthorne Experiments: First Statistical Interpretations." *American Sociological Review* 43 (1978), no. 5, 623–643.

Franz, Kathleen. *Tinkering: Consumers Reinvent the Early Automobile*. University of Pennsylvania Press, 2005.

Freyssenet, Michel. "'Reflective Production': An Alternative to Mass Production and Lean Production?" *Economic and Industrial Democracy* 19 (1998), 91–117.

Freyssenet, Michel, Andrew Mair, Koichi Shimizu, and Giuseppe Volpato, eds. *One Best Way? Trajectories and Industrial Models of the World's Automobile Producers*. Oxford University Press, 1998.

Fridenson, Patrick. "Ford as a Model for French Car Makers, 1911–1939." In *Ford: The European History, 1903–2003*, ed. Hubert Bonin, Yannick Lung, and Steven Tolliday. Éditions P.L.A.G.E., 2003

Friedel, Robert. *A Culture of Improvement: Technology and the Western Millennium*. MIT Press, 2007.

Frum, David. *How We Got Here*. Basic Books, 2000.

Fuessle, Newton. *Gold Shod*. Boni and Liveright, 1921.

Fujimoto, Takahiro. *The Evolution of a Manufacturing System at Toyota*. Oxford University Press, 1999.

Fujimoto, Takahiro. *Competing to Be Really, Really Good: The Behind-the-Scenes Drama of Capability-building Competition in the Automobile Industry*. International House of Japan, 2007.

Gabor, Andrea. *The Man Who Discovered Quality*. Random House, 1990.

Garson, G. David. "Automobile Workers and the Radical Dream." *Politics Society* 3 (1973), no. 1, 163–177.

Geertz, Clifford. *Works and Lives: Anthropologist as Author*. Stanford University Press, 1988.

Giedion, Siegfried. *Mechanization Takes Command: A Contribution to Anonymous History*. Norton, 1948.

Ginsberg, Allen. *Howl and Other Poems*. City Lights Books, 1956.

Goodrich, Carter. "Power and the Working Life." *Annals of the American Academy of Political and Social Science* 118 (1925), March, 97–99.

Gorer, Geoffrey. *The American People: A Study in National Character*. Norton, 1964 (revision of 1948 edition).

Graham, Laurie. "Subaru-Isuzu: Worker Response in a Nonunion Japanese Transplant." In *Lean Work*, ed. Steve Babson. Wayne State University Press, 1995.

Gramsci, Antonio. "Americanism and Fordism." In *Selections from the Prison Notebooks of Antonio Gramsci*, ed. Quintin Hoare and Geoffrey Nowell Smith. International Publishers, 1971.

Haber, Samuel. *Efficiency and Uplift: Scientific Management in the Progressive Era, 1890–1920*. University of Chicago Press, 1964.

Haddow, Robert H. *Pavilions of Plenty: Exhibiting American Culture Abroad in the 1950s*. Smithsonian Institution Press, 1997.

Hamper, Ben. *Rivethead: Tales from the Assembly Line*. Warner Books, 1992.

Harris, Herbert. *American Labor*. Yale University Press, 1938.

Harrison, Bennett. *Lean and Mean: the Changing Landscape of Corporate Power in the Age of Flexibility*. Guilford, 1994.

Haworth, Lawrence. "Focal Things and Focal Practices." In *Technology and the Good Life?* ed. Eric Higgs, Andrew Light, and David Strong. University of Chicago Press, 2000.

Head, Simon. *The New Ruthless Economy: Work and Power in the Digital Age*. Oxford University Press, 2003.

Heale, M. J. "Anatomy of a Scare: Yellow Peril Politics in America, 1980–1993." *Journal of American Studies* 43 (2009), no. 1, 19–47.

Hellebust, Rolf. "Aleksei Gastev and the Metallization of the Revolutionary Body." *Slavic Review* 56 (1997), no. 3, 500–518.

Helper, Susan. "Can *Maquilas* Be Lean? The Case of Wiring Harness Production in Mexico." In *Lean Work*, ed. Steve Babson. Wayne State University Press, 1995.

Herod, Andrew. "Implications of Just-in-Time Production for Union Strategy: Lessons from the 1998 General Motors-United Auto Workers Dispute." *Annals of the Association of American Geographers* 90 (2000), no. 3, 521–547.

Hines, Thomas. *Richard Neutra and the Search for Modern Architecture.* Oxford University Press, 1982.

Hixson, Walter. *Parting the Curtain: Propaganda, Culture, and the Cold War, 1945–1961.* Palgrave Macmillan, 1997.

Holweg, Matthias, and Frits K. Pil. *The Second Century: Reconnecting Customer and Value Chain through Built-to-Order.* MIT Press, 2004.

Homburg, Heidrun. *Rationalisierung und Industriearbeit: Arbeitsmarkt, Management, Arbeiterschaft im Siemens-Konzern 1900–1939.* Haude & Spener, 1991.

Hoogvelt, Ankie, and Masae Yuasa. "Going Lean or Going Native? The Social Regulation of 'Lean' Production Systems." *Review of International Political Economy* 1 (1994), no. 2, 281–303.

Hooker, Clarence. *Life in the Shadows of the Crystal Palace, 1910–1927: Ford Workers in the Model T Era.* Bowling Green University Popular Press, 1997.

Hounshell, David. *From the American System to Mass Production, 1800–1932.* Johns Hopkins University Press, 1984.

Huang, Yasheng. "Rethinking the Beijing Consensus." *Asia Policy* 11 (2011), January, 1–26.

Hu-Dehart, Evelyn. "Globalization and Its Discontents: Exposing the Underside." *Frontiers* 24 (2003), no. 2/3, 244–260.

Hughes, Thomas P. *American Genesis: A Century of Invention and Technological Enthusiasm.* Viking, 1989.

Hunter, Louis C. *Steamboats on Western Rivers.* Harvard University Press, 1949.

Huxley, Aldous. *Brave New World.* Chatto and Windus, 1932.

Ingrassia, Paul, and Joseph B. White. *Comeback: The Fall and Rise of the American Automobile Industry.* Simon and Schuster, 1994.

International Directory of Company Histories. St. James Press, 1988.

Jackson, Kenneth T. *Crabgrass Frontier.* Oxford University Press, 1985.

Jay, Martin. *The Dialectical Imagination*. Little, Brown, 1973.

Jolas, Eugene. "The Industrial Mythos." *transition* 12 (1929), November, 123–124.

Jones, Bryn. *Forcing the Factory of the Future: Cybernation and Social Institutions*. Cambridge University Press, 1977.

Jones, Franklin D., ed. *Engineering Encyclopedia*. Industrial Press, 1941.

Juran, J. M., and Frank M. Gryna. *Quality Planning and Analysis*, third edition. McGraw-Hill, 1993.

Karp, Hal. "Manufacturing Genius." *Black Enterprise* 29, no. 2 (1998), 54–57.

Katznelson, Ira. "Participation and Political Buffers in Urban America." *Race & Class* 14 (1973), 465–480.

Keene, A. Perry. "Production—A Dream Come True." *Journal of the Institute of Production Engineers* 7 (1928), 385–399.

Kendrick, J. W., and E. S. Grossman. *Productivity in the United States*. Johns Hopkins University Press, 1980.

Kenney, Martin, and Richard Florida. *Beyond Mass Production: The Japanese System and Its Transfer to the U.S.* Oxford University Press, 1993.

Kesey, Ken. *One Flew Over the Cuckoo's Nest*. Viking, 1962.

Khurana, Anil. "Managing Complex Production Processes." *Sloan Management Review* 40 (1999), no. 2, 85–97.

Kimble, James J., and Lester C. Olson. "Visual Rhetoric Representing Rosie the Riveter: Myth and Misconception in J. Howard Miller's 'We Can Do It' Poster." *Rhetoric and Public Affairs*. 9 (2006), no. 4, 533–570.

Kinni, Theodore B. *America's Best: Industry Week's Guide to World-Class Manufacturing Plants*. Wiley, 1996.

Kirstein, George G. "The Manpower Revolution." *The Nation*, February 10, 1964, 140–142.

Klein, Naomi. *No Logo*. Picador, 1999.

Kline, Ronald. *Consumers in the Country*. Johns Hopkins University Press, 2000.

Kochan, Thomas A., Russell D. Lansbury, and John Paul MacDuffie. *After Lean Production: Evolving Employment Practices in the World Auto Industry*. Cornell University Press, 1997.

Koritz, Amy. "Drama and the Rhythm of Work in the 1920s." *Theatre Journal* 53 (2001), 551–567.

Kotkin, Stephen. "Modern Times: The Soviet Union and the Interwar Conjunction." *Kritika: Explorations in Russian and Eurasian History* 2 (2001), no. 1, 156–162.

Kottgen, Carl. *Das wirtschaftliche Amerika.* VDI-Verlag, 1925.

Kouwenhoven, John. *Made in America.* Doubleday, 1948.

Kracauer, Siegfried. *The Mass Ornament: Weimar Essays.* Harvard University Press, 1995.

Krafcik, John F. "Triumph of the Lean Production System." *Sloan Management Review* 41 (1988), fall, 41–51.

Kroes, Rob. "Americanization and Anti-Americanism." *American Quarterly* 58 (2006), no. 2, 503–517.

Kuhn, Thomas. *The Structure of Scientific Revolutions.* University of Chicago Press, 1996.

Kuisel, Richard F. *Ernest Mercier, French Technocrat.* University of California Press, 1967.

Kuisel, Richard F. *Seducing the French: The Dilemma of Americanization.* University of California Press, 1993.

Lawrence, D. H. *Studies in Classic American Literature.* Viking, 1964.

Lecher, Wolfgang, and Johann Welsch. *Japan-Mythos und Wirklichkeit.* Bund-Verlag, 1983.

Lederer, William J. *A Nation of Sheep.* Norton, 1961.

LeGrand, Rupert. "Ford Handles by Automation." *American Machinist* 92 (1948), no. 22, 107–122.

Leonard, Jonathan Norton. *The Tragedy of Henry Ford.* Putnam, 1932.

Leslie, Deborah, and David Butz, "'GM Suicide:' Flexibility, Space, and the Injured Body." *Economic Geography* 74 (1998), no. 4, 360–378.

Levasseur, E. "The Concentration of Industry and Machinery in the United States." *Annals of the American Academy of Political and Social Science* 9 (1897), no. 2, 18–24.

Levine, Philip. *A Walk with Tom Jefferson.* Knopf, 1988.

Levine, Philip. *What Work Is.* Knopf, 1992.

Levine, Philip, interviewed by Gary Pacernick. "Staying Power: A Lifetime in Poetry: An Interview with Philip Levine." *Kenyon Review*, new series 21 (1999), no. 2, 9–29.

Levine, Philip, and Andrew Moore, *Detroit Disassembled.* Akron Art Museum, 2010.

Lewchuk, Wayne. *American Technology and the British Vehicle Industry.* Cambridge University Press, 1987.

Lewchuk, Wayne. "Fordist Technology and Britain: The Diffusion of Labour Speedup." In *The Transfer of International Technology*, ed. David J. Jeremy. Elgar, 1992.

Lewis, David L. *The Public Image of Henry Ford.* Wayne State University Press, 1976.

Lewis, Robert. "Redesigning the Workplace: The North American Factory in the Interwar Period." *Technology and Culture* 42 (2001), no. 4, 665–684.

Liker, Jeffrey K. *The Toyota Way.* McGraw-Hill, 2004.

Ling, Peter. *America and the Automobile: Technology, Reform and Social Change, 1893–1923.* Manchester University Press, 1990.

Linhart, Robert. *The Assembly Line.* University of Massachusetts Press, 1981.

Littmann, William. "The Production of Goodwill: The Origins and Development of the Factory Tour in America." *Perspectives in Vernacular Architecture* 9 (2003), 71–84.

Livingston, Jessica. "Murder in Juarez: Gender, Sexual Violence, and the Global Assembly Line." *frontiers* 25 (2004), no. 1, 59–76.

Loeb, Harold. *Life in a Technocracy: What It Might It Be Like.* Syracuse University Press, 1993 (reprint of 1933 edition).

Lomax, Alan, Woody Guthrie, and Pete Seeger. *Hard Hitting Songs for Hard-Hit People.* Oak Publications, 1967.

Long, John C. "Motor Transport and Our Radial Frontier." *Journal of Land and Public Utility Economics* 2 (1926), no. 1, 109–118.

Lubar, Steve. "Machine Politics: The Political Construction of Technological Artifacts." In *History from Things: Essays on Material Culture Studies*, ed. Steven Lubar and W. David Kingery. Smithsonian Institution Press, 1996.

Lucic, Karen. *Charles Sheeler and the Cult of the Machine.* Reaktion Books, 1991.

Lyman, Stanford M. "The 'Yellow Peril' Mystique: Origins and Vicissitudes of a Racial Discourse." *International Journal of Politics, Culture and Society* 13 (2000), no. 4, 683–747.

Lynch, James. "Some Expectations of the Workers." *Annals of the American Academy of Political and Social Science* 91 (1920), no. 1, 108–120.

Lynd, Robert S., and Helen Merrell Lynd. *Middletown: A Study in Contemporary American Culture.* Harcourt Brace, 1929.

Lynn, Barry. "Unmade in America: The True Cost of a Global Assembly Line." *Harper's Magazine*, June 2002, 33–35.

Macdonald, Dwight. "A Theory of Mass Culture." *Diogenes* 1 (1953), June, 1–17.

Madison, Charles. "My Seven Years of Automotive Servitude." In *The Automobile and American Culture*, ed. David L. Lewis and Laurence Goldstein. University of Michigan Press, 1983.

Maier, Charles S. "Between Taylorism and Technocracy: European Ideologies and the Vision of Industrial Productivity in the 1920s." *Journal of Contemporary History* 5 (1970), no. 2, 27–61.

Maltz, Albert. *The Underground Stream*. Little, Brown, 1936.

Marchand, Roland. *Creating the Corporate Soul: The Rise of Public Relations and Corporate Imagery in American Big Business*. University of California Press, 1998.

Marchand, Roland. "*Life* Comes to Corporate Headquarters." In *Looking at Life Magazine*, ed. Erika Doss. Smithsonian Institution Press, 2001.

Marchand, Yves, and Romain Mefre, *The Ruins of Detroit*. Stiedhl, 2011.

Marx, Karl. *Capital: A Critique of Political Economy*. Translated by Ben Fowkes. Penguin, 1990.

Mathy, Jean-Philippe. *Extrême Occident: French Intellectuals and America*. University of Chicago Press, 1993.

Maynard, Micheline. *The End of Detroit: How the Big Three Lost Their Grip on the American Car Market*. Doubleday, 2003.

McCarren, Felicia. *Dancing Machines: Choreographies of the Age of Mechanical Reproduction*. Stanford University Press, 2003.

McCarthy, Tom. "Henry Ford, Industrial Ecologist or Industrial Conservationist? Waste Reduction and Recycling at the Rouge." *Michigan Historical Review* 27 (2001), no. 2, 52–88.

McCauley, Karen A. "Production Literature and the Industrial Imagination." *Slavic and East European Journal* 42 (1998), no. 3, 444–466.

McDonough, William and Michael Braungart, *Cradle to Cradle*. North Point, 2002.

McGraw, Bill. "Historians in the Streets: Life in the Ruins of Detroit." *History Workshop Journal* 63 (2007), 289–302.

McKersie, Robert B., and Werner Sengenberger. *Job Losses in Major Industries: Manpower Strategy Responses*. OECD, 1983.

McKinsey & Company, *Lessons from the US Automobile Industry*. Available at http://origin.mckinsey.com.

McLeod, Mary. "Architecture or Revolution: Taylorism, Technocracy, and Social Change." *Art Journal* 43 (1983), no. 2, 132–147.

McNeill, William H. *The Pursuit of Power: Armed Force, Society and Technology, since A.D. 1000*. University of Chicago Press, 1982.

Meier, August, and Elliott Rudwick. *Black Detroit and the Rise of the UAW*. Oxford University Press, 1979.

Meikle, Jeff. *Twentieth Century Limited: Industrial Design in America, 1925–1939*. Temple University Press, 1982.

Meyer, Stephen. "The Degradation of Work Revisited: Workers and Technology in the American Auto Industry, 1900–2000." Available at http://www.autolife.umd.umich.edu.

Meyer, Stephen. "'An Economic Frankenstein': UAW Workers' Responses to Automation at the Ford Brook Park Plant in the 1950s." *Michigan Historical Review* 28 (2002), no 1, 63–89.

Meyer, Steve. "Rough Manhood: The Aggressive and Confrontational Shop Culture of U.S. Auto Workers during World War II." *Journal of Social History* 36 (2002), no. 1, 125–147.

Milkman, Ruth. *Farewell to the Factory: Auto Workers in the Late Twentieth Century*. University of California Press, 1997.

Miller, Clyde R. "Radio and Propaganda." *Annals of the American Academy of Political and Social Science* 213 (1941), 69–74.

Mishel, Lawrence, Jared Bernstein, and Heidi Shierholz. *The State of Working America*. Cornell University Press, 2009.

Mitchem, Carl. "Of Character and Technology." In *Technology and the Good Life?* ed. Eric Higgs, Andrew Light, and David Strong. University of Chicago Press, 2000.

Mokyr, Joel. *The Lever of Riches: Technological Creativity and Economic Progress*. Oxford University Press, 1990.

Monden, Yasuhiro. "What Makes the Toyota System Really Tick?" *Industrial Engineering*, January 1981, 37–46.

Moody, Kim. "American Labor in International Lean Production." Working paper, Center for Social Theory and Comparative History, University of California, Los Angeles. Available at http://escholarship.org.

Mulhall, Michael. "The Increase of Wealth." *North American Review*, January 1885, 78–85.

Mumford, Lewis. *The Myth of the Machine: The Pentagon of Power*. Harcourt Brace Jovanovich, 1970.

Muther, Richard. *Production Line Technique*. McGraw-Hill, 1944.

Nevins, Alan, and Frank E. Hill. *Ford: The Times, the Man, the Company.* Scribner, 1954.

Noble, David F. *America by Design.* Oxford University Press, 1979.

Noble, David F. *Forces of Production: A Social History of Industrial Automation.* Knopf, 1984.

Nolan, Mary. *Visions of Modernity: American Business and the Modernization of Germany.* Oxford University Press, 1994.

North, Douglass C. "Institutions." *Journal of Economic Perspectives* 5 (1991), no. 1, 97–112.

Nye, David E. *Henry Ford: Ignorant Idealist.* Kennikat, 1979.

Nye, David E. *The Invented Self: An Anti-biography, from the Documents of Thomas A. Edison.* Odense University Press, 1983.

Nye, David E. *Image Worlds: Corporate Identities at General Electric.* MIT Press, 1985.

Nye, David E. *Electrifying America: Social Meanings of a New Technology.* MIT Press, 1990.

Nye, David E. "Yesterday's Ritual Tomorrow." *Anthropology and History* 6 (1992), no. 1, 1–21.

Nye, David E. *American Technological Sublime.* MIT Press, 1994.

Nye, David E. *Consuming Power: A Social History of American Energies.* MIT Press, 1998.

Nye, David E. *Narratives and Spaces.* Columbia University Press, 1998.

Nye, David E. *America as Second Creation: Technology and Narratives of New Beginnings.* MIT Press, 2003.

Nye, David E. *Technology Matters: Questions to Live With.* MIT Press, 2006.

Nye, David E. "Energy in the Thought and Design of F. Buckminster Fuller." In *New Views on R. Buckminster Fuller,* ed. Hsiao-Yun Chu and Roberto G. Trujillo. Stanford University Press, 2009.

O'Malley, Michael. *Keeping Watch: A History of American Time.* Viking, 1990.

O'Neill, Eugene. *The Hairy Ape.* In *Complete Plays, 1920–1931.* Library of America, 1988.

Oates, Joyce Carol. *The Gravedigger's Daughter.* HarperCollins, 2007.

Official Guide Book, New York World's Fair. Exposition Publications, 1939.

Official Guide: Book of the Fair, 1933. A Century of Progress, 1933.

Ohno, Taiichi. "How the Toyota Production System Was Created." *Japanese Economy* 10 (1982), no. 4, 83–101.

Olson, Byron, and Joseph Cabadas. *The American Auto Factory*. Motorbooks International, 2002.

Ortiz, Chris A. *Kaizen Assembly: Designing, Constructing, and Managing a Lean Assembly Line*. Taylor and Francis, 2006.

Parker, Mike, and Jane Slaughter. *Choosing Sides: Unions and the Team Concept*. Labor Notes, 1988.

Partner, Simon. *Assembled in Japan: Electrical Goods and the Making of the Japanese Consumer*. University of California Press, 1999.

Pells, Richard. *Not Like Us*. Basic Books, 1997.

Perlo, Victor. "'People's Capitalism' and Stock Ownership." *American Economic Review* 48 (1958), no. 3, 333–347.

Person, H. S. "Man and Machine: An Engineer's Point of View." *Annals of the American Academy of Political and Social Science* 149 (1930), 88–93.

Peterson, Joyce Shaw. *American Automobile Workers, 1900–1933*. State University of New York Press, 1987.

Peterson, Sarah Jo. The Politics of Land Use and Housing in World War II Michigan: Building Bombers and Communities. PhD thesis, Yale University, 2002.

Potter, David. *People of Plenty: Economic Abundance and the American Character*. University of Chicago Press, 1954.

Pursell, Carroll. "The Technology of Production." In *A Companion to American Technology*, ed. Pursell. Blackwell, 2005.

Pursell, Carroll. *Technology in Postwar America*. Columbia University Press, 2007.

Rabinbach, Anson G. "The Aesthetics of Production in the Third Reich." *Journal of Contemporary History* 11 (1976), 43–74.

Rae, John B. *American Automobile Manufacturers*. Chilton, 1959.

Raff, Daniel M. G. "Productivity Growth at Ford in the Coming of Mass Production: A Preliminary Analysis." *Business and Economic History* 25 (1996), no. 1, 176–185.

Raff, Daniel M. G., and Lawrence H. Summers. "Did Henry Ford Pay Efficiency Wages?" *Journal of Labor Economics* 5 (1987), no. 4, S63–S75.

Rauchenbush, Carl. *Fordism*. League For Industrial Democracy, 1937.

Reed, John. "Why They Hate Ford." *The Masses* 8 (1916), October, 11–12.

Reese, Lyn. "Nimble Fingers: From Nineteenth Century New England Mills to Twentieth Century Global Assembly Lines." *Magazine of History* 3 (1988), no. 3/4, 45–49.

Reich, Charles A. *The Greening of America*. Random House, 1970.

Richards, Gene. "On the Assembly Line." *Atlantic Monthly*, April 1937, 424–428.

Riesman, David. "The Nylon War." *Common Cause*, February 1951, 67–79. Reprinted in Riesman, *Abundance for What? and Other Essays* (Doubleday, 1964).

Riesman, David. *The Lonely Crowd*. Yale University Press, 1950.

Riesman, David. "The Suburban Sadness." In *The Suburban Community*, ed. William Dobriner. Putnam, 1958.

Rifkin, Jeremy. *The End of Work*. Putnam, 1995.

Rinehart, James, Christopher Huxley, and David Robertson. *Just Another Car Factory? Lean Production and Its Discontents*. Cornell University Press, 1997.

Ritzer, George. *The McDonaldization of Society: An Investigation into the Changing Character of Contemporary Social Life*. Pine Forge, 1995.

Rivera, Diego. *Portrait of America*. Covici, Friede, 1934.

Robinson, Ian. "The China Road: Why China Is Beating Mexico in the Competition for U.S. Markets." *New Labor Forum* 19 (2010), no. 3, 51–56,

Rodgers, Charles T. ed. *American Superiority at the World's Fair*. John J. Hawkins, 1852.

Rodgers, Daniel T. *Atlantic Crossings*. Harvard University Press, 1999.

Roediger, David. "Americanism and Fordism—American Style: Kate Richards O'Hare's 'Has Henry Ford Made Good?'" *Labor History* 29 (1988), no. 2, 241–252.

Roethlisberger, R. J., and William J. Dickson. *Management and the Worker*. Harvard University Press, 1939.

Roger, Philippe and Sharon Bowman. *The American Enemy: The History of French Anti-Americanism*. University of Chicago Press, 2005.

Rosenberg, Nathan, and Manuel Trajtenberg, "A General Purpose Technology at Work: The Corliss Steam Engine in the Late-Nineteenth-Century United States." *Journal of Economic History* 64 (2004), no. 1, 61–99.

Roszak, Theodore. *The Making of a Counter Culture*. Doubleday, 1969.

Rothstein, Jeffrey S. "Economic Development Policymaking Down the Global Commodity Chain: Attracting an Auto Industry to Silao, Mexico." *Social Forces* 84 (2005), no. 1, 49–69.

Rubenstein, James M. *Making and Selling Cars: Innovation and Change in the US Auto Industry*. Johns Hopkins University Press, 2001.

Rubin, Joan Shelley. "A Convergence of Vision: Constance Rourke, Charles Sheeler, and American Art." *American Quarterly* 42 (1990), no. 2, 191–222.

Rydell, Robert, and Rob Kroes. *Buffalo Bill in Bologna.* University of Chicago Press, 2005.

Sandeen, Eric. *Picturing an Exhibition: The Family of Man and 1950s America.* University of New Mexico Press, 1995.

Sandler, Richard Lyle. You Can Sell Your Body But Not Your Mind: A Sociolinguistic Examination of the Folklore of the Automobile Factory Assembly Line. PhD dissertation, University of Pennsylvania, 1982.

Say, Jean-Baptiste. *A Treatise on Political Economy.* Lippincott, 1855.

Sayre, Henry M. "American Vernacular: Objectivism, Precisionism, and the Aesthetics of the Machine." *Twentieth Century Literature* 35 (1989), no. 3, 314–315.

Schoenberger, Karl. *Levi's Children: Coming to Terms with Human Rights in the Global Marketplace.* Atlantic Monthly Press, 2000.

Schor, Juliet B. *The Overworked American.* Basic Books, 1991.

Schrenk, Lisa D. "'Industry Applied': Corporate Marketing at A Century of Progress." In *Designing Tomorrow: America's World's Fairs of the 1930s,* ed. Robert W. Rydell and Laura Burd Schiavo. Yale University Press, 2010.

Shaiken, Harley. "Lean Production in a Mexican Context." In *Lean Work: Empowerment and Exploitation in the Global Auto Industry,* ed. Steve Babson. Wayne State University Press, 1995.

Shaiken, Harley. "Motown Blues: What Next for Detroit?" *Dissent,* spring 2009, 50–56.

Shearer, David. *Industry, State and Society in Stalin's Russia, 1926–1934.* Cornell University Press, 1998.

Shearer, J. Ronald. "Talking about Efficiency: Politics and the Industrial Rationalization Movement in the Weimar Republic." *Central European History* 28 (1995), 483–506.

Shearer, J. Ronald. "The Reichskuratorium für Wirtschaftlichkeit: Fordism and Organized Capitalism in Germany, 1918–1945." *Business History Review* 71 (1997), no. 4, 569–602.

Shimokawa, Koichi. *Japan and the Global Automotive Industry.* Cambridge University Press, 2010.

Shimokawa, Koichi, and Takahiro Fujimoto, eds. *The Birth of Lean: Conversations with Taiichi Ohno, Eiji Toyoda, and Other Figures Who Shaped Toyota Management.* Lean Enterprise Institute, 2009.

Shpotov, Boris M. "Ford in Russia, from 1909 to World War II." In *Ford: The European History, 1903–2003*, ed. Hubert Bonin, Yannick Lung, and Steven Tolliday. Éditions P.L.A.G.E., 2003.

Sigfried, André. *The United States Today*. Translated by H. H. Hemming and Doris Hemming. Kessinger, 2005 (reprint).

Simpson, George. "Bureaucracy, Standardization, and Liberal Arts." *Journal of Higher Education* 20 (1949), no. 3, 129–136, 169.

Simpson, Janice C. "The Robot Revolution." *Time*, December 8, 1980, 72–83.

Slade, Giles. *Made to Break: Technology and Obsolescence in America*. Harvard University Press, 2006.

Slichter, Summer L. *The Turnover of Factory Labor*. Appleton, 1919.

Sloan, Tod S., and Sherrie Brownstein Schroder. "Beyond Cross-Cultural Psychology: The Case of Third World Factory Women." *Psychology Developing Societies* 1 (1989), no. 2, 137–151.

Smith, Adam. *The Wealth of Nations*. Prometheus Books, 1991 (reprint of 1776 edition).

Smith, John P. "Preparing Students for Modern Work: Lessons from Automobile Manufacturing." *Mathematics Teacher* 92 (1999), no. 3, 254–258.

Smith, Merritt Roe. "Eli Whitney and the American System of Manufacturing." In *Technology in America*, ed. Carroll W. Pursell. MIT Press, 1981.

Smith, Suzanne E. *Dancing in the Street: Motown and the Cultural Politics of Detroit*. Harvard University Press, 1999.

Smitter, Wessel. *F.O.B. Detroit*. Harper and Row, 1938.

Snyder, Rachel Louise. *Fugitive Denim: A Moving Story of People and Pants in the Borderless World of Global Trade*. Norton, 2008.

Sombart, Werner. *Why Is There No Socialism in the United States?* M. E. Sharpe, 1976.

Sørensen, Peter, Jesper Strandskov, Kurt Pedersen, and Per Boje. "Ford Denmark and the Scandinavian Market: From Regional Export Base to Periphery." In *Ford: The European History, 1903–2003*, ed. Hubert Bonin, Yannick Lung, and Steven Tolliday. Éditions P.L.A.G.E., 2003.

Spode, Hasso. "Fordism, Mass Tourism and the Third Reich." *Journal of Social History* 38 (2004), no. 1, 127–155.

Stamp, Daniel. *The Invisible Assembly Line*. Amacom, 1995.

Staudenmaier, John M. Review of Linhart, *The Assembly Line*. *Technology and Culture* 24 (1983), no. 3, 503.

Stead, W. T. *The Americanization of the World; or, The Trend of the Twentieth Century*. H. Marckley, 1902.

Steele, James. *Conveyor*. International Publishers, 1935.

Steinbeck, John. *The Grapes of Wrath*. Viking, 1939.

Steinbeck, John. *Travels with Charley*. Viking, 1962.

Steinberg, Ted. *Down to Earth: Nature's Role in American History*. Oxford University Press, 2002.

Steiner, Wendy. "The Diversity of American Fiction." In *Columbia Literary History of the United States*, ed. Emory Elliott. Columbia University Press, 1988.

Stiglitz, Joseph E. *The Roaring Nineties: A New History of the World's Most Prosperous Decade*. Norton, 2003.

Stilgoe, John. *Common Landscape of America, 1580–1845*. Yale University Press, 1982.

Stolberg, Benjamin. *The Story of the CIO*. Viking, 1938.

Strasser, Susan. *Satisfaction Guaranteed*. Pantheon, 1989.

Stross, Randall. "When the Assembly Line Moves Online." *New York Times*, October 30, 2010.

Stuart, Arthur A. "It's Here—The All-Steel House." *Popular Science Monthly*, November 1928, 33–35, 155.

Sugrue, Thomas J. *The Origins of the Urban Crisis: Race and Inequality in Postwar Detroit*. Princeton University Press, 1996.

Swados, Harvey. *On the Line*. Dell, 1957.

Swados, Harvey. "The Myth of the Happy Worker." In Swados, *A Radical's America*. Little, Brown, 1962.

Swett, Pamela E., Jonathan Wiesen, and Jonathan R. Zatlin, eds. *Selling Modernity: Advertising in Twentieth-Century Germany*. Duke University Press, 2007.

Tauranac, John. *The Empire State Building*. Scribner, 1995.

Teague, Walter Dorwin. *Land of Plenty*. Harcourt, Brace, 1947.

Tedlow, Richard S. *New and Improved: The Story of Mass Marketing in America*. Basic Books, 1990.

Terkel, Studs. *Hard Times*. Avon Books, 1970

Thomes, Paul. "Searching for Identity, Ford Motor Company in the German Market, 1903–2003." In *Ford: The European History, 1903–2003*, ed. Hubert Bonin, Yannick Lung, and Steven Tolliday. Éditions P.L.A.G.E., 2003.

Thoreau, Henry David. "Walking." In *The Oxford Book of American Essays*, ed. Brander Matthews. Oxford University Press, 1914.

Thurston, Robert H. "Our Progress in Mechanical Engineering: The President's Annual Address." *Transactions of the American Society of Mechanical Engineers* 2 (1881), 415–422.

Thurston, Robert H. "The Trend of National Progress." *North American Review* 161 (1895), September, 297–313.

Toller, Ernst. "Ford through German Eyes." *Living Age*, May 1, 1930. Translated from *Berliner Tageblatt*. Reprinted in Mary Moline, *The Best of Ford: A Collection of Short Stories and Essays* (Rumbleseat Press, 1973).

Tolliday, Steven. "Management and Labour in Britain." In *The Automobile Industry and Its Workers: Between Fordism and Flexibility*, ed. Steven Tolliday and Jonathan Zeitlin. St. Martin's Press, 1988.

Tolliday, Steven, ed., *The Rise and Fall of Mass Production*. Elgar, 1998.

Tolliday, Steven. "The Origins of Ford of Europe: From Multidomestic to Transnational Corporation, 1903–1976." In *Ford: The European History, 1903–2003*, ed. Hubert Bonin, Yannick Lung, and Steven Tolliday. Éditions P.L.A.G.E., 2003.

Tolliday, Steven. "The Rise of Ford in Britain, from Sales Agency to Market Leader, 1904–1980." In *Ford: The European History, 1903–2003*, ed. Hubert Bonin, Yannick Lung, and Steven Tolliday. Éditions P.L.A.G.E., 2003.

Tsutsui, William M. "W. Edwards Deming and the Origins of Quality Control in Japan." *Journal of Japanese Studies* 22 (1996), no. 2, 295–325.

Turner, Fred. *From Counterculture to Cyberculture*. University of Chicago Press, 2006.

US Department of Commerce. *Fifteenth Census of the United States, Report on Manufacturing*, volume 2. 1933.

US Department of Commerce. *Historical Statistics of the United States*. Washington DC, 1975.

Updike, John. *Brazil*. Hamish Hamilton, 1994.

Utterback, James M. *Mastering the Dynamics of Innovation*. Harvard Business School Press, 1994.

van den Haag, Ernest. "Notes on American Popular Culture." *Diogenes* 5 (1957), March, 56–73.

Vonnegut, Kurt. *Player Piano*. Scribner, 1952.

Wada, Kazuo, and Takao Shiba. "The Evolution of the 'Japanese Production System': Indigenous Influences and American Impact." In *Americanization and Its Limits: Reworking US Technology and Management in Post-War Europe and Japan*, ed. Jonathan Zeitlin and Gary Herrigel. Oxford University Press, 2000.

Walker, Charles, and Robert H. Guest. *The Man on the Assembly Line*. Harvard University Press, 1952.

Wallace, Anthony F. C. *The Social Context of Invention*. University of Nebraska Press, 2003.

Waters, Frank. *Pumpkin Seed Point*. Swallow, 1973.

Watts, Steven. *The People's Tycoon*. Vintage, 2005.

White, Donald W. *The American Century*. Yale University Press. 1996.

Wiener, Norbert. *The Human Use of Human Beings*. Free Association Books, 1989 (reprint of Houghton Mifflin edition of 1950 and 1954).

Wilkins, Myra. *American Business Abroad*. Wayne State University Press, 1964.

Williams, Karel, Colin Haslam, and John Williams. "Ford versus 'Fordism': The Beginnings of Mass Production?" *Work, Employment, and Society* 6 (1992), no., 4, 517–555.

Williams, Karel, Colin Haslam, and John Williams, with Andy Adcroft and Sukhdev Johal. "The Myth of the Line: Ford's Production of the Model T at Highland Park." *Business History* 35 (1993), no. 3, 66–87.

Williams, Whiting. "The World's Got to Have Me!" *North American Review* 228 (1929), no. 4.

Williamson, Jack. *The Humanoids*. Simon & Schuster, 1949.

Wilson, Amy. "GM, Lear Make History in Brazil." *Automotive News* 74 (2000), July 4, 4.

Wilson, Edmund. "Detroit Motors." *The New Republic*, March 25, 1931. Reprinted in Wilson, *American Earthquake* (Da Capo, 1996).

Woirol, Gregory Ray. *The Technological Unemployment and Structural Unemployment Debates*. Greenwood, 1996.

Womack, James P., Daniel T. Jones, and Daniel Roos. *The Machine That Changed the World: The Story of Lean Production*. Free Press, 1990.

Wood, Stephen, ed. *The Transformation of Work*. Unwin Hyman, 1989.

Woodhouse, W. B. "Electrical Driving of Textile Machinery." *Cassier's* 38 (1910), May, 24–38.

Wright, Carroll D. *The Industrial Evolution of the United States*. Chautauqua Century Press, 1895.

Yarrow, Andrew L. "Selling a New Vision of America to the World: Changing Messages in Early U.S. Cold War Print Propaganda." *Journal of Cold War Studies* 11 (2009), no. 4, 3–45.

Zangrando, Joanna Schneider, and Robert L. Zangrando. "Black Protest: A Rejection of the American Dream." *Journal of Black Studies*, December 1970, 141–159.

Zeitlin, Jonathan. "Flexibility and Mass Production at War: Aircraft Manufacture in Britain, the United States, and Germany, 1939–1945." *Technology and Culture* 36 (1995), January, 46–79.

Zieger, Robert H., and Gilbert J. Gall. *American Workers, American Unions*, third edition. Johns Hopkins University Press, 2002.

Zuboff, Shoshona. *In the Age of the Smart Machine*. Basic Books, 1988.

INDEX